The Divided Family
in Civil War America

CIVIL WAR AMERICA

Gary W. Gallagher, editor

The Divided Family

in Civil War America

Amy Murrell Taylor

THE UNIVERSITY OF NORTH CAROLINA PRESS | CHAPEL HILL

© 2005 The University of North Carolina Press
All rights reserved

Designed by April Leidig-Higgins
Set in Bulmer by Copperline Book Services, Inc.
Manufactured in the United States of America

The paper in this book meets the guidelines for permanence and
durability of the Committee on Production Guidelines for Book
Longevity of the Council on Library Resources.

Library of Congress Cataloging-in-Publication Data
Taylor, Amy Murrell.
The divided family in Civil War America / Amy Murrell Taylor.
p. cm. — (Civil War America)
Includes bibliographical references and index.
ISBN 0-8078-2969-2 (cloth: alk. paper)
1. United States — History — Civil War, 1861–1865 — Social
aspects.   2. Family — United States — History — 19th
century.   3. United States — Social conditions — To 1865.
I. Title.   II. Series.
E468.9.T38 2005   973.7'1 — dc22   2005010248

A portion of this work appeared earlier, in somewhat different
form, as "Union Father, Rebel Son: Families and the Question of
Civil War Loyalty," in *The War Was You and Me: Civilians in
the American Civil War*, ed. Joan Cashin (Princeton:
Princeton University Press, 2002), and is
reproduced here with permission.

09 08 07 06 05   5 4 3 2 1

For my family

Contents

Illustrations

Acknowledgments

I HAVE MANY PEOPLE to acknowledge for their support and guidance over the years. As an undergraduate at Duke University, I had the good fortune to work with Anne Firor Scott and Nancy Hewitt, who opened my eyes to the history of women and families. I have them to thank for inspiring me by their example — and for teaching me how to be a historian.

My friends and mentors at the University of Virginia provided a wonderful community in which to develop intellectually. Ten years ago I was lucky to begin graduate school there and to study with Edward Ayers, a truly inspiring teacher and scholar. His always patient and enthusiastic advice made it possible for me to become the author of this book, and I am greatly indebted to him for all the time he spent reading and rereading the drafts of this work. I only hope I can be as dedicated an adviser as he has been. One of the best aspects of studying at the university was that so many others showed a similar dedication. Paul Gaston shared his passion for the South while guiding me through the history of civil rights. Peter Onuf took an interest in my Civil War research early on and, in one especially pivotal conversation, urged me to launch this full-blown study of divided families. Once I got this project under way, Cindy Aron, Gary Gallagher, and Stephen Railton read drafts and shared their expertise — each has influenced the final outcome in ways for which I am grateful.

My fellow graduate students in the History Department taught me a great deal, as well as provided much-needed social outlets. I am thankful to my friends from History 701 and 702, the Southern History Seminar, and the members of my dissertation "support group" — Andy Morris, Steve Norris, Josh Rothman, and Andy Trees. I also appreciate my conversations with Taylor Fain, Valerie Garver, Robert Ingram, Kathy Jones, Peter Kastor, Matt Lassiter, Andy Lewis, Maire Murphy, Anne Rubin, Lori Schuyler, and Lara Diefenderfer Wulff. The Virginia Center for Digital History and, in particular, its director, Will Thomas, were very good to me. I started working there in the hope of paying my bills and left with a new appreciation for servers, scripts, and source codes. I am thankful for the friendships formed while transcribing and tagging documents, especially with Susanna Lee and Watson Jennison. My many lunches with Holly Shulman, during which we brainstormed about our projects, are especially memorable.

My new friends at the State University of New York at Albany (SUNY-Albany) deserve thanks, too. Iris Berger, chair of the Department of History, rolled out the welcome mat when I arrived and has since provided much support—from tracking down money to listening to the stress of a junior faculty member. My transition from graduate student to professor was also made easier by the friendship of Richard Hamm, Jennifer Rudolph, Harriet Temps, Ivan Steen, and Julian Zelizer. Allen Ballard deserves special thanks for his frequent inquiries about my progress on this book and for teaching me how to carve out more time for writing.

I have been very fortunate to receive the advice of many other distinguished historians over the last decade. Particularly helpful were the comments I received on portions of this work from Peter Bardaglio, Catherine Clinton, Lynda Crist, Drew Gilpin Faust, Robert Kenzer, Peter Kolchin, Virginia Laas, Jan Lewis, James Marten, Stephanie McCurry, Sandy Treadway, and Mark Wetherington. I am also grateful to Joan Cashin for several detailed readings of the first chapter. Reid Mitchell, James Marten, and the anonymous readers for the University of North Carolina (UNC) Press all graciously took time out of their busy lives to read the entire manuscript and provided suggestions that greatly improved the outcome. Catherine Clinton read several different sections but deserves special thanks for her constant encouragement over the last few years. I also thank David Perry, Ron Maner, Stevie Champion, and other members of the staff at the UNC Press for taking an interest in this project and patiently guiding me through the process of turning it into a book.

I would not have gotten very far with all of this advice, however, without financial support. I thank the following institutions for their generosity: the American Historical Association for an Albert J. Beveridge grant, the Virginia Historical Society for a Mellon Research Fellowship, the North Caroliniana Society for an Archie K. Davis Fellowship, and Duke University for a Women's Studies Research Grant. The University of Virginia was a constant source of support while I was a student; I thank the Center for Children, Families, and the Law for a summer fellowship, as well as the Graduate School of Arts and Sciences for DuPont, Southern History, and travel fellowships. SUNY-Albany helped at the final stages with a Faculty Research Award Program grant, and the United University Professions provided assistance with an Individual

Development Award. Special thanks go to SUNY-Albany's College of Arts and Sciences and the Office of the Vice President for Research for last-minute support that made possible the reproduction of the images in this book.

Tracking down the scattered private papers of divided families required the help and expertise of many people. I am indebted to the following archivists and librarians for taking the time to identify these families: Karen Kinzey of Arlington House; Elizabeth Dunn at Duke University's Rare Book, Manuscript, and Special Collections Library; James Holmberg, Rebecca Rice, and Mark Wetherington at The Filson Historical Society; Claire McGann at the University of Kentucky's Margaret I. King Library; Martha Bennett at the Fort Delaware Society; Mary Herbert of the Maryland Historical Society; Dennis Northcott at the Missouri Historical Society; John Coski at the Museum of the Confederacy; Marilyn Hughes and Wayne Moore at the Tennessee State Library and Archives; Michael Plunkett at the University of Virginia's Albert and Shirley Small Special Collections Library; Graham Dozier and Frances Pollard at the Virginia Historical Society; Diane Ayotte, Jennifer Lukomski, and Cindy Stewart at the Western Historical Manuscript Collection of the University of Missouri; Nancy Baird and Pat Hodges at the Kentucky Library of Western Kentucky University; and the staffs of Woodruff Library of Emory University, the Southern Historical Collection at UNC–Chapel Hill, the Hagley Library in Wilmington, the Delaware Public Archives, the Library of Congress, and the National Archives in Washington, D.C., and College Park, Maryland. I am also grateful to the wonderful interlibrary loan staffs at the University of Virginia's Alderman Library and at SUNY-Albany's University Library for tracking down newspapers and novels.

A number of Civil War historians offered additional suggestions for finding divided families. Thanks especially to Jonathan Berkey, Peter Carmichael, Catherine Clinton, Robert Krick, Susanna Lee, Cora MacVilla, James Marten, Chandra Miller Manning, Anne Rubin, and David Smith. My search for these families was also facilitated by wonderful friends who opened their homes and gave me places to stay while I visited the archives. Thanks to Margaret and David Brackett, Allison Cowett and Dave Adams, Jessica and Jason Dasher, Preston and Elizabeth Kim, and Duncan and Sherri Murrell.

It almost seems appropriate, given the topic of this book, that my own family pitched in to help. My parents, Darwin and Joyce Murrell, took an interest in this project from the beginning. I will always remember the time they spent with me in the archives, learning about the Civil War and weeding through voluminous documents and microfilm. Together they were my best research assistants. How my brother Duncan and I, two siblings who showed no interest in the Antietam battlefield when we drove through it frequently as children, both ended up writing about the Civil War at the same time is still a mystery to me. But I have enjoyed our numerous and enlightening conversations about our newfound mutual interest. I am unsure how to begin thanking my husband, Scott Taylor. His humor, patience, and shared love of history have been the greatest support while I worked on this project. He may be happier than I am that this book has come to an end. I look forward to collaborating on our new project together — our daughter Katie, who came into our lives just in time to provide the final push for me to finish this work. To my entire family I dedicate this book.

Albany, New York
March 2005

The Divided Family
in Civil War America

Introduction

ABRAHAM LINCOLN WARNED in 1858 that a "house divided against itself cannot stand." His words, prophetic of the war that was to come three years later, continue to resonate today. That phrase — just one part of a much larger address — has become one of Lincoln's most recognizable contributions to our American political vocabulary. But those words were not unique to the nineteenth-century president. The image of a "house divided," or a family in conflict, was a timeless one that drew on a long tradition in literature and political thought. From the Bible to Greek tragedies to Shakespeare's works to the political theories of John Locke, the family has offered a common language for understanding the complexities of human relationships. For Lincoln, the family provided a rhetorical shorthand, allowing him in just six words to convey what slavery might do to the relationship between Northern and Southern citizens.

Lincoln was not alone in describing a nation in family terms. Historians across the globe have uncovered numerous moments in which family language and metaphor figured centrally in the imagining of nations — particularly nations in conflict. We can see this in the French Revolution, Russian propaganda during World War I, and the Cold War, to name a few examples. The widespread use of the family image raises important questions about national identity — where it comes from, how it is defined, and how attachments to family and nation coexist and reinforce one another. In the United States we can trace the roots of the family metaphor at least to the Revolution, as colonists imagined themselves as children of a tyrannical British father.[1] The Civil War only amplified this association of nation and family with an outpouring of speeches and stories that joined Lincoln in comparing the nation to a divided house. Even today, in movies, Web sites, children's literature, and John Jakes novels, we continue to see the warring nation as if it were a quarreling family — or a war of "brother against brother." It has become a cliché, easily recognizable and frequently invoked. Less understood is why this image has taken root in American culture.

This book offers the first sustained historical study of the divided family in the American Civil War. It takes what we often consider to be just rhetoric or common sense and finds within this image something more meaningful for those who lived through the war. It was meaningful, on a profound level, because it was real. Thousands of families did divide in what was widely considered to be a shocking dimension of the Civil War. Brothers did fight brothers; even Abraham Lincoln had relatives in the Confederate army. The image of the divided family therefore captured something tangible and authentic about the experience of war. But, on another level, it offered to Civil War Americans a framework for making sense of new and unprecedented problems. How could a country that was once one nation be carved into two? How could fellow citizens kill one another? Americans looked to the vocabulary of family — deference and authority, affection and conflict — for guidance in framing those difficult questions. This book follows the interplay of these two levels — experience and language — to provide a social and cultural history of the divided family in Civil War America.[2]

WE NEED NOT REACH FAR into the vast library of Civil War history to find evidence of divided families. The idea that two brothers, or a father and son, or a husband and wife could assume opposing stances in the war has both captivated and perplexed scholars, writers of fiction, and filmmakers since the first shots were fired over Fort Sumter.[3] Family division has become one of the "curiosities" of the war, filling out war narratives with colorful images and dramatic flourishes. Stories of divided families almost always appear in some form in anecdote books, a staple of Civil War popular culture, under titles such as "Love and Treason" and " 'Brother against Brother' Was Real."[4] Biographies of some of the most prominent Civil War political and military leaders rarely fail to mention a personal connection to the enemy side. Many central figures of that era were split from a family member, including Confederates Robert E. Lee, Thomas J. "Stonewall" Jackson, and their Union-sympathizing sisters, and U.S. Senator John J. Crittenden and his Confederate son. Indeed, the more one looks for evidence of divided families in the war, the more numerous they appear.[5]

This book thus began with the impossible search for all — or almost all — instances of family division in the American Civil War. Finding these families involved searching for references in the many books that have preceded this one, reading anecdote books and following short leads, drawing on the memories of archivists, and taking seriously what have become, in many minds, folkloric tales and legends. The writings of contemporary observers energized this search. "There is scarcely a family that is not divided," one woman wrote from St. Louis in 1861, and a Virginian noted of his own divided family, "There are thousands of families in the same situation."[6] Statements such as these, however, quickly made it apparent that this subject needed to be narrowed along several lines. I turned first to those families in which "division" meant open allegiance to the opposing sides during the four years of war. Many more families argued about the merits of secession and slavery prior to April 1861 or disagreed on the course of the war. But the families considered here are those in which disagreements translated into opposing national loyalties, evident through service in the army or an overt display of allegiance at home.

These families tended to live in one region of the country: the border states of Missouri, Kentucky, Tennessee, Virginia (and later West Virginia), Maryland, and Delaware, as well as Washington, D.C. These states—all slaveholding states of the Upper South—were widely acknowledged during the war for having the greatest concentration of divided families. As one Missouri newspaper observed in 1861, "Secession has broken up the dearest social relations in every community of the border slave States, turning son against father, brother against brother, daughter against mother, friend against friend." These words echoed what would become a popular belief during the conflict: that divided families were a border state problem that set this region apart from states farther north or south.[7] The "border slave States," indeed, had become an increasingly self-conscious region by the eve of the war, known alternately as the "border states," the "middle states," and, in the words of a Virginia legislator, "the tier of friendly states" between the Union and the Confederacy. They comprised the area immediately north and south of the Union-Confederate border, where, as a Virginia newspaper explained, national loyalties in the 1860s could "give rise to . . . reasonable doubt." It was here that slavery and abolitionism, Democrats and Republicans, industry and agriculture, urban and rural communities all existed side by side. This was the crossroads of American travel, too, as Northerners moved south to obtain land or to vacation, Southerners went north for education or employment, and Easterners moved west to seek new land.[8]

The different cultures, economies, and politics of the nation coincided in this region, making it difficult, when the war came, to draw a political border between the Union and the Confederacy that would mirror the geographic border between North and South. Latent divisions within the border states instead gave rise to the protracted secession crisis. This was a region where some of the most significant compromises to stave off sectional conflict originated in the 1850s and where voters supported moderate candidates over the more radical Republicans or Southern Democrats in 1860. Yet it was also where consensus was elusive once secession came, as states either seceded reluctantly after months of debate, like Tennessee and Virginia (which eventually splintered in two), or remained in the Union despite vocal secessionist minorities. The governor of Kentucky, for instance, supported efforts to establish an alternative Confederate government in his Union state, while in Missouri guerrilla warfare continually drew citizens into violent confrontations. In this region where, as one Kentuckian put it, "treason & loyalty overlap," and where reluctant Confederates and latent Unionists lived side by side during the Civil War, the line between Union and Confederacy fell in unexpected places, dividing towns, cities, and rural communities. It almost made sense, then, that families living in this diverse and conflicted region would divide, too.[9]

The people who experienced a schism in their families were not satisfied with that conclusion, however. Mid-nineteenth-century Americans idealized the family as the foundation of social and national stability — it was not supposed to give in so easily to the weight of adversity. Family members, of course, were known to have their differences and to argue about politics in the years leading up to the war. But many expected that in a time of war, when it became necessary to assume a public stance on one side or the other, their families would close ranks and present a united front. Americans believed then — as some historians do now — that men and women would act as a cohesive family unit, that their loyalty to family would coincide with their loyalty to country. Yet quite the opposite occurred when border-state residents chose to put a nation before their family and to become their kinsmen's public enemy. The division of Civil War families thus struck a powerful blow to popular expectations, forcing people to step back, question old assumptions, and reconsider the meaning of family and its role in shaping national loyalty.[10]

To explain what they called this "tragedy" and "horror" of war, border-state men and women looked deep within themselves to understand why their family members assumed opposing national allegiances. They turned to personal letters and diaries, at times writing long, introspective analyses of their conflict. A close reading of their words, particularly those of the white middle and upper classes who left behind the most extensive written record, anchors this study. The first three chapters explore how members of these families tried to understand one another's motivations and actions during the latter part of the sectional crisis and the first few years of the war. Chapter 1 examines conversations between fathers and sons, Chapter 2 follows the interactions between men and women during courtship and marriage, and Chapter 3 explores the relationships between brothers and sisters. Each of these chapters reveals that family division went beyond the oft-cited "brother against brother" and centers instead on particular relationships that triggered the greatest dispute about two critical — and still debated — questions of the Civil War: What motivated individual family members to align themselves with one side or the other? And why did they fight? Few agreed on the answers to these questions, and many argued vigorously about the meaning of their division.[11]

The story that emerges from these families is one of borders tested and boundaries challenged. Attempts to understand why a Union-Confederate border had broken through their household inevitably led these individuals to search for answers in the deeper social borders between gender and generations. To varying degrees, family members came to view their divided national loyalties through the more familiar lens of family conflict, as crises of duty and authority rather than of slavery and secession. Coming-of-age struggles between sons and their fathers, for example, were a part of everyday life in midcentury families; it followed then, in some minds, that this generational conflict, rather than something strictly political, could explain why sons assumed public stances in opposition to their fathers. Border-state families thus turned to the language of gender and generations to describe their internal breakdown: they took what was unfamiliar — wartime division — and made it familiar by cloaking their arguments in the existing vocabulary of domestic conflict. Their words, expressed in moments of frustration and candor, articulated beliefs about family life that often went unspoken in nineteenth-century sources. They talked about what it meant to be a son or a father, a wife or a daughter, and the meaning of those positions in the context of a military and political war.[12]

This book focuses on individuals who often lived in the same household and were bound together by close emotional, financial, and blood ties of kinship. Certainly "family" meant many other things, too, and could encompass a wide range of relationships. But relations between extended family or intimate friends are relevant to this study only when those relationships appear to have been a significant part of a man or woman's wartime life. The reason for this focus is simple: wartime divisions within the nuclear family were the most intense and surfaced in family correspondence far more clearly — and with far more frustration — than divisions involving extended kin. This may reflect the high expectations that had come to surround nuclear family relations in mid-century America. Between the Revolution and the Civil War, the combined forces of political independence, religious awakenings, and commercial and industrial expansion all helped foster an idealization of the father-mother-child family structure. Such a family was meant to be an emotional sanctuary, a small and child-centered refuge from public life that replaced traditional patriarchal authority with affection and love. Few families ever measured up to that ideal; those that came the closest were typically members of the white middle or upper classes, especially those in the urban North. Yet far more people across the nation, and in the border region, embraced this ideal anyway and grew frustrated when their wartime divisions exposed their inability to achieve it. Their attachment to this domestic model both exacerbated their conflicts and, as we will see, offered a guide to reconciling their divisions. The nuclear or "modern" family, and particularly the gap between that ideal and the reality, is therefore critical to understanding the domestic dramas that unfolded in border-state society.[13]

One aspect of their ideal that troubled divided families the most was the relationship — or the border — between public and private life. The family was defined in part by its physical and emotional distance from political, military, and economic affairs: these two "spheres" — the private and the public — were not to overlap but were to be separate and distinct. Yet, as numerous historians have documented in recent years, the line between public and private was far more permeable in reality and never as neat as promised.[14] This insight has led to a reconsideration of some of the most significant events and trends of the nineteenth century, and the Civil War is no exception. Wars, by their very nature, transcend public-private boundaries. An acknowledgment of this has led historians to argue that the war looks different when the connections between "homefront" and "battlefield" are considered. For some, pressures emanating from the homefront proved to be a drag on military progress; for others, families helped explain how and why men took up arms and fought the way they did. The war was not fought solely on the battlefield but also penetrated — and depended on — the most intimate facets of life.[15]

Divided families are intriguing in part because they openly acknowledged the permeability of the border between homefront and battlefront long before historians began to see it in hindsight. Divided relatives viewed the presence of war in their families as an intrusion, a sign of dysfunction, and they responded with a vigorous defense. Their translation of the conflict into domestic terms was, in part, an effort to reinscribe a division between their private lives and the public world of war. They tried to minimize their discussion of politics and redraw boundaries that would, they hoped, restore normalcy. They continually defined and redefined, in explicit language, what was "private" and what was "public," what was "domestic" and what was "military" or "political." And their words are revealing. Not only did these men and women acknowledge the connections between these two spheres, but also, driven by the war to document their daily experiences in diaries and letters, they went a step further and resisted these linkages. Their eagerness to defend a border between public and private — their use of it to deflect wartime stress — may be one reason why this domestic ideology continued to resonate throughout the nineteenth century despite a much more complicated reality for most families.[16]

Most divided families found it difficult to keep their affairs private as the war progressed. They did not live or act in isolation but instead were surrounded by other wartime pressures that forced their problems into the open. In the view of some contemporary observers, such as neighbors, newspaper writers, and politicians, the idea that a family had members with opposing political loyalties raised questions about that family's character, reputation, and, most significantly in this time of war, potential for disloyalty and even treason. Who knew whether someone in a divided family might utilize their kinship connections to spy or otherwise subvert a national cause? Many regarded divided families with a combination of lament and suspicion, wondering whether to sympathize with or condemn their alignment on opposing sides. Chapter 4 of this study examines how divided families became an acknowledged public problem. It pays particular attention to border crossing, to how military and political leaders in both the Union and the Confederacy passed laws limiting contact across the military border — via travel and mail — between family members. Such policies reflected a belief that the idealized boundaries between public and private life could be, and would be, subverted easily by these families, a subversion (or treason) that would threaten the wartime border between the opposing sides.

An additional tension in their own domestic ideals made it even more difficult for divided families to protect their privacy. The family, despite its role as a private refuge, had simultaneously served a very public function for the nation since the Revolution. American national identity was not self-evident in the decades after independence; it was defined less by the traditional components of nationalism, such as ethnicity, religion, or even a strong nation-state, and more by the diffuse ideas and values of its citizenry. The new republic is better described as an "imagined community," to borrow the words of Benedict Anderson; it was a nation of citizens who may have never known or met one another but who nonetheless thought they shared "a deep, horizontal comradeship." Certainly the republican values of liberty and equality drew early Americans together into such a "comradeship," but in an effort to nurture those values, and to represent them in a tangible and easily identifiable way, Americans turned to the idea of family.[17]

The family became a model and a metaphor for the youthful nation. Republican leaders held up the family as an incubator of civic and political values — of virtue and affection — deemed essential to the welfare of the republic. As "republican mothers" and "republican wives," women were to epitomize such values and inculcate them in their kin, thus serving the public interest while safely ensconced in the private sphere. John Adams, reflecting such expectations, once explained that "the foundations of national Morality must be laid in private Families."[18] Early national leaders such as Adams were not alone in linking a nation's welfare to the family, but this connection was particularly resonant in postrevolutionary America. Early Americans grasped for symbols and metaphors that would help them imagine their republican nation as a cohesive whole. They tried to build a society and a government of free and equal individuals, but, without an absolute monarch to bind them through deference and authority, Americans needed to envision some other ligament of national loyalty. They found this in the metaphor of the family, a concept familiar to every citizen, which offered a more voluntary and affective model for bringing together citizens of different backgrounds and interests. Americans were to be, according to many republican spokesmen, loyal members of one great "family."[19]

Abraham Lincoln's references to the "house divided" helped sustain this popular association of nation and family well into the Civil War. It might be tempting to attribute this continuity to rhetorical habit, to a tradition so engrained in American culture by midcentury that it naturally appeared again, and to some extent this was the case. But the particular circumstances of the Civil War also gave added meaning to the long-standing imaginative connection between nation and family. A civil war is, after all, a crisis of loyalty, and the U.S. Civil War revealed the failure of the American people to generate a common bond of national unity. It also, as the experiences of divided families reveal most dramatically, marked the failure of family. The affection, duty, and other attachments that were to be nurtured in the family proved vulnerable to the stresses of war. The family turned out not to be the stable, fixed model for the nation that early leaders may have hoped but instead an institution rife with conflict and disloyalty. Family and nation thus experienced parallel and interconnected crises of loyalty in this war that gave new intensity to the metaphoric connection between them.[20]

No one did more to promote the imaginative link between family and nation during the Civil War than the authors of wartime fiction. In both the North and the South, publishing houses churned out short stories and novels that offered ways of understanding the divided nation. Family comprised a dominant theme of these tales, as writers depicted the Union and the Confederacy as warring brothers, or father and son, or husband and wife. Divided families helped writers tell the story of the warring nation and examine the existence — or absence — of loyalty among its people. Chapter 5 of this book begins with one theme that was especially popular within this body of wartime literature — the failed romance of men and women on opposing sides of the Union-Confederate divide. These stories called on gender to depict the failed affections between Civil War Americans North and South. Other stories used the motif of family dysfunction with race more clearly in view, exploring the loyalty or disloyalty of African American slaves in interracial families. Chapter 6 examines how the metaphor of family and marital strife fed into a closely related theme by the late 1860s: intersectional marriage across the lines of battle. The message of this simplified postwar imagery was that kinship would heal all wounds, that ingrained and long-standing loyalties would resurface to trump any lingering division. No matter what remained of a Union-Confederate border, no matter what it was about slavery and sectional politics that once pulled the nation apart, all could be easily set aside and the national family restored.

But here the image diverged from the reality. The national family reunited in fiction offered an idealized version of what actual divided families aspired to over the course of the war. In both, Americans sought to domesticate the war, to translate the divisive issues of slavery and sectional politics into more manageable familial dramas. But real families did not find this so easy to accomplish. Chapter 6 continues the theme of reconciliation by examining these families' attempts to remain united from the first moments of their division. Despite their best efforts to defuse their political differences, most divided families found that the war would continue to intrude and tear them apart emotionally for years to come. Their personal loyalties were damaged by the war, though popular images still celebrated them more strongly than ever as models of unity. Family loyalty, and the reconciliation it promised, was something more easily imagined than achieved in reality.

It was easily imagined because writers of fiction could sidestep the war's divisiveness with little difficulty. Chapter 7 of this volume examines how these writers, in transforming the war into a family affair, avoided a serious reckoning with the most fractious aspect of the war — the destruction of slavery. In tales of intersectional marriage, African Americans become peripheral members of the national family: they are loyal but dependent, loving but subordinate to whites. The family metaphor helped Americans who were anxious to preserve the nation's racial borders as four million black men and women became free. This chapter also considers the subject that white authors managed to bypass in these postwar tales: the process of emancipation and the reunification of ex-slave families. The testimony of freed blacks exposes as fantasy the view that African Americans were loyal dependents of white families. Rather, these men and women now focused on repairing their own family divisions and demonstrated loyalty to their kin that paralleled that seen in other divided families. When image and reality are scrutinized together, then, what emerges is the origins of white Americans' selective memory of the war, and of a culture that celebrated the reunion of a divided white population at the expense of a serious engagement with the status of African Americans.[21]

The history of divided families is therefore not just a story of family or of the nation at war, but a story of the powerful intersection between the two. A writer for *Harper's New Monthly Magazine* observed in 1863 that "we are taking the nation *home* with us as never before, and making our public interests a part of our private welfare."[22] Americans took the nation home both in their real families and in the popular imagination. On each level the family figured prominently in their thinking about Civil War loyalty by absorbing, translating, and making understandable the divisions of the nation. Sometimes the family inflamed those divisions and at other times it smoothed over them. Sometimes it reinforced the nation's political, social, and geographic borders, and other times it reached across them. Subsequent generations continued to make the family — especially the divided family — central to their percep-

tions of the Civil War. This book begins to explore where that association
came from.

IN THE YEARS LEADING UP to the war, and as secession became imminent,
many observers joined Abraham Lincoln in regarding the United States as a
"house divided." Family language pervaded newspaper stories and speeches
aired during secession conventions; the view that the nation was embroiled
in generational conflict between children and their parents was especially
popular. Both unionists and secessionists found in the language of generations a way of arguing for the righteousness of their political stance. Both
sides proclaimed their obedience to the Founding Fathers — George Washington, Thomas Jefferson, James Madison — while calling their opponents
rebellious "children" who were working against that paternal legacy. These
images cast Civil War Americans as the "children," leaving their parents in
the past, whereas other metaphors centered on the older generation. The state
of Virginia, for example, was widely described as the "mother State" or the
"old mother Virginia," which had given birth, in the migration of its citizens,
to states farther south and west. "Virginia, that old mother of heroes and
statesmen!" proclaimed the *Southern Field and Fireside*, "How grandly she
breasts the storm! . . . she bears her bosom to receive upon it strokes which
are aimed at her children." This statement offered the Confederate view:
that Virginia's secession upheld its proper position as a protective "mother,"
geographically buffering states farther south from the invading North. But
New York's *Harper's New Monthly Magazine* saw things quite differently: this
"*Mother of Presidents*," who had given "birth to the disloyal subject, *Nullification*," and "cherished [it] in her bosom," should now be called the "*Nurse of
Disunion*." The seceding state of Virginia was, depending on one's sectional
perspective, a good or a bad mother.[23]

These generational metaphors drew together, in one succinct image, several diverse and conflicting questions that were paramount in the secession
crisis: who had a legitimate claim to the political legacy of the founders?
who interpreted the Constitution correctly? and who had the authority to
determine whether disunion was allowable or not? These images explored
the more amorphous subject of duty and loyalty, too, considering what claim
each section could make on the other. They also suggested, most simply, who
was right and who was wrong in the ongoing debates. Generational imagery,
through the personae of parent and child, created a dichotomy between right

and wrong, maturity and youthfulness, wisdom and carelessness. This distinction at once reflected the reality of the secession crisis and suggested a widespread desire to exaggerate those differences at the beginning of hostilities. At the same time, though, these images mirrored a real generational crisis taking place within border-state families as the nation fell into civil war.

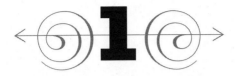

Union Father, Rebel Son

WHEN NINETEEN-YEAR-OLD Henry Lane Stone joined the Confederate army, he did not just turn against the Union, or what he called the "cursed dominion of Yankeedom." He also defied his family, especially his father. Stone's parents were natives of Kentucky, but by 1861 they were living in southern Indiana with Henry and his four brothers. They were staunch Unionists, and at least one of Henry's brothers volunteered for the Union army. But in August 1862 Henry, a middle child, felt drawn to fight for the Confederacy. Knowing that his family would try to stop him, he kept his decision secret and departed without even leaving a note. To make his way past Union pickets, he disguised himself as a poor farmer and headed for Kentucky to join the cavalry of John Hunt Morgan. A month later he revealed his whereabouts to his father: "Pap, I do not regret one practical my leaving home and every day convinces me I did right," he explained, yet he realized the personal cost of his actions. "I can imagine how your feelings are, one son in the Northern and another in the Southern Army," he acknowledged. "But so it is. . . . Good times will come again." He signed the letter, "Your rebelling son, Henry."[1]

Stone may have acknowledged that he was "rebelling" when he enlisted in the Confederate army, but he did not say why. Was he, like so many other Confederate soldiers, rebelling against the United States? Or was his a more personal rebellion against his family, especially his Union father? Or both? These questions vexed the Stone family and many other border-state families whose sons enlisted in the Confederate army despite their fathers' Union sympathies. Their division, which mirrored the greater conflict between the long-established Union and the youthful Confederacy, earned the notice of newspapers for its startling frequency across the border states. Few families knew how to respond to their sons' departure and spent the early war years trying to sort out the various meanings contained in the word "rebellion."[2]

Portrait of Confederate soldier Henry Lane Stone taken in Kingsville, Canada, January 1864, after his escape from the Union prison at Camp Douglas, Illinois. Stone's frequent letters to his Union family document his journey back to the South later that year to rejoin his regiment for the duration of the war. (Courtesy of the Filson Historical Society, Louisville, Ky.)

The personal papers of these border-state families offer few straightforward answers as to why their political allegiances settled along generational fault lines. These families were, like so many others in the border region, landowners who made their living by raising livestock and wheat. They generally lived in the low-lying areas and tended to own fewer than twenty slaves. They did not engage in the large-scale plantation agriculture of the Lower South but were still fairly wealthy, educated, and prominent in their communities. In most cases their nuclear families were intact, with mothers, stepmothers, sisters, and brothers sharing their households and generally working together on the family land. Yet when war came numerous sons, who averaged twenty-two years of age, enthusiastically left home to volunteer for the Confederate service, while their fathers remained Unionist advocates of compromise and moderation.

Fortunately these Union fathers and their rebel sons argued freely on paper during the war, explaining in vivid detail why they believed their loyalties were divided. Even though the sons who split from their fathers in most cases left their siblings and a mother too, it was conflict between father and son that inspired the most introspection. Male kin disagreed in particular about how personal their conflict was and to what extent the sons' national loyalties were linked to or contingent on their loyalty to their fathers.

Rebellion

The brewing rebellion of the sons became apparent to border-state observers even before the fall of Fort Sumter. As early as February 1861, twenty-one-year-old Josie Underwood noticed that in her hometown of Bowling Green, Kentucky, "all the men . . . of any position or prominence whatever are Union men — and yet many of these men have wild reckless unthinking inexperienced sons who make so much noise about secession as to almost drown their fathers wiser council." Border-state newspaper editors eventually took note of this family dynamic, including the *Louisville Daily Journal*, which months later declared the father-son conflict an "epidemic" and began writing lengthy essays on its pervasiveness.[3]

What these observers witnessed was the climax of a generational conflict that had been mounting throughout border-state society in the decade prior to 1861. During the secession crisis some of the most vigorous proponents of slavery and states' rights were men born in the 1830s and 1840s. These were young adults who had never known a time without sectional conflict, who had lived through tenuous political compromises in Missouri and violent threats to slavery in "Bleeding Kansas" and in Harpers Ferry, Virginia. What they saw all around them was the elusiveness of a national consensus on slavery and a political landscape where division was the norm. In such an environment it was almost impossible not to take a vigorous stance on the issues of the day. These young border-state advocates of slavery and Southern rights, though not unique, developed a passionate enthusiasm for secession that set them apart from older generations and, in the cases considered here, from their own fathers.[4]

Their fathers, meanwhile, were fixtures of the border-state political establishment: among them were a Maryland governor, two Kentucky senators, and several congressmen. Most were either Whigs or, as the war approached, Constitutional Unionists and Democrats intent on forging compromises to stave off civil war. Their political affiliations generally reflected the ideological and geographic middle ground in which they lived, and it appears that most tried to impart that same moderation to their sons. "I would caution you against imbibing all the notions put forth by your advocates for slavery," was how Samuel Halsey responded in 1857 to his son Joseph's blustery antiabolitionist rant. To make his case, Samuel sent Joseph a "sensible tract" written by a Kentucky minister. Fathers like Halsey detected their sons' radicalism early, but rather than demand outright conformity they generally permitted an open debate on sectional issues. Their letters reveal an energetic but tolerant exchange of ideas throughout the 1850s, as the fathers apparently believed that beneath their sons' political vigor was a deeper agreement on national loyalty.[5]

By 1861, however, the letters of these fathers and sons took on a starkly different tone. Any political difference was no longer something as benign as words on a page; in wartime, it could mean opposing allegiances across a deadly battle. As war seemed imminent, fathers grew less tolerant of their sons' independent political expression. They did not expect their sons to think exactly like themselves, but they did draw a line at specific actions. Service in the Confederate army was unacceptable. "Do not resign under any circumstances without consultation with me," one Kentucky father demanded of his son, whom he feared would leave the U.S. Army for the South. Other fathers struck compromises, even promising to support their rebel sons financially if they did not volunteer for Confederate service. Still others, hopeful that the war would last only a few months, made their sons promise to stay at home for a year before enlisting in the Confederacy.[6]

Union newspapers challenged fathers to prevent their sons from leaving for the Confederacy and to compel them to join the Union forces. "If the young men are slow to enlist in the cause of human freedom," advised the *Louisville Daily Journal*, "let the old men step forward, and by their patriotic example shame their degenerate sons and grandsons." In this paper's view, the mechanism of paternal authority was the most effective deterrent to a young man's military support of the Confederate cause. After all, mid-nineteenth-century society considered it a father's duty to nurture his son's political allegiances. A mother might instill a general sense of civic duty and consciousness, but in matters of partisanship a father's example was to be paramount. Fathers must live up to those expectations, the *Journal* exhorted, and most fathers did in demanding political obedience. Initially, many Confederate-minded sons complied, but over time they found complying with their fathers' wishes intolerable. In the first year of the war the awkward promises of these sons set the stage for the "epidemic" lamented by the *Journal*.[7]

Twenty-three-year-old Matthew Page Andrews of Shepherdstown, Virginia (later West Virginia), promised his father Charles, a pro-Union Episcopal minister, that he would not volunteer for Confederate service and would remain in law school. But this became difficult for him when his classmates began to enlist. "My position is getting more and more embarrassing every day," Matthew wrote his fiancée. "All the young men in town have joined one of the three companies formed here," and they did not understand why Matthew failed to sign up. Peer pressure was severe; indeed, it had prompted many other young men to fight for the South. Yet Matthew vowed to remain out of the service because he did not want to "offend" his father. Meanwhile, Charles Andrews took the opportunity to reinforce his political authority in letters to his son. "I am much more calm than you are, & have a much more intelligent & impartial survey of the whole question," he argued on one occasion and suggested that Matthew would come to share his opinions within weeks. Charles was overly confident, for Matthew never accepted his beliefs, although he did not volunteer for Confederate service.[8]

Sons like Matthew Andrews soon faced additional obstacles to obeying their fathers and retaining their civilian status. In 1862 and 1863 both the Union and Confederate governments passed conscription laws that compelled all men between the ages of eighteen and forty-five to serve in the military.[9] This made it impossible to simply remain at home, since almost every young man had to enlist in the army supported by his state. For sons in the Union states of Delaware, Kentucky, Maryland, and Missouri, the idea of being forced to join the Union army became an additional inducement to act on their Confederate sympathies and quickly head south. Henry Stone, who opened this chapter, explained to his father that while at home in a Union state he "was in great danger of being drafted where I could not have served." After leaving in 1862 and joining the Confederate army, he wrote, "I'm contented."[10] Sons in the Confederate states of Virginia and Tennessee had the conscription laws on their side, which, in many cases, did encourage a son's enlistment. But even in these regions some fathers stepped in to prevent the laws from affecting their sons. Matthew Andrews's father, for example, used his connections to preempt conscription and to find his son a job in the paymaster's office in Richmond, reasoning that a government job was less odious than service as a combatant against the Union.[11]

Other sons resorted to sneaking away from their fathers when it became too hard to resist the pressure of their peers or the law. The experience of twenty-year-old Ezekiel "Zeke" Clay was fairly common. Before the war, Zeke was schooled by several prominent Unionists. His family, in fact, offered a model of sectional compromise: his father, Brutus Clay, was a Whig member of the Kentucky legislature and a slaveholder, while his paternal uncle, Cassius Clay, was a vigorous abolitionist, and his distant cousin, Henry Clay, was the architect of several plans to prevent slavery from destroying the Union. On the other hand, Zeke had a significant circle of friends his age who attended pro-secession speeches and rallies and encouraged him to join them. His family knew of his dalliance with secession ideas but was openly tolerant of his views, even during the first months of the war. His stepmother, Ann, kept her own Union opinions to herself even while venting to her husband that Zeke talked about secession "like some one crazy." Brutus maintained his silence, apparently confident that his son would uphold his agreement to stay home and manage the family land while Brutus served in the legislature.[12]

Over several weeks in September 1861, however, Zeke secretly plotted his departure. He approached a Confederate officer about obtaining a commission in the army, yet denied having done so when his stepmother heard rumors about the meeting. He also set about making gun cartridges to take with him — working deviously right under his stepmother's nose — but claimed that they were for his father. Then one night the same month, after telling his step-mother that he was going loon hunting, Zeke rode off on his mare, taking along the blanket from his bed, one of his father's rifles, and a small amount of clothing. In a note found in his bedroom, he explained his departure this way: "I leave for the army tonight. I do it for I believe I am doing right. I go of my own free will. If it turns out that I do wrong I beg forgiveness. Good bye. E."[13]

Brutus Clay could hardly contain his anger when he learned what his son had done. Zeke had acted with the same hotheaded zeal as the South Carolinians whom Clay and other border-state Union men condemned. He had failed to show a moderation in politics that Clay expected of all his sons and, more personally, he had reneged on his promise to remain at home during the war. Zeke evidently preferred to follow the lead of "every scamp in the country" rather than his own father's, Brutus thundered to his wife. Ann agreed with his assessment, having already vowed to find out what it was that had "induced a boy to take sides against a father." To the Clays, this was no ordinary disagreement of two individuals over sectional politics; rather, it was a very personal case of filial defiance.[14]

Other Union fathers had the same angry reaction to the secretive departures of their rebel sons. Although they had given their sons latitude to develop independent political views, few had known how seriously to take their sons' expressions of Southern loyalty; fewer yet expected that their worst fear — Confederate service — would be realized. Union fathers therefore had difficulty knowing how to respond. If they accepted their sons' defection as an independent act of political conscience, then they would be acknowledging the outright rejection of their own political views. But if they attributed it to reckless and defiant behavior, as Brutus Clay seemed to do, it would be much easier to remain secure in their position as fathers. The sons' action would still represent a serious betrayal, but a more familiar and manageable one: it was just another coming-of-age struggle set against the dramatic backdrop of war.[15]

Fathers of the Civil War generation were well acquainted with this kind of conflict. Little consensus existed in midcentury prescriptive literature about the ideal relationship between fathers and sons. The historic tradition of paternal authority was being eroded gradually by an antebellum trend toward a less authoritarian and more affectionate model of child rearing. This left fathers and sons caught between expectations of paternal dominance and the impulse toward companionship. Where a father's authority and a son's deference met was rarely clear, and this created what historian Bertram Wyatt-Brown has called an "inherent ambivalence" between fathers and sons. Conflicts with fathers thus became a ritual of growing up for nineteenth-century sons, and this is what Civil War fathers often saw in their sons' defection to the Confederacy: a very familiar and personal challenge to their paternal authority.[16]

Newspaper observers encouraged Union fathers to view their sons' Confederate service as a deliberate act of filial defiance. In one of the first analyses of divided fathers and sons in 1861, the *Louisville Daily Journal* published a series of articles, entitled "Letters of a Father," elaborating on why the present rebellion of sons was a normal stage in life. The American "political and social system" contained an inherent contradiction, the series argued, one in which sons were required to defer to their fathers while at the same time were instilled with republican values of liberty. The most readily available expression of that liberty was the rejection of "filial piety" in the home, and for that reason father-and-son conflicts were a natural creation of the republican system. The rebellion of sons in wartime was merely a reflection of this greater flaw in the American "national character"; worse, however, was the Confederacy's exploitation of this phenomenon with "specious appeals to the natural love of liberty."[17]

Indeed, the Confederacy's call for independence meshed well with this younger generation's desire for autonomy. At least one study of secession has found that young men felt a natural affinity for the Southern cause precisely because of the desire for liberty nurtured in their own homes. Fathers, the guardians of their inheritance and future livelihood as the owners of land, slaves, and family businesses, at times posed a substantial obstacle to their sons' transition to adulthood. A father who was unwilling to give up land or otherwise assist his son in building an independent life for himself left him in a dependent position. This aroused a resentment and frustration that made the Confederate rhetoric of "independence" and "liberty" all the more resonant.[18]

The rebel sons considered here had reached this uncertain juncture in their lives. The majority were unmarried and between the ages of sixteen and twenty-five — the transition period between the dependence of childhood and the independence of adulthood. Zeke Clay, for example, had recently dropped out of college from lack of interest and had returned home to work his father's land. Henry Stone also worked on his family's property, having not yet taken up the legal career that would occupy him later. Census returns from 1860 show that roughly two-thirds of the border-state rebel sons also resided in their fathers' households, perhaps hoping to inherit land or eventually purchase acreage of their own. Their financial prospects ranged from being in debt, to working as apprentices, to relying on their fathers to put them through school, to striking out on their own for new land in the

Texas Southwest. Almost without exception, these young men had not yet settled into their lifelong careers and were self-conscious of their continued dependence on their fathers. Service in the Confederacy — acknowledged or not — allowed them to embrace the promise, if not the reality, of liberty. As one son informed his father, "Your boy who left you six or seven months ago a mere child has now grown to manhood." In this euphemistic declaration of independence, the son suggested that his father accept his service to the Confederacy as a defining moment in his emergence into adulthood.[19]

Personal liberty may have attracted sons to the Confederacy, but few fathers were willing to view this attraction as a deep ideological commitment. Much more popular was the belief that their sons possessed no ideas at all and were deluded or coerced into the Confederate service. After learning of Zeke's departure, Brutus Clay speculated that his son had been influenced by a "scamp"; other Union fathers similarly directed their frustration toward an anonymous influence. One father complained that "older & more wicked men" had "seduced" his son into service. The *Louisville Daily Journal* concluded that one Unionist's son probably would not have fought for the South "had not poisonous sophistries been poured into his ears by older men who had a design to corrupt his mind and seduce him into the paths of treachery."[20]

These "older men" who rivaled fathers for their sons' attention were no anomaly of war. Commonly known as "confidence men," "tricksters," or "seducers," they were a fixture in the minds of nineteenth-century fathers. Fathers were fearful that once a son was old enough to strike out on his own, whether to purchase his own land or to begin a career, unscrupulous strangers might take advantage of him, corrupt him, and destroy his character. Nothing, in a father's view, was more threatening to a son's republican liberty. Young men who were eager to make their mark on the world were susceptible to the words of designing men, and the confusion of war, these fathers believed, provided an ideal opportunity for such individuals to do their work.[21] Sometimes these wartime confidence men were known to the family, such as a cousin, an uncle, or a longtime friend who talked "secesh" and encouraged sons to accompany them to secession rallies. Other times they worked at a distance, as did the fire-eating secessionists of the Lower South. Indeed, Unionists across the North, even those without rebel kin, often blamed the fire-eaters and other Confederate leaders for duping the Southern people into supporting secession. Such arguments not only faulted confidence men for their sinister influence but also insulted their victims by minimizing the depth of their own commitment to the Confederacy. Union fathers, however, had little trouble applying this derisive argument to their sons' wartime service.[22]

No one worked harder to attract their sons' attention, these fathers became convinced, than the leaders of Confederate cavalry. These men, reputed to be more daring and more talented than their Union counterparts, cut dashing figures and appealed to young men's desire for adventure. One of the most influential in the border region was thirty-six-year-old John Hunt Morgan of Kentucky. Already legendary among Southern partisans as an embodiment of "chivalry" and "bravery," Morgan and his men swept through Kentucky and Tennessee in July 1862 on a raid that resulted in the imprisonment of 1,200 Union soldiers — with only 95 Confederate casualties. Morgan's words were as bold as his actions. In a circular entitled "Kentuckians!," he made the rousing declaration that he had "come to liberate you from the despotism of a tyrannical faction and to rescue my native State from the hand of your oppressors. Everywhere the cowardly foe has fled from my avenging arms." Crowds gathered along his route to catch a glimpse of the man who would become a folk hero of the Confederacy. His reputation awed young men. "You can't hurt a Morgan man," one Kentucky son boldly concluded after signing on to Morgan's cavalry. At least one hundred men, later referred to as the "sons of our best and strongest Union men" by a Kentucky woman, followed him.[23]

Morgan and his men, according to Union fathers, preyed on their sons to become followers. "My son," as one father described his departure with Morgan, "was seduced into the Rebel service by designing men." Also referred to as "Morgan's gang" and "Morgan's guerrilla party," this band of rebel soldiers unnerved Union families. They were persuaded that their sons were too young and too impressionable to resist Morgan's overtures, despite the best efforts of the sons to convince them otherwise. One Kentucky son tried to reassure his family that Morgan's men were "gentlemen of the best families of Ky.," and therefore honorable comrades in battle. But few parents accepted this notion. As one father explained, his son was a "victim" of Morgan's "folly & delusion."[24]

Other troubling influences, fathers discovered, lurked within their own homes and were of a decidedly feminine cast. Indeed, in some cases the "scamp" luring their son to the opposite side was none other than his own mother. Union fathers had good reason to suspect their wives: Who else had such close contact with and influence over their sons? While one Virginia father was attempting to dissuade his son from volunteering for the Confederacy, his wife was sending him letters laced with prosecession sentiment. "What is the benefit of plunging Ben [Matthew] into this certain destruction?" Charles Wesley Andrews asked his wife Sarah, demanding that she protect, rather than endanger, their son. In a Tennessee household, Louisa Brown Pearl chose to remain in the South with her rebel son rather than follow her Union husband north to escape the hardships of war. Pearl remained in contact with the son throughout the war and effectively condoned his behavior, despite his father's ardent Union stance.[25]

Women like Sarah Andrews and Louisa Brown Pearl occupied an uncomfortable position, caught between the conflicting roles of mother and wife. In accordance with antebellum political culture, they were responsible for their sons' development into moral, civic-minded, and patriotic individuals; many sons also looked to their mothers for guidance in the sectional crisis. At the same time, however, mothers were expected to defer to their husbands on all matters of public affairs. In the two cases cited above, the women put motherhood ahead of wifely duty and thus competed with their husbands in influencing a son's political choices. But, in other cases, the idea that such influence might result in a father and son meeting on a battlefield was agonizing and, as one mother put it, "pursued me like a ghost." For that reason, some mothers chose to suppress their own Confederate sympathies and to seek family unity by urging their sons to uphold their fathers' patriotic legacy. "Your dear Father never took sides either way," wrote one Missouri mother to her son in a plea for neutrality. "Try and follow the bright example your beloved Father has set you."[26]

Whether it was a family member or a cavalryman who deterred a son from that example, Union fathers found a way to explain familial conflict. To blame someone else's influence was to place the blame on the society that produced unscrupulous men (or women) and on sons too young or inexperienced to know better. A son's Confederate service was therefore not an expression of political conscience but instead symptomatic of a separate struggle over a father's paternal authority.

Political Conscience

This reading of the sons' behavior would seem to explain the common defection of the younger generation to the South, but the sons themselves provided an entirely different perspective. They repeatedly and adamantly denied that taking the Confederate side was in any way a deliberate act of defiance against their fathers. As Henry Stone exclaimed when he heard of his father's anger: "Father, when you look over my career in the past eighteen months, do you feel that I am a traitor? Have I not done my duty, and have I not followed your teachings of right? Do you feel that I'm unworthy to be your son? God forbid!" While condemning what he called the "despotism" that his father supported, Stone still rejected the notion that he might be "unworthy" as a son. If anything, he believed that, by following the dictates of his conscience, his service to the Confederacy was wholly consistent with his father's teachings.[27]

Obviously, a son would have every reason to deny a personally motivated rebellion against his father. But his denials did indicate a serious disagreement between the generations over the relationship between their family and national loyalties. Whereas fathers saw the two as intertwined — national loyalty was merely a reflection of their personal relationship — sons argued that the two were entirely separate. "I am a secessionist, but that shall not conflict with a duty I owe my father — that of being respectful, and kind," Virginian William Thomson told his father in February 1861. His loyalty to the Confederacy was unconnected to his ties to his father. Dividing his loyalties allowed Thomson and other sons to view their Confederate service more innocently than their fathers did.[28]

Sons accordingly explained their defection as a pure act of political conscience. Zeke Clay seemed to know that his father would attribute his departure to youthful rebellion when he assured his parents in the note explaining his flight south: "I do it for I believe I am doing right." "I know I'm right," wrote another son, though it is impossible to determine how much influence this sense of political "right" actually had on the mobilization of sons. The same question has confronted historians who study why soldiers fought in the Civil War, and it is likely that both ideological convictions and personal considerations motivated most soldiers. But in letters to Union fathers, rebel sons suggested that ideology was *all* that guided them in war. They wrote about fighting "tyranny," "Black Republicanism," and the "despotism of Lincoln," calling on popular political rhetoric to emphasize that their military service was guided only by politics. Their differences with their fathers could be explained simply as the divergent conclusions of two rational, thoughtful men.[29]

Behind those words, however, the political-first principles of the sons did not differ significantly from those of their fathers. On the most crucial and divisive issue of the war — slavery — Union fathers and rebel sons were, for the most part, in striking agreement. Census records show that three-quarters of the fathers were slaveholders themselves, and thus the majority of sons grew up in households in which slavery was openly accepted or tolerated. Rebel sons therefore could associate slavery with their fathers' interests and could see in secession the protection of something on which their fathers depended. Although their fathers, in contrast, may have predicted the eventual "doom of slavery," as one Virginia father put it, or believed that it was best protected in the Union, the sons still could argue that their wartime service realized their fathers' true ideals. The question that divided them was less ideological than practical: How could slavery be best protected — by an independent Confederacy or by the Union?[30]

Such ideological congruence on the issue of slavery may have helped sons downplay any filial rebellion that may have influenced their behavior. William C. P. Breckinridge of Kentucky, for example, had been instructed by his Unionist father, Robert, to remain at home during the war to care for the family's slaves (whom Robert once claimed were "faithful to union Masters"). It hardly seemed a violation of his father's orders, then, to go off and fight to preserve the master-slave relationship. Yet generational tensions may still help explain why common support for slavery gave way to opposing stances in the war. Border-state sons were raised in a white, landowning society that saw slavery as the path to upward mobility, the thing they needed to become independent and achieve manhood. To see a challenge to slavery was to see a challenge to their inheritance, to their future, to their whole way of life; it is understandable, then, that men of this generation would join the Confederate defense of that institution. Meanwhile, their fathers' generation had lived through threats to slavery before and had seen compromises worked out between the North and the South. These men had more faith that slavery could be preserved *within* the Union — indeed, some border-state fathers, such as John J. Crittenden, of Kentucky, a slaveholding U.S. congressman, had forged the compromises themselves. Different generational concerns could thus shape divergent outlooks on slavery and the war, suggesting a direct link between family position and wartime politics in the lives of border-state men.[31]

The sons still denied this link, however, and preferred to view their national loyalty separately from their filial relationship. In their letters home, they rarely attacked their fathers' choice to remain in the Union but strongly objected when their fathers tried to punish them for their Confederate service. Union fathers, indeed, considered punishment a necessary response to the personal rebellion they detected in their sons' enlistment. "Just as he has acted, he will be dealt with," was how Brutus Clay furiously explained his decision to withdraw his son Zeke's inheritance after his departure. Since Zeke had denied Brutus his authority as a father, Brutus would reciprocate by refusing what he owed in return: protection. Although disinheritance was rare among divided fathers and sons, fathers like Brutus Clay refused to send the customary aid to their sons, such as clothing or money, or forbade their sons from visiting their homes. These and other punishments served the indirect purpose of restoring the paternal authority that Union fathers believed was lost when their sons joined the Confederacy. Zeke Clay, however, did not take his father's threat of disinheritance seriously. With humor, he asked his stepmother if he could still keep his wristwatch.[32]

For other sons, punishments were no laughing matter. A father's disapproval was devastating enough, but many sons believed that their fathers' punishments were unwarranted. They saw little purpose in lessons on respect or obedience when they believed that they still upheld these values. One penalty was deemed especially unfair: a father's refusal to correspond with his rebellious offspring. Certainly the wartime security measures of the Union and Confederate governments made it more difficult to communicate frequently, but some fathers deliberately withheld their letters as a form of punishment. After all, in peacetime letter writing was an important means of sustaining a personal relationship. The failure to write regularly had always been a basis for chastisement, and not to write at all was an act of profound significance: the severing of emotional ties. Given the insecurity of wartime, when soldiers found themselves lonely and threatened with death, this punishment could be devastating.[33]

One Virginia father resorted to this step after finding his son's letters "full of the lies [of] Rebel Genl. Bobby Lee." Warner Thomson, a slaveholding farmer trying to maintain a living in the path of war, became fed up with his son's rebel allegiance after his own livelihood was threatened. Thomson suffered financial losses when advancing Confederate troops forced him to flee his Shenandoah Valley home temporarily in 1863. To make matters worse, his secession neighbors—especially the women—had grown increasingly hostile. An outcast, Thomson found it impossible to extend pleasantries to a son who allied himself with the Confederates and opted for silence over false sentiments. His son William, an eighteen-year-old aspiring teacher and a soldier in a Tennessee regiment, recoiled at his father's mindset. "Pa has ceased to think of me as his son," he complained to his stepmother, declaring that his father obviously cared more about Abraham Lincoln than his own son.

This was especially traumatic for him when his brother, Jonathan, who also joined the Confederate army, was imprisoned by Union authorities. Without his father to comfort him, William became dependent on the kindness of strangers to help him cope with his brother's incarceration. "For all intents and purposes," William concluded, "I am a lone orphan."[34]

In his father's silence, William detected that he had been consigned to the most desperate position of unwanted child. He saw the worst in the absence of his father's letters, revealing the extent to which he relied on Warner's love. His reaction was yet another reflection of the tension between authority and affection that characterized antebellum families. Whereas Warner, stunned by his son's defection to the Confederacy, chose to reemphasize his parental authority, William found his father's love increasingly important once he endured the foul weather, loneliness, and tainted food of his life in camp. In pleading letters, William accused his father of violating an obligation to extend that goodwill toward his children. "No one is capable of more devotion to a parent than I am," he wrote, "but in order that this feeling have *full* force, there must be a corresponding affection on the part of the parent."[35]

Warner Thomson's silence was not an adequate measure of his true sentiments, however. He was, in fact, more conflicted than his son believed and found it difficult to condemn William outright, even if his cause was "entirely wrong." Warner frequently turned to his diary to wrestle with their relationship. "My natural affection for my sons & love for my country," he once wrote, "cause a struggle in my mind—it is a painful one." Warner had difficulty reconciling his son's act with his own desire to continue as a family. "I feel as if I am committing wrong to allow an active enemy of my country to remain in my house," he wrote of the idea of permitting William to visit, but "than [*sic*] I am met with the feelings of affection natural to a parent—it is a trial—sore trial." His loyalty to the Union—as well as his own economic security—compelled him to react as a stern patriarch, but deep down he possessed more complicated feelings toward his son. He temporarily resolved this conflict by asking family members for frequent reports on William.[36]

Thomson's reliance on other family members was not unusual. When relations between fathers and sons became strained, mothers, wives, and sisters—whether they wanted to or not—sometimes assumed a mediating position. In the Thomson family, Warner's wife and William's stepmother, Josephine, eventually became a surrogate correspondent. William believed that Josephine's intervention was essential to save him from permanent orphan status: "I hope you will not fail to improve it," he wrote of his relationship with his father, asking that she encourage Warner to communicate with him. Some women eagerly embraced this mediating role, writing letters, sending supplies, and even appealing to fathers on their sons' behalf. But Josephine Thomson seemed to resent being used as a surrogate. "You seem to wish me to write only that you may hear from him," she complained to William on one occasion, demanding that he carve out a separate place for her in his thoughts and feelings.[37]

Women in other families sometimes became irritants, exacerbating the estrangement between father and son rather than relieving it. Issa Desha Breckinridge, wife of Confederate soldier William C. P. Breckinridge, once intervened when it became evident that her husband and his strongly pro-Union father, Robert, had resumed contact. William wrote his father on Robert's birthday in 1864, sending his "love" and suggesting that, in the case of his death, Robert should care for William's wife and young daughter. Robert complied with the request, writing next to Issa to assure her that he would "do for his wife & child all that I am permitted to do, and able to do." But Issa resisted his overture. In the first of a three-way exchange of letters, she fired back: "Neither I nor our child expect or desire any thing from you." Issa was angry with her father-in-law for initially cutting off contact with his son and for having treated her daughter with "profound indifference." Calling this behavior "I can never forget," Issa was no mediator in this father-son split but instead positioned herself as defender of her husband's integrity. She urged him to recognize that his father's punishment was too severe to be forgiven quickly. William agreed but ended a letter to his wife with a request of his own: "Darling do not allow any thing to make you widen the breach."[38]

Widening the Breach

Union fathers faced additional pressures that complicated their relationships with their sons. A son's Confederate service was to his father even more than a private crisis of filial defiance: it was a potential source of public embarrassment as well. In a region influenced by a Southern honor culture that forced people to think about how their friends and neighbors judged them, an errant son could be a black mark to the family name. This was particularly true for men of military or political prominence, who contended daily with the scrutiny of both their allies and their pronounced enemies. Mid-nineteenth-century political culture revolved around establishing the reputations and character of men who became leaders. To what extent an individual's private or family life should affect or shape that public reputation, however, was not settled in the popular mind. So when wartime newspapermen floated rumors about the divided loyalties of some of the nation's most prominent families, Union fathers were placed in an awkward position.[39]

Nothing illustrated this more vividly than one episode in Kentucky. It involved John J. Crittenden, a member of the U.S. House of Representatives who had achieved national recognition for trying to prevent the Civil War through compromise while previously serving in the Senate. Crittenden was respected by his Whig colleagues for his integrity, eloquent speeches, and cautious political skills and was frequently referred to as "noble" and a "great statesman" in the border-state press.[40] But Crittenden had failed to exercise these conciliatory skills in his own household. Although his youngest son Thomas dutifully became a soldier for the Union, his oldest son George joined a Confederate regiment. George had disappointed his father before, with his weakness for alcohol and his penchant for debt, but his defection to the Confederacy made George the subject of press attention for the first time. In May 1862 George D. Prentice, editor of the *Louisville Daily Journal*, published a scathing attack on George Crittenden's Confederate career. Crittenden had joined the Union's "malignant enemies" and had become one of the "most malignant of those enemies," Prentice wrote. His "treachery" was "sad" and had brought unknowable pain to his friends in Kentucky. For this, Prentice concluded, the name Crittenden "can no more be dishonored." The *Daily Missouri Democrat* went even further, suggesting that his rebel son "may somewhat affect his [John Crittenden's] patriotism."[41]

John Crittenden was infuriated by these attacks. "My son is a rebel — I defend him not," he wrote three days later in a private letter to the *Journal*'s Prentice, "but what public good can such denunciations, as that article contains, do?" What angered him most was not the article's censure of George's decision to go south — Crittenden himself had stopped writing to George for having done so — but its suggestion that the Crittenden family honor had been damaged as a result. In keeping with his stature as an honorable statesman, Crittenden corrected Prentice's assessment of his family: "Geo. B. Crittenden, save his act of Rebellion, & the occasional habit of intemperance, is beloved by all his family as one of the *best* & noblest of their race." Even though his son was "deluded" into rebellion and his behavior deserved condemnation, Crittenden acknowledged, his family had come to believe that George was serving his cause well and had acted with "honorable" intentions. Family honor, he claimed, was not necessarily damaged by a wayward son if that son acted honorably in his new position. For this reason Crittenden pronounced the article "most cruel."[42]

Equally galling to Crittenden was Prentice's apparent belief that there was some public benefit in revealing the Crittenden family's problems to his readers. In a note at the bottom of his letter, he urged the editor to keep this matter "private" in the future. Crittenden thus claimed for himself and his family the right to privacy that some Americans believed was inherent in the idealized division of society into separate spheres of home and world. Domestic life was to stand distinct from the disruptions of work and politics, and this, Crittenden evidently thought, afforded him a wall around his private life to protect him from the prying eyes of journalists. Such a demarcation, however, was never as neat as promised in ideal terms.[43]

George Prentice continued to exploit that murky distinction between public and private life. He remained vigorous in his exposés of rebel sons, once advocating the hanging of the U.S. assistant surgeon general's son to restore that family's honor. His attention to family life appears on the surface to be nothing more than the zealous behavior of an extremely patriotic Union man. In fact, Prentice was, in the words of the *Richmond Enquirer*, "one of the most decided enemies of the Southern cause" and one of Kentucky's loudest Democratic voices against secession. To police the loyalty of families was in Prentice's view to defend the interests of the Union. But even as he delved into the private lives of others, Prentice soon found himself in the same position as other Union fathers: he, too, was placed on the defensive by the actions of *his own* rebel sons, twenty-three-year-old Courtland and twenty-year-old Clarence.[44]

Months after his attack on George Crittenden, Prentice learned that the *Cincinnati Commercial*, his strongest Republican rival, had published rumors that Courtland had stolen Prentice's prized silver mounted rifle when he joined John Hunt Morgan's cavalry. The paper speculated that Prentice found his son's behavior "disgraceful." Taking a page from John Crittenden's book, Prentice immediately fired off a note to the *Commercial*, which subsequently appeared in other border-state papers, denying that his son had stolen a rifle. He never owned such a rifle, Prentice explained, adding that he was sorry to see his "lamented boy" slandered. Prentice jumped to his son's defense, his position as a protective father temporarily outweighing the demands of his own politics. Prentice was motivated partly by the fact that Courtland lay defenseless in a hospital bed, the victim of friendly fire in Augusta, Kentucky. Prentice and his wife went to visit their son days after he wrote the response and witnessed Courtland's eventual death. A few days later Prentice asked readers to spare his family from additional newspaper coverage. "The tears of weeping eyes," he asserted, "are not for the public gaze."[45]

Observers likely would have respected his request, given that death and mourning were widely accepted in midcentury society as private matters. But Prentice undermined that status by publishing a three-column eulogy of his son in the *Louisville Daily Journal*; the piece later traveled in an abridged form to newspapers across Missouri and Ohio. In "William Courtland Prentice: A Brief Sketch," Prentice extolled his son's virtues. Courtland was "manly" and possessed "the strength of a young Hercules." He was constantly in search of outdoor adventures and recognized as a skilled marksman after moving to Texas in 1860. He was also a "wild" and adventurous youth, who early on had grown impatient with school discipline. This, Prentice explained, made it difficult for Courtland to resist taking up arms when his loyalty directed him to the South during the war. Although initially Courtland curbed his impulse to leave home in deference to his father, he became miserable, "like an imprisoned lion." Although Prentice sympathized with his son, he believed that Courtland would have remained in the Union had it not been for those ubiquitous "bad men" who were able to lure him away. His family would remember Courtland as a "brave and noble though misguided youth."[46]

Prentice did not explain what compelled him to delve into a character study of his son in the pages of the *Journal*. Perhaps he believed that it would blunt the stinging criticism of Courtland's defection from the Union. The eulogy effectively established that his son's Confederate service was an aberration in an otherwise harmonious father-son relationship: Courtland had been a loyal son despite his misery, George was a watchful father, and only outside influences had pushed Courtland into the rebel army. Not unlike John Crittenden's defense of his own son, Prentice went even further to prop up Courtland's reputation with details about his sense of adventure and manly honor. He may have hoped that his essay would silence the question of his family's honor once and for all, but instead his seemingly apologetic stance toward his son's behavior opened the floodgates of suspicion and innuendo.[47]

In March 1863 it was rumored that Prentice's other son, Clarence, was feeding him information about the movements of Confederate troops. The *New York Times* charged that Prentice was en route to Europe to escape the rebel troops that, he had been warned, were making their way into Kentucky. The paper accused him of withholding this information from other Union partisans and thus using his connection to the Confederacy for his own self-interest. In a letter to the editor, Prentice hotly denied the accusation and disparaged the paper for subjecting his family to such "malignant calumnies." Months later, a rival border-state newspaperman, Unionist William G. Brownlow of Tennessee, published a blistering attack on Prentice's loyalty based on the Confederate service of his surviving son. "You are but one degree removed from a rebel and a traitor," Brownlow declared, and for that reason "your paper is no longer a Union authority." This time Prentice chose silence rather than openly respond to censure that undoubtedly wounded him as a proud Union man.[48]

The Prentice and Crittenden exposés were part of a larger journalistic trend of invoking family division to question the reputation of public men. Most common were articles written by Union partisans to evaluate the position of Confederate leaders. Typical was a March 1862 story that originated in the *New York Tribune* and was circulated by the border-state press stating that Confederate leaders President Jefferson Davis and Vice President Alexander H. Stephens were "of Yankee . . . paternity." The writer traced both men's parents to the town of North Killingly, Connecticut, where they reportedly lived until finally settling in the South. Relatives of Davis and Stephens still resided in the town, the article noted, including an eighty-year-old man named Stephens who made the dubious claim of being a cousin of both leaders. "What could more forcibly exemplify the foolishness of the rebel cry of 'mudsills,' 'pedlers,' 'slaves,' 'cowards,' 'poltroons,' against Northern Society!" exclaimed the *Louisville Daily Journal*. Family ties made it impossible to draw the sharp distinctions between the two societies on which Southerners depended. It was hypocritical, the paper therefore charged, for these Southern leaders to distance themselves from a society to which they were so intimately related.[49]

Rumors of political division in the families of Southern leaders played into the Northern critics' hands. After all, it was the veneration of lineage and kinship, so central to Southern conceptions of honor and gentility, that Confederate leaders and writers often identified to distinguish themselves from the corrupt and degenerate Yankees. The Confederate nation was a perfected land of cavaliers, descended directly from English bloodlines both noble and pure. Yet, Northern critics charged, this revealed nothing more than a distorted genealogy. "The parents of Jeff Davis and Alex Stephens were probably no better than the average of Yankee men and women," the *Louisville Daily Journal* asserted. Although the paper actually was mistaken — Davis's parents were born and raised in South Carolina, and Stephens's were from

Georgia—the point underlying the attack was more credible. It was fallacious for Confederates to suggest that their family identities were as distinct as their political ones.[50]

Stories about Jefferson Davis's bloodlines, and in particular his alleged illegitimate progeny in Union territory, abounded. He was rumored to be the father of an Indian child in Wisconsin, the product of a relationship with a "Menomonee squaw" when Davis was a U.S. Army officer stationed at Fort Winnebago in the 1820s. Other articles indicated that Davis was the father of a Minnesota boy. The *Louisville Daily Journal*, for example, reported that Davis had seduced a "Minnesota girl" while stationed at Fort Snelling, and that the son who resulted from this liaison had become a "mysterious assassin." Such stories may have been more easily exaggerated than documented, although Davis did work in these regions of the old Northwest while in the U.S. Army, including service as a construction superintendent at Fort Winnebago. According to one contemporary recollection, he was once confronted by the brother of an Indian girl for having taken "improper liberties" with his sister while stationed at Fort Crawford (also in Wisconsin). Regardless of the facts behind the rumors, such stories allowed Union newspapers to characterize Davis as a promiscuous man, one who actively blurred the genetic lines that supposedly existed between North and South.[51]

Private family histories linking Northerners and Southerners provided a useful means of undermining the South's legitimacy as a separate nation. Confederate lineage thus captured the Union imagination, and the family trees of some of the most prominent Southerners were scrutinized by the Northern press. Most accounts centered on families in which recent generations appeared to "betray" their ancestors' national loyalty. The Lees of Virginia made frequent appearances, with articles praising Revolutionary War hero Henry "Light Horse Harry" Lee while condemning his son, Robert E. Lee. The Keys of Maryland were also noticed when it became known that the daughter of Francis Scott Key, author of the "Star Spangled Banner," was under investigation as an alleged spy for the Confederacy. The Breckinridges of Kentucky likewise were subjected to a point-by-point comparison of two family members: Unionist and Danville Theological Seminary professor Robert J. Breckinridge—a "great *thinker*"—and his nephew, Confederate general (and former U.S. vice president) John C. Breckinridge—a "great *talker*" and "soul-sacrificing, vote-catching villain." Kentuckian Henry Clay, long identified with his compromises for staving off civil war, was featured for having several grandsons who fought for the Confederacy. Their service was a "sad" postscript to the storied life of that "illustrious statesman," according to the *Louisville Daily Journal*. Most troubling, however, was the family of Thomas Jefferson. "Alas, how his descendants are divided in this war!" exclaimed the *Nashville Daily Press*, noting that all of the former president's grandsons were fighting for the Confederacy while his granddaughters sided with their Union husbands.[52]

TRACING THE POLITICAL LINEAGE of these prominent families reminded Southerners of where they came from and gave Northerners additional ballast for their charge of Confederate treason. The newspaper articles, regardless of their veracity, illustrate the high value that midcentury Americans placed on inheritance and genealogical ties as a source of national loyalty. It was difficult, in many minds, to separate family identity from national identity or kinship from citizenship. To do so was to raise uncomfortable questions about the origins of national identity. The rebel sons of Unionist fathers were therefore sorely tested when they volunteered to fight for the South. They were forced to argue either that their family ties had little bearing on their national sympathies, or that they understood more clearly than their fathers how that family inheritance translated into Confederate loyalty (rather than fidelity to the Union). Few Unionists, if any, were willing to accept their rebel sons' defection as an expression of rational political calculation. They chose instead to see a disturbing connection between nation and family in their sons' Confederate service and to interpret their wartime division as a familiar, yet lamentable, generational conflict. In this way, they could contain their wartime division as a more manageable form of domestic strife.

Neither the fathers nor the sons may have seen it, or may have wanted to see it, but in their arguments they hit upon common ground. Both wanted, in contrasting ways, to protect their family from the pressures of war: fathers focused on restoring their lost paternal authority, whereas sons wished to maintain their filial position regardless of their political stance. Both saw something wrong in the mixing of domestic and political affairs and sought to restore normalcy again by defending the border between their private and public lives. Exactly where that border should fall was unclear, something that other families would encounter as they faced other types of division.

Marriage and Courtship

THE CIVIL WAR represented a marital crisis for Catherine Brown Hopkins. By the time the first shots were fired on Fort Sumter, her year-old marriage was showing strains despite the recent birth of her first child. Looking back on her relationship with her husband Henry, she began to wonder if their union had been doomed from the start. Catherine was a native of Philadelphia, whereas Henry was born and raised in Virginia. The marriage seemed like a good one at the beginning, but it quickly disintegrated into conflict. Their mixed backgrounds proved troublesome just months after their wedding, when the couple began to argue over secession. "Our sentiments on political subjects were entirely opposed," Catherine recalled; on one occasion in December 1860 she had even grown fearful for her safety when Henry "urged his secession views with such violence." Although she would never accept secession, Catherine decided from that day forward to suppress her thoughts and to "soothe" rather than "excite" their differences. In doing so, she sank into a position of self-described "martyrdom."[1]

Catherine might have remained silent had Henry not acted on his secession sentiments. In March 1862 she surprised him while he was gathering clothes and money for a trip to Virginia. He assured her that the journey was a temporary excursion to see how his mother, a slaveholding widow, was holding up in the midst of war. But when she noticed that he had packed *all* of his clothing and had thrown a collection of papers into the fire, she became suspicious. When he did not return after the promised seven days, Catherine notified the Federal government's detective force of Henry's trip. Within days Henry was arrested in southern Maryland, charged with disloyalty, and incarcerated at Fort McHenry prison in Baltimore. Catherine then sought to sever her ties with her husband permanently and filed for divorce based on his disloyalty to the Union.[2]

The very suggestion that an institution as sacred as marriage could give way to the division of civil war was unprecedented. Disloyalty or political conflict was not a ground for divorce anywhere in the United States; to file on this basis in Pennsylvania, Catherine Hopkins had to take the unusual step of circumventing the courts and appealing to the state legislature. The members initially responded to her petition with patriotic enthusiasm. One sympathetic senator proclaimed: "The man is a traitor and his wife is loyal; they ought to be divorced."[3]

This "singular" and "curious" case attracted close press coverage in Philadelphia, Louisville, and as far west as St. Louis.[4] Yet its newsworthiness may have stemmed less from its singularity and more from what the Hopkinses shared with other couples. The articulated tension in their marriage was fairly common at the crossroads of North and South, where the lines between slavery and freedom, Cavalier and Yankee, were blurred. The border region's diversity made for unions of mixed backgrounds, which, although rarely ending in divorce, led to significant conflict during the war. The result, in the words of one Missouri man, was "domestic pandemonium" along the Civil War border.[5]

"Pandemonium" seized border-state households when war intruded in the intimate relations of marriage and courtship. This was startling to contemporaries for its threat to their idealized division between public and private life that rendered marriage antithetical to political and military affairs. Most troublesome was the role that women played in transcending this divide. In assuming a national loyalty distinct from their husbands or suitors, women such as Catherine Hopkins not only challenged the prerogatives of male authority but also redrew the boundaries around wartime combat. They shifted the national dispute over slavery and secession from newspaper columns to their personal letters, from battlefields to their own households. In doing so they raised questions similar to those confronted by fathers and sons—particularly, what did a woman's dissenting loyalty mean? Men and women across the border states debated whether a woman's national loyalty was an assertion of independent political views, as Hopkins suggested, or a more personal stance derived from her position as wife, mother, or daughter. Different families reached different conclusions, though most found some way to manage the war's intrusion into their intimate lives.

Marriage

The seeds of some of these marital conflicts were sown at the beginning of the relationships. Throughout the antebellum period the setting of the border region, especially its transience, encouraged unions of men and women who had been raised with different ideas and values. In some cases marriages resulted when a Northern man traveled to the South in search of new economic opportunities and remained there for life. In other cases it was a woman from the Northeast who sought a teaching position in the South and married a man she met there. The popularity of resort towns also brought together men and women from different places. Even extended families that stretched across state boundaries from Virginia to Kentucky introduced men and women with contrasting views on slavery and sectionalism. This region thus nurtured latent divisions between men and women not necessarily acknowledged when they married—at least not in the case of Catherine and Henry Hopkins.[6]

According to Catherine's petition, she and Henry met in the late 1850s in Philadelphia, where she was living with her mother and father, a prominent pharmacist. Henry had moved north from Virginia to pursue a medical education; by 1860 he was practicing medicine in the outlying town of Germantown, Pennsylvania. Henry apparently was smitten with Catherine from the start, but it took his promise to attend church for her to agree to marry him in February 1860. The marriage ostensibly began smoothly, as Henry related well to Catherine's parents; indeed, he called her mother his "mother-in-love." The only visible source of discord was their finances—Henry had not achieved the financial independence expected of a husband and could contribute only $250 to their expenses during their first two years of marriage. Catherine's parents compensated by giving them $100 each month and by purchasing the house in which they lived. That arrangement worked well at first, Catherine stated in her petition, and the couple went on to have a daughter within a year of their marriage.[7]

In December 1860 Catherine took an interest in the secession crisis heating up around them. She began to notice that Henry's views on the issue would often "excite the indignation of his neighbors," and, after reading a newspaper article outlining the views of fire-eating Georgian Thomas R. R. Cobb, she initiated a discussion with her husband. This led to their ill-fated argument when Catherine grew fearful of Henry's anger and insults. It proved to be a turning point after which Catherine began viewing their relationship through the lens of war. Henry's ongoing desire to visit his slaveholding mother suddenly seemed less innocent; Catherine's suspicions were confirmed when the government detectives found him with a supply of "rebel clothing" and a stash of Confederate money. His behavior forced her to question other aspects of their marriage, such as whether he had really married her for her money and whether he had neglected her health during several fainting spells. Having inherited "the blood and principles of 'revolutionary patriots,'" Catherine's petition concluded, it was impossible to resume normal relations with her "traitor husband." "A traitor to his wife, his country, and his child," she wrote bluntly. "I can never look upon union with this man, with any other feeling than that of abhorrence."[8]

Henry Hopkins was shaken by his wife's divorce petition. The public airing of their private problems was "painful" yet inevitable, he conceded, but the challenge to his national loyalty was another matter. He was particularly troubled by Catherine's assertion of loyalty to the Union and questioned its sincerity. The sentiments expressed in her application could not be her own, he argued in his responding petition, but instead must have been "directed by others," namely her parents. His wife — with whom he emphasized he was still "in love" and wanted to reconcile — had become a mouthpiece for her father's Union politics. Even during that infamous argument in December 1860, he asserted, her parents were in the room. To Henry, this was evidence that Catherine's parents — especially her father — exerted a stifling influence over her wartime loyalties. This was lamentable, because it showed that "my influence was entirely superseded . . . [by] the principle of filial obedience." Catherine had chosen her father over her husband.[9]

With these words Henry recast their marital conflict not as a clash of political loyalties, as Catherine had argued, but rather as the more familiar crisis of male authority. Henry had always believed that his wife's family interfered too much in their marriage, from their financial help to their insistence that Catherine live with them after giving birth. Her father made it impossible for Henry to be the "master of my own house," forcing him to assume instead the humiliating position of a "dependent." To add insult to his already injured ego, Catherine's petition requested that their child be made her father's adopted daughter. In Henry's view, then, his father-in-law was the "real and operative cause" of the proposed divorce. It was to get away from his father-in-law, and to build an "independent" life for himself and his family, that motivated him to pack up his belongings and travel to Virginia.[10]

Henry's view of his marriage would have been understandable to the state legislators. In midcentury America, a wedding ceremony may have symbolized the "giving away" of a daughter to a husband, but in reality this transfer of male authority rarely occurred without dissension. Fathers were uneasy about relinquishing their influence over their daughters, just as daughters proved unwilling to stop deferring to their fathers. Marriage often had the effect of pitting husbands and fathers-in-law against one another.[11] From Henry Hopkins's perspective, this conflict — not politics — was the only proper ground for divorce. "If mere sympathy for secession . . . is cause for divorce," he proposed, "who can estimate the misery that must inevitably ensue, how many families may be dissolved and demoralized by this new doctrine?" Acknowledging the "precedent" to be set in this case, the Pennsylvania legislators agreed with Henry and downplayed the political discord in his marriage. They dismissed Catherine's application days after receiving Henry's petition, arguing that the case was better treated in the courts like any other domestic conflict. Henry then urged Catherine to accompany him to Virginia for an affectionate reconciliation away from her father, but she successfully sued for divorce on the grounds of desertion three years later.[12]

Henry Hopkins's response to his wife's petition was not unusual for husbands dealing with wartime division. It was one thing for a wife to express political opinions that were different from her husband's in peacetime, but quite another to assume an opposing stance during a war. Disloyalty to a husband's wartime convictions was tantamount to becoming his public enemy and, if he was a soldier, to support his defeat (or, in Hopkins's case, his incarceration). This went too far in challenging a man's position as the head of his family, so other husbands joined Hopkins in deflecting the contest of political loyalty onto the familiar terrain of masculine power struggles. To do so was to take something shocking — a wife's political challenge — and turn it into something more manageable and, perhaps, more comfortable. Sometimes a husband reasserted his authority by prohibiting his wife from visiting her parents during the war or by loudly insulting her father's views. The most extreme case was Confederate cavalryman James Ewell Brown "Jeb" Stuart's demand that his son's name be changed so that he no longer shared it with Stuart's Unionist father-in-law, Philip St. George Cooke. His wife, Flora Cooke Stuart, refused and appeared to condone her father's Union views. "Dont [sic] call our son by his old name," Stuart continually admonished Flora, determined to rid their family symbolically of her father's influence. In ways such as this, a husband could defuse his wife's political expression by treating it as nothing more than the intrusion of her meddling father.[13]

There is no doubt that fathers nurtured their daughters' partisan political beliefs. Political socialization began in the family at a young age. Child-rearing manuals and other prescriptive literature of the period urged both fathers and mothers to inculcate in their children a sense of civic duty and consciousness, although it was typically the father who figured most prominently in defining a child's public partisanship. Fathers could vote and hold office and were the political ambassadors of their households; through a process of both direct instruction and setting the example, they taught their sons and daughters acceptable partisan behavior. This could create strong political affinities between fathers and daughters. Twenty-one-year-old Josie Underwood, the daughter of a former U.S. congressman from Kentucky, frequently quoted "Pa's [Unionist] position" in her diary and was straightforward about his influence on her beliefs. "I drew on Pa," Josie explained of a discussion about secession with neighbors, "for all the fine arguments and bright things I could remember."[14]

A father's influence was strengthened for the women considered here by the fact that many of them were not far removed from their fathers' households. In 1861 nearly two-thirds of these women were under age twenty-eight and had been married for less than ten years.[15] More than half were childless.[16] This indicates that these women had not been married long when the nation divided and had yet to develop the kind of identification with, or loyalty to, their new families that they had with their old. Indeed, in all but two cases of divided couples, a wife's dissenting political stance was the same as her father's. His memory might have lingered, and if that was not enough, then his letters might have continually reminded her of his example. In the spring of 1861, for instance, Caroline Lawrence Bedinger of Shepherdstown, Virginia, received weekly letters from her New York father, each containing at least a paragraph on current events. In one letter he declared that South Carolina's secession was "the most extraordinary rashness and folly," and in others he continued to condemn the South. Caroline had denied his request to leave her Confederate husband in Virginia to live at her parents' home during the war, so letters substituted as the vehicle for his political influence.[17]

Fathers were anxious about their daughters' marriages to men on the enemy side and in some cases went to great lengths to maintain their paternal influence. Some feigned illness to lure their daughters from their husbands' homes; others belittled the younger men's credibility. One East Tennessee Unionist wrote his son-in-law a letter shaming him into staying out of the Confederate service in order to fulfill his manly duty to "protect" his wife and children.[18] Such efforts even became the subject of campfire stories. A popular (and perhaps fictionalized) tale among Union soldiers in Tennessee told of a rebel man who tried to shoot his daughter to prevent her from marrying her Union-loving beau. The father apparently missed his shot and was arrested. In another story, a Union father from Washington, D.C., reportedly confronted his adopted daughter's Confederate husband at the First Battle of Manassas but was shot and wounded by the husband's comrades.[19] Such drastic scenarios underscore the ambivalence surrounding the transfer of male authority from fathers to husbands, and some fathers were forced to acknowledge their weakened position. Martha Clay Davenport, daughter of Unionist Kentucky legislator Brutus Clay, was an avowed Unionist herself during the secession crisis, but within months of marrying a prosecession, slaveholding Virginia farmer in 1860, she threw her support behind the Confederacy. Her father, already reeling from his son's enlistment in the Confederate army, was furious at her switch, and it took the unlikely intervention of his abolitionist brother to put him at ease. "I beg you to overlook her secessionism," Martha's uncle, Cassius Clay wrote, "because it is a virtue in a *woman* to go with her husband in all things."[20]

Such contests of influence between husbands and fathers reinforced traditional lines of male authority and effectively denied the existence of a woman's independent political views. Inevitably some women felt trapped in the middle, pressured into taking a neutral stand to placate the men in their life. In 1861 Josie Underwood described how her sister Juliet balanced the contrasting opinions of her husband and their father. When Juliet was with her husband, a Confederate soldier, she defended the right to secession; but when she was with her father, a Union spokesman, "she is union heart and soul." "So she stands on the line," Josie explained, "one foot on the either side." This mediating position might have helped to preserve family harmony, but it was taxing. It became so traumatic for Sarah Glasgow of St. Louis that her sister urged her to be "thankful" for their father's death in 1863. It meant that Sarah no longer had to endure the "serious disagreements" between her Union husband and Confederate father.[21] Other women desperately wanted to influence their men to think like them on politics. "Oh if I could only give you my advice," Maryland's Mary Macgill wrote of her desire that her husband take the oath to the Union, "but think I have no right to advise you what to do." Macgill paid lip service to the idea that a woman should remain silent on politics, but she nonetheless made her views clear.[22]

More assertive women refused to allow their husbands or fathers to ignore them and to elide their loyalties with the men in their lives. Unionist Anna Robinson sent her Confederate fiancé, Matthew Page Andrews, stars-and-stripes calico on the eve of the war and explained that her next dress would be made from it. The surprised and unnerved Confederate—who once referred to politics as "the subject you are likely to be bored with" and preferred to debate secession with Robinson's brother instead—vowed in return that they would "compare notes on the subject of politics" when they were next together.[23] Robinson forced Andrews to confront a troubling issue: Was the wartime loyalty of his wife-to-be only a reflection of her family's? Or did she have her own, independent political convictions? The contest of male authority could not always obscure the more disconcerting questions about the meaning of a woman's loyalty.

This became an increasingly salient issue for the generation of women who came of age and married in the 1850s and early 1860s. These women were exposed to many political influences—apart from the men in their families—when the subjects of slavery and secession became central to their everyday lives. Sectional politics was not contained within the halls of legislatures; it also entered passing conversations, discussions at dinner parties, and letters from friends. And these women were ready to absorb it. Their writings, almost without exception, suggest a level of education that prepared them to understand the intricacies of nullification and abolition. In their diaries they refer to newspapers read, editorials absorbed, and pamphlets obtained. Their leisure reading offered a form of political instruction, too, as sentimental fiction centered on decidedly political themes in the decades before the war. Politics also became visible when rallies and torch-lit processions passed through their towns, or when slaves on their farms and plantations seized their freedom by running away. Even the most avowedly apolitical women could not ignore the sights and sounds of the sectional crisis as it swept across the border states. As a result, these women were not solely dependent on men for their political opinions but instead had their own sources of information and could make their own judgments about it. It is not surprising that some of them had difficulty suppressing their partisan loyalties once war came.[24]

This lack of restraint raised uncomfortable questions for husbands and suitors. Benjamin Buckner, a twenty-five-year-old major in the 20th Kentucky Infantry and an aspiring lawyer, struggled to understand his fiancée's loyalty to the South. At first he conceded that such loyalty was "commendable" because "all your ties of relationships bind you to that side." Buckner was engaged to Helen Martin, the twenty-four-year-old daughter of a Kentucky physician. Yet when Martin revealed that she was reading newspapers and when she began airing her thoughts on presidential power, battle strategy, and emancipation, Buckner sensed that something else besides family bound her to the Confederacy. Her outspokenness on the war soon became frustrating. "When did you get to be such a politician as you seem to be from your reference to proceedings held in the various northern legislatures[?]" he demanded only partly in jest. To Buckner, a woman playing the role of a "politician" threatened to overstep her bounds.[25]

Contained in Buckner's statement was a subtle distinction between a woman having political loyalties and a woman being a "politician." The former could be, as Buckner suggested, an acceptable position for an educated woman raised in a politically aware household. But his use of the word "politician" implies that extending political loyalty to active participation in a partisan conflict was more problematic. A politician, according to midcentury custom, debated policy and was well versed in the minutiae of policymaking. The term also connoted someone who embraced politics too intensely, who pushed his or her own selfish interests too hard, or who engaged in secret and devious behavior.[26] This role was at odds with popular expectations of women. Women might be aware of public issues and attend legislative sessions, but when they expressed themselves they were to do so at the behest of their men and were to leave the actual work of politics to men. To assume the status of a partisan antagonist independently, as Martin seemed to do, was presumptuous and challenged the notion that a woman's politics was to emerge in partnership with her husband's. Realizing that she had overstepped her bounds in letters to her future husband, Martin quickly apologized for "talking secesh." Buckner accepted her apology, adding that "you know my sentiments upon the subject of wife management too well to make it necessary for me to elaborate."[27]

The two may have acknowledged boundaries around Martin's political expression, but something still kept Buckner from fully engaging in the practice of "wife management." He, and others like him, had reason to tolerate a political partnership with his spouse that was characterized less by her deference to him and more by her active engagement with politics. Political leaders sometimes found their self-interests served by wives who became agents of their patronage relationships or liaisons with their constituents. Men could thus benefit politically from an assertive wife.[28] But they also could, as Buckner would discover, benefit personally. By the mid-nineteenth-century, as numerous historians have documented, men like Buckner had begun to recognize that the promise of friendship in a marriage was almost as alluring as the exertion of authority. Men wanted to be more than patriarchs; they wished to enjoy the stimulation of a wife's companionship, too.[29] Respect for a woman's intelligent conversation, even on politics, was the "offspring of love," as Buckner himself once explained, and for this reason, he assured his fiancée that "I have never & will never desire to do your thinking." These dual aspirations, however, created a tension in marriage as men and women struggled to define where the egalitarianism of affectionate friendship left off and where a man's authority began. To Buckner, this is what the wartime conflict between he and Martin became: a contest between their companionship and his assertion of "husbandly" authority. As such, it was just another form of midcentury marital tension in political disguise.[30]

"Had I not been so much in love and so very anxious to hear from you," Buckner once wrote after an argument, "I would have been angry at you for believing me to have turned Abolitionist." Buckner then caught himself. "This is quite an imprudent admission for a lover to make to his sweet heart is it not?" he acknowledged, for women like Martin could potentially become "tyrants." "When they find out their power," he explained, they "are sure to make use of it." Buckner admitted that his desire for friendship gave Martin room to express herself. She could insult his war views all she wanted and he would still love and respect her. But at the same time, he sought to control that leverage. "Promise me not to be very tyrannical," he warned her, "for when we get married you know how I despise a henpecked husband." Buckner appealed to Martin's sense of feminine propriety to encourage her restraint. He also tried to defuse her political enthusiasm by pointing out that there was actually little difference in their views on the pivotal issue of slavery: he was no "abolitionist," he asserted; in fact, he believed that early proposals to end slavery during the war were a "violation of the Constitution." There might be other differences between them, but "a difference of opinion upon any political or other point can never diminish to the smallest extent the love which has grown up between us."[31]

The allure of companionship thus helped maintain a space for women's dissenting political expression in marriage. That expression was tolerable to husbands only so long as it was confined to the privacy of their household, in conversation with themselves or with neighbors, or in a letter. Indeed, letter writing was perhaps the most popular medium through which women could air their political views during the war. Their letters traveled across the border states to friends and relatives who often shared their political sympathies.

When necessary, these women went to great lengths to smuggle letters across the lines. Sometimes their messages were really packages containing food, clothing, or monetary assistance to a friend or family member on the other side.[32] But the letters themselves could be quite passionate about the politics of the war. The letters of Confederate Eugenia Phillips were apparently so revealing that Union government officials seized them in 1861 as evidence of "treason." Her house in Washington, D.C., according to newspaper reports, was known as a "Southern mail post office." Although her Union husband, former congressman Philip Phillips, was aware of her activism, he did not feel compelled to stop her.[33] Such lenience toward a wife's political expression elicited the concern of at least one Union newspaper. "The rebel women are talking too much," the *Louisville Daily Journal* declared in July 1862. "Men unfortunate enough to have rebel wives, sisters, and daughters, had better keep catsplasms on their mouths except at meal times."[34]

It is likely that the husbands of dissenting wives listened to such injunctions. Not only was confining their wives' opinions to private settings a matter of national interest, it was also a question of their own reputations. If a woman's contrary views became generally known, she might undermine her husband's public status—just as rebel sons threatened the respectability of their Union fathers. This was not taken lightly in a society where honor forced men to think about how their friends and neighbors judged them. Honor was especially important in wartime and for soldiers, who needed to command the confidence and respect of their comrades-in-arms.[35] But how could a man be trusted if he was intimate with an outspoken enemy? "My wife being such a rebel," one Kentucky Union officer confided to a friend in 1863, "I began to be suspected" of disloyalty. Her views eroded his credibility among the soldiers in his ranks. Even Abraham Lincoln faced similar criticism in newspaper editorials on account of his wife's Confederate kin.[36]

To the dismay of some men, however, the household proved inadequate as a private, contained space for women's politics. One Kentucky Union man was mortified when his wife "sang secessionism" to dinner guests at their home. One guest later declared him "a worse henpecked man" and his wife simply "unladylike." As news of the dinner spread through their neighborhood's gossip chain, the wife's expression in a private household became a public challenge to her husband's masculine authority.[37] In other cases where a wife's contrary views became public, a husband felt compelled to respond in a way that would restore his honor by showing himself to be in control of his spouse. Unionist James McKown opted to leap to his wife's defense after his family accused her of having an affair in order to spy for the Confederacy. He "rose in a great passion, and said we were all throwing out hints that his wife was not a virtuous woman," his mother later wrote, "and he swore bitterly he would never enter this house again." McKown simultaneously sought to defuse the allegations against his wife while bolstering his manly position as the protector of her virtue.[38] Other men erected very public restraints around a wife's political expression, such as the Confederate newspaper editor who convinced his Union wife to live in England for the duration of the war. Jeff Thompson, the commander of a Confederate army in Missouri, may have gone to a greater extreme; he reportedly had his Unionist wife committed, against her will, to a St. Louis mental asylum. Tellingly, subsequent newspaper reports touted his honor as a loyal Confederate.[39]

Benjamin Buckner was less sure about what to do when soldiers in his camp heard that his fiancée was a Confederate and accused him of being "lenient" on imprisoned rebel soldiers because of her convictions. (Buckner admitted to Helen Martin that he was indeed more lax on rebels because his "sweetheart" was of that "political stripe.") To make matters worse, Martin began urging him to resign from the Union army.[40] Buckner thus found himself caught between the dueling demands of his duty to the Union and his affection for his Confederate wife-to-be. Unable (or unwilling) to silence her, Buckner instead came to understand his dilemma in terms familiar to midcentury men—as a conflict between public honor and private love—and sought to finesse the two.[41] He decided to resign to please Martin but waited until he could find an adequate reason that would preserve his reputation and be acceptable to his military superiors. That reason presented itself with Abraham Lincoln's Emancipation Proclamation of 1863, which the proslavery Unionist proclaimed a "most abominable infamous document" for threatening the property of loyal Union men. "I cant fight against my principles and those of my friends in order to satisfy the absurd desire of a faction [the abolitionists] at the North," Buckner explained before submitting his resignation in January of that year. On the grounds of conscience, Buckner could honorably resign without publicly acknowledging the influence of his fiancée's political allegiance.[42]

Buckner was not unique in considering whether he should give up his military position in deference to his fiancée. Other men received similar pressures from their wives and their families. Union officer John Todd despaired when his Confederate fiancée said he "shan't have her unless I resign." (He eventually chose his military service over his fiancée.)[43] For some husbands with enemy wives, resignation from military service was an amenable resolution to the conflict between their love and honor, their family and national loyalty. This was especially true for officers, whose resignations were accepted even after the passage of strict conscription laws by both governments.[44] Kentucky Unionist June Holmberg resigned in 1863 after his Confederate wife announced that she "bitterly opposed" his service in an army that bore arms against her two Confederate brothers. Another Union man resigned from the army in 1864 on the official grounds of tending to a family business, although he privately admitted that he sought to placate his Confederate wife. A resignation properly framed allowed men like him to preserve his honor publicly while privately deferring to his wife's national loyalty.[45]

These men had good reason to guard their reputations, as gossip about men who resigned in deference to their wives and girlfriends surfaced across the border states in letters and newspapers. The Richmond correspondent to the *Charleston Mercury* gave one such resignation a prominent position in his column on Confederate politics.[46] In 1863 the pro-Union *Louisville Daily Journal* assigned the story of a Confederate soldier's resignation front-page coverage, applauding it as an act of loyalty. Under the headline, "A Yankee Girl Converts a Rebel Surgeon and Marries Him," the paper reported that a rebel soldier had resigned his post and then joined the Union army — all because of a woman's influence. "This lady has thus not only brought a valuable acquisition to the Federal service," the *Journal* concluded, "but has herself gained an excellent husband by her patriotic efforts." Conversely, accounts of women who failed to elicit a similar response from their men earned an audience, too; reports of frustrated women who dressed as men and joined the opposing army to neutralize their husbands' service appeared in Union and Confederate newspapers alike.[47]

Other publications seem to have hoped that the impulse to resign would extend to some of the nation's most prominent military leaders. Union newspapers in particular were fond of scrutinizing the political ties between Confederate leaders and their wives and of looking for any hint that these women might undermine their husbands' loyalty to the South. The *Daily Missouri Democrat* speculated that a trip to Washington, D.C., in 1862 had triggered feelings of Union loyalty in Mary Lee, wife of Robert E. Lee. "Mrs. Lee may be a strong secessionist," the reporter wrote, "but I doubt not that a still small voice will whisper to her woman's heart, 'Is it well that we do this thing?'"[48] Other papers took note when General P. G. T. Beauregard's wife visited her Northern family in Indiana and when the wife of Confederate navy secretary

Stephen R. Mallory reportedly became anxious to visit her sister in Massachusetts.[49] Also of interest was the fact that former Virginia governor Henry A.
Wise's wife was the sister of Union general George Meade's wife, and the two
women had visited one another during the war. Often these articles contained
little commentary and were merely matter-of-fact reports on a Confederate
wife's ties to the Union. But to position these accounts amid more weighty
political news was to remind readers of a wife's potential to distract or lure
her husband away from his public commitment.[50]

On occasion such accounts strayed too far from reality, as evidenced by
the treatment of General Thomas J. "Stonewall" Jackson and his wife. In
September 1862 the *Missouri Statesman* reported that Jackson's wife was
the daughter of a staunch Unionist, the Reverend Dr. George Junkin of Baltimore. The paper noted with a hint of glee that Jackson's Confederate stance
was "of deepest regret" to his father-in-law. Yet it was apparently overeager
to make this connection between Jackson and his Union in-laws. A week
later, a correspondent for *Frank Leslie's Illustrated Newspaper* clarified that
Junkin was in fact the father of Jackson's *first* wife, Elinor, who had died eight
years earlier. Jackson's current wife, Anna Morrison, was the daughter of a
proud Confederate, the Reverend Dr. Robert Morrison, a former president
of Davidson College in North Carolina. Despite this correction, other papers
did not hesitate to continue reporting a year later that Reverend Junkin sent
Jackson copies of his anti-Confederate tract, "Popular Fallacies."[51] No evidence was too small or insignificant when it came to searching for divided
marriages. The press was ready and willing to consider any way in which a
wife might—either directly or indirectly through her family—introduce a
dissenting political view into her marriage.

Such scrutiny was important to government officials, too. Records of civilians arrested for disloyalty show that the Union government investigated
officers' wives and at times were inclined to believe that these women were
acting independently on behalf of the Confederacy. The fact that one woman's
husband was a commander in the Union navy, for example, did not protect
her from having her mail seized and from being arrested for disloyalty in
1861.[52] Other government policies encouraged women to take a stand opposing their husbands'. In May 1863 Union general Ambrose Burnside issued
General Order No. 66 announcing that Kentucky women who were married
to rebel men would be presumed sympathetic to the Confederacy and would
be removed to the South unless they were willing to take an oath of loyalty to
the Union. Knowing, perhaps, that few women wanted to leave their homes,

Burnside effectively encouraged women to side with their husbands' opponents.[53] In this way, the Federal government institutionalized the notion that wives could stand apart from their husbands politically.

Yet the idea that men and women could divide over the war while remaining married still surprised some commentators. "Strange as it may seem," the *Nashville Daily Press* remarked in 1863 of one Kentucky couple, "difference in political sentiment . . . has never caused any interruption in domestic harmony."[54] Although this was an exaggeration, it was indeed significant to see husbands and wives working to assuage their conflicting loyalties in wartime. The imperatives of war may have called on men to defeat their enemies in battle, but these husbands proved more accommodating of their wives' dissenting politics. Because they did not want to divorce these women, they adjusted to their stances, as Union fathers had done with their sons, by translating their differences into more acceptable forms of domestic tension. Henry Hopkins attributed his wife's politics to the overwhelming influence of her father. Other men, such as Benjamin Buckner, balanced a desire for companionship with the accompanying need to give his fiancée room to express herself. Still others sought resignation from military service to preserve their public honor while privately deferring to their wives. A husband could follow the scripts provided by these already familiar marital dramas of authority, companionship, and honor to make his wife's dissent manageable. It is not surprising that he would do so. Given that these men were fighting a war to protect their families — as so much of the wartime rhetoric suggested — it follows that their families would take precedence.[55]

Courtship

As resilient as marriage may have been to political conflict, courtship was less forgiving. Popular attitudes weighed much more strongly against new romances of enemy men and women. When Confederate troops occupied Bowling Green, Kentucky, in 1861, for example, Josie Underwood found herself the object of a number of soldiers' attention. But as the daughter of prominent Union parents, Underwood was little inclined to respond to the Confederates' attempts to strike up conversations on her property or visit her at home. She rejected them at every turn and grew indignant at their persistence. When one rebel soldier wrote her a love letter, she fumed: "He wants to amuse himself with a flirtation with the enemy — a sort of sham Romeo and Juliette affair — to vary the ennui of camp life. I don't care to *play* the game."[56]

Underwood believed that this soldier's advances could never measure up to Shakespeare's classic story of romance across enemy lines. Romeo and Juliet might have found true love despite their families' bitter feud, but in the context of the Civil War, she suggested, no sincere romance could develop between two enemies. Some political opponents might be happy in marriage — her own sister was married to a Confederate soldier, and Josie respected their relationship — but only when their unions predated the war. The idea of developing a romance *after* the war had begun seemed disrespectful and false. "If he were not fighting against our country this might be possible," she reasoned in the case of the soldier who sought her affections, but his Confederate service undermined "any thought of him as 'my heart's hero.' " He did not have a history with her or her family that could reassure her that he truly respected and wanted to protect them. On the contrary, in her view he was indistinguishable from other Confederate soldiers intent on destroying her family's property and undermining its livelihood. Thus it would be extremely difficult, if not impossible, for the two to develop the trust and mutuality that midcentury Americans like Underwood thought were central to love.[57]

Josie Underwood was not alone in this opinion. Although there were no laws banning such relationships, social pressure across the border states — from newspaper editorials to warnings in private letters — strongly discouraged intersectional courtship. One Virginia man recalled urging a woman friend to ask about her new beau's values and "ascertain his political creed." "In these times," he emphasized, "that is a very essential part of a husbands [*sic*] good or bad qualities."[58] It was a matter of character and a patriotic necessity to reject the overtures of an enemy. It was also a question of security. Confederate women, particularly those in the Western states of Kentucky and Missouri, expected Union soldiers to rape their way through the South, destroying the dignity as well as the property of Southern women. Union civilians lived in fear of the Confederate guerrillas who were responsible for some of the most notorious violence during the war. These apprehensions proved well placed in the case of black women, who bore the brunt of soldiers' sexual assaults. Although violence against white women was apparently less common, white women were warned for the sake of their physical well-being to keep their distance from the enemy.[59]

In spite of these social pressures, courtships and wartime marriages did occur across the political divide. How common these relationships were is difficult to determine, though one can hardly pick up a border-state newspaper without seeing some commentary on this phenomenon. According to the

Daily Missouri Democrat, twenty such marriages had taken place in St. Louis in 1863 in one month alone; in 1864 the *Nashville Daily Press* reported that about thirty marriages had occurred in and around Charleston, West Virginia.[60] Also in 1864 the *Missouri Statesman* noted that marriages of "soldiers and citizenesses" are of "daily occurrence," and that "all single women under sixty are gobbled up as fast as the soldiers can find them." "What a world we live in," exclaimed the *Nashville Daily Press* in reference to these incongruous relationships, which generally evoked surprise and fascination.[61] How they could occur, and what they meant in a time of civil war, however, were questions that would continually vex border-state observers.

Certainly the military setting of the border states made courtship and marriage logistically possible. Here, enemy troops occupied local communities for sustained periods, bringing strangers into close proximity and daily interaction. In areas such as Nashville, Tennessee, Bowling Green, Kentucky, and northern Virginia, occupying soldiers and civilian women were forced to share public spaces. They passed one another on the street, shopped in the same markets, shared church pews as well as railroad cars. It was difficult for a woman living in an occupied region to avoid meeting the enemy face-to-face. In St. Louis a woman recorded her encounters with Federal soldiers at a "grand ball." (The Confederate women who attended accepted their presence but refused to join them in a waltz.)[62] Josie Underwood saw her family's property in Bowling Green turned into a Confederate encampment; she could not work in her garden without soldiers walking by or trying to talk to her. Their presence eventually eroded Josie's resolve to spurn them: "We don't want to treat the rebels as though we approved or countenanced them in any way," she observed, "and yet, I confess, I do enjoy the chance talks with them."[63]

The close proximity of enemy men and women in occupied regions of the border states nurtured a familiarity that sometimes mediated against hostility and bitterness. This was especially true between Confederate women and Union men, who were more successful in occupying their opponents' territory than their Confederate counterparts. Southern women in general have been legendary among historians for their bitter exchanges with Union forces, but border-state women also revealed a willingness — to varying degrees — to become acquainted with them. Their abstract view of the Union army as inhumane and uncivilized did not preclude them from looking at individual Union soldiers in a different light. The average soldier did not wish to harm them, some of these women discovered, but instead could be friendly and nothing more than a lonely man in search of conversation. Some soldiers even spared a woman's property from destruction. A Fairfax County, Virginia, woman admitted that despite expectations that a Union soldier would "beat the 'hull' out of us," while his army occupied northern Virginia, "on the whole he was candid and good-natured." Enemy soldiers even became a source of income for some civilian women when they were willing to pay for boarding or meals in the women's homes.[64]

Other Union troops were deemed sympathetic, as were the prisoners of war in hospitals who depended on Confederate women to feed them soup and change their bandages. Hospitals offered a unique setting that appealed to a Confederate woman's sense of humanity and Christian duty.[65] For some it was a temporary act of charity that would end when the men recovered, but other women may have found the intimate conversation nurtured in a hospital amenable to romance and even marriage. The *Nashville Daily Press* noted a number of such relationships that were rumored to have developed among volunteer nurses, patients, and doctors, noting in one 1864 account that "the M.D.'s seem to make the most headway in marrying the fair daughters of Dixie." The paper speculated that the army physicians' status as noncombatants made them more attractive to women determined to uphold their Confederate loyalty.[66]

Prisons also provided an insulated setting in which enemy men and women could interact peacefully. Especially in institutions in St. Louis, Louisville, and Washington, D.C., where numbers of women were incarcerated as political prisoners for their actions on behalf of the Confederacy, prisoners and guards became friendly, even flirtatious, as they shared close quarters for months at a time. Female prisoners depended on their Union guards to provide food, conversation, and privileges. But these women, who were supposedly the most rebellious of the rebels, also discovered a political utility in becoming extra friendly with Union guards. The *Missouri Statesman* reported in February 1865, for instance, that women in a Chariton County prison were marrying their guards to prove their allegiance to the Union and be released. Such marriages exploited popular expectations that women would assume the national loyalty of their husbands, so to marry a Union man was "undoubted proof of her loyalty," the paper concluded.[67] In a more well-known example, accused Confederate spy Belle Boyd became romantically involved with one of her captors, who subsequently helped her escape and continue her spying career.[68] Intersectional romance in these instances was a matter of expediency for Confederate women accused of spying or other acts of treason.

At least, that is how these romances were characterized in newspaper columns. The private papers of individuals involved in prison romances suggest that their dalliances with the enemy could be more complicated than a simple assertion of political self-interest. Twenty-five-year-old Antonia Ford, an inmate of Washington, D.C.'s Old Capitol Prison, attributed her romance with a Union guard entirely to the power of love and "Destiny."[69] Few of her fellow inmates might have believed her at first, as there was no doubt that Ford was a staunch Confederate. Her family of prominent merchants in Fairfax Court House, Virginia, was known to be loyal to the Confederacy. Her brother was a soldier in the Confederate army, and Antonia herself had been commissioned as an honorary aide-de-camp by General Jeb Stuart in October 1861. Her support for the South became a concern to Union authorities in March 1863, when she was arrested on suspicion of providing key information for a successful Confederate raid on the Union headquarters at Fairfax Court House earlier that month.[70] On her way to prison Ford was escorted by forty-one-year-old Joseph Willard, a Union major and native of Vermont. The two struck up a conversation that continued throughout Ford's six-month incarceration. The exact nature of their exchange is difficult to piece together, since much of it was face-to-face, but by the end of 1863 Ford vowed in a letter to Willard that she would "love you as long as I live."[71]

Ford had not forgotten that Willard was a Unionist when she made this unlikely profession of love. Her writing suggests that their divergent wartime loyalties were always on her mind and may have encouraged, rather than discouraged, her interest in Willard. There was something about Willard's Union position that appealed to her. "What a reputation you have," Ford exclaimed in a letter to Willard of her fellow civilians who appreciated his "gentlemanly" treatment during the Union occupation of Fairfax; "none of them consider you an enemy." Ford drew a distinction between Willard and the ugly stereotype of the aggressive Yankee. Willard's ability to act in ways that countered that "enemy" image deserved respect, and Ford felt proud to have won his attention.[72] Certainly there may have been a degree of opportunism behind Ford's praise: within six months of her arrest she was released from prison with Willard's help. But she also continued to claim a sincere attraction to the Union officer, addressing her letters to "my dearest Major," rather than to "Joseph," because, she explained, it was the army officer who "protected me in danger."[73]

Within a year of their first meeting, Ford and Willard began talking of marriage. But before taking this step, they were concerned about how

Antonia Ford (above) and Joseph Willard (facing page). This suspected
Confederate spy and her Union prison guard were joined in marriage in 1864.
The two then moved to Washington, D.C., where they ran the Willard Hotel,
had a son just weeks after the South's surrender, and remained married
until Ford's death in 1871. (Courtesy of the Library of Congress)

people around them — their family, friends, and especially his military colleagues — would react to such a union. Public opinion proved a significant
obstacle to intersectional courtships like theirs. Ford and Willard were most
concerned that Confederates might see their marriage as a conversion of one
of their women to the Union and seek retaliation, perhaps in the form of a
guerrilla attack on Willard. Ford had no plans to change her national loyalty;

she took the oath to the Union as a condition of her release from prison, but in her view that was a promise to act—rather than think—loyally to the Union. This became clear in her negotiations with Willard over the terms of their marriage. Willard first proposed that they be married secretly, telling only their closest family members, but Ford refused. "I can *never* consent to a private marriage," she wrote, calling it "wrong" and a step she could not take "without compromising myself." There had to be another way to seek public approval of a marriage of acknowledged political opposites. "I know you are true to the [Federal] government," she acknowledged, promising that "I love *you none the less for it*." But, she argued, the obstacle to their marriage "is with you, not me" — Willard would have to resign his commission from the Union army.[74]

Willard had reason to consider resignation, and thus defuse probable Confederate anger at his impending marriage, even though he would run the risk of angering his Union comrades. He owned a business in Washington, D.C. — the Willard Hotel — that needed his attention, his own mother frequently begged him to leave the army, and he wanted a more fulfilling private life. Willard was recently divorced and had seized opportunities to be in the company of women. In 1862 he wrote in his diary of attending a party with Virginia women — or, as he termed them, "terrible, wicked Secessionists" — and was intrigued to learn that they "could be approached by Yankees."[75] He apparently did not hesitate to approach Ford and found in her a woman described as "intelligent" by other Union officers, "decidedly good-looking" by the U.S. Secret Service, and, according to census records, prosperous in her economic background.[76] Willard did decide to leave the army within two months of Ford's request: his public reason for doing so was to tend to his family's hotel, but privately he admitted that his real intention was to make Ford "as happy as in my power."[77]

Willard's decision to leave the army followed a thought process similar to the other men examined here. He agreed with Ford that either they could be married publicly *or* they could be publicly Union and Confederate — but not both at the same time. Popular opinion, particularly in time of war, did not clearly support the idea that a husband and wife could safely and openly disagree on politics, so part of their lives had to become private. They therefore acted to subdue their public partisanship with Ford's oath and Willard's resignation. Having done so, the two were married on March 8, 1864, with the approval of their families. Their marriage was no secret, as it was announced in at least two city newspapers. Afterward they concentrated their energies on the relatively neutral occupation of running the Willard family hotel. Their retreat to Washington, D.C., free of their official, public duties as spy and military officer respectively, allowed Ford and Willard to maintain their divergent national sympathies as a married couple without fear of criticism or retaliation. It was no easy retreat, however. "I do very much wish to know what the people say of me," Ford later wrote, still anxious about the opinion of fellow Virginians.[78]

The public criticism that Ford and Willard had feared could have been quite vocal. Confederate partisans, for one, argued that only desperation for a man's companionship after the Confederacy's own population of eligible men left to fight could compel a Southern woman to drift toward Union soldiers. "I did not think she would marry a *yankee*, even though she were anxious to marry," one Virginia man wrote of a friend who at age twenty-eight had wed a Union officer. "I suppose she felt in need of a protector," he continued, adding that she "has been rather unfortunate in her love affairs." There was a degree of truth in these statements: in occupied areas Confederate men of marrying age had become scarce, leaving Union soldiers to fill the void in the marriage market. Yet Southerners remained critical of women who accepted Union men. A woman in Virginia wrote that at one wedding "I felt vexed that any southern girl should have so little self-respect as to be willing to marry one who was a soldier in the army of our oppressors." She attributed the union to the woman's "ignorance and want of sensibility." The *Southern Field and Fireside* did not hesitate to pronounce such marriages "reckless" and condemned women for engaging in hasty relationships. "Is there a village of fifty houses in the land wherein a plausible, well-dressed adventurer, of whom nobody knows anything, cannot marry a girl of spotless character, after a residence of six weeks?" the paper demanded in a veiled reference to occupying Union troops in January 1864. In failing to hold off the advances of Union soldiers, Confederate women, the writer suggested, had exhibited a weakness tantamount to disloyalty.[79]

Union observers, in contrast, frequently poked fun at the neediness of Southern women. Typical was the sentiment conveyed in the poem, "I'm in Want of a Beau," which appeared on the front page of the *Missouri Statesman* in January 1864. The humorous verse projected the voice of a Confederate woman, as in this first stanza:

> I'm in want of a beau,
>   Heigho, heigho!
> And should be very happy to gain one,
>   But no suitors appear,
>   And I really fear
> I shall find it hard work to obtain one.

The *Daily Missouri Democrat* further claimed that a "new social arrange-ment" had evolved in 1863 from the longings of such women. Soldiers in St. Louis were willing to court "secesh" women and even marry them on the condition that the union would last only "while the war lasts." A more drastic step, wrote the *Louisville Daily Journal*, was a rumored attempt by unmar-ried women in St. Louis to have the state assembly legalize polygamy in 1864. The assemblymen apparently viewed the appeal as "an excellent joke," but the paper assured readers that the women were actually quite serious.[80]

The image of desperate Confederate women served a useful purpose for Union partisans. To suggest that they were so focused on their romantic lives that they would resort to polygamy, or even worse, a relationship with a Union man, was to raise questions about the sincerity of their devotion to politics. "When we see a young lady waving the war flag of the South," the *Louisville Daily Journal* commented just as the conflict began, "we conclude she is anxious for an engagement with some good-looking Union man."[81] A Con-federate woman's patriotism was simply an expression of her desperation, according to the *Journal*, and to Union readers this was a significant point. From the outset, Confederate women had distinguished themselves as among the most outspoken and patriotic Southern partisans; Union soldiers were often surprised by their public displays of support for Confederate troops. Yet, in an article aptly titled, "Converting Lady Rebels," the *Missouri Statesman* explained how Union soldiers could easily defuse that hostility. Acknowledg-ing that but for the women "the spirit of the rebellion would soon die out," the paper suggested that by "wooing and marrying the fair ones," Union soldiers could succeed in "striking at the root of the evil." In other words, with an offer of marriage a soldier could attack Confederate women where they were most vulnerable. To convert them to the Union side would erode the strongest foundation of the Confederacy.[82]

A popular target of such commentary was the female population of Nash-ville, Tennessee. It was here that Union forces, in the winter of 1862, cap-tured a Confederate state capital for the first time, guaranteeing, by virtue of its geography, Union control over much of Tennessee and Kentucky. For the next three years, longer than anywhere else in the South except northern Virginia, Confederate residents of Nashville witnessed the daily presence of Union troops.[83] During that time the female residents developed a reputation for their bitterness toward Union soldiers. The *Louisville Daily Journal* re-ported that women carried "unconcealed pistols" in the streets, and an Ohio paper maintained that it was impossible for a Union soldier to be outside "for ten minutes without being insulted by word or deed by some of the fair sex."[84] These exchanges could be nasty: the twenty-year-old daughter of the proprietor of the St. Cloud Hotel reportedly was brought before the military governor, Andrew Johnson, on the charge of spitting on Union officers from the front porch of the hotel.[85] But the *Journal* refused to take such antagonism seriously. "Tell the rebel beauties of Nashville that making up unpretty mouths at the gallant Federal officers is no way to win kisses," the paper teased that spring. Six days later it noted gleefully that "a number of young ladies of Nashville who were at first very fierce toward the U.S. officers have come to. We said they would."[86] A six-day turnaround in their sentiments was unlikely, but these reports effectively defused the significance of Confederate women's patriotic expressions.

The *Missouri Statesman* contributed to the domestication of Nashville women's patriotic fervor. In June 1865 it published a letter of dubious authenticity from a woman named "Marie" to her brother "Tom" in which she broke the news that women in Nashville were quickly "dropping off" in the arms of Union soldiers. Among them were several of their female friends who had become "willing victims" of the "ruthless invaders." "Mollie," who was known to wear a breastpin with the likeness of General Beauregard and sleep with a Bonnie Blue Flag under her pillow, was now the wife of a Union soldier. "Sue," who once claimed to want to imitate Charlotte Corday, the heroine of the French Revolution, and to assassinate the Union soldiers around them, had married a Union officer. Most upsetting of all were the actions of "Anna," Tom's former sweetheart, who had previously resisted the orders of occupying officers. After her marriage to a Yankee, she had taken down the Confederate flag from in front of her house and had started singing "Union Forever" in the streets. Convinced that Tom, a Confederate soldier, would be devastated by the news, Marie urged him to "take it like a man" and come home immediately to reverse the trend. She added: "Tell the boys down in Dixie, if they do not return soon they will not find a single girl or widow below conscript age in these parts." In a postscript, she announced that she too planned to marry a Union captain "to make a martyr of myself."[87]

Newspapers had reason to exaggerate, but at least one Union soldier substantiated the behavior described in Marie's letter. According to Gates Thruston of the 1st Ohio Infantry, by March 1865 the women of Nashville were through "playing the part of nuns and being true to their southern lovers and allegiance." After years of separation from their men and living alone, they now "smile upon the Federal beaux." They danced to Yankee Doodle without complaint and "are always ready for a flirtation," Thruston told his mother. Although there was some truth to this, based on the public announcements of the marriages of Nashville women to soldiers from Indiana, Michigan, and Ohio, Thruston concluded that "they are all beginning to be subjugated." Essentially he argued that Confederate women had been conquered politically by appeals to their romantic selves. Yet, to what extent these women actually suppressed their political instincts or were indeed converted to the Union side is unclear. When months later Thruston himself married the daughter of a prominent Confederate family, Ida Hamilton, she made sure to have portraits of Confederate generals Lee and Jackson decorating their reception room.[88]

The idea that Confederate women could be converted through romance likely bolstered the masculine pride of Union soldiers in their war with Southern men. Stories of intersectional romance commonly depicted Union men as the saviors of desperate Southern women when Confederate men failed them. A typical story, under the headline "War and Romance," appeared in the *Daily Missouri Democrat* in February 1863 and was based on an actual intersectional marriage. Captain Edwin W. Sutherland of the U.S. steam ram *Queen of the West* became attracted to the "snapping black eyes" of a Confederate widow he encountered along the banks of the Mississippi River. Mrs. Harris was an "intense, red-hot" advocate of the Confederacy and the owner of over 150 slaves. One day the two struck up a conversation during which Harris lamented the impending loss of her slaves when the Emancipation Proclamation declared free all slaves residing in Confederate territory. The captain, overcome by her beauty, proposed that if they married, the slaves would not have to be freed since his loyalty to — and residence in — the Union was undeniable. Harris agreed to the plan, the two were married, and both her property in slaves and her principles were saved. A Union man had stepped in when her male compatriots failed to protect her property.[89]

Union partisans clearly enjoyed playing with the idea that Union men were better protectors of Confederate women. In a tongue-in-cheek announcement, the *Louisville Daily Journal* attributed the romances between Union men and Southern women to the extraordinary number of Southern men who had died in battle. "Some of our officers in the South are marrying Southern women for the philanthropic purpose of preventing the Southern race from becoming extinct," the paper stated, for if Union military might rendered Southern men unable to propagate their sectional race, then Union men would have to take their place.[90] Union men beat back the threat of Confederate men by portraying them as inadequately equipped to fulfill their first obligation to their women. By romancing Southern women, Union men could prove themselves more virile and more masculine than their Confederate counterparts. Union soldiers thus boasted of "conquering" Southern women; one Kentucky Union soldier told friends that "I have a rebel sweet heart & have one every place I go to."[91]

THIS REPEATED EFFORT to translate single women's patriotic declarations into more intimate expressions of love and romance paralleled the efforts of husbands in divided marriages. Men deflected what they feared was politics into more personal domestic conflicts: a single woman's defiant patriotism was really a desire for a husband, or a wife's dissenting views were a demonstration of her father's overbearing influence. To what extent a woman's national loyalties were indeed political or more domestic in nature is difficult to untangle; it is likely, as in the case of rebel sons, that they were really a combination of the two.

What is more significant is that politics was addressed at all within the most intimate relationships between men and women. Border-state women essentially pulled politics in the opposite direction from the typical historical narrative of women's political activity in the nineteenth century. Rather than moving outward from the household into the public sphere, here we see politics turned inward and private, intersecting with and exacerbating domestic relations and forcing men to accommodate their differences.[92] Women generally found that they did not have to adopt their husbands' loyalties as long as their marital differences remained sheltered from public view. As one Maryland woman recalled, "Politics, which had been fearlessly public, became an entirely private affair, to be discussed behind drawn curtains and well-locked doors."[93] Women in divided marriages redrew, along with their husbands, the boundary between their public and private lives that allowed some room for the politics they brought home. As a result, marriage and courtship, two institutions idealized for their distance from the rancor of politics, proved somewhat resilient to the intrusion of war.

Brothers and Sisters

SOMETIME DURING A BATTLE at Perryville, Kentucky, in October 1862, two opposing regiments from that state exchanged gunfire. Among them was a soldier with the last name of Hopkins. Hopkins stood only twenty feet away from a group of enemy soldiers when he aimed, fired, and mortally wounded a soldier who, it turned out, was his own brother. It was no tragic coincidence. According to the *Louisville Daily Journal*, immediately after shooting him Hopkins approached his brother and told him that "he had done it on purpose"; then he gave him water and a blanket and left soon after. Later that day, however, Hopkins returned to the scene of the fight and stayed with his ailing brother for half the night. The paper explained Hopkins's actions by the fact that he was "a man of family."[1]

How could a man simultaneously shoot and embrace his own brother? The *Journal* did not provide an answer in its matter-of-fact retelling of this alleged incident, but many readers might have been startled by the juxtaposition of violence and affection. The confrontation of two brothers on a battlefield, ending in the death of one at the hands of the other, epitomized everything that divided families feared about the Civil War. The public rules of combat forced these two men to suppress their kinship ties and to become enemies. It was precisely the desire to avoid such a public face-off, and to maintain a private relationship, that prompted fathers to keep their sons out of the service and encouraged some husbands to resign from the army and return home to their wives. It is striking, then, that in the Hopkins case the worst fear of divided families was only partially realized. Hopkins may have shot his brother, but he also managed to remember his family ties; their fraternal bond was not destroyed by the war but instead existed alongside their new position on opposite sides of the battle line. This begs the question of how and why these two seemingly conflicting identities — kinsman and enemy — could coexist.

Many other sets of border-state siblings joined the Hopkins brothers in raising this issue. Instances where brothers, and to a lesser extent other horizontal kinship relations such as those between sisters and cousins, assumed opposing stances in the war are notable in that they could not keep their conflicts within the protective walls of the private household in the same way that fathers and sons, and husbands and wives, often could. This partly had to do with their age: averaging about thirty-five years old, these men and women did not share households but instead were established in their own marriages and careers. They had grown apart, a trend encouraged in roughly half of the cases by the death of both parents, and they were not as reliant on each other as children were on their parents or wives on their husbands. The absence of this dependency, and the existence of more voluntary attachments of fraternity and affection, uniquely affected how these family members managed their personal relationships amid the stresses of war.[2]

Brothers in Conflict

Brothers were accustomed to conflict. Nineteenth-century ideals encouraged male siblings to maintain active, even confrontational relationships with one another. From an early age they were part of what historian E. Anthony Rotundo has termed a "boy culture," a world of energy, noise, and violence in which male peers socialized by challenging one another to be better and stronger. Brothers hunted together, played games, and fought one another; they participated in any and all activities that centered around direct competition. Through such challenges they tested their physical strength and mental aptitude and, in the process, came to define themselves independently of their male siblings. Young men's coming of age thus encompassed, in large part, conflict and rivalry with their brothers. Fraternal competition was regarded as healthy and an important exercise in the progression to manhood.[3]

For many mid-nineteenth-century brothers, sibling competitiveness extended quite naturally into the realm of politics and public affairs. The young men considered here grew up in border states that had witnessed significant sectional turmoil in the 1830s and 1840s; they could not ignore the issues of slavery and sectionalism being debated around them. From boyhood these brothers incorporated politics into their everyday play, with name-calling and role-playing games encouraging them to stake out opposing positions in the sectional conflict.[4] As they grew older, their games gave way to more sophisticated arguments; intellectual engagement with public affairs was considered an important part of a young man's educational and civic development. These men joined debating societies to learn the fine art of argumentation and political thought, but, in most cases, they found that challenging their own brothers, at home or in a letter, was an equally satisfying outlet for attempting to understand the events around them. There was little consequence to disagreeing with one's brother. Men could argue with their brothers without fear of offending them; they were not limited by the demands of deference and duty that bound them to their fathers and mothers. Their brothers were roughly their equals socially and intellectually, and therefore fair opponents in the rhetorical battles of politics. For these reasons young men sought active, even contentious, political debate with their brothers.

Letters between male siblings tended to be more explicit on the subjects of slavery and sectional conflict than those between other family members. In their near-weekly correspondence throughout the 1850s, for example, the three Halsey brothers —Joseph, Samuel, and Edmund —of Virginia and New Jersey continually discussed questions relating to abolition, tariffs, John Brown, and disunion. These siblings were natives of New Jersey, but Joseph, the oldest, had moved to Virginia in the 1840s to purchase land and become a planter. Joseph Halsey married a Virginia native, Mildred Morton, went into partnership with her father as a landowner and slaveholder, and declared his intention to remain in Virginia for the rest of his life. His outlook on sectional politics differed from his younger brothers' in direct relation to his geographic distance from their New Jersey home. Joseph sympathized with the South's growing disaffection with the Union (and, in particular, its antipathy toward Northern abolitionism), whereas Samuel and Edmund were Republicans and firmly committed to the Union. In their letters, often eight-to-ten pages long, the brothers challenged one another to think more deeply and clearly on the pressing political issues. When Joseph linked the Republican Party to abolitionism, for instance, Samuel sent him a copy of the party's 1856 platform and asked him to "sift it, criticize it minutely, and tell me if it smacks of abolitionism." Samuel contended that Republicans —himself included —had no intention of ending slavery in the South but only sought to prevent its expansion in the West.[5] The Halsey brothers demanded from one another more precision and evidence for their arguments and often referred one another to newspaper clippings, historical texts, and biblical passages to substantiate their points. Their letters thus read like pamphlets, the product of significant research and deliberation rather than casual conversation.

The Halseys' letters were as much displays of political savvy as arguments over the merits of slavery or secession. The brothers seemed to relish the opportunity to hone their debating skills. "I like the idea of your sending me questions to answer," Samuel told Joseph. "It is an excellent exercise & a very pleasant method of improvement."[6] The brothers monitored the content as well as the style of one another's writings and offered criticism when they felt it was necessary. "In argument it is very essential to make statements as much to the point as possible," Edmund chastised Joseph when the Virginia brother appeared to use the word "fanaticism" too freely.[7] Edmund was perhaps more attuned to the intricacies of debate than either Samuel or Joseph. As the youngest brother, Edmund entered college in the late 1850s and was new to political argument. In fact, the Halseys' father supported their letter exchanges specifically as a means of cultivating Edmund's speaking and debating skills. "I am glad you correspond with Edmund," the senior Halsey wrote his Virginia son, "and though you may not derive much profit from his rather crude letters he will no doubt be greatly benefitted."[8] Edmund, for his part, began to wonder if his letters annoyed Joseph. In the margin of one notably long discussion of slavery, he scribbled, "Do you think I had better join a debating society?"[9]

Edmund Halsey was concerned that his often strident opinions somehow violated a code of etiquette surrounding brotherly debate. His writing was particularly energetic — long, impassioned, full of strong language — and it was possible that it might offend Joseph personally. "If henceforth anything should be said that seems rather blunt," Edmund wrote him in January 1857, "remember its [sic] all in politics."[10] He did not want his passion for politics mistaken for anger or frustration with Joseph. More significantly, though, Edmund wished to make sure that his brother recognized a boundary implicit in their exchanges. Their discussions were "in politics" — something easily contained that did not have to spill over into their personal relationship without their consent. The brothers routinely spoke of this boundary and tried to reinforce it by depersonalizing their debates with humor. Edmund, for instance, sketched a skull and crossbones in the upper corner of one letter to Joseph and labeled it "Abolitionist crest" after Joseph wrongly accused him of advocating emancipation in the South.[11] Samuel injected a light-hearted jab in another letter to Virginia, signing himself "your affectionate brother though a Black Republican."[12] Samuel claimed that he could still be a brother even while staking out a divergent stance on the sectional crisis. Division over slavery might play a significant role in their correspondence, but the Halsey brothers believed that they could contain their divisions under the rubric of "politics."

Most brothers similarly accommodated politics in their relationships and were not surprised when their antebellum divisions led to opposing stances in the war. "We have so often, and so radically differed upon the subjects of party politics," Tennessean William Cooper wrote about his brother Edward, "that it is not surprising that we should differ again now, when the Union seems in actual peril." William still did not condone Edward's pro-Union position. "How he can come to such a conclusion passes my comprehension," William continued, "but that he is honest no one who knows him can doubt." William acknowledged, based on numerous letters and conversations, that Edward's position was sincere and therefore deserved respect.[13] Few brothers tried to change one another's minds about the sectional conflict. "We probably shall never think alike and must agree to pity and try to respect each other's blindness," concluded Baltimore mayor George Brown in an 1862 letter to his brother-in-law and close friend.[14] Brown admitted that both of their opinions might be the product of "blindness," that neither man was necessarily right about the war. He resigned himself, as did many brothers, to their opposing views as a familiar and understandable part of a fraternal relationship.

Any optimism that brothers had about containing their wartime division as just "politics" was encouraged by another facet of their relationship — brotherly love. Affection was an important component of fraternal relations in midcentury America, one that was closely connected to the competitiveness among men. Fights and debate may have promoted division, but they also bred respect and an admiration for the fortitude exhibited in the course of a competition. Respect and admiration, in turn, fostered intense loyalty and affection among brothers that differed from the bonds they shared with their wives or mothers. "Brotherly love" was a spiritual bond, rather than a physical one, one that centered on loyalty and sacrifice rather than intimacy. Brothers might alternately fight and protect one another; they were allies beneath the rough-and-tumble world of boy culture.[15] Fraternal affection therefore acted as a yoke that restrained the competitiveness of male siblings.

Brothers talked openly and self-consciously about the importance of affection when the Civil War exacerbated the divisions between them. "I never took enough interest in the present or future condition (whether temporal or spiritual) of the American Negro-Slave," Samuel Halsey assured his Southern brother, "to generate feelings inconsistent with brotherly affection." He later promised that "a difference of political opinions shall make no difference in the brotherly affection which has always existed between us."[16] Similar statements appear repeatedly in brothers' letters with only slight variation. "Do not let a political creed and difference of sentiment," Kentuckian Valentine Stone urged his Confederate brother in 1862, "divide the love which we shared as companions in youth, as brothers and as friends." There was something reassuring in this notion of fraternal love. Brothers looked to affection as something that could reinforce the boundary around "politics" and protect them from estrangement. Another brother, fearing that he might not see his sibling again if the war took one of their lives, was consoled by realizing that "he knows well how I have loved and do love him."[17] In this case, as in others, expressions of affection offered a defense against guilt over brotherly division.

References to fraternal "love" were prominent in wartime letters in part because male siblings feared that it might be threatened. The war appeared to promote one side of their relationship — competition — at the expense of their more affectionate side. Brothers read one another's letters carefully, looking for any sign that their affection was waning or that they were becoming emotionally detached. Here, the experience of John and Jabez Pratt is illustrative. The Pratt brothers descended from an old Maryland family that produced a governor and several other prominent men. In April 1861 John, the oldest, lived in Boston, where he supported Republican politics, while Jabez lived in Baltimore, where he shared the city's pervasive pro-Confederate sentiment. In the months leading up to the war the two corresponded weekly, delving into the merits of slavery, Lincoln's election, and secession. Their letters, like so many others between brothers, mixed vigorous and sometimes angry debate with professions of affection and friendship. At the outbreak of hostilities, for example, John invited Jabez to live with him in Boston, where, he believed, his brother would be safer than in the line of battle in Maryland. But Jabez turned down the offer, explaining that he and his wife had no desire to run into the arms "of infernal abolitionism." The younger Pratt rejected the offer of fraternal assistance in a way that equated it with abolitionist oppression. This was "cruel and unkind," John wrote in response, since Jabez had obviously allowed politics to take precedence over fraternal love.[18] Jabez quickly recognized the error of his ways and apologized, promising that "I can hold no other than brotherly affection though we may differ and be separated." He concluded with the plea that he "not be compelled to meet you in hostility," since he would "prefer to meet you as a brother."[19]

Jabez Pratt's choice of words is significant. He drew a distinction between meeting his brother in "hostility" and as a "brother," or between interacting in the public arena of the battlefield and in the private confines of their letters and households. The two situations, he suggested, were different and required distinct modes of behavior. Privately, the brothers might be able to rein in the familiar competitiveness of their relationship with expressions of affection and love. But in wartime that competition — their division over sectional politics — might overpower the restraints of affection. Jabez recognized that if he met John in "hostility," or on the battlefield, he would be forced to shed his brotherly identity and treat him as an enemy; the war introduced new pressures that disrupted the accustomed balance between competition and affection shared by male siblings. Jabez indicated that he would rather meet his sibling as a "brother" in an intimate setting that was insulated from the larger, public battles of war. He leaned on the idealized boundary between public and private life to create an acceptable space for maintaining their familiar relationship.

Brothers generally agreed that keeping their relationship private and preventing any public encounters between them was essential to maintaining their rapport. But this reliance on privacy was difficult when the source of their differences — slavery and sectionalism — was so overtly public in nature. It was a constant challenge for brothers to extract the war's issues from the hostility and emotion that surrounded the military war. The Pratts' arguments over Lincoln and the fate of border states such as Maryland became increasingly angry and bitter. "Dear Brother," Jabez wrote in frustration after the South's secession, "You are fast driving me to consider that term inappropriate." The two brothers resorted to name-calling when their attempts to discuss the war reasonably failed. John called Jabez a "fool and a boor," to which Jabez replied, "You are crazy," and asked John to stop writing until "you get your senses."[20] Their language disintegrated, a sign that the emotional intensity of war had intruded. Even worse, perhaps, was the unusual and drastic step taken by John of sending one of Jabez's letters to the *Boston Daily Journal* for publication in April 1861. Here John broadcast their conflict in the most public medium — the press — and undercut the privacy that was to preserve their relationship.[21]

Jabez Pratt viewed his brother's action as first and foremost a violation of a tacit understanding between them. He fired off a furious letter in which he questioned John's "personal honor" and "oft-repeated assurances of affection for me." Jabez believed that John's action revealed that he had been insincere in his previous expressions of brotherly love; moreover, it was nothing other than "dishonor and private treason." His brother had published a private letter only to inflame the public mind — a serious breach of their relationship, since letters were a primary mechanism for reinforcing the bonds of fraternal loyalty. Letters were so crucial in this regard, Jabez argued, that he himself would "suffer death before I would violate the confidence of a brother's correspondence." Jabez Pratt drew on the language of honor — "dishonor" and a willingness to "suffer death" — to emphasize the insult behind his brother's action and to remind him of the fraternal bond that should have guarded against such a public embarrassment. Jabez was skeptical that his brother could redeem himself. "I fear you have broken the chain which should unite brothers forever and that we must part," he concluded with a touch of drama. "This is a bitter cup. It cuts me to the quick and I can hardly see through my tears which flow as I write these lines."[22]

John Pratt quickly apologized but tried to minimize the seriousness of his action. "I am sorry, very sorry, if I hurt your feelings," he wrote, "if I did it was an error of judgment and not of the heart." John claimed that he had published the letter on a whim, after a *Journal* reporter asked him if he had had any news from Baltimore. The paper was always eager to receive reports from places farther south, especially that week when there had been no mail or telegraphs from Baltimore. John believed that Jabez's letter would be informative to Boston readers, especially because it dealt almost exclusively with public affairs in that border city. He rejected the notion that anything private between them had been violated. "You gave me the *public* sentiment," he pointed out. "There was nothing *private* about it." (He did not mention the additional — and relevant — fact that the paper had withheld his brother's name and published the letter anonymously.) Because this was a uniquely nonprivate letter, John reasoned, Jabez should not be concerned about any breach of brotherly honor or "private treachery." Instead, he might take pride in the fact that the newspaper held him up as "an exponent of public sentiment in Baltimore." At the same time, John promised not to publish any more letters and urged his brother not to "make such a fuss over a small matter."[23]

Brothers in Combat

The larger issue here was no "small matter" to Jabez Pratt or other brothers in his position. How could brothers maintain a private relationship when the public pressures of war increasingly weighed upon them? It was not the conflict itself that troubled these men, but rather the potential for their division to slip beyond their control — into a newspaper or, more commonly, onto a battlefield. This posed a troubling dilemma for the majority of brothers examined in this study, who were between the ages of eighteen and forty-five and eligible for military service. Many had been educated at West Point; others had dedicated years of their lives to soldiering and had developed a strong sense of duty to military life and to the men with whom they served. If these brothers followed their politics and joined the army of the opposing side, then their private division would become irrevocably bound up in the conflict between the Union and the Confederacy. Indeed, the brothers might meet on the battlefield and be forced to choose between their loyalty to their sibling and their loyalty to a nation. In the worst scenario, they might have to shoot their brother in the heat of combat or, in the words of Unionist Charles Henry Lee, whose first cousin was Robert E. Lee, "engage in fratricidal strife."[24]

Fratricide was a powerful image looming over border-state families. Letters written early in the war are full of references to "fratricidal animosity" and the "fratricidal war."[25] For some Americans, the specter of brother killing brother was an apt metaphor for the nation turning on itself.[26] But to border-state families whose brothers were divided in the war, fratricide was dangerously close to becoming a reality. Fratricide was not common in midcentury America, but it was widely written about and discussed. Occasionally, newspapers would report the shocking death of one brother at the hands of another.[27] Fictional accounts of fratricide could be found in the works of James Fenimore Cooper and William Shakespeare, who depicted the murder of brothers in *Hamlet*. In the Bible, stories about brothers such as Cain and Abel were often moral tales that pitted a good brother against a bad brother and ended in an ignominious death. This was death filled with rage, hate, guilt and jealousy; it was the deadly culmination of a brotherly rivalry gone bad.[28] To invoke the image of fratricide in the context of two brothers on opposing sides of the Civil War, then, was to see the worst possible outcome of their division. This possibility preoccupied border-state families.

Brothers paid close attention to one another's military decisions at the start of the war and tried to influence their male kin not to enlist against them. "He must not take sides *against* me," a Confederate wrote to his sister about their Union brother. "I am the *oldest* and have a right to the first choice." (No brothers in this study appear to have honored birth order seniority in the decision to fight, however.)[29] The specter of fighting one another on the battlefield drove others to plead with their brothers not to serve in the military. "The fact that we may meet you in an opposing regiment is not a very pleasant one," Samuel Halsey wrote his brother Joseph with understated concern. "I hope and fervently trust you will keep clear of military honors & positions of all kinds." Brothers like these tried to talk their kin out of fighting rather than avoiding service themselves. Confederate soldier Henry Stone, whose

brother Valentine Stone served in the Union army, told his Unionist father
in 1862 that "I wish to God he would resign." In the next sentence Henry
declared his own intention to remain in the Confederate army until the end
of the war.[30]

The prospect of resigning and sitting out the war posed a tough alternative
for these men. Union and Confederate conscription laws beginning in the
second year of the conflict made refusal to serve illegal unless the individual
had a proper exemption, and rarely were family relationships considered an
acceptable reason to grant such a privilege. Officers did have some leeway to
resign their commissions, as did men over forty-five, but even they found it
difficult to break away from military duty.[31] For men at midcentury, military
service was very meaningful. To serve in the army or the navy was an exercise of bravery, honor, and duty — all the markers of masculine authority. To
avoid service was to undermine one's claim to manhood and, in wartime,
to shirk one's manly duty or, as some contemporaries put it, to be guilty of
"skulking."[32]

Men who had served in the military for a considerable time previously
were torn by an additional sense of obligation to their comrades. Such was
the case of West Point graduate Alfred Mordecai, a fifty-seven-year-old major
in the U.S. Army and an ordinance chief serving in Watervliet, New York,
in 1861. A native Southerner, Mordecai had brothers and sisters living in
Virginia with whom he corresponded during the secession crisis. Moreover,
as a prominent military officer, his skill was well known to the leaders of the
new Confederacy. In January 1861 the governor of North Carolina had made
overtures to Mordecai to return to the South and in March he received a letter
from aides of Confederate president Jefferson Davis offering him the command
of either the South's Army Corps of Engineers or Corps of Artillery.[33] The
offer was tempting and was made all the more so by the repeated urgings of
his siblings to return home, but Mordecai was disinclined to resign his U.S.
commission. "I would not take sides against the south," he wrote to his brother
in Richmond, "but I confess that I should be almost equally reluctant to enter
the ranks against those with whom I have been so long associated on terms
of close intimacy & friendship."[34]

Mordecai found himself caught between competing familial bonds — both
literal and figurative. His army comrades were also, as so many men termed
them at the time, his "brothers." He was bound to them by the military's code
of honor and had sworn to serve and protect them. In fact, military custom
at midcentury encouraged soldiers and officers to view their duty to one an-

other in family terms; a commander assumed authority akin to an "uncle" or "father," while enlisted men were bound to respect him like a "son." Among fellow soldiers — or "brothers in arms" — this familial-military organization fostered a closeness, a companionship, and, in Mordecai's words, an "intimacy" that was not easily broken.[35] In a private letter to the head of the Ordnance Department, Mordecai announced his intention to resign from the U.S. Army, but he balanced this difficult decision by also abstaining from service in the Confederate army. Mordecai wanted to avoid meeting either his military or his familial brothers on the battlefield, and he hoped that by initiating this compromise he would "be permitted by both sides to retire quietly to private life."[36]

This longtime soldier relied on the popular belief that private life offered a place where his family's differences could coexist peacefully. Initially, however, Mordecai's resignation offered him no quiet retreat. He satisfied few people with his compromise — both his Virginia family and his military colleagues opposed it and told him so. His brother George continued to urge him to take up arms for the Confederacy, while his sister Ellen urged him to recognize his duty to the South, noting that "all eyes at the South are turned towards you."[37] He also received a number of letters from U.S. Army colleagues expressing their "sorrow," "pain," and "regret" at his resignation.[38] Several Union newspapers questioned his motives, with some wondering if he might use his knowledge of U.S. arsenals to aid the rebels and spy for the Confederacy. Residents of Troy, New York, even threatened arrest or violence to prevent him from going south.[39] The *Troy Daily Times* saw the resignation as evidence that Mordecai was not a "true and loyal officer," because he did not put his country before his family. A "true officer," the paper declared, "would stand by the Union as his mother, dearer than the mother of his blood."[40] But Mordecai did have both of his "mothers" or, in this case, his "brothers," in mind when he acted, as he explained in a seventeen-page letter to his family written shortly after the newspaper commentary died down. Here Mordecai acknowledged his commitment to the Union but made a case for his family loyalty by pointing out that, in resigning, he had just given up "the labor of a whole life."[41]

The issues surrounding Alfred Mordecai's resignation — competing families, public pressure, conscription laws, and a military career — were common to border-state men. Others found their situations equally difficult, but rarely did they respond with a resignation that pleased their family. Indeed, three-quarters of the divided brothers examined here did enlist and serve on opposing sides. The prospect of confronting a brother in battle may have been sufficiently lamentable to urge him to resign, but it was not strong enough to induce one's *own* resignation. Of the cases in which one or both brothers did not serve, only two (including Mordecai's) involved resignation from the military to avoid facing siblings in battle. In the remaining cases, brothers did not serve for different reasons: two were clergymen, some held political office, and others had reached the age of military retirement.[42] It is difficult to estimate how many sets of brothers actually served in opposing armies, but these divided enlistments may not have been uncommon. In Company F of the 24th Tennessee Union regiment, for example, at least five soldiers had brothers in the Confederate army.[43] Brothers such as these likely hoped that the prospect of seeing their siblings in battle was slim. Yet one pair of brothers reportedly met twice in combat during the war, and such incidents prompted a Confederate in Missouri to comment that "literal fratricidal strifes" were taking place all around him.[44]

The possibility of a battlefield encounter was never far from opposing brothers' minds as they went off to war. They imagined how these meetings might occur and how they would respond. "When the knife of my best friend is at my brother's throat," Confederate William Cooper of Tennessee wrote hypothetically to his brothers, "reason ceases to act and instinct must take its place." He would, he admitted, have "no choice" but to let his friend proceed and kill his Yankee brother in the interests of the South.[45] By Cooper's reasoning, the laws and duties of military service would compel him to put his comrade before his brother, his nation before his family. It was a necessary evil. Similarly, when a Missouri Unionist heard that his Confederate brother was in a Federal prison, he told another brother that "if he is ever exchanged and meets me on the battlefield I will fight him or anybody else."[46] Virginian Unionist James Welsh made no distinction between his Confederate brother and any other enemy soldier: "I would strike down my own brother if he dare to raise a hand to destroy that flag."[47] Most brothers, like this one, avoided putting a personal face on his adversaries, preferring to elide their brothers with the anonymous "enemies." "If I should meet any of my relatives on the battle field," wrote another soldier, "they will there be considered as my enemies and treated as such."[48] Once their conflict entered the public arena of battle, these men suggested, a whole different way of relating to family would necessarily take over and "brother" would be replaced by "enemy."

Public opinion initially embraced (and sometimes celebrated) reports that two brothers had met one another on the battlefield. Personal letters and newspapers told of such encounters in various battles in the first year of the war—from Manassas, Virginia, to Rolla, Missouri, to the coast of South Carolina.[49] Often these accounts praised the men for their fortitude in confronting a sibling. Noting that "several brothers" had met on opposing sides at Manassas in 1861, one Confederate soldier wrote that although "the scenes are affecting . . . the Southerners have never to my knowledge flinched from their patriotic duty." There was something noble in being willing to sacrifice the bonds of kinship for one's country.[50] Confederate Virginian Matthew Page Andrews, who witnessed the deaths of two brothers in the same battle, called it the "most glorious" kind of death.[51] The men's very willingness to confront one another exhibited a courage, bravery, and toughness to which all soldiers aspired. The *Louisville Daily Journal* pronounced the loyalty of Union officer John W. Tydings "zealous" in "contrast with the disloyalty of his brothers," who had both joined the Confederate army.[52] The latter statement suggests that the ultimate test of one's national loyalty—and one's courage as a soldier—was a willingness to turn against and fight one's family members.[53]

Newspaper editors in the border states were especially interested in reports of sibling battlefield encounters. Stories describing these incidents, which appeared under such provocative headlines as "Brother against Brother," "Brother Shoots Brother," and "Brother's Blood," played on readers' fears and likely sensationalized any element of truth behind them. Such articles told of siblings taking aim at one another in literal acts of fratricide.[54] It was this "encounter," the meeting and recognition of brothers in battle, not merely their sectional division, that fascinated observers. In one of these "strange events," as the *New York Herald* termed it, a Union soldier bearing the colors of his regiment was captured by his brother's Confederate regiment. In another "strange scene," a Union officer leading his company across a battlefield in Missouri heard his name called out by a wounded Confederate soldier and discovered that the dying man was his own brother. He continued marching. In other stories brothers were captured by one another's regiments, shot by one another's bullets, or involved in some conspiracy against the other.[55] The press generally characterized these incidents as curiosities of war, and, at least in the first year of hostilities, implicitly urged brothers to be courageous against their brothers' opposing army. In October 1861 the *Louisville Daily Journal* published a story about Richard Williams, a Unionist, who had grown tired of being driven from his Kentucky home by the Confederate army, of which his brother was a member. Provoked by the brother's aggressive actions, Williams announced his intention "to do a little driving himself" and joined the Union army in order to fight back. The paper was optimistic about Williams's chances against his "traitor-brother."[56]

By 1862, however, the enthusiasm for these sibling encounters started to wear off. Newspapers were more attentive to the dark side of these stories — the bloodshed and hostility — and began to view them as something to be lamented rather than celebrated. In February 1862, for example, the *Louisville Daily Journal* described a battle at Fort Donelson, Tennessee, in which two opposing Kentucky regiments met face-to-face. A Union man was "dangerously wounded," whereas his Confederate brother "escaped unhurt and was taken prisoner." Although their lives were spared, the Union paper condemned the fact that they "were forced to shed each other's blood by the infamous authors of this infamous rebellion." The brothers' near-fratricide highlighted the treachery of Southern leaders, a notion reinforced by the story's headline, "Horrors of Civil War."[57] Articles such as this one emphasized the immorality of fratricidal encounters and used them to cast aspersions on enemy leaders. In April 1862 the same paper reported the death of Union brigadier general William Pegram after a "bloody" battle in Tennessee. William Pegram was the brother of Robert Pegram, commander of the privateer *Nashville*, who fought for the Confederacy. The encounter of two Southern brothers on opposing sides, the *Journal* suggested, should undermine any leaders' claims that the Confederacy "is founded on any deep or universal conviction." It concluded that there "is certainly no feature of the present war so tragic as when brother is thus found arrayed against brother."[58]

The idea that battlefield confrontations between brothers were "tragic" became increasingly popular in the press as the war progressed — and as border-state residents grew weary of the destruction around them. Indeed, later stories of such encounters in battle emphasized their inhumanity rather than bravery, as well as friendship and kinship threatened rather than courage displayed. The *Daily Richmond Examiner* declared in 1863 that the "meeting of brother against brother" was one of the "evils" of the war.[59] Furthermore, newspapers tended to highlight episodes in which such "evil" was overcome by the strength of brotherhood. In May 1862 the *Louisville Daily Journal* printed from the *Nashville Union* a story of two brothers who met in battle at Lebanon, Tennessee, and immediately fired. Both missed their mark. Afterward the Union brother reportedly said: "I'm d — d glad that I didn't kill my brother, though he is a traitor and deserved death." The reporter, who called this a "tragic incident" and likened it to the men who unknowingly — and regretfully — killed their kin in Shakespeare's *King Henry VI*, commended the Union brother's restraint.[60] The *Missouri Statesman* saluted an Ohio pastor who, after confronting his brother at the Battle of Stones River in Tennessee, resigned from the Union army to avoid meeting him again. When the Confederate brother was later imprisoned at Camp Chase, Ohio, the pastor provided him counsel and material comforts. These acts revealed him to be a "true and loyal brother."[61] In both articles the "true" or noble brother was a man who saw beyond the division between siblings and embraced their common humanity.

Other stories, which also emphasized the friendship of brotherhood over division, told of brothers reuniting in affectionate embraces on the battlefield. In October 1862 *Harper's Weekly* published a poem, entitled "At South Mountain," in which the last two stanzas describe two brothers dying in one another's arms in Maryland:

> Their hands are clasped together,
>   Their bloody bosoms show
> Each fought with a dauntless purpose,
>   And fell 'neath each other's blow!
> They fell, and the crimson mingled,
>   And before the paling eye
> Back rolled the storm of the conflict
>   To the peaceful days gone by.
>
> Each thought of the mystic token —
>   The talismanic sign;
> Each recognized a Brother!
>   Two firm right hands entwine!
> The fire of the noble order
>   Touched not their hearts in vain.
> All hate fades out, uniting
>   Two hearts with the triple chain![62]

Newspaper articles similarly highlighted expressions of eternal love amid violent encounters. In 1864 the *New York Herald* described a Confederate brother's tearful remorse at the death of his Union brother. The soldier had died from a wound inflicted by the brothers' Confederate cousin, whom the Confederate brother then shot and killed in revenge. The grieving soldier was overheard lamenting, "I weep for my brother and my bosom friend."[63] In early 1865 the *Louisville Daily Journal* and the *Nashville Daily Press* reported that two "close friends" who commanded opposing regiments at the Battle of Mission Ridge both fell mortally wounded. When the fight was over, a Union captain, and a former classmate of the two brothers, found them lying on the battlefield with their right hands clasped. "They had evidently recognized each other after being wounded, and the old ties of friendship had asserted their supremacy," the article concluded, "side by side, in the same grave, they slept their last sleep."[64]

The likelihood that some of these accounts depicted events exactly as they occurred is probably small. The authors no doubt took creative license in depicting actual encounters and clearly romanticized the battlefield as a place where soldiers could recognize and reach out to one another (when, in reality, fighting was mostly an anonymous experience). Added elements of melodrama helped produce stories with several layers of meaning, from an uneasiness with the war's violence, to a message about humanity and civility in the midst of war, to a reaffirmation of family. But even though these stories appear to be semi-fictionalized, there is good reason to believe that they still mirrored a reality of war. Throughout the conflict soldiers both Union and Confederate tried to define their enemies as savage and cowardly in order to justify their own aggressive warfare, but, as historians Reid Mitchell and Gerald Linderman have argued, the war itself sometimes undermined their attempts to do so. Soldiers came to recognize that although their opponents could be savage in battle, they could also exhibit enormous courage. This recognition of common humanity occasionally led to fraternization among troops on opposite sides in such forms as truce agreements for burials, the swapping of money and equipment, and even casual conversation. The experience of combat ironically nurtured a fraternity that many soldiers — especially those with brothers in the enemy camp — had felt the need to suppress in the interests of war.[65]

The few brothers who did have close encounters on the battlefield found it difficult to ignore reminders of their personal ties. In most cases they did not share the tearful embraces described in newspapers but offered one another more practical gestures of fraternity. Brothers on both sides used their influence with military authorities to help their siblings when help was needed. News of a brother's imprisonment, wounding, or other setback incurred in combat prompted his sibling to seek aid on the brother's behalf. Sometimes this assistance involved appealing for a brother's parole, sending money, or guaranteeing proper medical care; in most cases, the aid came from a distance and not through the brothers' direct contact in battle.[66] In one of the more dramatic examples of a brother's help, Confederate William M. McFarland was within minutes of being executed in Missouri in September 1862 when a commander at the site read an order that he be spared. "This is a tribute to the patriotism and sense of duty of your brother," who had appealed to Union authorities on his brother's behalf. The commander hoped that McFarland would prove himself "worthy to be called brother by an honest man" by renouncing his Confederate loyalties. McFarland's Union brother acted on his fraternal kinship ties, but, interestingly, he did so in a way that reinforced the distance between them. He did not communicate with his brother personally, and the Union authorities acting on his wishes carefully distinguished between his own "patriotism" and his Confederate brother's disloyalty.[67]

This Union brother may have been concerned that his act of fraternal love would be construed as disloyalty to the Union. Other brothers like him also restrained their gestures of fraternity in accordance with the rules of combat. When brothers explained the temptation to assist, or even to think about, their brothers on the opposing side, they often spoke of it as an act of loyalty, not to their brothers, but to their mothers. To illustrate, a Union soldier at Gettysburg wrote his cousin after the battle that he was surprised to learn that his brother in a Confederate regiment was only one day behind him. "Had we met, had our Regiments fought," the Union brother observed, "how harrowing would the remembrance be to our precious Mother." It would not, he implied, be "harrowing" to himself.[68] This soldier obscured the emotional bonds of brotherhood behind the loftier attachment of a son to his mother. Similarly, when a Union soldier came upon his brother's wounded body on a battlefield in Kentucky and carried him off to safety, all he could say was, "What will mother say when she hears of this?"[69] In Missouri, another Union soldier, on discovering his wounded sibling lying on a battleground, "tarried with his brother a moment, dropped a tear for mother's sake, and hurried off to rejoin his command."[70] In their mention of "mother," these soldiers acknowledged the profound blood ties that bound brothers. Yet her presence also deflected their feelings for one another in a cautious nod to the rules of combat that separated these men.

Brotherhood could be so powerful that it drew together other military "brothers," especially graduates of West Point, in similar gestures of intersectional fraternity. The U.S. Military Academy earned notice during the war for its divided alumni, which, according to an 1862 study, split three-quarters for the Union and one-quarter for the Confederacy. The graduates — officers in their respective armies — repeatedly came into contact with one another over the course of the war. Henry DuPont, a West Point graduate of 1861 who

Two West Point "brothers" and a slave. A photographer with Mathew
Brady's studio took this image of divided West Point classmates when
Confederate James B. Washington (left) was captured by Union forces that
included his friend, George Armstrong Custer. The two friends sat side by
side in a symbolic representation of the two sides of the war, while the cause
of that conflict is evident in the young slave at their feet (sitting closer to
the Confederate side at Washington's request, according to the memoirs of
Custer's wife, Libbie). Custer later used his influence to obtain an exchange
for Washington that allowed the Confederate to return to his
regiment. (Courtesy of the Library of Congress)

fought for the Union, visited classmate William H. Browne of the 45th Virginia
Infantry, after hearing that he had been wounded and taken prisoner during
a battle in Virginia in June 1864. The two talked tactics and military strategy
before DuPont returned to his command, leaving Browne with a ten-dollar
bill. In a similar case, General Robert E. Lee personally arranged a truce in
1862 that guaranteed the delivery of his classmate Philip Kearny's body to
Union lines and made sure that Kearny's sword and other personal effects
were sent to his widow.[71] Such gestures of assistance, transmitted between the
highest authorities on both sides of the lines, occasionally stirred concern in
the press. In 1862 the *Philadelphia Inquirer*, alarmed that "curious contacts of
old friends transformed into bitter foes are everywhere observed," reminded

Union officers that "no man who stands in arms against his country and her cause can be a patriot's friend." Officers, such as Confederate Simon Bolivar Buckner and Union general Ulysses S. Grant, two "affectionate friends" specifically named by the paper, must strive to forget their friendship temporarily and become a "relentless foe."[72]

The *Inquirer*'s unease may have been misplaced, as such gestures of intersectional fraternity, according to those who bestowed them, did not necessarily mean that soldiers in any way fought the opposing side less vigorously. Rather, these men explained their simultaneous desire to fight their opponents and assist their brothers by finessing their definition of the "enemy." Many "brothers" drew distinctions, as one Confederate soldier did, between "my friends & relatives" and "the wicked & merciless leaders."[73] They separated individuals with whom they were personally acquainted from leaders and other anonymous enemy soldiers. There was a difference between the abstraction of the "Yankees" or the "Rebels" and a Union or Confederate brother; brothers could thus withhold their aggression for certain individuals even while they fought vigorously against an enemy regiment. Not all enemies were the same, and this distinction was important. It allowed brothers — siblings and friends alike — to maintain their relationship as it shifted from the privacy of letters and household to the public battle of war. And it enabled them to balance the familiar elements of competition and friendship, division and love, that had always comprised their fraternal relationships. As General William T. Sherman put it to West Point classmate Thomas Hunton, even as he declined to help reclaim Hunton's runaway slaves in Memphis in 1862, "We are Enemies, still private friends."[74]

Women and Sisters in Conflict

Women faced a different set of challenges when it came to maintaining their relationships as "private friends," but their situation was no less complicated or emotionally charged. Sisterhood, defined here as the bond between blood sisters as well as between female friends and cousins, was considered one of the most central relationships in a midcentury woman's life. It was an emotional and intimate friendship, often begun in childhood and extended into adulthood, one that could be intense, even sensual, in the exchange of love and affection. Women shared their innermost thoughts with female peers through letters and conversations and supported one another through births, deaths, and other life changes. Sisterhood offered a network of relations that complemented marriage, as it provided an environment of relative equality: women could enjoy each others' company free of the subordination that bound them to their husbands. Above all, sisterhood—in contrast to brotherhood—idealized love and affection over competition. Women may have recognized differences, even political differences, between them, but they did not concentrate on their disagreements in quite the same way that men did. As a result, when war came, and public affairs inevitably intruded, women confronted the difficult problem of finding a place for wartime division in their sisterly relationships.[75]

At first women did not always see their divisions coming. "I have no idea Hattie dear that *your surprise* was greater on reading my views . . . than mine on learning *you* were a *Black Republican*," twenty-four-year-old Emma Berry, of Orange County, Virginia, wrote her sister, Harriet Read, in Vermont, during March 1861.[76] Emma acknowledged a mutual element of surprise in becoming aware that Harriet had assumed a political stance so contrary to her own. Similar discoveries of difference were common in women's correspondence, but these revelations emerged slowly, sometimes a year or more into the war. "You seem *surprised* that I see this wretched war in a different light from you," one woman wrote to her sister in Virginia in August 1862, "but I am sure that I have expressed myself just so to you more than once when we have met."[77] How clearly or forcefully she expressed herself is another question. These sisters, like others, tended to explain away their wartime differences by their geographic distance or by the different loyalties of the families into which they had married. These explanations, however, did not mitigate the awkwardness that inevitably arose from the unfamiliarity of wartime division. "I am sure she still loves me," twenty-one-year-old Josie Underwood, of Bowling Green, Kentucky, wrote of her friend Lizzie in 1861, "but there is restraint in our intercourse now . . . so visiting together isn't so pleasant."[78]

Many women tried to avoid discussing the war. A Union woman of Lebanon, Missouri, urged her Confederate cousins to "not let difference in political views interfere with our friendship."[79] Unionist Sarah Bibb of Frankfort, Kentucky, devised more specific guidelines. She managed to remain on a "decent social footing" with her Confederate friends by initiating a ban on war conversation. "If we were to visit," Bibb told a niece, "the subject [of war] must be dropped." This had succeeded in the past and "we go on as usual."[80] Most of these women seemed to believe that if they prevented the war—or "politics"—from intruding in their conversations, they could maintain their normal sisterly relations. Harriet Archer Williams, of Harford County, Maryland, was pleased to report in 1864 that "my southern friends are always kind as ever & I have never noticed any change." Williams promised to return the kindness. Months later she explained that "until they say or do something to offend I consider it my duty to treat them all as I have always done."[81] There was an implicit quid pro quo in these wartime friendships: if a woman was treated with understanding and restraint by her friends, then she would respond in kind. Accordingly, Sophie DuPont of Delaware welcomed into her home a Virginia relative, Charlotte Cazenove, who contained her Confederate loyalties. Cazenove may have been a "warm little rebel," but DuPont was pleased to see that she "behaves admirably here, never breathing a word about politics."[82]

Other informal rules emerged to govern divided women's friendships. Some women objected to any hint that a friend was becoming less amiable or distancing herself socially. Agnes Babb, a Unionist in Baltimore, noticed in 1862 that her friend Mary did not visit as often as usual. Several months later, Babb learned that other friends had hosted two large parties the previous winter to which she was not invited. "I feel rather vexed with them," Babb wrote her brother John, "I don't like to be slighted." She vowed to treat her friends the same way and refused to visit them again. It was not her friends' Confederate sympathies that alienated Babb but rather their unwillingness to keep their differences on the war out of their relationship.[83] Other considerations, such as the military progress of the war, sometimes prompted women to be extra thoughtful and compassionate when interacting with their friends. "I am on the victorious side; our troops hold the town," Josie Underwood mentioned in her diary, and for that reason she would be "ungenerous" if she did not make special overtures to her Confederate friends. "I *will go* to see her this very night!" she decided, referring to one such friend.[84] Some women also were extra kind to sisters and friends dealing with the absence of husbands and close male kin in the military. In an 1864 letter to her husband, who was serving in the Union army, Harriet Archer Williams noted that none of her sisters in Mississippi "have ever mentioned politics to me since you left home."[85] The very divisions that women tried to obscure still influenced—in indirect ways—how they related to one another in wartime.

Fighting the temptation to discuss their differences could be a struggle. Emma Berry of Virginia was startled when her sister Harriet slipped political talk into a letter in 1861. "I am not angry with you Sister dear for expressing your opinions so fully—although so entirely different from mine," Emma replied. "Though my face did burn whilst first perusing it[,] I have also taken the liberty of giving you some of my thoughts." Once Harriet broached the subject of politics, Emma was not about to ignore her challenge.[86] Indeed, the propriety of remaining silent on the war cut against a very natural desire among women to talk about what was happening around them. Young Josie Underwood wrote in 1861 that she and two friends had to "let ourselves out once or twice" during a recent encounter because "we couldn't stand not knowing how each of us stood."[87] An earlier conversation about the war with another friend, however, had created tension, and the two did not kiss good-bye as usual. This unnerved Josie. "We have never had a disagreeable word pass between us in all our lives before," she wrote in her diary later that day. "I'll be careful not to let it happen again."[88] The suppression of politics and war was even more difficult for women who lived together. Anna Dupuy, who resided with her married sister and family in Prince Edward County, Virginia, recognized the challenge posed by physical proximity after the Confederate victory at Manassas in 1861. Her sister's family celebrated all around her, and Dupuy, a Unionist, had "no sympathizers" with her views on the war. Anna retreated to her bedroom, where, she wrote a cousin, "I feel as if confined in a prison."[89]

Not sharing political differences could be unsatisfying. Josie Underwood's literary club decided that it would be better to disband than to search for something acceptable to discuss at meetings. "We can't talk of indifferent things when the war is the all-absorbing subject of our thoughts," she wrote.[90] Women such as Josie were well intentioned in their silence on politics — they wanted to keep their friendships intact — but that silence, ironically, could also be damaging. It meant deliberately withholding their thoughts and feelings from their sisters and friends. This, according to Josie, "spoils a friendship," because the bond between female friends was built in part on "frank confidence."[91] She and others like her knew that their sisters and friends' silence was often intentional rather than the product of apathy or ignorance. This was a war about which women, from the beginning, were outspoken, and they participated in it in unprecedented ways as observers of legislative debates or as spies and smugglers of important military information. Women had war on the mind, and not to discuss it with friends was not to confide and share in their accustomed ways. It was, in short, to strain a fundamental ligament of women's friendship.

For this reason, women carefully watched for any sign of permanent estrangement from their friends. One Wheeling, Virginia, woman was thankful that her friend "has not seceded from me yet" and hoped that their relationship would not go the way of the nation.[92] Other women did notice such a secession. Alice Ready, of Murfreesboro, Tennessee (the sister-in-law of Confederate general John Hunt Morgan), lamented that several of her friendships were "severed" by the war. Her only solace was the hope that "some of them . . . will be renewed at the close of this terrible war."[93] Eleuthera DuPont of Delaware passed around a letter from her friend, a Mrs. Fowle, which stated that she would stop visiting for the duration of the war. "My dear friend," Fowle wrote DuPont, "when I was with you last, there were things said to me & before me, by you & other members of your family, that it was very trying for me to listen to." Fowle's letter took the female members of the DuPont family by surprise, but they resigned themselves to the breach and hoped that the friendship would resume when the war ended.[94] Indeed, few women in this position would have identified with the story, which circulated in Union newspapers in Missouri and Tennessee in 1864, of a fight between two young women in front of a Missouri church. The antagonists, frustrated by their opposing views, reportedly screamed, punched, and rolled over one another on the ground. Men nearby tried to part "the Amazons," as the papers termed the participants in this departure from feminine restraint, but they continued fighting and soon their "beautiful tresses of hair were mixed with blood from dainty noses." Bystanders were said to watch intently. "The combatants fought long and well, until Miss Union seized Miss Secesh by the throat, when she fell to the ground and gave up the battle."[95]

Women were more likely to argue about the war with their brothers or male cousins than their sisters. In fact, women's letters to brothers are much more open and detailed on political matters than their letters to other family members. Ellen Coolidge, a granddaughter of Thomas Jefferson and resident of Boston, for example, found in her correspondence with her brother, Benjamin Randolph of Virginia, a unique opportunity to share her thoughts on her native South's secession. "I cannot tell you how unhappy I am in the present conflict between the North & South," she wrote in a typical letter in 1861. "The idea of Civil War makes all the blood in my body run cold." Weighing the South's right to secede, she admitted that the region had reason to complain but concluded: "I do think South Carolina greatly to blame for her violent measures."[96] Letters from sisters to brothers likewise discussed secession and the legitimacy of the Confederacy, as well as the competence of various military leaders. "I do not think that we are over-fond of Lincoln any more than you are," Marylander Mary Davis told her Confederate brother, "but I see no reason for avowing dead hatred for the poor man[,] for I think he is indeed to be pitied."[97] Coolidge and Davis seemed to welcome the audience offered by their brothers, as well as the forum for debate. This was also evident in Confederate Martha Tipton's decision to copy portions of her correspondence with her male cousin into her diary, interspersing the passages of each writer in a debate format. One exchange in 1863, in which the two disputed whether Southern women should be punished for the South's secession, reveals the intensity of their argument. Tipton's words, "Would you hang me?" appear just before her transcription of her cousin's response: "Well, Mattie, I would not like to hang you but if I commenced the work, I guess you would share the fate of your friends."[98] Letters to brothers (or male cousins), especially to those with whom they disagreed, thus offered women an outlet for speaking out on the war.

Women could speak more freely to their male kin because brother-sister division did not convey the same meaning as other types of family conflict. For one thing, sisters were not restrained by the deference due their fathers or husbands that often required them to choose their words carefully. Mid-century ideas about the relationship between brothers and sisters were more fluid and forgiving than between parents and children or husbands and wives. Consider the attempt of the *Southern Literary Messenger* to define the meaning of "sister" in 1862. Calling sisters "a pleasant invention," this paper explained that "she does not demand the reverence of a mother, but she can feed you just as well. You don't have to pay her expenses, but at the same time you can quarrel with her almost as if she were your wife. She has no special claim on your gallantry, but she can comb your head as well as if she were your sweetheart." Because of this, the paper concluded, "Sister is a most ingenious and acceptable contrivance."[99] Brothers and sisters shared a complicated relationship in which the bonds of kinship and gender interacted in diverse ways. Some brothers and sisters acted more like friends, some like parents and children, and others like husbands and wives. They generally enjoyed a more egalitarian and less hierarchical relationship with each other than with other family members.[100] For this reason, many brothers and sisters engaged in vigorous debates on the war.

Women did not restrain themselves from using bitter language with their brothers. Maria I. Knott, a Unionist and widow from Lebanon, Kentucky, for instance, had two brothers who supported what she termed the "blood thirsty savage and cruel" Confederacy. "I want nothing to do with them," she wrote in 1861. "I am sorry to own such as brothers." Knott wrote these words to her son and daughter-in-law, who also shared her brothers' pro-Confederate sympathies. Knott was apparently less willing to cast off her children than her brothers.[101] Unionist Mary Davis, of Brookeville, Maryland, wrote her Confederate brother outright that she and her sister "are sorry and ashamed to be obligated to own a *traitor* and a *turn-coat* as our brother."[102] Davis, like Knott, not only condemned her brother's actions but also questioned her desire to "own," or to share, a kinship with him. Even brothers who had achieved public recognition for their military leadership in the war were not immune from their sisters' scorn. Union general George H. Thomas, a native of Virginia, had two sisters, Judith and Fanny, who reportedly turned his portrait to the wall and stopped writing him letters when he decided against service in the Confederacy. Rumors of the sisters' tough stand made their way into newspapers. Not long after Thomas gained fame at the Battle of Chickamauga, the *Staunton Spectator* gleefully reported that one of his sisters had refused to send him a prized sword, as she "would prefer to see it thrust through his traitorous heart."[103]

Sisters sometimes had specific expectations for their brothers that could trigger these angry outbursts. Some of them viewed their brothers as objects of their maternal care after the death of one or more parents. Quite naturally, their letters were tinged with parental commands or warnings. "I really think you had better leave politics alone and attend to your *books*," Mary Davis advised her Confederate brother.[104] Unionist Laura Jackson Arnold, the sister of General Stonewall Jackson, left behind few direct insights into her reasoning, but she may have possessed a similar sense of sibling duty when she severed ties with her Confederate brother. Throughout their lives Arnold and Jackson had maintained a very close relationship, a bond created when they became orphans before the age of ten; for two decades before the war they had corresponded regularly. Their letters dealt with the most personal subjects, from religious beliefs to health to Jackson's experience as a soldier in the Mexican War. In the words of a Jackson biographer, Arnold had become the general's "closest confidante." Yet immediately after Virginia's secession in 1861, Arnold cut off their correspondence and, according to rumor, would not allow her brother's name to be spoken in her presence. Their uniquely intimate relationship and the natural expectations of loyalty that went along with it may have fueled—rather than quelled—Arnold's sense of betrayal and anger when her brother sided with the Confederacy.[105]

For other women, a brother's service for the enemy betrayed the patriotic investment they had placed in him. Unable to participate in the military war, these sisters sometimes looked to their brothers as their families' surrogates in

battle, as representatives of their parents and their heritage. The experience
of Lucy Henry Underwood, of Bowling Green, Kentucky, is thus revealing.
When the war began, Lucy was the forty-four-year-old wife of a former U.S.
congressman and the mother of six; her one brother, Winston "Wint" Henry,
was enrolled at West Point. Lucy and Wint came from a distinguished military
family in Virginia: their grandfather, William Henry, fought in the Revolution under George Washington, and their father served in the War of 1812.
Lucy was proud of her family's military heritage and, after the death of her
parents, "inherited the combined patriotism of the family," according to her
daughter Josie. When war came, Lucy threw her support behind the Union
and assumed that her male kin would do the same. But not all of them did.
Two cousins enlisted for the Confederacy, a fact that "nearly kills her," Josie
observed in 1861. Lucy initially took solace in the decision of her brother to
remain in the Union — a decision "she glories in," according to Josie — but
within four months of the South's secession, Wint also enlisted in the Confederate army. This news devastated Lucy, and she vowed never to say his
name again. "All her patriotic family pride had been centered in Wint," Josie
noted, "and his resignation nearly kills her."[106]

Josie Underwood took an interest in her mother's reaction and documented
it in her diary. Lucy apparently wept, shut herself up in her room, and forbade
her family from saying her brother's name as well. "Oh! if he had only died
or been killed defending the flag and the country for which his fathers fought
before he turned traitor," Lucy reportedly exclaimed on several occasions.[107]
For nearly a year, from August 1861 to July 1862, she kept her vow and did
not talk of her brother. Meanwhile, however, she welcomed a Confederate-
sympathizing brother-in-law into her home and kept in close contact with
her daughter and son-in-law, a Confederate soldier. It was the betrayal of
her brother, not any other relative, that most upset Lucy. In July 1862 she
received a letter from her sister saying that Wint might have been injured
near Richmond. According to Josie, her mother turned "white" on reading
the news; she had "tears often in her eyes" and remained in her room for long
periods. "I know she is praying for the brother of whom she will not speak,"
Josie remarked of her mother's time alone.[108] Eventually, word came that Wint
had not been seriously injured and would be able to return to his post. Lucy
Underwood defiantly exclaimed that her brother would "be better dead than
fighting against his country." "She thinks she feels that," Josie commented,
"but I don't believe she does way down in her tender heart."[109]

LUCY UNDERWOOD vacillated between frustration and understanding in much the same way that other brothers and sisters did. The sibling relationship proved both resistant and accommodating to the intrusion of war, from brothers who embraced their differences to sisters who suppressed their disagreements with one another while arguing freely in the presence of their male kin. As their stories demonstrate, along with those of fathers and sons, husbands and wives, divided families adopted specific strategies for managing the war's presence in their intimate lives. They took what was unfamiliar to them—political division—and translated it into more familiar forms of domestic conflict. Preexisting ideals about generation, gender, brotherhood, and sisterhood provided men and women with a clear sense of what was permissible and what was not when it came to expressing their differences to each family member. There was never an easy solution for managing those differences; it took constant effort to contain the disruptive effects of war.

What is most significant is that these strategies existed at all. Divided families reacted to the war rather conservatively: they tried as much as possible to continue a sense of normalcy, to maintain a boundary between their public positions and their private lives that would protect—and shelter—their personal relations from the destruction of war. It was a shifting boundary that accommodated, to varying degrees, a certain amount of politics in their family life. Yet it also reveals just how strongly midcentury men and women relied on their domestic ideals as a defense against the war. Whether any separation between public and private could be sustained in reality, however, depended largely on the families' ability to control their fate—and to control the momentum of war for four long years. That would prove increasingly difficult.

Border Crossing and the
Treason of Family Ties

THIRTY-YEAR-OLD Martha Clay Davenport of Charlestown, Virginia, discovered by 1862 that having a divided family carried certain risks. A secessionist married to a Confederate soldier, Davenport did not like but accepted her Kentucky family's Union loyalties and continued to write regularly to the Clays, just as she had done before the war. Yet by March 1862 she came to realize that not everyone around her viewed her correspondence as innocently as she did, and so she decided to send shorter, less frequent letters in the future. "I am afraid to send a letter," Martha explained to her stepmother, "as I know it will be opened and perhaps myself arrested for treason."[1]

Davenport's fears were not misplaced, as government and military leaders on both sides came to view divided families with suspicion. Many of these families were divided by geography as well as by loyalty, living on opposite sides of the Union-Confederate border. That border, and the area surrounding it, witnessed some of the largest and bloodiest battles of the war, as both sides fought to protect their geographic boundaries and to resist incursions from the other side. The border was challenged, defended, and constantly under siege. Adding to the military hurdles were those geographically divided family members, like Davenport's, who tried to cross the lines by traveling or sending letters to their kin. In the eyes of Union and Confederate officials, such border crossing intruded on military operations and posed a significant problem — among other things, as a potential source of treason — and had to be stopped.

Military restrictions on the passage of people and information from one side to the other affected divided families from the beginning of the war. Neither government cut off contact entirely and selectively permitted some communication across the lines. Families had to obtain permission to travel or send letters, and their requests were often denied. It became extremely difficult to mail letters or to visit relatives living in the opposing section, and, for many families, these obstacles were intolerable. They had, after all, relied heavily on letters and personal visits to share their opinions and feelings about the war and ultimately reinforce the ties that bound them as a family; personal communication, then, was crucial to the resolution of intrafamily conflicts. The absence of contact would only foster estrangement — and potentially sever their family ties for good. Few were willing to accept such an outcome, and they set out to challenge the travel and mail policies.

A vigorous debate ensued between geographically divided families and the Union and Confederate governments over the propriety of border crossing. The dispute centered on whether sending a letter or visiting a relative was inherently an act of treason — offering "aid and comfort" to the enemy — or whether such contact had no bearing on military concerns. The answer to this question depended on one's view of family ties: were they private and personal? could they be separated from military affairs? This was a key issue, already considered within families, that now had serious implications for public policy. Families argued for the private — and thus, innocent — nature of their communications, whereas government officials, skeptical of claims that loyalty to a nation would not be compromised by domestic ties to the opposing side, increasingly guarded against the possibility that divided families might conspire to commit treason. Intersectional travel and mail thus pit the interests of the nation against the interests of families. And divided families, despite their best efforts to keep their affairs private and contained, became a public problem.

Travel

Travel always had been important in maintaining relationships among families separated by geography; with the insecurity of wartime, divided relatives grew desperate to see one another. Rumors and newspaper reports on the destruction of battle-plagued areas made people worry about the well-being of their kin. "We tremble for your safety and wish you were safely here amongst your friends with your family," Samuel Halsey wrote in 1861, urging his son Joseph in northern Virginia to move his family north. "Here you would be safe from danger."[2] Families implored their kin to leave their homes and cross the lines, as if there was relief in being able to see or personally guarantee the safety of a relative. When a brother and sister in Washington, D.C., lost both parents to the war in 1862, Virginia relatives encouraged the siblings to visit them. The sister, in considering the offer, admitted to her brother that "every day of my life I see more closely the value of those close blood ties."[3] There were other reasons for family members to travel, too. Some men and women desired to leave a boarding school, or an asylum, and return to family in the other section. In some cases health and medical care prompted a mother or father to go live with an adult child on the other side, but more commonly the need for financial support and subsistence drew family members across the lines.[4]

Permission to make these trips came in the form of a passport, or "pass," issued by military authorities in the traveler's home section. Beginning in 1861, according to similar Union and Confederate regulations, any individual desiring to cross the lines had to file a formal petition with either a provost marshal, the secretary of war, or initially in the Union, the secretary of state. The petition outlined in detail where the individual planned to travel, when, and for what reason. Officials then reviewed the application and, if it was acceptable, issued a slip of paper that the traveler would show to railroad conductors or military pickets along his or her route. The purpose of the pass system was to preclude "the passage of dangerous or disaffected persons," as Confederate secretary of war James Seddon put it, or, more specifically, to prevent spying and smuggling. It also was meant to bolster the manpower of each army by guarding against desertion and the departure of able-bodied men evading conscription.[5] But at times petitioners felt that the system infringed on their freedom to travel, and to some white Southerners it was an insulting extension of travel restrictions ordinarily imposed only on African Americans.[6]

Those who sought to travel across the border despite these obstacles did not know how officials determined who was "dangerous," and thus ineligible for a pass, and who was not. Not only did both the Union and Confederate governments fail to issue any specific guidelines for assessing the loyalty of petitioners, but also both left the decision largely up to the discretion of individual officials. The result was a haphazard and largely inefficient system, in which some officials required that petitioners take oaths of allegiance to prove their loyalty, whereas others did not; still others, recalled a frustrated Confederate War Department clerk, issued passes to anyone willing to pay the right price. Petitioners thus were left to guess about how to frame their application—and their case for loyalty—effectively.[7]

Petitions to the Union government, more so than to the Confederacy, have survived and reveal what pass applicants believed the authorities wanted to hear.[8] In various ways they made cases for their patriotism and thus their intention never to use the pass to betray the Union. Some applicants made blanket statements such as "I am now and always have been devoted to the Union," but typically they also provided letters from a prominent person or a known Unionist who vouched for their loyalty.[9] Sometimes this person was a newspaper editor or a politician — a mayor, city councilman, or congressman — or someone in a profession known for its integrity, such as a lawyer or a clergyman.[10] Others emphasized their kinship with a known patriot. In one of the more striking examples, a Baltimorean stated: "I am the son of the late Surgeon Henry Lee Heiskell (USA) also a grandson of J. Monroe, Ex-President of the United States. My God father Genl Winfield Scott will vouch for me." A female applicant noted that "I am the widow of Col. Foule who served in the United States Army, through the War of 1812," without attesting to her own loyalty.[11] Both of these petitions implied that the applicant was loyal by association, that an ancestor or family member's loyalty was enough to establish his or her own allegiance. Yet there was an inherent weakness in this argument, as revealed in the petition of a Washington, D.C., man writing on behalf of his mother, who wanted to travel South to be with her husband in Richmond, Virginia. To establish his mother's loyalty, the man pointed out that her son-in-law was a soldier in the U.S. Marine Corps and had "shed his blood on the field of Manassas" for the Union. "Her relationship to this meritorious officer," the man wrote, "will, I trust, plead in her behalf." But what about her relationship to her husband in Virginia?[12]

Here was the basic problem that divided families faced when applying for a travel pass. How should applicants portray their relationship to Confederate family members while trying to convince officials of their indisputable loyalty to the Union? Most applicants did not hide the fact that visiting their Confederate families was the primary reason for their travel. Three-quarters of them explained that they desired either to care for a sick relative, provide companionship, or perform general family "maintenance," as one Baltimore man put it.[13] In the applicants' minds, it might not have been difficult to view this duty to family as disconnected from their loyalty to a nation. Many families had sought to erect a border between private and public affairs within the confines of their households or within their intimate conversations. How to make such a separation convincing to government officials who were looking for any evidence of disloyalty, however, was another question. How could they persuade the officials that crossing the geographic border between the

Union and the Confederacy was not a simultaneous crossing of the boundary between domestic and military spheres?

Some applicants tackled this problem by reminding officials of popular domestic ideals. They argued that travel for family reasons was by its very nature insulated from the war. "The object of my visit is *purely* of a *private nature*," explained William Bayne of Baltimore in a typical petition. Thus, Union officials could be assured that "I will not *aid* or *abet* the enemy in *any way.*" Bayne was applying for a pass to Virginia to search for his widowed sister-in-law, who had not been heard from in almost a year. Another man asserted that his prospective trip related solely to family "duty" and therefore was "actuated by no motives detrimental to the public good."[14] All of these petitioners were asking officials to stand by the idealized separation between public and private spheres. A family visit should be seen as inherently apolitical and would have no influence on the war around it.

The friend of another applicant, however, suggested why it might be difficult to make this distinction during a time of civil war. In 1863 George W. Cullum refused to support the request of Mary Wagner Faulkner, of Martinsburg, West Virginia, to visit her children in Virginia. According to Cullum, no one — not even his good friend Mrs. Faulkner — should be allowed to visit relatives on the enemy side. "It is hard for a mother to be separated from her children," he acknowledged, "but if families divide and a part espouse the side of rebellion, it is hardly to be expected that the government will give aid and comfort to those who have forgotten their obligations to that government." Cullum's words, although polite on the surface, made a damning statement. He suggested that by visiting her children, Faulkner would provide "aid and comfort," a phrase echoing the Constitution's definition of disloyalty, and she would "help those who had forgotten their obligations," a kind euphemism for traitors. In Cullum's view, then, Faulkner's proposed family trip would be inherently an act of treason. He asked his friend to think with her "head" and not with her "heart," and to remember the "injury" that could be caused by "free intercourse with those in arms against us." This was a sacrifice she must make in wartime, Cullum argued, conceding that "War is a harsh thing."[15]

Most pass applicants naturally claimed that they could be trusted to act loyally while visiting their Confederate families. Many did so by focusing on the related question of character. In one case, three townsmen writing on behalf of a woman trying to go to Alabama could "vouch for her integrity."[16] Another man declared that the applicant — a relative — was of "the highest respectability" and "may be implicitly confided in" not to endanger the Union.[17]

These statements implied that a principled individual could be trusted to *act* faithfully, even if, as officials would be inclined to suspect, he or she did not *think* in ways that were loyal to the Union. To some extent this was a smart strategy, as most civilian arrests in the Union were triggered by disloyal acts rather than by disloyal beliefs alone.[18] But given that the applicants for passes made these promises before they traveled, before they had the opportunity to act disloyally, such avowals likely carried little weight with government officials. Other prospective travelers tried to make a convincing case by turning it into a moral issue. A New Yorker writing on behalf of his cousin stated that her "religious principles" were too strong to permit her to divulge any information that would betray the Union.[19]

Numerous women apparently believed that being female would help them make the case for integrity. Eighty percent of the applications to Union authorities were from women, many of whom argued that their gender gave them a unique claim to being trustworthy. "I pledge as a lady to take nothing nor carry anything whatever with me," wrote a Baltimore woman seeking a pass to see her husband in Virginia. Being a lady, or a "Lady" with a capital "L," as one applicant made sure to emphasize, offered, in these writers' view, a respectability that should be honored by Union officials. Some women grappled with the language to describe this unique female integrity. "My daughter & myself pledge our word & honor," one woman attempting to visit her son began, "if it is a proper term to express the obligation of a female." "Honor" was generally associated with men, but this woman argued that she could indeed promise to "carry no secret information." Other individuals, particularly men writing on behalf of women, drew on other feminine stereotypes to justify a woman's travel across the lines. One woman was described as "entirely ignorant" of the war and therefore incapable of betrayal; another was "too simple hearted to understand or communicate intelligence." Female ignorance guaranteed that a woman would not participate in subversive activity, a notion reinforced by another woman with admitted Confederate loyalties. "I think inasmuch as ladies did not make this war," this woman began her justification for a pass, "they are silly in the extreme to mix themselves up in it." She vowed to abide by the idea that the public affairs of war were not a woman's concern. (She even encouraged Secretary William H. Seward to "shoot up" those who assumed otherwise.)[20]

Yet professions of ladylike behavior or female ignorance cut against growing evidence that women were deeply involved in the conflict. Women did "mix themselves up" in the war's intrigue, as historians Drew Gilpin Faust, Catherine Clinton, and others have shown, to become some of the most successful spies and smugglers.[21] Newspapers across the divided nation reported cases of women smuggling goods and letters with the help of a pass, and some papers began to speculate that the pass system permitted women to slip through unnoticed. In early 1862 the *New York Tribune* reported that women's applications for passes "quadrupled" just before a planned expedition by Union general Ambrose Burnside into Tennessee. Although female pass applicants were generally "well armed" with letters of endorsement from Union men, the *Tribune* acknowledged, "they are sure to present themselves in fullest force when the information they can carry will be most valuable to the rebels."[22] Within days the *Tribune* announced that the Federal government had decided to stop issuing passes to women. The reason given was that "in nearly every instance" in which women received a pass, "letters and other documents have been concealed in their clothes." Nothing in the Union records suggests that this change in policy actually occurred in 1862, although by 1864 General Henry Halleck informed a commander in the South that fewer passes were being issued because "we have a superabundance of female spies among us now."[23]

Union officials were inclined to see the worst in almost every application that came before them and to doubt claims that a family visit was inherently innocent. Indeed, over ninety percent of the applications for which the Union government's answer is clear were denied.[24] The standards governing why officials issued passes to some people and not to others are unclear, and it may be that there were no objective reasons for those decisions. In some cases having the right connections appears to have helped an applicant, but in others it did not. Sometimes it mattered whether the person would be traveling in the direction of a battle—and thus into danger—but, again, this was not always true.[25] Even disloyalty was not a clear-cut ground for rejection. It may not be surprising that Juliana Gardiner, of Staten Island, New York, was denied a pass in January 1862. Her application stated that she wanted to go to Virginia to visit her daughter, "who is in deep affliction and needs a mothers attention & sympathy." Her daughter was Julia Gardiner Tyler, the wife of former president John Tyler, who, the petition did not bother to state, had just died and left his wife a widow. But Julia Tyler was known in Washington, D.C., and Virginia circles for being an outspoken, even troublesome, secessionist. With this in mind, perhaps, the secretary of war wrote "Inexpedient" at the top of Juliana Gardiner's application.[26] Yet in the same month Esther Tiffany, the sister of Baltimore's Confederate-sympathizing mayor, George

W. Brown, apparently received a pass to visit her Southern family without much trouble.[27]

The Lincoln Case

No doubt fueling the suspicion surrounding family members seeking passes was a widely publicized case involving President Abraham Lincoln and his family. In late 1863 and early 1864 Martha Todd White, a half sister of Mary Todd Lincoln and a loyal Confederate, visited Washington, D.C. Martha was fifteen years younger than Mary and, according to biographers, was not particularly close to the first lady. She had married a Southerner and during the war lived in Selma, Alabama, while her husband served in the Confederate navy. In late 1863 White traveled to Washington and then asked President Lincoln for a pass that would allow her to remain there for an extended period. It is unclear why White solicited help from the very man who commanded the forces opposing her husband's army (although bypassing the formal petitioning channels would certainly have been expedient). In her letter to Lincoln, she described her prolonged visit as a way to "recruit my health, to replenish my wardrobe, and to take for my own use articles not now obtained in the South." Her words seemed to be those of a war-worn woman who desired a temporary escape from the battle-scarred South. She was also careful to explain that only she would benefit from her stay, as it would rejuvenate "my" health and wardrobe and would result in items for "my own use." In other words, Martha White did not intend to use the visit to assist other Confederates. Lincoln approved the pass, and White remained in the North until at least February 1864.[28]

White's journey to Washington and her extended stay in Union territory excited little comment in the press. Her return trip to Alabama, however, sparked a publishing frenzy, starting with Confederate newspapers. On March 2, 1864, the *Daily Richmond Examiner* described White's trip home from Washington. In just a few sentences it noted that she had been allowed to bring back only one item from the North — a uniform that she intended to give to "a very dear friend of hers" who was fighting for the Confederacy. The uniform made it safely to the South and a few days later revealed itself to be worth more than originally thought. "All the buttons were found to be composed of gold coin," the *Examiner* reported, as a series of gold pieces had been set in the wooden buttons and "covered with Confederate cloth." Altogether the gold was said to be worth between thirty and forty thousand dollars. The paper applauded White's smuggling caper as "a remarkable instance of woman's ingenuity."[29] This was indeed a remarkable story, although several aspects were questionable: How could White have been allowed to bring into the South what was obviously a *Confederate* uniform? Where did she get it, and where did she obtain the gold? The article did not answer these questions, nor did it reveal who had come upon this bit of information or who had made it available to the *Examiner.* Alarmed, Union newspapers from St. Louis to Chicago to New York picked up the story and reprinted it over the next two months.[30]

At first glance this account did not differ substantially from others published about the divided Todd family during the war. Newspaper editors were fascinated by the fact that the Union's first lady had three half brothers in the Confederate army and four half sisters who openly supported the Confederacy.[31] The Todds not only dramatized the nation at war — the "house divided," in the words of Abraham Lincoln himself — but also raised questions about the loyalties of the Union's first family. Did Abraham and Mary Lincoln harbor any secret, potentially subversive allegiances to Mary's Confederate relatives and thus to the Confederacy? The press, especially Northern papers, kept close tabs on the movements of the Todd family, documenting the military service of Mary's half brothers and brothers-in-law, as well as the travels of her stepmother and half sisters between their home state of Kentucky and states farther south.[32] The stories often carried hints of suspicion about what those traveling Todds might do, or what they might induce the Lincolns to do, and in the account of Martha White's gold smuggling many papers found confirmation for their fears. Whispers about the Lincolns' complicity in the incident — especially the president's — followed the story as it traveled from paper to paper and erupted into a full-blown scandal.

By the 1860s scandals involving national politicians and members of their family, particularly the women, were nothing new. Thomas Jefferson and Sallie Hemings, Alexander Hamilton and Maria Reynolds, Andrew Jackson and Rachel Donelson all found their intimate lives subjected to the scrutiny of journalists concerned with the private lives of their leaders.[33] But what was different about the Martha Todd White affair was that it did not involve sex or a woman's virtue. It involved politics — a *woman's* politics — and a woman's potential to induce a man to act against his political inclinations. Did this Southern woman influence the Union president to be her accomplice and thus to act disloyally? This question had a powerful impact in the spring of 1864, dramatizing for a wider audience the same issue — family loyalty versus national loyalty — that other border-crossing families grappled with in their applications for passes. It also resonated with other press accounts of wives who induced their husbands to resign from military service.[34] The imagination of the Union press ran wild with this story, and for a brief time Martha Todd White became the most talked about Southern white woman in Northern newspapers.[35]

Each paper characterized White differently. To the *Daily Richmond Examiner* she was an ingenious patriot, but to Union editors, who agreed that her patriotism was strong, she was also a devious woman. One of the first Northern papers to publish her story was the *New York Tribune*, which, after several weeks of investigation, reluctantly concluded that "the chuckling of the Rebel press . . . was founded in truth." "It is stated in best-informed circles," the paper reported in March 1864, that White had indeed crossed the lines with "Rebel uniforms and buttons of gold" and thus had outsmarted Union military officials. The *Tribune* called for an inquiry into the affair and titled its story, "Aid and Comfort for the Enemy," indirectly accusing the Lincoln administration of treason.[36] The next day Washington, D.C.'s *National Intelligencer*, also a pro-Union paper, placed blame squarely on Lincoln himself: after suggesting that the clothing she carried was a "rebel general's" uniform, it pointed out that White "was sent through . . . by a special pass from the President."[37] The pass was indeed "special" and perhaps indulgent on Lincoln's part, given how difficult it had become for the average Union citizen to obtain one.

Was this favoritism toward Martha Todd White merely a gesture of family loyalty, with no further meaning attached? Lincoln may have thought so, but because it occurred during the stormy electoral season of 1864, members of the Northern press were inclined to be skeptical. *Tribune* editor Horace Greeley, an outspoken Republican (and abolitionist) critic of Lincoln, had long argued that the president was not aggressive enough in suppressing the rebellion and abolishing slavery. Now the Martha White story appeared to connect Lincoln to an act of subversion against the Union and, on a small scale, dramatized what Greeley had feared would result from Lincoln's wartime policies — the Union's collapse at the hands of a designing South. Publicizing this story, and thus casting aspersions on Lincoln's loyalty, might open the door to a different Republican presidential candidate in 1864 (something Greeley had already been seeking behind the scenes). It may not have mattered to newspaper editors how solid the evidence was of White's smuggling, for her action was consistent with other rumors and reports about Lincoln and his wife's family and friends in the South. Throughout the war Lincoln had been willing to bestow favors on Southerners with whom he was personally connected. He previously had issued passes to another Todd sister, Emilie Todd Helm, as well as to his wife's stepmother, Elizabeth Todd, for their own visits to Washington, D.C. Moreover, his published papers contain numerous orders to Union commanders to allow a friend to cross the lines or to retrieve furniture taken by Union soldiers — despite the government's reluctance to grant such privileges to others.[38]

Martha White's story thus touched a nerve in Northern electoral politics in 1864, and press depictions of her became proxies for Lincoln himself, consuming editors' commentaries on the president's politics.[39] White next emerged as the innocent victim of a Confederate prank in a story first printed on April 2. The *New York Herald*, a Democratic paper, stepped up to challenge the *Tribune* by publishing a letter from someone called "Veritas." "The [*Tribune*] article does not contain one word of truth," the appropriately named Veritas wrote, explaining that an investigation had turned up another Southern newspaper containing the exact same story — but one dated two weeks *before* White ever returned to Alabama. The entire story apparently was the clever invention of a Confederate journalist. Under the headline, "Mrs. Lincoln's Sister," the *Herald*'s story defused questions about smuggling and treason and returned White to the less politically charged position of Todd sister.[40] There may indeed have been "truth" to the *Herald*'s account, but this paper also had its own reasons for publishing the story. Although it was a Democratic paper, the editor, James Gordon Bennett, generally supported Lincoln during the war and defended him against attacks by mutual rivals such as Republican Horace Greeley. Bennett later endorsed Lincoln in the 1864 presidential race and received a diplomatic appointment in return. In the meantime, he cast Martha White as an innocent in the story, thereby vindicating the president from charges of disloyalty.[41]

The *Herald*'s explanation did not end the suspicion, however, as a much less innocent Martha Todd White reappeared a few days later. Journalists who were "peace Democrats" (or copperheads), Lincoln's most vocal critics to the other extreme, published still more new details about White's behavior. "The facts," according to the *New York World*, "are even worse" than originally reported. Without question, White "was a rebel spy and sympathizer." Not only did she carry a uniform through the lines, but also her trunks were full of "all kinds of contraband goods," such as medicine, newspapers, and letters. Even worse, when General Benjamin Butler, the commander at Fortress

Monroe where White crossed the lines, asked to inspect her trunks, White shoved in his face an order from President Lincoln exempting her from the customary inspections that accompanied passes and exclaimed, "I defy you to touch them." The *World* found White's impudence distasteful, but equally objectionable was the president's role in "giving aid and comfort to the enemy." It was bad enough to give White a pass, as reported before, but to take the additional step of exempting her from inspection was far worse. This made Lincoln more than a passive accomplice — he was now her devious partner, giving White outright permission to smuggle. The Union "is thus betrayed in the very White House," the *World* concluded, calling for the president's impeachment.[42]

Copperhead papers relished the opportunity to accuse the president of treason. These Democrats, with their calls for compromise during the war, often found themselves accused of disloyalty by Republicans. Now they turned the tables. But in the telling of this story, they also gave Martha White a great deal of influence over her brother-in-law, the president of the United States, which was more unusual for the time. Would any readers, beyond the most ardent Lincoln haters, really believe that a woman could persuade a male relative — the *president*, no less — to permit her to smuggle and thus to act in ways that countered his political inclinations? It was, as we have seen, a common expectation among mid-nineteenth-century Americans that women would follow the partisan loyalties of their male kin, who, in turn, were to represent their interests in the political arena.[43] But the *Daily Missouri Republican*, another Democratic paper (despite its name), responded, under the headline "Disloyal Relations," that maybe it was time for readers to reconsider their assumptions about women and politics. Since it was customary to "judge a man disloyal because his father, son, brother or cousin may be a secessionist," the paper wrote, "we don't see why the rule . . . should not have a universal application." In other words, a woman's partisan loyalty was no different than a man's: it was not necessarily weaker or more deferential but could, in fact, influence the men around her — in this case, a presidential brother-in-law.[44]

This view of Martha Todd White might have been believable to readers. There were plenty of other rumors circulating in the North, as seen in cases of divided marriages, about women luring the men in their families from one loyalty to another. Many Americans viewed women in divided families — not just wives, but mothers, sisters, and aunts, too — with suspicion: they might use their familial position to influence or undermine the loyalties of their men. So why not suspect Martha White of doing the same?[45] Another aspect of the latest Martha White portrayal might also have resonated with readers: her unladylike and spiteful partisanship. White shoved her pass in Benjamin Butler's face and spoke rudely—a familiar scenario, especially for Butler, who had already had well-documented confrontations with the women of New Orleans. White embodied what historian Nina Silber has called "the northern myth of the rebel girl," the belief in an "angry, defiant southern woman" that helped diminish sympathy for Southern women and encourage their treatment as legitimate targets of warfare.[46] White herself had offered additional reasons to be viewed as an ardent "rebel girl." In 1863 Northern papers reported that she had presented a Confederate flag to a gunboat in Mobile, Alabama. Later the Washington, D.C., rumor mill contended that she had been obnoxious in expressing her rebel sentiments at a local hotel while visiting Washington.[47]

This image of an assertive, spiteful sister-in-law had serious ramifications for the president. His reputation had become intertwined with Martha White's: as her portrait shifted from devious patriot to unladylike and dangerous spy, so too did Lincoln's deteriorate from ineffectiveness to outright treason. Newspaper editors equated the president's private loyalty to his sister-in-law with public loyalty to the Confederacy, holding Lincoln and his wife's family to the same standards as other border-crossing families. The administration's strict pass system did not distinguish between family and national loyalty or between private and public life, and neither did the newspapers when they wrote of White's trip. But in Lincoln's case, the overabundance of partisan bickering, not to mention outright fiction, surrounding the articles gave the president some room to extricate himself from the scandal. Naturally in an election year, as each account served the interests of different partisan groups, Lincoln felt compelled to respond. (He may have been encouraged by the fact that average citizens had begun asking him whether the accounts were true.)[48] Lincoln dispatched his secretary, John Nicolay, to investigate and rewrite the story.

The articles had granted Martha White a great deal of political agency, and that was the very point Nicolay set out to challenge. The president was "not conscious" of having given White any "extraordinary privileges," Nicolay wrote in an initial letter of inquiry to Benjamin Butler, and thus he had not been influenced by her to facilitate any smuggling. But the secretary needed more evidence and turned his attention to White's behavior. "Did she use the language alleged?" Nicolay asked, concerned with whether White had indeed acted as a defiant Confederate woman. Responding the next day, Butler refuted many charges in the articles. He pointed out, for example, that White's bags had in fact been inspected and that the only items found were "bridal presents," which he determined were "of no possible use to the Southern army." Throughout his letter to Nicolay, Butler referred to White as a "lady" and noted that her behavior was not "different from the usual courteous and ladylike deportment" he had observed by other women with passes. Martha White was not an assertive Confederate partisan, in Butler's view, but instead a perfectly deferential lady (meaning one who did not overtly challenge men's political loyalties).[49] This was just what Nicolay wanted to hear. He quickly drafted Butler's response as an editorial and sent it to Horace Greeley for publication in the *New York Tribune*. Frustrated by how his Democratic rivals had distorted his original report, Greeley printed Nicolay's editorial the next day under the headline, "The Story about Mrs. White."[50]

The president himself never publicly refuted the stories but, with Nicolay's help, guided the newspapers' gossip mechanisms to work in his favor. (The latest *Tribune* version referred only vaguely to its source as the "highest authority.") Nicolay later told Butler that "the whole canard was too silly and trivial to merit an official contradiction," but that this clarification was certainly "due and proper."[51] Yet his statement belies how seriously the administration did take this story. Lincoln had to depoliticize Martha Todd White, to recast her as an innocent lady rather than a strong Confederate partisan, to protect his own reputation. The new version of the story suggested that the president and his sister-in-law could have a personal, familial relationship without any impact on his political loyalties—an argument that was similar to the one made by families seeking travel passes. Lincoln's, though, was more successful: the whispers and stories about Martha White stopped with the *Tribune* editorial.[52]

So what really happened during Martha White's trip? Her original letter to Lincoln asking for a pass claims that she needed time in the North for rejuvenation and shopping, an assertion substantiated by a friend in a letter to Lincoln during the press firestorm. Angered and determined to do "justice" to White by assuring the president that the story was "absurdly false," Mrs. S. B. French wrote that "Mrs. White was too feeble to go out of the house for ten days before she left this city." The only items she carried with her from the North were "vials of medicine" to care for her (unnamed) medical condition. White, in French's view, was weak and innocent. She concluded that "we are all convinced the report sprang from some political enemy to injure you." French appears to have been right in this judgment, but her letter also reveals another complication: that White likely never visited the Lincolns during her trip and therefore required her friend to reassure her family of her motives. This fact, coupled with the need for John Nicolay to investigate her behavior, suggests that the Lincolns may have harbored some suspicion of their relative and did not trust her to act so innocently. A year later White herself gave them reason to suspect her willingness to exploit familial connections, when she asked the president for special permission to bring thirty thousand bales of cotton out of the South in order to sell it.[53]

Lincoln's personal encounter with all the public suspicion of border-crossing families did nothing to change his administration's policy on the issuance of passes. Applications continued to be rejected at a high rate, and, in response, divided families grew bolder and sought illegal means of crossing the border. One petitioner revealed as much in his pass application when he threatened to travel one of "several routes" to reach the South "clandestinely" if he did not receive a pass. He did not.[54] Underground routes were widely known by people in the border region, especially by those whose families had lived there for decades and knew the terrain. In their papers these men and women reveal many different methods for crossing the lines secretly, including sneaking through wooded areas, lying to Federal pickets, forging passes, or, in the case of Warner Underwood, a U.S. congressman, waving a piece of paper in the faces of guards that looked like a pass but was not.[55] It was impossible for military authorities to guard the entire border, but covert travel still required great care to avoid detection. When Maria McGregor Smith left her home near Richmond in 1864 to live with her father in Washington, D.C., she gave her two children a dose of "paregoric" to help them sleep (and not make noise) while their boat made a middle-of-the-night trip across a fourteen-mile stretch of the Potomac River into Maryland.[56]

Networks of residents of the border states mobilized to help families that were desperate to cross the border. For instance, Millie Halsey, of Culpeper County, Virginia, the mother of two young daughters and the wife of Confederate army captain Joseph Halsey, stumbled on a "sudden and unexpected" opportunity to send her children to live with her husband's family in New Jersey. In Halsey's view, it was essential that her daughters leave home, as Union troops were camped on their property and their food supply was dwindling. It was simply not safe there anymore. In the summer of 1864 she got word that "Old Mr. Smith," a man on crutches, was heading toward the

Washington, D.C., border. She quickly paid the man, a total stranger, $160 to take her daughters and their friend, Miss Holmead, with him to Warrenton, Virginia. Once in Warrenton, the girls donned outfits and accessories provided by their mother to make them look like market women. With Miss Holmead they crossed the border and headed toward Holmead's sister-in-law's house in the city, where they then telegraphed their uncle in New Jersey. To help them along the way, Halsey had given them $35 in gold and $20 in state currency.[57]

It all happened so fast that Millie did not inform her husband of the plan until after their daughters had left. Joseph was furious, and his reaction reveals some of the reasons why other divided families might not have crossed the border illegally. After receiving his wife's letter informing him of the trip, Joseph fired back a reply enumerating everything he thought was wrong with her decision. First, as the girls' father, he was upset that he had not been consulted first; he could not believe that Millie had allowed two young girls to travel three hundred miles near battlefields and into the "enemy's country." This risked their safety, especially as they were guided most of the way by strangers. He chastised his wife for "throwing your children out as beggars" on other people's charity, which not only threatened their "family pride," but also subjected them to dangerous people. "What if [they were] betrayed in Washington & forced to take the oath," he demanded. Even worse, their departure put him in an "embarrassing position" in Virginia. A Northerner by birth, he was already suspected of disloyalty to the Confederacy, "and here goes the report that two of my daughters have been sent to Yankeedom to live & be educated."[58]

Upset by her husband's reaction, Millie defended her own loyalty to the Confederacy: "The step I took was conceived in patriotism being the only way I *could invade and weaken* the enemy." Millie did not explain how this was possible, nor did she make it clear how she differentiated the "enemy" from Joseph's family. Millie probably knew that such a distinction was difficult in wartime; had she applied for a pass, Union officials might have agreed with her husband's inclusion of their family in the "enemy's country." The overlap of these terms — enemy and family — and the unwillingness of government officials to distinguish between them led many other families to abandon travel to the North and to channel their energy toward other means of communication.[59]

Intersectional Mail

Correspondence between husbands and wives, parents and children, siblings and cousins, had traditionally maintained a lifeline among families, bringing news of life changes, of marriages or children born, as well as expressions of love and kinship. Wartime offered no exception, as letters became for many families a surrogate for the intimacy they had enjoyed in peacetime.[60] A New Jersey woman urged her brother in Virginia to write because "I need your loving sympathy now more than ever before in all my life."[61] At this tumultuous time family members wanted support and love; even where anger or estrangement existed, they longed for reassurance that their relatives were alive and well on the other side of the lines. The words of a family member could be an enormous source of relief. To her sister in Washington, D.C., a Roanoke, Virginia, woman wrote: "I cannot express the feelings of delight which filled my heart at the sight of your beloved handwriting yesterday."[62]

Like travelers, however, letter writers confronted official barriers while trying to maintain contact. Not long after the South seceded, both governments moved to prevent mail from crossing the lines. First, Union postmaster general Montgomery Blair ordered that all postal communications with the seceded states (except western Virginia) be discontinued after May 28, 1861. Any letter sent to the North from the South, even if it contained a U.S. stamp, was to be sent to the Union's dead letter office. On June 1 the Confederacy weighed in with its own restrictions, establishing a separate postal service to carry mail only within Confederate lines. For a time these policies created confusion, as residents of both sections did not know whether they would be able to get a letter across the lines, and mail accumulated in border-state post offices. Some people continued to send mail through private express companies, such as the Adams Express Company and the American Letter Express Company, that operated along the North-South mail lines from Washington to Richmond and Louisville to Nashville. But even these routes were discontinued on August 10, 1861, when President Lincoln ordered the arrest of anyone carrying mail across the lines via private express. This directive marked the establishment of what became popularly known as the "paper blockade."[63]

Wartime postal policies mirrored the restrictions on travel by preventing the contact of individuals on opposite sides of the lines. Even though mail was inherently limited in the kind of sedition it could transmit, with small envelopes binding a letter's content, authorities recognized that the written word could convey dangerous secrets. Yet, as with travel, the two governments also recognized the need for some contact between individuals North and South, that most friends and families would want to maintain communication. Accordingly, in 1861 officials on both sides adopted a policy akin to the pass system that allowed for the selective transmission of letters on "flag-of-truce" boats sailing between Maryland and Virginia through Fortress Monroe. Anyone on either side could send a letter via flag of truce as long as it conformed to three standards: (1) it contained both Union and Confederate stamps to cover the cost of postage on both sides, (2) the writer's name was signed in full, and (3) it did not exceed one page and related only to "family and domestic affairs." Any letter that failed to meet these criteria was either returned to the sender, forwarded to a dead letter office, or used as evidence in arresting an individual for disloyalty. Packages were unacceptable.[64]

The flag-of-truce mail policy created a time-consuming postal inspection system that remained in place for the duration of the war. Union and Confederate postal authorities carefully monitored the mail that came through their offices and employed postal clerks for the sole purpose of reading every letter to look for anything suspicious. This was a laborious task, as thousands of letters circulated daily; to accomplish it, postal officials employed more clerks than ever before. (Union authorities even considered hiring "citizen detectives" to assist the postal clerks.) The one-page restriction on length was intended to expedite the clerks' work, but occasionally sympathetic inspectors accepted longer letters. As a result, it could take anywhere from a few weeks to almost a year for a letter to cross the lines. Many letters never made it to their destinations after being rejected by censors. The uncertainty of whether a letter would successfully cross the lines prompted one Union man to say that he wrote "with the same feeling which a sailor has when he seals up something in a bottle & throws it overboard."[65]

Even more guesswork surrounded the acceptability of a letter's content. "Write no military matters or I shall not get your letters," was how one Confederate woman explained the guidelines to her Union sister in 1863. Sallie Knott, of Jefferson City, Missouri, told her mother-in-law: "There is much to tell in the way of rumors & war news. . . . but 'twould be *treason* to tell you anything, as you are not exactly a *friendly power.*" Others simply warned their kin to self-censor their correspondence, deleting mention of "public affairs" or anything "derogatory of President Abraham Lincoln."[66] All of these writers were correct—some surviving letters rejected by Union and Confederate postal clerks reveal that references to politics and the military were consid-

ered in violation of the "family and domestic" rule. (Union authorities asked
a Baltimore man who referred to Lincoln as a "vulgar dictator" to be more
"respectful" in his letters.)[67] The two governments, in a departure from their
travel pass policies, initially appeared to consider "family and domestic" letters innocent by nature and easily distinguishable from all others. But they
failed to define what they meant by "family and domestic," assuming perhaps
that this arena was self-evident, focusing on the household or the idealized
"woman's sphere." The fact that some letter writers bothered to advise their
families on acceptable content, however, suggests that "family and domestic"
content was not self-evident at all.[68]

Few people knew where postal clerks drew the boundary around domestic
life in this civil war, and the uncertainty only grew as the majority of flag-of-
truce letters wound up in the dead letter office. This was especially true in
cases where there was mention of hardships suffered in the war. To write of
losses incurred in battle was on one level a domestic matter, particularly when
it involved the destruction of a home or the death of a family member. But on
another level, such information implicitly referred to the actions of the enemy,
which made it a military or political matter. A Kentucky woman grappled
with this difficulty when writing to her sister in 1862. She wanted to recount
the recent "outrages" committed near her home but refrained from doing so
because of her "fear" of being arrested. Thus she would not "particularize"
on her hard times because "such news . . . is now contraband." This woman
was aware of the danger of describing her privations, so by simply alluding
to them she updated her sister on her welfare without offending the censors.
Her letter made it through the lines.[69] Other subjects such as slavery and a
soldier's death required similar care in distinguishing domestic from political
and military news.

Unease about the content of flag-of-truce letters was compounded by the
knowledge that a stranger would be reading personal mail — an act of "vil-
lainy," in the words of one Kentucky woman. Virginian George Bedinger
stopped himself from commenting on the war in a letter to his sister because
"a cod-fish eater may inspect this." (Bedinger did not direct his insult to anyone in particular, and perhaps for this reason the censors allowed his letter to
pass.) Matthew Page Andrews of Richmond preferred to mock the censors'
work in a letter to his mother in western Virginia. While complaining about
the postal restrictions, Andrews wrote a general family letter on a 14" × 17"
sheet of paper with the words "The Rebel News Sheet" scrawled at the top.
Nothing in its content was objectionable, and the letter passed inspection.

Other people were simply uncomfortable with censorship. As one Confederate woman told her Union father, "I have a very great dislike to my letters being read by strangers."[70]

A letter might also be read by the general public if a postal clerk sent it to a local newspaper. Throughout the war mail on ostensibly "domestic" subjects made its way from post offices into newspapers, excerpted under headlines such as "From a Sister in Augusta to Her Brother in New York." A letter from a Richmond woman named "Mary" to her sister in Kentucky appeared in the Democratic *New York Herald* under the banner headline, "Important from Rebeldom," detailing the death of relatives, her lack of food, and general unhappiness in Richmond society. The *Herald* prefaced the account by calling it an "intelligent and reliable source" on the "mournful condition of affairs in the South," suggesting that domestic letters indeed could be of military or political significance. Such firsthand descriptions of wartime problems could offer military authorities a unique glimpse of the enemy's situation, as well as influence public opinion at home.[71] For this reason, perhaps, Union officials took steps early in the war to prevent similar letters from being used against them. An 1861 order required Confederate prisoners incarcerated in the North to include the following statement in all of their letters: "It is my express desire that the contents of this letter or any part of it will not be put in such a situation as to be published in any newspaper."[72]

A Union woman in St. Louis spoke for many when she declared it an "awful thing . . . to have a private letter published." But the publication of these letters, as well as the postal inspection system itself, was more than merely unpleasant. These actions threatened the wall of privacy that was supposed to surround mid-nineteenth-century families, protecting them from the intrusion of politics, war, and other public affairs and ensuring stability and happiness in their personal lives. Privacy assumed an even more important meaning during the war, as we have seen, but when families found themselves divided along Unionist and Confederate lines, the rupture allowed government officials and newspaper editors unprecedented access to their private lives. This transgression — a rude violation in the minds of many — prompted divided families to protect the privacy promised by their domestic ideals.[73]

Self-censorship offered one means of shielding private thoughts and news from the eyes of strangers. Writers simply omitted "gossip" and other intimate news, waiting until the war was over to share information freely again. "I could give you a nice little dish of family gossip," a Tennessee man wrote to his wife in 1862, "but in these times what is intended for the eyes of one person alone has to pass the inspection of those for whom it was not intended."[74] It was potentially embarrassing for this man to air his family's affairs, as he had no way of knowing how the information might spread. Similarly, a Baltimore man would not express his feelings of affection to his mother because the gesture was "not agreeable to have subjected to the inspection of a stranger."[75] At the same time, though, stripping family letters of interesting news frustrated the relatives who received them. "Why on earth didn't you say something to me I wanted to hear," Josephine Owen, a Confederate, demanded of her sister Jennet Tavenner, who resided in Union territory and had written a bland letter. "Give me a discription [*sic*] of *all* your doings all day till you go to bed so that I can imagine I have spent the day with you."[76]

Other correspondents set out to deceive the inspectors. "Hold the blank part of my 'flag of truce' letters to the fire," a Kentucky man instructed in a letter secretly delivered to his parents by a friend, "for I'll write in milk." (Unable to obtain milk, a Tennessean in Fort Delaware prison opted to write in "onion juice" instead.)[77] Some people asked family members to write their letters on the inside margins of newspapers, which, they thought, were more apt to escape the censor's notice. A Missouri man told relatives to direct his letters to his wife, implying that as a woman she was less likely to have her correspondence scrutinized. (The records of intercepted letters, however, suggest that women were not immune from postal inspection.)[78] Sometimes the deception merely involved a more careful parsing of words — a Virginia woman, for example, asked her brother in the Union army to describe his movements "individually," rather than referring to his regiment as a whole. "Surely there is nothing imprudent in *such* details," she concluded.[79] All of these ploys pushed the boundaries of postal rules and sometimes violated them. In 1863 the *Daily Richmond Examiner* instructed readers to "never append their signatures to their letters" when writing to someone in the North. Initials or a "private mark" would suffice and, if a letter did not pass inspection, would protect the sender from Union retaliation. But this tactic probably achieved only limited success, given that Union policy explicitly required a full signature.[80]

Each of these strategies tried to regain the privacy that families had lost to wartime postal policies. With milk, cryptic writing, or other methods, people could redraw private boundaries around their letters while insulating themselves from charges of disloyalty or treason. At the same time, these were also attempts to outsmart postal authorities who, many believed, were overzealous and too eager to read other people's mail. Indeed, there is evidence that postal censors occasionally reveled in their task. In Lexington, Kentucky, Henrietta Morgan, the mother of Confederate cavalryman John Hunt Morgan, was forced to endure the humiliating (and unusual) experience of having a Union officer visit her house and read aloud excerpts from her son's letters.[81] Despite such incidents, some citizens accepted the loss of privacy as a patriotic necessity. A letter "may be opened and its lines scaned by the curious eyes of some post office official," a Virginia woman wrote to a sister in Vermont, but "I care not. I am willing to put up with even that inconvenience for the good of any country."[82]

Privacy was not the only issue at stake in the mail censorship system. Also in question were the basic freedoms to which Northerners and Southerners alike felt they were entitled. "When freedom of correspondence between friends & members of the same family, even those most nearly related, ceases to be a right, and becomes a privilege," Confederate soldier Thomas Hall told his Union father in 1862, "it may not cease to be a pleasure to receive letters — it certainly is no longer one to write them." Hall, who was writing from a Union prison, invoked the language of constitutional rights to suggest that the current postal policies were violating his "freedom of correspondence." Many other people avoided the flag-of-truce system altogether.[83]

A more dramatic alternative to ensure privacy was to smuggle mail across the lines through secret — and illegal — routes. One option involved conveying letters on blockade-running ships that traveled to Nassau, Bahamas, and transferred mail to British ships. More common, however, was the more informal and discreet system of stashing letters in the belongings of anyone traveling across the lines, either secretly or with a pass. Divided families seized on this option and created what became a widespread underground mail system that crisscrossed the border states. Letters sometimes changed hands several times and followed circuitous routes: for instance, a letter from Virginia might travel west into Kentucky before heading back east to a family member in Washington, D.C.[84] Use of these routes, which could take as much time and certainly more effort than the flag-of-truce system, was desirable because it allowed families the privacy to write freely and fully about their lives during the war. For this reason, family members were constantly on the lookout for word of a secret route. A Virginia man promised his cousin in Washington that "I shall most gladly avail myself of every channel that seems to offer a reasonable prospect for the interchange of letters between us."[85]

Letters that survived the journey across the lines described the smuggling process. Writers often sealed their letters in two envelopes — the inside addressed to the recipient; the outside, to whoever was to carry the letter. The carrier would then take the letter across the lines, tear off the outside envelope, and either deliver the letter personally or drop it in the mail. Considering the risks involved, it was remarkably easy to find someone willing to transport letters. In some cases sympathetic military or postal officials helped families send letters, either by looking the other way or by knowingly forwarding them across the lines. In Missouri, the Southern-sympathetic Knights of the Golden Circle managed to have some of its members appointed to key positions in post offices and steamboats to facilitate the flow of illegal mail. Prominent figures, such as ministers, state legislators, and in one case a British consul, also smuggled mail across the lines.[86] Their reputation for integrity and loyalty shielded them from suspicion; at the same time, their official positions could give them access to useful mail channels. When Jeb Stuart, one of the Confederacy's most celebrated cavalry officers, heard via the "underground R.R." that his mother-in-law, a Unionist living in Baltimore, was longing to hear of his wife's welfare, he devised the following plan. "If you will write a small letter [and] put it in a *small* envelope," Stuart wrote his wife, "I can have it put under your Ma's breakfast plate . . . & she will never know who brought it." The willingness of men like Stuart to smuggle mail — not unlike President Lincoln's tendency to issue passes to his own family — indicates that a gap could exist between an official's professional and personal approaches to border crossing.[87]

Also called on to carry mail were individuals who were above suspicion based on their position as noncombatants. Among them, according to military officials, were enslaved African Americans. In one instance, Captain B. P. Wells of the 2nd Michigan Cavalry reported the capture of a "black boy" who had been observed "crossing and recrossing" the Tennessee River carrying "rebel mail."[88] The letters' authors were perhaps aware that slaves often had experience with underground travel. Such cases, however, likely diminished over the course of the war, as increasing numbers of African Americans seized the opportunity to escape from the writers of rebel mail. More significant were the efforts of white women, who may have hoped that by virtue of their gender they would not be suspected. Stories abound of women stuffing letters in the folds of their skirts or even in the curls of their hair. One woman baked letters inside a cake.[89]

In fact, white women became the focus of investigations into mail smuggling. In 1862 the *New York Tribune* reported that the practice had become a widespread problem and attributed it largely to "female agency."[90] Military officials across the border states, already concerned about women's travel, concentrated on the activities of women. "I find that a large number of women have been actively concerned in both secret correspondence and in carrying on the business of collecting and distributing rebel letters," reported F. A. Dick, the provost marshal of St. Louis, in 1863. Most of these women were "wealthy and wield a great influence" — among them, the wives of judges, a senator, and several Confederate officers — and were doing everything they could "to keep disloyalty alive." Dick advised that they be exiled to the South as a consequence of their activities.[91] A number of other border-state women were arrested and imprisoned for allegedly smuggling mail, and sometimes they had indeed carried valuable secrets across the lines.[92] Most notorious was Rose O'Neal Greenhow, the widow of a prominent Washington, D.C., attorney and friend of various Union officials, who was apprehended in August 1861 for conveying letters that may have led to the Union army's failure at the First Battle of Manassas. At the time of her arrest Greenhow was found tearing up mail and throwing it into a fire.[93]

Union officials were especially vigilant in their investigation of mail smuggling. "I have ordered the parties guilty of conveying these papers to be held as spies," wrote John McNeil, a Union brigadier general in Springfield, Missouri, in July 1863, after discovering a cache of smuggled mail. McNeil gave no indication that he had actually read the letters in question nor did he know for sure that the smugglers had seditious motives. But his quickness to condemn and punish mail smugglers as "spies" was not unique. Union authorities were determined to stop the spread of illicit mail, and they did so by restricting the issuance of travel passes, learning the aliases and other tactics of the smugglers, and taking rumors of smuggling seriously. In Lexington, Kentucky, for example, the news of a smallpox outbreak was considered evidence of mail smuggling; a similar outbreak had occurred in Richmond, and officials speculated that the virus had spread to Lexington via smuggled mail. Union authorities also targeted popular smuggling routes, such as the Potomac River between Maryland and Virginia, where an estimated six hundred letters passed daily.[94] Here investigators cracked two popular smuggling rings in 1863 after interviewing the slaves of men who had devised an intricate system of flag and light signals to help boatloads of mail cross the river undetected.[95]

Union officials may have been tougher in their enforcement of mail smuggling than their Confederate counterparts. Despite the fact that the Confederacy's mail policies were similar to those of the Federal government, few reports appear in newspapers of Confederate arrests for illicit mail, and it is likely, given the South's disadvantage in manpower and other resources, that mail enforcement was not a priority for the Confederacy. In fact, some Confederates found it advantageous to look the other way — and even support — underground mail. J. B. Jones, a War Department clerk, noted in his memoirs that some individuals who smuggled mail out of the Confederacy received "special" passes specifically for that purpose. The hope was that these smugglers would return with Northern newspapers and other information about the enemy.[96]

Individuals involved in mail smuggling still took precautions to avoid arrest by either side, however. Letter writers often chose their carriers very carefully, preferring delay over sending mail through a hasty and perhaps dangerous channel. "I have not had an opportunity which I was satisfied with" was the reason one man gave for not writing to his relative sooner. "In these times no communication is safe."[97] He and others waited for someone they knew they could trust to deliver their letters, or for a time when the planned route of travel seemed safest. In the meantime, writers often kept letters open and added new information periodically until they found the right opportunity to send them; as a result, letters that made it through the lines often read like small diaries, covering a month or two at a time. Men and women who did the carrying protected themselves, too — in some cases by instituting the very system of censorship that letter writers tried to avoid. One Richmond man told his son that he could not seal his letter before sending it because the carrier wanted to inspect it first for anything that "might give him trouble." "Very few now take letters unless they are sent open," he explained. Other carriers purposely did *not* inspect the letters so they could proclaim their ignorance of the contents if arrested.[98]

That so many people risked arrest for the sake of a letter indicates how powerful was the desire for private communication. Yet a closer look at the content of these "private" letters reveals that something very public often prompted the need for secrecy. Some individuals felt it was their duty to educate family members about the war around them and to counter perceived misinformation. Southerners in particular expressed frustration with the reports — or "lieing humbug," in the words of one woman — that their Northern relatives read in Northern newspapers. "Don't believe anything you see in the newspaper," Matthew Andrews of Richmond advised his mother. "It is all the Northern version of affairs." Letter writing, then, filled a need to correct a perceived bias of the press. Proctor Knott, a Confederate in Jefferson City, Missouri, regularly sent his version of events to his mother in Kentucky. Calling her

newspapers "subservient to abolition fanaticism," Knott concluded in one letter that she "cannot get a syllable of truth" about the war in Missouri. He was
especially concerned about a recent report in Kentucky's Union papers that
many Confederate Missourians had died in a skirmish with Federal troops.
In reality, Knott claimed, only two Confederates were killed, whereas the
Union lost more than sixty men. He urged his mother to rely on his account
"as being true or as near the exact truth as can be arrived."[99]

At the same time, conveying the "truth" could also involve purely domestic matters. People wrote letters to correct misinformation about the health
and well-being of their kinsmen. Border-state families states often looked to
newspapers for reports on the injury or death of a relative in battle, but such
reports were unreliable: for example, the name of a family member appearing on a casualty list might actually refer to someone else, or the information
might be totally inaccurate to begin with.[100] People frequently did not want
to believe reports in the newspaper and sought clarification. When Mary Ellet
of Washington, D.C., read that a "Brig. Gen. Baldwin" had been captured
at Vicksburg, she wondered if it was her cousin John Baldwin of Staunton,
Virginia, who had been appointed a brigadier general in the Confederate army.
Ellet wrote to her brother in the Union army and asked him to find out "who
this General Baldwin is." "Make every enquiry in your power," she begged
him.[101] Similarly, Kentuckian Brutus Clay feared that his son had been killed
after seeing his name in newspaper accounts of the Battle of Chickamauga
in 1863. Fortunately for Clay, a friend in Richmond wrote him not long after
to confirm that the newspapers were wrong—Clay's son was alive.[102] If the
friend's letter had not crossed the lines, Clay would have been left in the dark,
like so many other families, and grieved needlessly. The desire to convey the
"truth" about the fate of family members thus provided a strong incentive to
send letters across the lines despite the risk of arrest.

Advertisements

The frustrating limits on travel and mail compelled some families to employ
yet another alternative for crossing the border: communicating with family
and friends through newspaper advertisements. On May 27, 1864, the following ad appeared in the *Richmond Enquirer*:

Edward C. Huntley, Richmond, Va. — Folks all well; no news from Kate; Aunt
Sarah dead; money in bank for you, Holmes, Executor; I am keeping hotel at
Catskill. Have started twice to see you; couldn't get there. Heard from you some
time ago, and answered per directions. Let us hear from you again. JACK.

The writer, a New Yorker identified only as "Jack," paid two dollars to place
his ad in the *New York Daily News*, knowing it would then be reprinted by the
Richmond paper and read by his Confederate relatives. This might seem to
have been an unlikely medium for writing to family, as it was both public and
impersonal, but Jack only followed the lead of many other men and women
trying to contact family members across the Union-Confederate border. "Lost
all my children to yellow fever. Kate and I are well," a Confederate soldier
informed his Union brother in a similar ad. "Dear Brother. I am well, but
have been severely wounded twice," wrote a Confederate soldier in another.
"Father and brother William died during the siege of Vicksburg. . . . Would
like to hear from you." The authors of these notices thought that they had
found a reliable means of communicating with distant kin in the face of strict
military regulations on travel and mail.[103]

It is unclear what first prompted these ads, which originated in the *New York
Daily News* on December 4, 1863. But within a month the *Richmond Enquirer*
began publishing the New York paper's ads and soliciting similar notices from
Southern families. The *Daily News*, in turn, reprinted the *Enquirer*'s ads and
thus began a reciprocal arrangement between the two newspapers that resulted
in the publication of over two thousand family advertisements in 1864. The
notices comprised both direct communications to relatives and open appeals
to readers for information on a particular family. Few readers could have ignored such appeals; some issues contained over one hundred ads covering five
columns and over a page of newspaper space. The ads helped a wide range of
families, including prisoners of war temporarily separated from their relatives
at home, but at least one-third were placed by families residing permanently
on opposite sides of the lines.[104]

These ads offered what families could not get from any other mail system
— reliability. "None of your or our truce letters came to hand," one writer
reported in an ad directed to a relative in Norfolk, Virginia. "Continue them,
however, but use personals when certainty is required."[105] While flag-of-truce
letters could take anywhere from a few weeks to a year to reach their desti-
nation and smuggled letters might be seized, personal ads were printed in

full in a timely manner, as the newspapers promised to publish every ad for which they received payment. If a relative wanted to inform a family member of something as important as a death, he or she was better served doing so in an ad rather than waiting months for a flag-of-truce letter to be delivered. Moreover, families could also anticipate a quick response to the ads. In less than a week, for example, a woman in New York had placed an ad for her Richmond father and received his reply.[106]

Placing an ad in a newspaper, which could be read by thousands of people, might seem an odd choice for families anxious to protect their privacy. But writers of ads found ways of shielding their intimate lives from public exposure. Many withheld their emotions from the text of their ads. They may have been constrained, in part, by an eight-line limit imposed by the newspaper editors, as well as the two-dollar charge, but even those who did share feelings often obscured their identities by withholding their names. One notice read: "To T. M. A. Sherwood, Virginia. . . . I was delighted with your personal. It relieved me of a weight of anxiety — such cheering news of you all. . . . T. G. L." A woman wrote: "To E. M. . . . Your letter of the 6th instant received yesterday. It gave us great joy. . . . Mother."[107] It would take a great deal of knowledge about these families for a reader to figure out exactly who was involved. Some writers referred to individuals in their ads only as "father" or "brother," an uncertain strategy given the large number of fathers and brothers who might read the paper. Indeed, the desire to obscure an individual's identity may have rendered some ads useless. The following is all that appeared in one space: "To S. S. H. — Your mother and sisters are well, and desire to hear from you."[108] Without an address or a signature it is questionable whether the right "S. S. H." found this ad. Still, through the use of careful language, family members at least attempted to make the public medium of advertising private.

But this language raised the suspicion of some Union officials. In late 1864, after the ads had appeared for one year, Union secretary of war Edwin M. Stanton called on his department's Bureau of Military Justice to investigate the ad exchange and report back on its propriety. It is unclear what prompted his request, but on January 20, 1865, Judge Advocate General (and former postmaster general) Joseph Holt sent him an extensive analysis of the ads and recommended the immediate termination of personal advertising. Holt argued that the ads were first and foremost a "deliberate evasion and open defiance" of existing Union regulations on communication across the lines. The newspapers had created this system without government permission and had provided individuals with a form of intersectional contact unregulated by military authorities. For this "violation of the laws of war," Holt blamed both the families who wrote the notices and the newspapers that published them. The families, he declared, had acted in a "most deliberate and criminal nature," since they had most likely resorted to ads when their letters failed inspection by the flag-of-truce censors.[109]

Judge Holt pointed to the families' efforts to conceal their private lives as evidence that the ads were vehicles of illicit aid and comfort between families. He pointed to the use of initials, "fictitious names or designations," and "eccentric language" as clear indications that something "improper" lurked beneath the ads. In Holt's view, rather than an innocent attempt to maintain privacy, the careful use of language in the ads was an indication of something illicit. As corroborating evidence, he pointed to places where writers discussed how to convey money and supplies from one relative to another. One objectionable ad featured a son in a Confederate regiment near Richmond asking his father in the North for one hundred dollars because he was "very much in need of money." In other notices, writers offered instructions on where to pick up payments of money, advice on investments, and news that a package of clothing and provisions would soon make its way across the lines. These ads themselves did not transmit the money or goods directly but appeared to help make possible such transfers via separate — and illegal — routes. And that, Holt maintained, was reason enough to end the ads: they were a vehicle for conveying treasonous "aid" to the enemy.[110]

More disturbing to Holt was the exchange of "comfort," or what he termed "expressions of personal sympathy and encouragement," apparent throughout the ads: "I am so glad to hear you are improving." "Am truly glad you are all well." "I am so distressed about you all." "My heart is aching to see your children." Such sentiments, all written by Unionists to Confederates, were troublesome because they implied support for Confederate family members and "have a very great effect in inducing them to persevere in their disloyal and traitorous purposes." Holt had a personal appreciation of the meaning of divided family ties, as he himself was a member of a divided Kentucky family and had a Confederate brother. But his own experience did not stop — and even may have encouraged — his vigorous prosecution of disloyal activity in the Union, earning him a reputation as a zealous pursuer of traitors and spies. With regard to the advertisements, he was unrelenting in his view that an "impassable barrier" needed to be constructed between divided families. Not only should the ads be pulled, he argued, but also the entire flag-of-truce system should be eliminated (it never was). "Shut out from all communion with those to whom they were bound by ties of kindred and friendship," the Confederates would become "far sooner discouraged in the vain but desperate struggle in which they have engaged." Secretary Stanton agreed and ordered the *New York Daily News* to pull the ads on January 22, 1865.[111]

Virtually no type of family correspondence was acceptable to Judge Holt, even if the letters or newspaper ads showed no intent to subvert the national cause. The very *act* of communicating was dangerous. In this view, Holt was not alone. Other Union officials such as Secretary Stanton, the postal clerks who rejected flag-of-truce letters, and the investigators who arrested smugglers all appear to have grown convinced over time that "family and domestic" concerns were less innocent than their policies first assumed. To communicate with a family member on the opposing side was to write to the enemy. Federal government officials did not, as the families themselves had done, distinguish between a person's private identity as a family member and their public identity as a Unionist or Confederate. The two were one and the same.

The *Daily News* complied with Stanton's order but not without lashing back at Union officials. In an editorial published a few days after pulling the ads, the paper called the directive "one of the worst phases of the despotism that sways at Washington." It speculated that the Lincoln administration was acting on a grudge it had held against the *Daily News* from the beginning of the war. The paper was headed by the strongly Democratic and anti-Lincoln Benjamin Wood, a member of Congress who made a name for himself by denouncing the war and the use of force against the Confederacy. Back in the summer of 1861, after it had published a series of highly critical articles, the Union government denied the *Daily News* postal privileges, which forced the paper to suspend operations for eighteen months. The order to terminate ads was only the latest in an ongoing effort of the Lincoln administration to stifle its critics in the press, the *Daily News* declared, this time in direct retaliation for a recent series criticizing the Union's treatment of Confederate prisoners. The paper vowed to fight to get the ads reinstated and to remain a "watchful sentinel" against the tyranny of Lincoln's government.[112]

A subsequent series of articles shifted the focus toward what the *Daily News* believed was Washington's inhumane attack on American families. The paper dismissed the notion that the family ads in any way transmitted illicit information and pointed out that the system was in keeping with the flag of truce in the limits on length and the public inspection of the contents. The paper defended its own motives as simply to provide a "means of family communication." In an editorial entitled "Warring on Women and Families," the *Daily News* called Secretary Stanton's order to suppress the ads "a wanton outrage on the ties which still connect brother and sister, mother and son, though they may be separated by the boundaries which divide the Northern and Southern States." To illustrate this point, the writer related the story of a woman who had reportedly gone to the newspaper's office to inquire about placing an ad for her son in the South. On hearing that personals were now illegal, the woman "burst into tears," anguished that another channel of communication had been cut off. Evidently, the paper concluded, the War Department regarded "a mother's affection as treason."[113]

The *Daily News* printed other testimony from a variety of citizens and other newspapers that demonstrated the Federal government's "cold-blooded cruelty" against families. As far away as England, the *London Times* criticized the Lincoln administration for seeing "treason in these affectionate letters." Closer to home, a reader from Jersey City, New Jersey, wrote a letter to the editor to express his "pain" and "anger" at the suppression of the personals. One couple he knew had news from their daughter in the South for the first time in three years after she had inserted an ad. Another reader, who signed himself "A Foreigner," informed the editor that the ads had been "relieving" amid "all the sickening horrors of this fearful war." He called on Union officials to recognize that personal feelings among families still existed on both sides of the war's divide. An article published in the *Richmond Whig*, and subsequently reprinted in the *New York Daily News*, used similar language, contending that the ads had helped to "mitigate some of the horrors of civil war." Still, despite the "mission of philanthropy" behind the paper's efforts, the *Richmond Enquirer* told its readers on February 8, 1865, that it was "useless" to continue placing ads.[114] Indeed, no more personal advertisements appeared in either of these papers for the duration of the war.

THE AD CONTROVERSY marked the most drastic break between divided families and the Union and Confederate governments over the propriety of crossing the border. On one side were the judge advocate general and Union officials, who all saw treason in a family's desire to maintain contact through the personals. On the other side were the families and the newspapers defending them, which claimed to see only humanity in the proliferation of personal ads. A similar polarization surrounded intersectional travel and mail. Officials regulating pass applications believed that individuals were traveling to see an "enemy," whereas the petitioners themselves argued that they wished to make innocent trips to visit kin. Similarly, mail censors tended to see political or military significance in what was often to families only of domestic interest. In each of these contexts divided families were viewed in contrasting ways: either too treasonous to cross the border or too insulated from the war to influence its progress.

The disparity between these two views continued throughout the war, reflecting a fundamental disagreement about the relationship between family and military affairs, private and public life. Families fought an uphill battle, as they had within their own households, to maintain their privacy and the distinction between family life and the public world of war. U.S. government officials, on the other hand, collapsed that distinction and saw only disloyalty and treason in the actions of these families. Union policymakers thus took an unconventional stand that challenged popular ideals about the separate spheres of home and world. Although their reason for doing so was to stop the spread of sedition in wartime, their ability to do so testifies to how fluid such boundaries may have always been in the minds of midcentury Americans. Union, and to a lesser extent Confederate, leaders easily implicated divided families in the public battle of war. And, as we will see, fiction writers joined them in finding a larger significance in the private experiences of divided families.

Border Dramas and
the Divided Family in the
Popular Imagination

THE PRIVATE ORDEALS of divided families captured the attention of popular fiction writers almost as soon as the Civil War erupted. In 1862 Delphine P. Baker, a Union woman living in Illinois, published *Solon; or, The Rebellion of '61: A Domestic and Political Tragedy*, the tale of two fictional characters — one a daughter of Abraham Lincoln, the other a son of Jefferson Davis. The two are in love and want to marry but are thwarted temporarily while their fathers confront one another in war. This leads to both "domestic" and "political" tragedy, as the domestic bliss of the lovers becomes fatally intertwined with the wartime politics around them.[1]

Baker's story depicts the experience of men and women who are torn between their family and national loyalty. Yet the author also finds in these families something larger and more significant for the warring nation. The political divide between the fathers, the two figureheads of the Union and the Confederacy, ideally should have been clear-cut, Baker suggests, but instead is challenged by the competing social bonds of the son and the daughter. A vigorous effort on the part of both presidents is necessary to keep their intertwined domestic lives from subverting their political divide. And in that effort Baker dramatizes a question that consumed individual families, government officials, and the nation as a whole: Could a definitive and secure boundary be drawn between the Union and the Confederacy? Or did deeper attachments hold people together across the sectional border, even in the middle of a civil war?

Other midcentury writers joined Baker in examining this question of Civil War loyalty. The authors, both male and female, soldier and civilian, Union and Confederate, and almost always white, produced no masterpieces, but their stories were widely read across the warring nation. Fictional and semi-fictional articles published in newspapers, plays produced on local stages, and novels printed in New York, Baltimore, and Richmond satisfied a widespread desire to visualize and understand the war on a large scale. Wartime fiction, as one Confederate woman writer indicated, assumed "a potency far beyond facts and figures" in shaping public opinion and, as historian Alice Fahs has argued, comprised a "vital part of a larger, public, patriotic culture." Fiction also served as propaganda, so important in a time of war, helping to define what it meant to be a "Unionist" or a "Confederate" and how the two should relate to one another. But wartime fiction also participated in a deeper "cultural work," to borrow the words of literary criticism, exploring how different individuals might interact both within each section and throughout the nation, across borders of gender, race, and generations. These works drew on the same dialogue evident in the private letters of divided families but infused their words with a larger, public meaning for the nation as a whole.[2]

Writers like Delphine Baker saw in the wartime experiences of divided families an allegory for the divided nation. Tales of warring kinsmen appeared throughout the war in both sections of the country and dramatized the problem of dividing one nation into two.[3] The authors may have been influenced, in part, by a sentimental literary tradition in which the family was central, but their focus on kinship relations also reflected a reality of the Civil War.[4] The war had stripped the family of at least some of its sentimental mystique and permitted men and women little escape from the harsh truths of military battle. The family became deeply implicated in the war's division, politics, and violence, often amplifying, rather than moderating, the war's presence in people's lives. It followed, then, that writers, who often claimed to represent "truth" and "fact," found in the family a source of raw, authentic war experience.[5] In their stories the divided family engages in adventure, guerrilla warfare, and political debates as well as romance. Their fiction occasionally revolves around actual events, real battles featuring real people, and, appropriately, is set in the place where the boundary between Union and Confederacy was disputed most heavily — the border states.[6]

These border dramas center on divided families' struggle with the meaning of loyalty. To dramatize the wartime border between Unionists and Confederates, one group of stories draws on what may have been the most easily identifiable border in their cultural vocabulary — gender — and overlays this on the contested boundary between Union and Confederacy. With titles such as "Love and Disloyalty—A True Tale" and "Sad Affair—Love, Desertion, Suicide," these dramas compare the warring sections to men and women and elaborate on an existing literary association of the Union with a marriage. Yet these wartime stories are instead tales of romantic dysfunction, rarely ending in a harmonious marriage of Northerners and Southerners.[7] The relationships between men and women offer a figurative language for discussing the relationship between North and South—and the way in which the war threatened to undermine those attachments. These stories deal mainly with the loyalties of white Americans; a second group of stories examine the place of African American slaves in the warring nation, asking to which section they were most loyal and using the family metaphor to dramatize their allegiances. Writers both Union and Confederate, to varying degrees, wrote of slave men and women as the figurative—and often literal—kinsmen of their white Confederate masters and explored how the war either destroyed or sustained any attachment between them. Family dramas in all of these stories thus captured the complex loyalties—political and sectional, gendered, generational, and racial—that both challenged and sustained the borders between mid-nineteenth-century Americans.

Seduction Tales

In May 1863 the Union-leaning *Nashville Daily Press* published a fictional piece entitled "Love and Disloyalty." It is the story of Charles Granger, the son of Pennsylvania farmers who travels South in the late 1850s to launch his legal career. He eventually settles in Nashville, despite the misgivings of his parents, who fear he will "become contaminated with unholy principles." Charles ignores their warnings and moves in with distant relatives, the Clayburns, one of the city's most prominent families. He sets up his law office and is instantly charmed by one of the Clayburn daughters, Frances, who not only is beautiful but also possesses "all the living fire and energy characteristic of the high-born southern woman." In short order a romance ensues between Charles and Frances and proceeds harmoniously until the climax of the secession crisis in early 1861. Frances, or "Frank," reveals herself to be a "fierce defender of the rebel cause," whereas Charles openly asserts his loyalty to the Union. The two debate politics daily, until Frank becomes frustrated and lays down an ultimatum: "I want proof of your devotion to me," she declares, demanding that Charles support the South. After some reflection, Charles agrees. "He was not a champion of Southern Rights," the narrator says of Charles's Confederate service, "but a champion of her he loved." A month later, however, he learns the painful truth: Frank married another man, and all along her romance with Charles had been a sham. The story ends as Charles is stuck in the Confederate army, full of "anguish" and hoping to be killed in battle.[8]

At the time this story appeared, a pro-Confederate press in Richmond published a similar tale of love and conflict, entitled *The Aid-de-Camp: A Romance of the War* (1863) by James Dabney McCabe Jr. Here we meet Mary Worthington, another "beautiful" daughter of a celebrated Southern family, who is "greatly admired by the gentlemen of Baltimore," her hometown. At a party in early 1861 Mary makes the acquaintance of Henry Cameron, a native of Philadelphia, whose "handsome" features and "attentive" manner pique her interest. They strike up a conversation that leads to frequent visits in Mary's home. At first Mary does not realize that Henry, in addition to being a loyal Union man, is "decidedly unprincipled" as well as "cold and heartless." Over the course of several weeks, however, Mary's loyal Confederate instincts alert her to his base motives and she refuses to see him again. "Maddened by his failure" to win her heart, Henry flies into a rage, accepts a commission in the Union army, and hatches a plan to make Mary his forever. With the help of fellow Union soldiers, he has her kidnapped. But Mary manages to foil her captors almost immediately and frees herself from Henry's clutches. She goes on to marry a Confederate soldier, who later confronts Henry in battle and shoots him dead.[9]

The tales of Frank and Charles and Mary and Henry, written by authors on opposite sides of the sectional divide, agree on the incompatibility of Union men and Confederate women. Other stories like these, with titles such as "All For Love — A Federal Officer Seduced" and "A Sad Case of Seduction," follow one of two story lines that vary according to the sectional loyalties of the authors. In the Union version, a brave and innocent Union man succumbs to the advances of a charming Southern woman, only to learn that her motive has been to ensnare him in some rebel plot. In the Confederate tale, the reverse occurs: a dark and sinister Union man is close to attracting a Southern woman by similar means but is rebuffed when she proves wise enough to resist his overtures. Both accounts are pessimistic that true romance can unite Union men and Confederate women; instead, as revealed in the titles, they are cast into the alternative literary motif of "seduction."[10]

By the eve of the Civil War seduction had a long history as an American political metaphor. For decades in literary works and political essays the contentious relationship between a man and a woman evoked a central concern in the founders' republicanism that was later amplified by Jacksonian democracy: the tension between liberty and power, equality and inequality.[11] Americans — particularly white Americans — worried that a nation built on the political independence of its people would one day fall victim to the excessive power of a few; the Civil War seemed to confirm those fears. We can see this in the political rhetoric of secession, which was steeped in allusions to illegitimate power, most noticeably in the popularity of the terms "Slave Power" and "Black Republicans" to depict the slaveholding South and the Republican Party in the North respectively. Each side viewed the other as wielding excessive power over the American people and grew suspicious when its opponent's influence appeared to be manipulative and dishonest. Both sides saw in the other's cause a conspiracy to deprive Americans of their liberty.[12]

With the coming of war, Americans looked everywhere for these expressions of illegitimate power and found ample evidence along the border between Union and Confederacy. Here, Americans paid close attention to one another's loyalties and tried to explain what induced people to take one side or the other. Fathers with Union loyalties, for example, commonly blamed cavalrymen and other so-called unscrupulous men for having lured their unsuspecting sons into the Confederate army; husbands accused their fathers-in-law of triggering their wives' dissenting loyalty.[13] Others tried to explain why certain border states, such as Maryland, Virginia, and Kentucky, went with one side or the other. Maryland was, one Confederate paper lamented in 1862, "wedded" to the Union "sorely against her own heart" because of Abraham Lincoln's threats of force.[14] Both Union and Confederate writers dramatized this type of coercion in seduction narratives, accusing their enemies of exercising everything from illicit power to deception to immorality to win the minds — and especially the hearts — of people over to their side. To suggest that someone had been "seduced" to the Union or Confederate side was to assert that the individual's loyalty was false and the cause to which he or she adhered, illegitimate.

The main story line in seduction tales turns on the success or failure of a conspiracy, or of an attempt to entice an innocent individual to abandon his or her national loyalty. In "Love and Disloyalty," for example, Charles Granger is inclined to remain "neutral" in his adopted Tennessee home rather than join the Confederacy, but Frank's perfect features and jet-black hair cause "a great struggle in his mind between his love and what conscience told him was his duty." Frank is relentless in her expressions of "love" and equally relent-less in her demands that he prove his love in return by fighting for the South. Charles is slowly persuaded by her overtures until, "under the impulse of her violent love and fervent kiss," he takes the fatal step of accepting a Confederate commission. "The syren had accomplished her purpose," concludes the nar-rator. Through false overtures of love, Frank had deceived a man into casting his lot with the Confederacy. Other Union stories tell of Southern women luring Union soldiers with false professions of affection in order to smuggle gold, solicit Union secrets, or even free them from prison.[15] In Confederate tales, love is also the vehicle of deception, usually when a Union man makes a promise of marriage to separate an innocent and desperate Southern woman from her loving Confederate family — and sometimes to lure her into a house of prostitution.[16]

The seducers succeed when they can persuade their victims to betray their causes. Success depends not on any particular weakness of the victim but on the unique strengths of the seducer. Authors of these tales are explicit about what makes the "vile seducer" and "syren" so effective. In *The Aid-de-Camp*, Henry Cameron is "tall and elegantly formed" yet wears a "foul and sinister expression about the mouth." In other stories the seducers are both "beauti-ful" and "dark" or "comely" with "black eyes." The seducers thus exhibit a dual nature of physical beauty and darkness — put most succinctly by one author in describing a "charming secesh siren."[17] Their ability to slip easily between their appealing and sinister natures is what makes seducers so effec-tive in the art of deception; in doing so, they can easily lure their victim from one political loyalty to another. The seducers are melodramatic to be sure, but in the Union and Confederate imaginations they also embodied something very real. Deception through expressions of "love" by a sinister yet beautiful character offered an allegory for the demagoguism that each section accused the other of exercising over the American public.

But seduction was more than a metaphor for political demagoguery. It also spoke to growing concerns about perception and appearance in midcentury society. The nation had become more anonymous as its area and population expanded, bringing strangers together in new towns and cities and eroding the familiarity that once bound men and women in their local communities. Western plantation settlements witnessed the arrival of new landowners, just as northeastern cities enticed men and women from across the United States to work in their factories. Unable always to be certain who people were and where they came from, men and women placed a premium on "sincerity," or the truthful outward expression of one's inner character. A "cult of sincerity" surrounded midcentury Americans, and in the wartime figure of the seducer, writers North and South suggested how the war's political intrigue threatened this ideal.[18]

Americans had substantial evidence in their daily lives of the prevalence of insincerity in the war. Not only were the overtures of Abraham Lincoln and Jefferson Davis commonly read as false promises by their opponents, but also along the Civil War border residents did not always know where friends, neighbors, or even family members stood on wartime politics. The questions lingered—who are you really? and where do you stand?—as reports of spying and smuggling became an everyday aspect of the border war.[19] In places where men and women had to endure the constant intrusions of the enemy, lying about one's national loyalty became necessary to survival. Moreover, along the paths of North-South travel, in railroads, boats, and carriages, masking one's national identity was at times a matter of expediency.[20] This dissonance between one's public and private expressions of loyalty was a part of everyday life along the border. For this reason we might view contemporary works of fiction as cautionary tales, urging men and women to be more discerning in recognizing the overtures of the enemy. The author of "Love and Disloyalty" concludes his essay by urging readers to stand fast against the duplicity of Confederate seductresses because "there is many a young woman in Tennessee whose deeds of like character will rise up before her in the last day."[21]

This particular quotation is noteworthy, too, because of the role women play in tales of seduction. In "A Sad Case of Seduction," first published in the *Daily Missouri Democrat* in late 1864, border-state readers were treated to an apparently fictionalized news story of a sixteen-year-old boy, the son of a Union general, who had been won over to the Southern cause by none other than the Confederate first lady, Varina Davis. The boy was in Richmond when the war began and his father took up arms for the Union. At that point "Mrs. Jefferson Davis set herself deliberately to the work of seducing the young man from his allegiance." According to the narrator, Davis took the boy into her home and, through "the flatteries and cajoleries that women so well know how to use," persuaded him to accept a Confederate commission. The piece is vague on details—although the persons involved were real—but pronounced the boy "ruined" as a result of Davis's actions. It goes on to chastise the first lady for carrying out the seduction only to "plant a thorn in the side of the loyal father" but gladly reveals that the boy eventually became "free" from the "wiles of the traitress." This story captured the attention of readers across the border states, appearing in the same form in St. Louis and Louisville papers.[22]

This story might have startled readers for its sexual innuendo — that the Confederate first lady had "ruined" the innocence of a young boy. But in other ways it fit comfortably with the narratives of seduction, particularly in its implication that Varina Davis, a symbolic figurehead of Southern womanhood, was a primary conspirator for the South. To Union readers, this would have epitomized what many believed was a true conspiracy of Southern women to lead Union soldiers astray. Confederate women did pose a very real temptation to Union soldiers in occupied areas, where, despite the well-documented antagonism between the two groups, opportunities for intimate contact flourished. In hospitals and prisons, as well as at ballroom dances, Confederate women found plenty of room to work on behalf of their cause, a Missouri woman explained, as "many a bit of information was cajoled from their admirers . . . and forwarded to their own generals." Confederate women literally lured men to resign their commissions or to share Union secrets. By virtue of their gender, which provided a cloak under which they could hide their true motives and therefore disarm Union men, Southern women became some of the most effective practitioners of patriotic deception during the war.[23]

The Varina Davis story was likely a gross exaggeration of anything the Confederate first lady might have actually done, but consider what it shared with other seduction dramas: Davis is front and center and, as in other narratives, the main protagonist and the symbolic presence of the South. In other seduction tales the Southern woman is "young," "spunky," and "extremely beautiful," the epitome of refinement.[24] She is usually wealthy — either the favorite daughter of a planter or a widow with a plantation of her own — and lives among slaves in an elegant mansion. She is, in short, the physical embodiment of the aristocratic South, which had tempted migrants throughout the antebellum years. She is also the voice of the Confederate South. In conversations with Union men, some of the stock phrases of secession tumble out of her mouth in the form of a lecture. In the seduction narrative, the South is almost always represented as female, suggesting an imaginative link between Southern women and secession in the minds of Civil War writers.

The Southern woman is different in each version, however. In the Varina Davis story, she reflects only the Union viewpoint: she uses her "flatteries" and "wiles" to achieve ends both devious and immoral. In other cases the Southern woman takes on an overtly sexualized role, using her "heaving bosom" and "burning kisses" to lure a man into the Confederate fold or her "sudden passion" to make him recklessly abandon his principles. This persona of the Southern seductress, so common in Northern tales, was in stark contrast to the image portrayed by Southern writers. In the Confederate view, she is not a seductress but instead the seducer's dramatic foil: a stalwart, moral presence who resists a Union man's temptations. This version of the Southern woman is "innocent" and "confiding," a less sexualized and passionless figure who closely resembles her Revolutionary foremothers in her Spartan determination to remain true to her convictions. Her resolve can be powerful. In one story, a woman jumps off a pier and drowns herself when her other attempts to fend off a Union seducer fail. Death is preferable to giving in to the Union cause. In other dramas, the woman enlists in the Confederate army and risks her life to confront a Union man on the battlefield.[25]

These opposing images of Southern womanhood converge on several questions: Is the Southern woman inclined to seduce and ensnare, or will she resist the seducer and protect her feminine purity? In other words, will her virtue be violated or protected? The weight of all the seduction narratives falls on women's virtue and, in doing so, draws a familiar idealized connection between women and the political stability of the nation. First through the vaunted position of the "republican wife" and "mother," then as the guardian of the domestic sphere, women were expected to set a moral example that would build a healthy foundation on which liberty and equality could flourish and illicit power would vanish. Women, themselves moral figures who thought only of the good of others, were to nurture that same selflessness in their sons and husbands. Men, in turn, would carry those qualities with them into the public sphere and foster an environment conducive to national unity.[26] The idea that national stability was rooted in the virtue of women thus remained intact in wartime seduction tales, where a woman's inclination to embrace or resist sexual immorality is a pivotal development. When she chooses to seduce, as in the Union view, she destroys the bonds of union; but when she resists, as in the Confederate perspective, she guarantees the protection of liberty as defined by Southerners. In both depictions, domestic ideals are inextricably linked to the nation's political crisis.

Certainly these representations may be — in varying degrees — literal reflections of how each side viewed Southern women's conduct in the war. Southern women were popularly considered to be among the most ardent Confederates; Union newspapers called them "the most rebellious," "more violent rebels than the rebel troops," or simply "She-Secessionists."[27] But the repetitive linkage of the South with women, rather than with men, points to deeper meanings shared by the Union and Confederate stories. Both versions commented on the South's right to secede through the figure of the Southern woman. The sexually deviant female described by Northern writers—an obvious violation of conventional gender norms—conveniently reflected what Union partisans argued was the illegitimacy of the South's secession. The morally pure woman in Confederate renditions, in contrast, symbolized what many Southerners believed was the Confederacy's righteous and determined claim to secession. The ideals of gender, so wrapped up in value judgments of morality and purity, offered a useful language for evaluating the South's secession. At the same time, though, this common association of the South with womanhood also acknowledged a military reality—that the South was on the defensive, both a victim and a resister of Northern invasion. The South's subordinate position in the military war was symbolized by the subordinate gender in nineteenth-century society: the Confederate woman either stays true to her principles and successfully resists the Unionist's overtures, or she oversteps her bounds and deserves punishment, depending on the author's point of view.

Imagery of sexual hostility also dramatized the feelings of aggression and danger inherent in the war. Writers of seduction narratives set aside the expressions of love and affection so common in private letters of this period and opted instead for the contrasting language of "burning passion" to emphasize the conflict between Unionists and Confederates. Indeed, these authors often go to great pains to tell us that they are not depicting real love or affection at all. (One author maintains that a Union seducer "is incapable of experiencing such a pure emotion.")[28] This conscious suppression of sentimentality is significant. At midcentury true love was an idealized concept that promised individual fulfillment from one's affectionate bond with others. Affection was to be nurtured in marriage and projected onto the society at large, where it took on a political significance as the necessary force binding a society of free and equal individuals into a harmonious union.[29] The authors of seduction tales, in contrast, reveal the corruption of this affectionate bond through the false pretenses of sexual attraction. It is sex that binds—or attempts to bind—the Union man and the Confederate woman and proves a great irritant capable only of creating an unhealthy relationship. The sexual bond is a dangerous bond, a notion punctuated in these narratives by the frequent references to a seducer having "conquered" or "subjugated" his or her victim.[30]

The fusion of the languages of sex and war was not unique to Civil War fiction. The same connection appeared beyond the pages of popular literature, even in the vocabulary of the common soldier, who drew on sexual terms — such as "ravage" and "rape" — to describe military conduct. This intermingling of military and sexual hostility testified to the aggressiveness of the war fought in the border region. But its figurative translation of the military conflict into the more familiar tensions of male-female sexual relations did more than just that. It also called on a tradition in American warfare of conjuring up images of an enemy's sexual aggression — termed the "rape scenario" by one scholar — to excite a powerful sense of justice and revenge in one's own soldiers.[31] Sexual imagery could offer a simple rhetorical shorthand, allowing writers to convey in one easily identifiable representation the complex emotions of anger, fear, and vulnerability that often drive a military war.

Most authors, accordingly, leave it to the power of the military, and to battlefield heroics, to end the sexual intrigue of seduction in their stories. It is striking that nearly all of these stories end with the death or near death of a man, most often a Union soldier, in battle (occasionally accompanied by a woman's death, too). In "Love and Disloyalty," Charles Granger, having been seduced by a distant relative, hopes for death and eventually finds it in battle. His last words are that he is "repentant, beseeching heaven's mercy and forgiveness for my great crime." Henry Cameron, the slippery seducer resisted by Mary Worthington in *The Aid-de-Camp*, is killed in battle by Mary's heroic Confederate beau.[32] These dark endings reinforce the dysfunctional nature of seduction but also facilitate a resolution. The Union man's honor is put to the test in these stories, as he is either disgraced by seductive women or degraded in his own attempt at seduction. He can, in the end, redeem himself through the ultimate test of a man's honor — his willingness to confront death.[33] A battlefield death, and its recommitment of men to the dictates of honor, cleanses these stories of the taint of seduction and restores men and women to an idealized sense of domestic — and thus, national — stability.

Romantic Triangle Stories

On December 22, 1862, theatergoers at the Richmond Varieties Theater in Richmond were treated to the opening night of a new play, *The Guerrillas*, by James Dabney McCabe, also author of the novel *The Aid-de-Camp*. *The Guerrillas* is the story of Arthur Douglas, the son of a prominent Virginian and grandson of a Revolutionary War hero, who is engaged to Rose Maylie, a beautiful Southern woman. Their intended bliss is interrupted by the onset of the Civil War and by the intrusion into their lives of a brash young Union officer named Colonel Bradley. Bradley is immediately smitten by Maylie but is foiled by Douglas in his repeated attempts to win her favor. Scorned, Bradley vows to hunt Douglas "like a wild beast." Leading a band of Union guerrillas, Bradley travels to the Douglas home and burns it down, slashing the throats of the entire family. Arthur Douglas, who was away at the time of the attack, subsequently vows "vengeance" as the commander of a group of Confederate guerrillas. The play follows the ongoing attacks and skirmishes of these two bands in western Virginia, including the forcible advances on Maylie by Bradley's superior, General Fremont. Eventually Douglas is captured by the Union soldiers. While awaiting his hanging on a scaffold, he is rescued by his slave Jerry, who has disguised himself as an executioner. Jerry places a pistol in Douglas's hand, and the play ends with the bloody deaths of Bradley and his Union guerrillas. Douglas and Maylie are now guaranteed a lifetime of happiness.[34]

The play was a hit. According to the *Daily Richmond Examiner*, spectators were "yelling, whistling, stamping, and shouting" in the aisles; they "stormed and cheered incessantly" throughout the performance. The audience may have been under the influence of holiday eggnog, the paper speculated, but it embraced the portrayal of Confederate heroism and Yankee cowardice. The drama ran for a week — longer than most plays at the theater — and later traveled to Mobile, Alabama; Macon, Georgia; and Wilmington, North Carolina. It was one of the few original plays produced in the Confederacy during the war and received an inordinate amount of critical acclaim in the press.[35] A reviewer for the *Examiner* applauded "the thread of love and romance meandering like a refreshing stream through the recital of blood, and wrong, and outrage."[36] The love binding the Confederates in the drama offered a welcome counterpoint to the bloody battles taking place between two enemies.

The juxtaposition of love and violence in *The Guerrillas* was a central motif shared by other romantic triangle stories. McCabe's play presented the Confederate version of such tales: a brave, handsome Confederate man vies for the affections of an innocent woman but is temporarily thwarted by the aggressive overtures of a Union man. The two men, soldiers in the opposing armies, take their rivalry to the battlefield, and, in the end, the Confederate man wins the romantic contest by killing the Union man. In the Union version, of course, the theme is the same but the protagonists change: the good Union man defeats the bad Confederate man and in the end wins the woman's affection as his "reward."[37] In some ways this story line is similar to that of seduction tales, most notably in its focus on romantic discord between men and women and its portrayal of personal relationships between individuals of opposing national loyalties. One Confederate reviewer summed up the plot of *The Guerrillas* in the language of seduction, calling it the "rescue of innocent virtue threatened by Yankee lust."[38]

Yet the emphasis on "rescue" sets triangle stories apart from other tales of romantic conflict. In stories such as *The Guerrillas*, for example, the narrative centers not on the relationship between Rose Maylie and Arthur Douglas or Colonel Bradley, but on the relationship between the two soldiers: how they compete for Maylie's attention, how they both attempt to save her from the corruptive influence of the other. Romance is sidelined in this and other triangle stories, as the setting shifts from domestic scenes in the household to the front lines. The competition between men takes place in real-life battlefields in, for example, Chickahominy, the Shenandoah Valley, and northern Virginia. The men fight with all the accoutrements of male warfare — muskets, daggers, and swords — and their encounters highlight the corresponding martial traits of bravery and cowardice. The two men assume positions on the opposing sides, thus fusing the romantic contest to the military battle.

A woman's place in these stories is significant, but only to incite and exacerbate the conflict between men. The woman is the object rather than the agent of the conflict, and she often appears only at the beginning and end without weighing heavily on the course of the struggle. The authors describe her in various stances of neutrality, unable or afraid to choose between the men and, in some cases, uninterested in assuming a national loyalty of her own. She is open to a man's influence, a position underscored in many stories by something unique about her: she is an orphan. Indeed, with remarkable frequency the female protagonist has no parents and is living with a guardian. Thus she has no parental influence to guide her romantic life, which not only simplifies the story to a battle of two suitors, but also leaves her emotionally malleable to male overtures. She is also physically vulnerable to men. In one Union tale, the author gives a detailed description of the woman's body, telling us that her "bare and brown" arms were "a matter of congratulation to the male spectator." In another story, the woman is literally an object of male infatuation — her presence is delineated by a photograph over which a Union prisoner and his Confederate guard fight.[39] The women in these stories cast into relief the masculine nature of the conflict around them.

Romantic triangle stories generally open with a retrospective of the men's pasts. Mary Jane Haw's *The Rivals: A Chickahominy Story* (1864), a Confederate tale awarded one thousand dollars for winning the "best romance" contest sponsored by the *Southern Illustrated News*, begins with the boyhoods of Walter Maynard and Charley Foster, both of Hanover County, Virginia. The pair grew up in the same neighborhood, yet from a young age they had distinctive personalities. Maynard was less "polished" and "outgoing" than Foster, who was more "beloved" by his friends. Both attended West Point, where they acquired the same educational and military training, but Maynard received regular financial assistance from the wealthier Foster family. The two male protagonists thus had similar backgrounds, but more significantly, they shared friendship. Maynard and Foster spent much of their time together and over the course of their adolescence became "more like brothers than friends." Their comrades at West Point dubbed them "Jonathan and David," in a comparison to the intense and loving biblical friends. But by 1861 their close relationship has soured, as both men seek the affections of the "peerlessly beautiful" Nellie Gardiner. They carry their rivalry to the battlefield, where Maynard sides with the Union and Foster fights for the Confederacy — which is victorious in the end, allowing Foster to win Nellie's hand.[40]

This transformation of friends into enemies is typical of romantic triangle stories. With few exceptions, the Union and Confederate men have shared the bonds of friendship and brotherhood from an early age. They are not longtime enemies; the fight between Union and Confederate men is a fight between "brothers." Here the authors tapped into the traditional American view of relationships between men, particularly white men, in fraternal terms. The Revolution was waged by the Founding Fathers, according to antebellum orators and politicians, and its legacy was bequeathed to the following generations to uphold and defend. This common duty created what Daniel Webster once described as "the bonds of political brotherhood," a powerful kinship uniting Americans North and South as the sons of a common father. During the secession crisis, a poet for *Harper's Weekly* commented on how a civil war might affect this national brotherhood:

> For eighty-five years we have struggled and toiled,
> And manfully battled as brother for brother
> And 'tis hard to see all our felicity spoiled,
> By bickering fruitlessly one another.

The war, of course, demonstrated that the conflict among Americans was much more than "bickering," but this poet's characterization of the sectional crisis was shared by other writers who tried to make the nation's descent into bloody warfare seem understandable or even natural.[41]

Triangle stories embrace the battle of "brothers" as inevitable in the course of male relations. The conflicts usually begin when two young men have reached the end of adolescence and are starting down the path to adulthood. As *The Rivals* opens, Walter Maynard and Charley Foster are in the process of developing "their boyish forms into models of manly strength and vigor."[42] The author centers her story in the moment when young men typically experienced a coming-of-age struggle not only in relation to their fathers, but also in relation to their peers. Nineteenth-century men, as in the case of real brothers, generally enjoyed at least one intimate male friendship in their childhood, a relationship akin to a "rehearsal for marriage," in the words of historian Anthony Rotundo. This friendship could be contentious, even volatile, especially as men aged and their careers or marriage took precedence in their lives. Men's ascent into adulthood occasionally stimulated a break in the bonds of their childhood friendships, making the ensuing conflicts between the male friends, or "brothers" in these stories, a natural result of coming of age.[43]

It seems particularly fitting that Confederate writers would draw on a young man's desire to identify himself independently of his male peers as an allegory for the South. Secession, a writer for the *Daily Richmond Examiner* observed in January 1864, marked the "heart-rending divorce of brother from brother."[44] Southern writers could at once acknowledge the bonds that previously united the two sections while offering a validation of secession as a natural phase in the fraternal relationship. So why did Union writers, who certainly were interested in keeping these ties of brotherhood intact, find this imagery equally compelling? Here we must consider the different types of brotherhood depicted in Union and Confederate tales. Whereas Confederate writers are concerned with men as friends, as figurative brothers, Union authors often portray two men as *actual* brothers, bound by genealogy and blood. The men in Union tales may have enjoyed the close companionship of boyhood, but when it came time to go their separate ways in adulthood, something profound and natural still bound them. This brotherhood is thus deeper — and less vulnerable to dissolution — than the brotherhood depicted by Confederate writers.

Writers North and South both drew sharp distinctions between Union and Confederate men as good and bad brothers, however. The brothers portrayed in "Strategy," published in 1863 in a compilation of Union short stories, offer a good example. The author, who is not identified by name but is clearly pro-Union, informs us first that the Confederate brother, Wilbur, is younger. Consequently, he is full of "anger, reproach, and jealousy" and has a "fiery impetuosity." He has not yet developed the intelligence and reason that his older brother Leo, a Unionist, possesses, and he must look up to Leo as a "model of sageness." The author contrasts the "exacting and selfish" Confederate brother with the Union brother, "so generous, so self-denying" — a comparison that invoked popular conceptions of masculinity. Self-sacrifice, expressed through duty and obedience, was a primary marker of manhood to midcentury Americans and a quality men ordinarily sought to prove when they volunteered for military service. In "Strategy," the Union brother has achieved these attributes of manhood. Confederate stories offer similar distinctions, with a tendency to depict Union men as overly self-indulgent when trying to kiss or touch a woman.[45] The enemy in both versions is selfish and impulsive, in stark contrast to his virtuous and manly brother, echoing how each section viewed the conduct of the other in the secession crisis and the Civil War.

Biblical allusions helped authors, as well as journalists and political orators, portray these contrasts between the characters of Union and Confederate men. Stories such as that of Cain and Abel, especially popular with writers, offered models of brothers who similarly grew apart in ways that drew them into conflict. References to different pairs of biblical brothers convey sharp dichotomies of betrayal and loyalty, honesty and trickery, sin and virtue. The Unionist *Louisville Daily Journal* once compared Abraham Lincoln to Joseph and the Confederacy "to his brothers who had betrayed him [and] sold him to servitude." From the Confederate point of view, "The Union . . . has not been much unlike the womb of the venerable Rebecca," the *Southern Literary Messenger* observed, and the two sons she produced, Jacob and Esau, "are no bad exemplars of the North and the South." The South, it suggested, was like Esau, forced by the trickery of Jacob to renounce his birthright and standing in the family. Writers rarely bothered to elaborate beyond a quick reference to biblical brothers, as readers would undoubtedly understand the distinctions. Such allusions helped the authors establish brotherly ties between two men while suggesting that they were profoundly different and therefore could become mortal enemies.[46]

Physical combat was the logical culmination to this conflict of character in romantic triangle stories. Union and Confederate soldiers conduct themselves very differently in battle. Consider one author's depiction of the warring friends in "The Tory's Revenge: A Tale of the Shenandoah," a short story published in the Confederate *Magnolia Weekly* in 1863. The men, George Ashton and Isaac Walton, are prosperous farmers and longtime neighbors in Clarke County, Virginia. Years before the story begins, they fell in love with the same woman, and in a twist on the romantic triangle scenario, the woman actually chose one of the men to marry — George Ashton. For years Walton fumed about his rejection, even after the woman died, and "swore to be revenged." Now, as the story opens, he is preparing to meet Ashton in a skirmish in the Shenandoah Valley. His conduct is reprehensible, the narrator tells us, as he does not bother to enlist in a Union regiment; instead, he stockpiles his own guns and forms a guerrilla band. He also bribes one of Ashton's sons to serve with him and secretly leaves for the fight in the middle of the night. Along the way Walton kills a man in an exchange of gunfire and, in a display of bloodthirstiness, stabs the corpse repeatedly with a dagger for good measure. Ashton, on the other hand, officially enlists as a Confederate infantryman, puts on a proper uniform, and leaves for battle after waving a tearful good-bye to his family. Ashton's service is about duty and honor, whereas Walton's is about revenge.[47] This same contrast appears in other stories, where the good brother is disciplined in combat and the bad brother is vicious and overindulgent.

Readers might have appreciated this distinction between good and evil forms of combat. According to historian Charles Royster, Civil War Americans needed to draw moral absolutes between themselves and their enemies in order to validate their participation in what had become a very destructive conflict. The writers considered here generally penned their stories after some of the war's bloodiest battles — Shiloh, Antietam, and Fredericksburg — in 1862, when America had witnessed large-scale suffering unprecedented in its history. Readers sought, and writers tried to provide, a justification for the bloodletting, something to quell any ambivalence they might have had about violence. Through these clear distinctions, authors could blame the enemy for the viciousness of war while justifying their own aggressive response as a moral duty.[48] Perhaps for this reason, they did not feel compelled to cloak the despair of war in narratives of triumph.[49] Instead, their stories are graphic — most notably in the throat slashing of an entire family in McCabe's *The Guerrillas* — and in this way draw readers into the raw experience of war. Such unromanticized imagery also served a vicarious need of Civil War Americans, especially those distanced from combat, to know, understand, and experience their war.[50]

Violence typically ends Confederate tales and marks the final break between the "brothers." In the final scene of *The Captain's Bride: A Tale of the
War* (1864), written by W. D. Herrington of the 3rd North Carolina Cavalry,
a Confederate observer who witnesses a violent confrontation picks up a dagger and thrusts it into the Union man's heart. "With a slight tremor of his
frame and a horrid contortion of his countenance," the narrator concludes,
"his unmanly spirit past away." (This gory ending did not prevent an advertisement for the story from proclaiming it "charming" and "delightful.")[51]
In other Confederate tales, a hanging or some other public death ends the
Union man's life and bolsters the Confederate man's claim to manhood and
marriage. Sometimes the Union man will have a moment of reckoning, in
which he realizes the error of his loyalty and announces that he has become
a Confederate before throwing himself before gunfire or into a river. Violent
death, these stories suggest, is honorable when it eliminates the evil embodied
in the Union enemy. More significantly, in Confederate stories there is no
reconciliation between the warring brothers. Napier Bartlett's *Clarimonde*
(1863), for example, ends with the corpses of the two old friends lying on a
Virginia battlefield, "their blood refusing to mingle."[52]

In Union tales violence does not end in separation but, perhaps unsurpris-
ingly, is a catalyst for reunion. In "On the Kentucky Border," a short story
published in *Harper's Weekly* in 1862, two brothers, Dan and Maurice Byrne,
battle for the affections of their eighteen-year-old cousin known as "Harry."
The story begins when Dan, the Confederate brother, returns to his Union
home after several months of combat; he is missing an arm and is "haggard,
hollow-eyed, emaciated, unshorn, unshaven, faint with wounds and exhausted
with hunger and lack of sleep." (Even the family's dogs cower at the sight of
him.) Having seen the destruction of war firsthand, Dan has come back to
protect his family from expected Confederate raids. But he fails. In a climactic
scene, his Confederate comrades arrive, and, "thirsting for blood," ignore his
pleas to spare his Union family and fire on the house anyway. Their violence
wisens Dan to the Confederates' viciousness, and he turns his sword on them
to defend his family. He is beaten to his knees, but, in the end, is rescued
when his Union brother Maurice arrives on the scene accompanied by U.S.
cavalrymen. The fight that ensues "was short, sharp, and bloody," culminating in the capture of most of the Confederates by Maurice and his men.
The conflict ends with Maurice receiving the promise of Harry's affection
as "the reward of his love and loyalty" and the two brothers resuming their
friendship.[53] Similar reunions close other Union stories, although sometimes

more ambivalently. In one tale two brothers shake hands "if not in renewed friendship, at least in mutual forgiveness and kindly feeling."[54]

The Divided Interracial Family

Fictional portrayals of romantic dysfunction captured the unique problem of a civil war: how to draw a clear border between two sections that were once united as one nation. Writers examined the strength of the boundary between Union and Confederacy and considered what, if anything, still drew Americans together across sectional lines. Both Northern and Southern authors condemned the false attachments displayed in a seduction, such as deception and illegitimate power, that each side believed was operative in the war tactics of their enemy. Yet they disagreed on the extent to which the deeper, more sincere ties of brotherhood still may have bound together North and South. In romantic triangle scenarios, writers explored the persistence of these more natural attachments of blood, genealogy, and heritage, dramatized by the central position of "brothers" united since childhood. These authors collectively imagined just how "divided" the nation was and went on, in other writings, to consider how race and biological ties worked to unite or divide the two sections.

Union writers stressed the endurance of blood ties and genealogy that bound the sections together. The nation at war was "ONE POLITICAL FAMILY," asserted the *Louisville Daily Journal* in 1862, for the two sections maintained a "unity of race and natural origin," language, religion, republican political institutions, and the "common memories of early history." These commonalties were "the springs of reciprocal affection," which were indissolvable bonds among any people. Just as affection strengthened kinship ties in real families, the *Journal* concluded, its "influence is just the same in political communities." A letter in the *Missouri Statesman* concurred, calling the warring nation "a people bound together by every tie held sacred . . . the same blood . . . the same language . . . the same religion." To break these ties was not just "treacherous," but "altogether impossible."[55] Reunion was inevitable when it involved a family, the *Nashville Daily Press* agreed in 1863, and "this great family has been divided too long already."[56]

By the latter years of the war, however, Confederates stressed that no natural ligaments bound together North and South. In fiction, the death of one brother without remorse or sympathy from the other signaled the final destruction of what once might have been kinship ties. Newspaper writers echoed these stories by blaming Yankee aggression for severing those bonds. "How can we again shake hands with them over the slain bodies of our loved ones, and again embrace them in fraternal relations?" asked a correspondent for the *Southern Field and Fireside*. Confederate writers acknowledged kinship at the outset of the war but suggested that such attachments were ruined by the North's wartime conduct. To a poet for the *Southern Illustrated News*, the Union's Emancipation Proclamation was the final blow:

> Thou hast broken the tie that once bound me
> In fondest affection to thee;
> Thou hast wounded the heart that so loved thee,
> By making that awful decree —
> That we must be parted forever —
> That I must now love thee no more,
> And *this* world is more dreary than ever
> Was desert to pilgrim before.

"There is little love for the Yankee," a writer for the *Southern Literary Messenger* similarly concluded. And to any Unionist who continued to appeal to family ties, the *Daily Richmond Examiner* responded simply, "All men are not brothers."[57]

It was not just affection that Southerners claimed had disappeared. They also objected to Northern assertions that shared "blood" and "race" maintained a tight bond between the warring populations. In 1861, for example, the *Southern Literary Messenger* published an article declaring that the war was in fact the result of "ethnological idyosyncracies" between North and South. The populations of the two regions were not bound by blood, as Yankees were an "inferior race" characterized by "an admixture of force and finesse." Comparing the South to the Normans and the North to the Saxons, the writer maintained that the Civil War was a contest for the "supremacy of race." These arguments defied historical and biological accuracy, and other writers came forward to qualify them. Acknowledging "the earnest and natural eagerness of the South to disclaim any near kinship with the North," a Dr. Stuart, in the same journal in 1863, conceded that such reasoning was at times "ambiguous and paradoxical." It could not be denied that the two populations came "from the same stock," but even if the two sections were not "organically different," they were as different "as it is possible for races to be." Stuart suggested that "decided marks of innate, fixed, enduring difference" indicated that Northerners and Southerners were of two different races, even if they were both of Anglo-Saxon origin.[58]

Denying racial kinship with the North bolstered Confederate arguments for independence. According to these arguments, there was something more natural in the blood ties shared exclusively by Southerners, ties that would help consolidate another national "family" during the war—a Confederate family. Indeed, much of the Southern fiction examined in this study demonstrates the reinforcement of these Confederate familial bonds. Unacceptable relationships between Union men and Confederate women are destroyed in Confederate tales of seduction, leaving the women with the promise of marrying a Confederate man. Similarly, at the end of romantic triangle stories Confederate men marry the women in the middle and happily start a new family in the South. During this period marriages between Confederate lovers were a popular theme of Southern fiction, as were reunions of long-lost family members. In these stories, native Southerners living in the North on the eve of the war are spurned by their Yankee friends but subsequently find a home with family in the South. In "Kitty's Southern Relations," which appeared in the *Magnolia Weekly* in 1865, a native Virginian – turned – New York socialite experiences an epiphany with the coming of the war: "Her sympathies were alive in an instant, to the wrongs of a gallant South, and Northern bred and educated though she had been, all the warm Virginia blood flowing through her veins, answered to the appeal of her mother State." Treated poorly by her Union friends, Kitty quickly returns to Virginia. There was something powerful in the blood of Southerners, her story suggests, that united them regardless of time or distance apart.[59]

Furthermore, it united more than white Southerners. The idealized Confederate family supposedly encompassed loyal slaves as well. Southern writers drew on the "faithful slave," a stock character in their antebellum fiction, one who enjoyed a close and often loving relationship with his or her white master, and made it a central figure in their wartime stories. The slave Jerry in James Dabney McCabe's *The Guerrillas* is typical. Early in the play Jerry is distraught, almost hysterical, because he fears that his Confederate master has been killed by a rival Union man. (The master lived.) Later, Jerry helps the woman in the middle, Rose, when she is imprisoned and is subsequently rewarded with his freedom. But "I don't want to be free," Jerry defiantly tells his master. "I bin in your family eber since I bin born." Although that family was not bound by blood ties, McCabe suggests, it was nonetheless powerful.

Jerry concludes: "I lub you jis like you was my own son." The story ends when Jerry rescues his master from the scaffold. (According to the *Daily Richmond Examiner*, "the devotion of the negro is very beautifully illustrated in the play.")[60]

Jerry was more than merely loyal to the white people who owned him — he was like a member of their family, a figurative kinsman. This position for a slave hardly stretched the imaginations of white Southern readers, who would have been accustomed to references in fiction, proslavery theory, and even private letters and diaries to the plantation as one extended "family black and white," often with masters as figurative parents and slaves as perpetual children. This widespread image simultaneously defined the inequality and dependency so necessary for slavery to exist while masking the violence and cruelty that frequently characterized day-to-day relations between master and slave. It was an image that white Southerners invoked for their own benefit as well as for abolitionists, who loudly condemned the inhumanity of slavery. A mix of self-delusion and propaganda, such paternalistic language, as historian Eugene Genovese has argued, "lay at the core of slaveholders' world view and sense of themselves as good and moral men."[61] Indeed, this rhetoric appeared frequently throughout the personal writings of border-state Southerners during the war. A Kentucky soldier, for example, complained to his father that he had not received any news lately about "a single member of the family white or black."[62] A Tennessee woman recalled of a "mammy" whose portrait hung prominently in her sister's household that "we thought as much of her as if she were a member of the family."[63]

White Southerners appear to have latched onto this imagined "family white and black" even more intensely when the war threatened slavery in new, more aggressive ways. In private writings, and especially in fiction, they became increasingly convinced of the loyalty of slaves, suggesting that the arrival of Union soldiers in the South and the prospect of emancipation held little attraction for African Americans.[64] If given a choice, whites wrote, slaves would always choose to remain faithful to their masters rather than act on any newfound allegiance to the Union and Abraham Lincoln. It was assumed that slaves would extend their attachments to their masters to the Confederacy as a whole; indeed, Confederate supporters went so far as to hold up slaves as models of loyalty for all Southerners to emulate. In "The Old Mammy's Lament for Her Young Master," a poem that appeared in an 1863 issue of the *Southern Literary Messenger*, the title alone illustrates the way in which slaves came to represent for white Southerners a loving and selfless devotion to the South and, in this case, to a Confederate soldier.[65] Such depictions appear in other stories, such as Mary Jane Haw's *The Rivals: A Chickahominy Story*, in which a slave — "Uncle Thomas" — delivers the climactic speech, lecturing a Union man for abandoning his friends and family in the South. Black Southerners in these border dramas are often the most defensive of Confederate family sanctity and thus, the authors suggest, willing members of the Confederacy. Slaves — even more than white Southerners — are said to be the voice of Confederate family unity.[66]

This was a huge imaginative leap, however, as the reality of slavery in the wartime border states told a very different story, one of black *dis*loyalty to slaveholders and to the Confederacy. From the beginning of the war, and particularly after the 1863 Emancipation Proclamation, slaves made their willingness to abandon their masters abundantly clear, bolting from their plantations — and the Confederacy — by the thousands. They fled not to the Confederate army, as white Southerners might have wanted to claim, but to Union camps in Kentucky, Tennessee, and Virginia, where, despite the reluctance of many Federal troops to receive them, they found refuge as well as even a chance to enlist in the U.S. Army.[67] In the month of July 1864, for example, seventeen slaves of Kentuckian Robert J. Breckinridge headed for Camp Nelson, near Lexington, where several of the men enlisted in the Union army while their families set up their own lodgings on the edge of the Union encampment. Not all slaves left in such large groups, but even the departure of one, or the threatened departure of any, forced slaveholders to experience what has been termed a "moment of truth." They had always counted on the loyalty of slaves to their "family," so where had it gone? or had it ever existed? "i hope you have no Hard feeling," one of Breckinridge's slaves, Jacob Warren, wrote his master. "i lef for A good cause."[68]

Few masters acknowledged that "good cause" and tried to get their slaves back, punishing those who did return and lashing out at those who never left the plantation. These actions, however, did not obviate the need to explain the loss of their "loyal" slaves. One popular rationalization denied that the slaves had left of their own free will. A Kentuckian stated that slaves had "never thought or acted for themselves any more than children have done under the guidance of their parents." For this reason, the slaves themselves were not responsible for their departure; rather, it was "the whites who *seduce* them from home *in more ways than one*" who were to blame. Like this man, others attributed the slaves' apparent disloyalty to the sinister actions of Union soldiers, or other white Northerners, who "induced," "forced," or "enticed off" their otherwise faithful slaves.[69] The *Charleston Mercury* sounded the alarm in 1862, when it accused Union soldiers of "the seduction or forcible abduction of slaves." A year later the same paper reported that Union soldiers were offering to marry enslaved women to entice them away from their owners. Such charges of enticement and seduction, which also raised the specter of sexual assault, offered slaveholders a simple rationale. Their slaves were still loyal at heart; it was only the interference of aggressive Northerners that had divided master and slave.[70]

Southern writers of fiction also enlisted the popular literary device of seduction, so useful in dramatizing the divided nation, to explore this forcibly divided "family black and white." In a pro-Confederate novel entitled *The Elopement: A Tale of the Confederate States of America* (1863), twenty-four-year-old Celia Connelly, writing under the penname L. Fairfax, sketched this version of the seduction scenario. As the story begins, we learn that a light-skinned woman named Amanda is working under the direction of a brutal white overseer, a native of New England. By contrast, Amanda is treated very kindly by a neighboring plantation mistress, who teaches her how to read and showers her with affection. One day Amanda meets Jed, who is in town under the guise of peddling jewelry but is actually an abolitionist. Jed tells Amanda he has heard that her overseer is about to sell her and urges her to accompany him to New York. Amanda is thus torn between leaving the neighboring mistress and avoiding the auction block. Choosing the second option, she goes to New York, where, she quickly realizes, prejudice against blacks is much worse than she experienced in the South and abolitionists like Jed spread lies about slavery. Despite her disappointment, she stays, pretending to be Jed's sister, until she discovers the disturbing fact that he is also a gambler and runs away. Amanda then boards a train for the South and returns to the welcoming embrace of her friend, the neighboring plantation mistress. This melodramatic tale contains all the stock elements of deception and trickery that comprised a seduction. But in the end, it is clear that the only sincere relationship is the one between Amanda and her neighbor, that is, between a slave and a slaveowner.[71]

A striking aspect of *The Elopement* is that initially we are told that Amanda is of mixed-race parentage, that the lines between black and white blurred literally — not just figuratively — in her plantation "family." This would seem to be quite an innovation for a white Southern writer, as the reality of sex between master and slave and the production of mixed-race children was barely acknowledged in most Southern wartime fiction. But Celia Connelly, after several narrative detours following Amanda's attempt to pass for white in the North, ultimately reveals that Amanda is, in fact, a full-blooded "white" person, having been enslaved and led to believe she was of partial black parentage by the unscrupulous overseer. The overseer, who is the brother of Amanda's father, stands to inherit his dead brother's property on Amanda's death; he thought that making her "black" and a slave would drive her to suicide. (She does indeed kill herself in the end, when Jed, the abolitionist/gambler, returns and tries to accost her.) In this white Southerner's tale, then, a child of mixed-race parentage is still a fiction, a terrible lie made up by a devious and money-hungry New Englander. Mulattoes and master-slave sex are nonexistent.[72]

But, of course, they did exist. Thousands of slave children were born to parents of different races, often to white fathers and black mothers and often the result of rape. The illicit sex that produced these children revealed a double meaning to the phrase "family black and white" and earned the condemnation of many Northerners.[73] Northern newspapers exposed this hidden truth with shocking revelations of the black kin of some of the Confederacy's most prominent men and women. In 1865 *Frank Leslie's Illustrated Newspaper* reported that a man named Charles Syphax was — without question — "a *half-brother* to Mrs. General Robert E. Lee, and grandson of George Washington Parke Custis, who was a stepson of George Washington!" "That is quite a pedigree, is it not?" proclaimed the paper, adding that Syphax was now a messenger for Federal secretary of interior James Harlan, serving the very government that waged war against the army of Mrs. Lee's husband. The newspaper went on to repeat the "well-known fact" that Mrs. Lee had "some forty half-brothers and sisters of the same sort in and around Washington."[74] Some of these allegations may have been true, as Syphax family tradition holds that Custis, Mrs. Lee's father, did have a child named Maria Carter with one of his slaves and that a Syphax did serve Secretary Harlan. But details are confused: it was William Syphax, the son of Maria Carter and her husband Charles Syphax, who actually served Secretary Harlan, making this a division between Mrs. Lee and her black half nephew rather than her half brother. Regardless of its veracity, this account offered a useful weapon of war by tarnishing the image of one of the Confederacy's most respected families. Mrs. Lee is depicted as coming from a promiscuous familly (not to mention violent if rape was involved), a heritage that betrayed the noble legacy of George Washington.[75]

Mrs. Lee's story does not seem to have spread among other Northern papers, but a similar account about an even more prominent Southerner did.

This one portrayed Confederate president Jefferson Davis, already rumored to have fathered Yankees, actively blurring racial lines by having a son with one of his slaves in Mississippi. This story, which first appeared in February 1864, allegedly originated with a London reporter who was tipped off by an anonymous source "occupying a high position in the United States." The reporter, accompanied by an officer in the Union navy, traveled to Mississippi, conducted an investigation, and pronounced the story confirmed by the child's mother. The story then appeared in Union newspapers across the country, from the *Boston Journal* to the *Daily Missouri Democrat*, and changed from version to version.[76] Sometimes the mother's name was different, other times the circumstances of Davis's relationship with the enslaved woman varied. But in all accounts one detail was consistent: that the son was now serving in the Union navy under the name Purser Davis. One story, under the headline "Jeff Davis's Son in the Federal Service," noted the irony of the Confederate president facing his black son in battle. Another rendition, entitled "Miscegenation by Jeff. Davis," was not so amused but made no secret of the story's usefulness. "This same Jeff. Davis flaunts abroad his professions of Christianity, and sneers at the Puritanical habits of New England," the *Daily Missouri Democrat* pointed out, while "his own life is a fitting exemplification of the *Barbarism of Slavery*."[77]

Different layers of this story served different purposes. To an abolitionist, as the St. Louis paper suggested, it was another example of the sexual exploitation of enslaved women. To Republicans accused by fellow Northerners of embracing interracial sex in their calls for emancipation, it was proof that Southerners themselves were the worst practitioners of miscegenation.[78] (One newspaper coined the term "Davisegination.") And to patriotic Unionists, the idea of a white Confederate leader sharing bloodlines with a black Union soldier poked holes in Southern pretensions of racial and genetic purity. It did not matter whether this story was entirely true or not, or that Davis apparently ignored it and did not publicly respond. Those who latched onto it were searching for something with which to undermine Davis's, and other Confederates', claim to be fighting as a nation with loyal and contented slaves.[79]

Northern readers no doubt found irresistible the idea that the war gave black family members like Purser Davis a chance to confront the white kinsmen who enslaved them. This scenario also appeared in novels and short stories, especially after 1863, when the Federal government formally allowed black men to enlist in the Union army and take up arms against Confederates. In "My Boy Ben," a short story published in an 1864 issue of *Harper's*

Weekly, a slave named Ben takes advantage of his physical "resemblance" to his master, Perry Littlejohn, and poses as him, even wearing his Confederate uniform, while making his way toward Union lines. Once in a Union camp Ben pretends to be a deserting Perry Littlejohn and seeks safe haven among Union authorities, who are later confused when Littlejohn himself arrives to reclaim Ben. Unable to determine who is the real Perry Littlejohn and who is the slave — there is no discernible racial difference between them — the Union commander, Colonel Manning, arrests both men. Ben later owns up to his disguise but claims that, under the Confiscation Act of 1862, which allowed Union soldiers to seize the slaves of Confederates, he should be seized — and freed — by Manning. The colonel agrees, freeing Ben in an act that simultaneously thwarts a rebel slaveholder's attempt to reclaim his slave. The story ends with the black and white kinsmen on opposing sides of the Union-Confederate divide.[80]

The scenario of black and white kinsmen confronting one another across battle lines fused the nation's sectional and racial divisions. Ben is not only a runaway slave fleeing his master but also a former slave who seeks the power of the Union army to help him confront his master with unprecedented force. His alignment with the Union brings new intensity to the long-standing conflict between master and slave, white and black. Furthermore, there is actual evidence that African Americans were willing to mobilize Union resources against their white kin. Kentuckian Nannie Eaves, herself the daughter of her white master, recalled that her husband Ben ran away from his white master (and also his father, a rebel) to join the U.S. Army.[81] A woman named Ellen, the slave of the Clay family of Virginia and Kentucky, likewise sought leverage against her white master (and family) when running to the Union army. Her departure outraged Ellen's white half sister and mistress, Martha Clay Davenport, who asked their father, Brutus Clay, for any help he could provide in the difficult task of retrieving her. "The morning she left I told her you should know it," Martha wrote Brutus. "She told me then she cared nothing for you & was not afraid of you and said if her Father came for her, she would have him arrested." Apparently Ellen had told many Union soldiers that "her daddy was a white man" and was confident that they would mobilize on her behalf to fight him. (In this instance she may have been overly optimistic, for Brutus Clay remained pro-Union throughout the war and served in the U.S. Congress, beginning in 1863, despite the fact that he was a slaveholder.)[82]

Fiction and newspaper writers reveled in tales of divided interracial families — especially those that turned the moment of confrontation into an act of revenge. Louisa May Alcott's "The Brothers," which appeared in the *Atlantic Monthly* in late 1863, tells the story of a "contraband," an escaped slave named Bob, who vows to get even with his white half brother Ned, who is also his master. Ned had sold Bob's mother to the Deep South, raped his wife Lucy, and virtually destroyed his family. "I hate him!" Bob tells a nurse in the Union hospital where he works when she discovers that a rebel soldier whom she cared for was none other than Ned himself. Bob makes it clear that he intends to kill Ned—the ultimate revenge—but the nurse, Miss Dane, tries to help him find "a better way of righting wrong than by violence." With her encouragement Bob leaves for her native Massachusetts and soon enlists in a black regiment of the Union army. The story then fast-forwards to Fort Wagner, South Carolina, the site of a bloody but heroic battle between the 54th Massachusetts regiment of black soldiers and Confederate troops. Here Bob finds Ned in battle, and as soon as the two recognize one another, they "went at it." Both are fatally wounded, although Ned's injury was inflicted by a comrade of Bob's rather than by Bob himself. The story ends as Bob declares himself "satisfied" with the result before joining Ned in death.[83]

"The Brothers" contains the stock elements already seen in tales of white brothers confronting one another over the lines of battle: the good versus the bad brother, a deadly confrontation, and finally the death of the bad brother. But this story ends in the death of both brothers, as Bob dies along with his white half brother, an ambiguous conclusion suggesting a common fate for both blacks and whites. On one level, the ending eliminates the problem of divided interracial families by envisioning no future for them together—there is no place for such a family in American society. This message reflects an uneasiness among some Northern writers with how blacks and whites would coexist in postemancipation society. It also demonstrates the underlying discomfort with miscegenation that surfaced during the war and was condemned by Northern Democrats. But at the same time, by drawing two brothers into a bloody confrontation, this story sends a clear message about the fallacies of the white Southern imagination. The confrontation draws a sharp contrast between blood ties and loyalty: the very real blood ties between black and white Southerners that Northern writers set out to expose did not lead to loyalty, duty, or dedication between the races. These black kinsmen are willing to kill. Such a view directly countered the white Southern tendency to emphasize the reverse: to deny blood ties between the races in favor of a more nebulous "loyalty" between them.[84]

Unionist white observers continued to emphasize this absence of loyalty, even when a confrontation or an act of revenge fell short of death in battle. The year 1863 saw the publication of *Incidents of the War: Humorous, Pathetic, and Descriptive*, a book of short stories compiled from newspapers with some apparent embellishments by Alfred Burnett, a war correspondent for the *Cincinnati Commercial*, which document a number of acts of retribution by blacks against their white kinsmen-masters. In one, a black woman in New Orleans persuades Union officials to give her one of her father's confiscated houses. The father, a "wealthy rebel" whose property was taken over by the Union army, had made the woman not only his slave, but also his mistress and the mother of his son. In another story a "young and delicate mulatto girl" goes before Union authorities to charge her master-father with "inhuman castigation." On revealing the "sickening" scars he had inflicted, the girl wins her freedom from the officials, along with an additional judgment that her father create a $500 trust fund in her name.[85] This story mirrors a number of cases documented by the Freedmen's Bureau in which black families successfully filed paternity charges against white men to obtain support for their children.[86] These cases forced masters, quite literally, to pay a price for enslaving their black kin. In one instance, reported in *Frank Leslie's Illustrated Newspaper*, a "nearly white" woman appeared at the headquarters of a Union general in Lexington, Kentucky, seeking protection from her own aunt, a white woman who claimed her as a slave. The enslaved woman, who the paper referred to as "Sally," had previously left the aunt's home and in Lexington joined her husband, "a hard working, thrifty, black man," who provided her with a house and a "comfortable living." The Union general promised to protect Sally, since it was "improper for relations to hold each other in bondage."[87]

IN 1865 THE *Colored Tennessean* wrote: "We are part of this race, though our skins have a darker hue. . . . the best blood of the haughty South runs in the veins of her darker children."[88] These black journalists joined Northern writers in making clear that the ties between black and white Southerners were deeper, more complex, and less romantic than any surface loyalty celebrated by their white masters. This argument was similar to that of white Union writers concerning the relationship between Northerners and Southerners generally: blood, race, and genealogy created an inseparable bond between the sections, apart from any surface disloyalty. But Confederate writers offered contrasting views of loyalty that emphasized the imagined bonds — Southern tradition, as well as the "family black and white" — supposedly uniting black and white Southerners alike.

All of these stories' explorations of loyalty were captured succinctly by the metaphor of the divided family. Both Unionists and Confederates, who obviously had very different outlooks on the relationship between the two sections, found they could manipulate this familial imagery to represent their views. They used the same language of kinship to both reject and embrace secession, lament and celebrate the violence of war, and expose the loyalty and disloyalty of African Americans to the Confederacy. Family imagery also allowed them to examine the multiple layers of an individual's loyalty, from the bonds of blood and race to the attachments of tradition and heritage. The common tendency to use family metaphors called on a tradition that extended far beyond the United States but still suggests an important cultural overlap within the American nation. The family — so idealized as a private haven in midcentury society — assumed a very public role in the divided nation by providing a common rhetorical ground for thinking about the war. Its useful-ness stemmed from its ability to embody diverse and conflicting sentiments about loyalty and, perhaps for this reason, would continue to resonate publicly as the war came to a close and Americans tried to reconcile their conflicting loyalties.

Reconciliations
Lived and Imagined

THE CLOSING YEARS of the war tested the strength of family ties, both metaphoric and real, to reach across the nation's borders and restore national unity. As the death toll rose, Confederate losses multiplied, and the end of slavery seemed imminent, Americans began to talk about the reconciliation of the two sections. But what did "reconciliation" mean? What result could reasonably be expected, how quickly could it occur, and just how reconciled could the nation ever become? These questions, which provoked heated debate in the halls of Congress, state legislatures, and the press, also troubled divided families in their private correspondence. If reconciliation meant a return to the status quo, a resumption of the same conversations, activities, and feelings they had shared in peacetime, then divided families never reconciled. What most of them found instead was that reconciliation was a complex, and sometimes halting, process that involved both practical gestures of assistance and economic aid, as well as the emotional dimensions of forgiveness and understanding. The practical gestures were often quickly accomplished, but the emotional reconciliation proved more elusive in the long term.[1]

In the realm of emotions, and in their intimate conversations, divided families confronted the same question that had confounded them throughout the war: Could they continue to deflect politics and public affairs by erecting a shelter around their private lives and thus maintain their familial relationships? In the new context of the postwar period, this separation between private and public appeared even more difficult to achieve. Four years of war took a toll on these men and women, and inevitably, even if they resisted it, the conflict intruded on their most intimate feelings. Lasting emotional scars were evident in bitter words, testy exchanges, even estrangements, suggesting, at least on an emotional level, that the war forever changed these families. At the same time, however, a growing disjuncture emerged between the experiences of these real divided families and the image of them in fiction, where emotional bonds were forged more quickly between North and South and paved the way for a speedy national reunion.

Wartime Reunion

The impulse to reconcile did not begin, as it is tempting to believe, in 1865. It actually emerged much earlier, at the very beginning of the war, when most divided families did not abandon one another entirely and instead reached out with gestures of assistance across the lines. They did not use the word "reconcile" to describe these actions, but their attempts to help one another testify to an instinct to remain connected even as the war tore them apart. Division and reunion were thus simultaneous processes, and any examination of reconciliation must therefore begin long before the South surrendered at Appomattox.[2]

Constant reminders of the deadly nature of war sensitized family members to one another's welfare from the first days of the conflict. Border-state men and women lived amid some of the Civil War's largest and bloodiest battles as well as in the path of troops moving through the Shenandoah Valley and central Kentucky. They knew firsthand how vulnerable their families were to having their houses burned or their crops raided or their virtue insulted. This knowledge did not prevent tough public stances against enemy kin, as seen in the cases of brothers in particular, but, at the same time, the thought of relatives being harmed physically by the same forces for which one served could be very disturbing. Isaac Noyes Smith, a native of Charleston, Virginia (later West Virginia), had not hesitated to join the 22nd Virginia volunteer regiment early in the war, even though his father was a prominent Unionist. But by September 1861 he had become "depressed" by the fierceness of hostilities and found it difficult to rejoice at the prospect of Confederate success. "Virginia is to be red with blood before the end," he noted in his diary, "yet my source of constant trouble is that my father will be in danger." This was at times a terrifying thought, Smith continued, for "I am here actually leading a set of men one of whose avowed objects is the arrest and judicial or lynch murder of my father."[3]

Family members who shared Smith's sentiments often tried to mitigate the war's destructiveness with offers of direct assistance for their kin. This ranged from money, food, and medicine smuggled through illicit mail to offers of safe and comfortable shelter away from the battling armies.[4] Sometimes they appealed to army commanders to spare their relatives from impending raids. In 1864 one Union brother wrote directly to General William T. Sherman, requesting that he grant his sister-in-law in Nashville "consideration and protection," even though she was a secessionist at heart. He specifically asked Sherman to avoid the woman's household during future raids and to exercise leniency when interacting with his kin.[5] Army officers occasionally responded to such requests by issuing a letter of protection to the relative in question. The relative was to show the document to invading soldiers, who would, ideally, avoid damaging the individual's property.[6] These letters could be quite effective. The *Louisville Daily Journal* reported that Unionist Robert J. Breckinridge suffered no losses after Confederate Kirby Smith and his men raided central Kentucky in the fall of 1862. Smith had sent Breckinridge a letter of protection ahead of time, and, as a result, "not so much as a grain of corn has been taken from him." The *Journal* noted with a hint of envy that Breckinridge was more fortunate in this regard "than many of his Union neighbors." This protection had been arranged by his twenty-four-year-old son William, who, though an ardent Confederate, claimed to still care about his father's welfare. "I am glad that if we are driven from Kentucky," William wrote in October 1862 after the raid, "that you . . . will be benefited by our loss."[7]

Members of divided families, like William Breckinridge, derived satisfaction from being able to use their influence to protect their kin from military invasion. Not only could they save relatives from harm, but also, and perhaps more significantly, they could reassure them of the personal loyalty they believed still existed between them. This was the case when Christopher Clay, a twenty-seven-year-old rebel son of Kentucky Unionist Brutus J. Clay, wrote home to warn his family of Kirby Smith's 1862 Kentucky raid. The younger Clay advised the household to bury the silver and gave the alarm that Confederate leaders were plotting to take Brutus "hostage." He offered his assurance that he and his brother Ezekiel "Zeke" Clay, also a Confederate, would call on a "friendly rebel" to watch over their father. The brothers' efforts were successful, as the Clays lost no corn or other property during the raid, and Brutus remained free. Christopher expressed pride at having taken these measures to safeguard his family; as his stepmother conveyed to Brutus, "He & E[zekiel] say that you will yet be indebted to your rebel sons for saving your property." To Christopher and his brother, their actions exhibited the personal loyalty and filial duty that their Union father had accused them of abandoning when they sided with the Confederacy. Apparently, however, Brutus cared little about the meaning behind their support, telling his wife that "all the protection I want from my rebel son is to shoot the rogues who come to steal."[8] He accepted his sons' aid as a practical gesture but remained skeptical, as Union fathers like him had been since the beginning of the war, that it represented any deeper personal loyalty.

Most divided families did not take the time to consider the implications of their assistance, concentrating instead on the more immediate task of finding available channels to convey it. One of the most popular routes was through the gates of military prisons. The incarceration of a relative offered an opportunity to send material aid with the encouragement of government officials and without the suspicion of treason. This was particularly true for the families of Confederate soldiers who were being held in Union prisons, where inmates generally experienced a more efficient—or at least a less incompetent—bureaucracy.[9] From the beginning of the war, Union policy stipulated that Confederate prisoners could receive packages from "near relatives" who lived within Union lines and who could prove their loyalty to the Union. These relatives were permitted to send clothing, as long as it was gray, of an "inferior quality," and in no way resembling the uniforms of Union soldiers; food, but not liquor; and money for the purchase of various items from the prison sutler, such as tobacco, postage stamps, and brushes. Union relatives also could visit sick or injured soldiers in the prison hospital. Although in part a humanitarian gesture, this policy enabled the Federal government to exploit the mechanisms of family duty in order to reduce its own financial burden.[10] Men from border-state regiments detained in military prisons such as Camp Chase and Johnson's Island in Ohio, Camp Douglas in Illinois, Point Lookout in Maryland, and Fort Delaware in Delaware, as well as women imprisoned for political reasons in Washington, D.C., or St. Louis, benefited significantly when their Union relatives took advantage of this policy.

Word of a relative's imprisonment spread quickly through family communication channels, mobilizing members of the immediate household as well as extended relations such as aunts, uncles, and cousins. "I have just heard to-night, that you are a wounded prisoner," Fanny Warren of Maryland wrote to her Confederate brother Fred in 1863; "without a moment[']s delay I hasten to ask you what I can do for you." A few days later Fanny's other brother William wrote Fred asking how he could "alleviate your condition."[11] The Warrens, like other families, were aware that prison life was often unbearable, even life-threatening. News traveled throughout the military and civilian populations of the border states about the mistreatment—and death—of prisoners in both Northern and Southern prisons. The occasional sight of a paroled or exchanged prisoner returning home emaciated and in rags fueled concern about the imprisoned population. The opportunity to spare one's kinsmen from the same treatment was undoubtedly compelling, or at least seen as a duty. Many families thus sought to make their relatives more comfortable with donations of pants, shirts, socks, slippers, stamps, and all kinds of food. While imprisoned in a Pennsylvania hospital, twenty-seven-year-old Bennett Taylor of Virginia received a visit from an aunt living in Philadelphia. An uncle in the same city sent him periodic checks for twenty-five dollars along with magazines and newspapers. Sometimes these family packages could be quite large. The box sent to Virginian Mary M. Stockton Terry, a political prisoner in Massachusetts, by her New York family included three smoked tongues, one ham, three bottles of claret, sherry, two bottles of pickles, one English cheese, three bundles of crackers, seven pounds of tea, and one lot of peaches. The warden allowed her to keep everything except the alcohol.[12]

Occasionally these packages arrived after a Confederate family had made a considerable effort to find a relative who lived in Union territory and could send these goods lawfully. Eliza Preston Carrington, a resident of Virginia and the mother of a Confederate soldier, turned to her brother-in-law's family in 1864 when she was unable to assist her son in the Fort Delaware prison hospital. Her brother-in-law just happened to be Unionist Robert J. Breckinridge, a former member of the Kentucky legislature and, most importantly, a resident of Kentucky. Carrington asked Breckinridge to send aid to her son and to help her obtain a pass so she could visit him. Breckinridge did so without any apparent hesitation, using his friendship with Abraham Lincoln to obtain the pass, and Carrington made her trip to Delaware later that year. Breckinridge did not say why he so readily helped his Confederate kin (though he had already benefited from his Confederate son's protection in 1862), but he did expect that the favor would be reciprocated. A few weeks later, on learning of another (Union) son's confinement in a Southern prison, he asked the Carrington family to "get my son the means of existence during his imprisonment."[13] Breckinridge seemed to believe that families—even if separated across the lines of battle—were obligated to assist one another whenever requested. One Maryland woman wrote to Confederate relatives that she would be happy to help their son imprisoned in Baltimore, adding that "perhaps you may be called on to do the same duty" for her own two sons fighting in the South.[14] These families recognized the mutual benefit in their divided national loyalties and urged their kin to mobilize accordingly.

The search for Union relatives occasionally led to discoveries of previously unknown or unfamiliar kinship connections. A Confederate prisoner incarcerated in Elmira, New York, observed that because Union policy stipulated that "none but relatives" could send supplies to inmates, "a relationship to many was quickly discovered."[15] In some cases these connections may have been made between two unrelated individuals for the sole purpose of administering aid under the parameters of the law. (This would not have been difficult to pull off, as packages to prisoners need only be accompanied by a letter attesting to the family member's kinship — something that could be easily forged.)[16] But there is evidence that some people did genuinely discover new relatives. Families across the border states often knew about distant cousins or uncles and aunts, even if they had never met them or had any contact with them. Now, when the welfare of someone close to them was threatened, these men and women turned to their family trees with renewed interest and looked for any relation — however distant — who might lend assistance. In 1864 Marylander Rebecca Davis referred to her "newly found cousin," Lieutenant Bowie, a Confederate soldier incarcerated at Fort Delaware. Bowie, "having heard his father mention he had relatives in Maryland," wrote to her after spending three months in the prison. Although Davis and her family had never met Bowie, they packed him a box of rolls, canned peaches, writing paper, and flannel shirts. "He is a native of Virginia," Davis wrote in her diary. "What a treat it will be to find he has friends in a strange land to . . . supply his needs."[17]

It is striking how readily a distant family member, such as Rebecca Davis, would go to the aid of a "newly found" relative. In a similar case, Matthew Page Andrews, a paymaster for the Confederate government in Richmond, spotted the name of his wife's cousin on a list of prisoners in a newspaper in 1861. The cousin, John Mines, was an Episcopal minister from New Jersey serving as a chaplain in the Union army. "Poor fellow I am sorry for him," Andrews wrote his wife Anna on seeing the cousin's name. Andrews spent several weeks trying to locate Mines and then used his connections in the Confederate government to arrange a face-to-face meeting. Soon afterward Andrews gave Mines ten dollars; he also promised to write to Mines's wife and to help him retrieve a trunk seized at the time of his arrest. "As the Cousin of my darling wife," Andrews told Anna, "I feel it my pleasure as well as my duty to look after him and do what I can for him." This sense of "duty" to his wife's cousin did not come from any personal attachment to her kin. Andrews had never met this cousin before and had not yet formed a close relationship with anyone in his wife's family, as he and Anna had been married only a month. His act of kindness may have stemmed instead from a vicarious sense of duty to his wife or from a feeling of obligation to his own father, who was also a Unionist. So even while the war divided the Andrews and Mines families, and others like them, it could also offer reasons to cement new kinship attachments across the lines of battle.[18]

Yet it is likely that some people simply ignored imprisoned relatives and refused to help them. It is difficult to determine how often this occurred, as many of these family members would not have bothered to answer letters requesting aid and thus left no evidence of their refusal to do so. Only a few indications remain, such as the complaints of Confederate James Perry, a prisoner in Fort Delaware, who wrote a cousin that other relatives "have turned the cold shoulder" to his appeals. Another Confederate in the same prison informed his mother that a Union cousin had requested the return of forty dollars previously sent.[19]

Imprisoned men had little trouble accepting aid from their families on the other side of the lines. Simple desperation made such assistance essential. "I am almost naked and the weather is wet and cold," a prisoner wrote his cousin from Fort Delaware, calling his situation a "case of necessity."[20] To receive assistance from a Union family did not injure military pride; on the contrary, it was considered, in the words of one soldier, "a great favor" that might be repaid some day, or a "loan," rather than a "gift," as another soldier put it.[21] These Confederates did not want charity per se, nor did they want to be pitied, but they did recognize that assistance from family could keep them alive and maybe allow them to resume their military service at a later time. Perhaps for this reason some soldiers grew demanding, regarding aid as a requirement that their families must fulfill whenever logistically possible. "I hope every thing will work out right," Confederate William Thomson wrote to his Union parents in Virginia of his imprisonment, "which it will do if the clothes are forthcoming." To his dismay, however, that clothing was never sent, and he had to rely on "strangers" for help.[22] Soldiers sometimes grew angry when their families did not assist them. "For those who sympathized or expressed friendship without deeds which they could readily have performed," a Missouri Confederate wrote his mother, "I have contempt inexpressible." In this man's view, family connections were meaningless unless substantiated by concrete support.[23]

Those families who did provide for their imprisoned relatives, both close
kin and strangers, and the readiness of those prisoners to accept their aid,
still testify to a strong sense of family obligation at work during the war. It is
difficult to pinpoint exactly what triggered this perception of duty; no doubt
relatives acted for their own unique reasons. For some men and women, assisting a prisoner was simply an act of benevolence or Christian duty; for
others, it was a more symbolic attempt to reinforce the ties that bound them
to their families. For still others, though, aid to prisoners had a transformative
meaning: it was an investment not in a man's military future, as the soldiers
may have hoped, but in his political conversion. A West Virginian, in a letter
enclosing money to his rebel son imprisoned at Fort Delaware, implored the
young man to "become a loyal citizen of the U.States." Other fathers similarly provided help along with pleas that a prisoner had a reciprocal duty to
leave the military service, renounce his present sectional loyalty, and accept
that of his family.[24] Indeed, some people viewed their assistance as merely
conditional — protection in exchange for the prisoner's willingness to become
"loyal" to their cause.

A number of border-state families initiated such a conversion by seeking
their relative's release from prison. A Confederate could be paroled, according
to Union policy, if he would take an oath of allegiance to the United States. In
so doing the prisoner swore to never again take up arms against the Union and
to defend its interests.[25] Federal authorities, knowing how desperate Confederates were to be released from prison, and how easily a soldier might lie about
his loyalty and return to his unit, did not distribute paroles indiscriminately.
They instead sought confirmation that a prisoner was sincere in his profession of loyalty to the Union, in many cases relying on the word of relatives
for that assurance. Union policy stipulated that a prisoner could be granted
a parole "as a favor to his family or friends, they being all loyal people and
vouching for his sincerity in desiring to take the oath of allegiance." All the
family had to do was file a petition testifying to its own Union loyalty; the
document moved first through the Commissary General of Prisoners' office
and then to the secretary of war for approval.[26] The Union government thus
recognized — in a marked departure from its travel and mail policies — the
usefulness of divided families. In this specific case, it acknowledged that
numerous Union households had kinsmen in the Confederate army and thus
would be able to serve the Union's strategic interests.[27]

No one took more advantage of this policy, perhaps, than Union fathers
with Confederate sons. In 1863 the *Nashville Daily Press* urged "every sensible

man . . . to get his son out of the rebel army." Those loyal men with "deluded relatives" in the Confederate service could use the parole system to reassert their authority over their sons.[28] The *Daily Press* understood how well such policies meshed with mechanisms of family authority, as sons, desperate for relief after military losses and conscious of their fathers' disappointment in them, were growing increasingly ready to seek aid on their fathers' terms. And fathers, by pursuing their son's parole, could end their conflict as they defined it at the beginning: a personal rebellion that should end with a decisive reassertion of their paternal authority. A clear example of reconciliation through this mechanism occurred in 1863, when a failed raid through Kentucky resulted in the arrest and imprisonment of hundreds of Confederate cavalrymen led by John Hunt Morgan. Many soldiers escaped with General Morgan, but others who had been captured heeded the pleas of their fathers to take the oath to the Union and be released from prison. Petitions testifying to their newfound Union loyalty poured into government offices. In February 1864 Kentucky congressman Brutus J. Clay, painfully aware himself of the ordeal of these families, received thirty-three petitions from Union fathers in his congressional district seeking the release of their rebel sons.[29]

The authors of these appeals often attributed their sons' service in Morgan's cavalry to the naïveté of youth. Their sons had been "seduced" by "designing men," they wrote, echoing the language of wartime fiction, but after two years of war their sons now regretted their errors. One man explained that his son was intoxicated when he joined the rebel army but was immediately sorry when he became sober and realized what he had done. A more typical letter was that of A. H. Calvin of Fayette County, Kentucky. His son had enlisted with John Hunt Morgan the previous year, but once imprisoned he wanted to return home as quickly as possible. At first Calvin was unwilling to help his son escape the hardships of war because "I thought he had not repented enough." But after receiving numerous letters from his son claiming to be sorry for fighting with the Confederacy, Calvin became convinced that he was ready to become a "good and Loyal citizen." Calvin promised that his son would be true to his word. Calvin would make sure of it. This language of repentance suffused descriptions of sons' behavior, as fathers listened carefully for evidence that their offspring were prepared to renounce the Confederacy. Another petitioner concluded that his son "has repented for the sins that he commited in joining the rebellion." These fathers accepted nothing less than a son's complete submission to the Union.[30]

Certainly the fathers wrote their letters with the readers in mind, knowing that Union officials would want to hear that the sons were truly remorseful. But their references to "sin" and "repentance" also hint at a deeper meaning that the Union fathers might have invested in the paroles. This unmistakably Christian language recalls the biblical tale of the prodigal son, in which an errant offspring is welcomed back into his father's household. The son recognizes the error of his ways, atones for his sins, and yields to the authority of his father, who, in turn, embraces the son and restores his own status as patriarch. This story offered a useful allegory for Union fathers, a way of connecting the military-political question of a son's Confederate service to their own concern about his filial rebellion. The rebel sons' likeness to the rebellious son in scripture was not lost on the younger generation, either. In 1862 one Kentucky son, broken and exhausted from fighting, declared himself to be "prodigal & poor." Newspaper and magazine editors also compared the increasingly desperate position of rebel sons to the prodigal son. As early as December 1861 the *Missouri Statesman*, under the headline, "Return of a Prodigal Son," reported that the Hannibal mayor's son had returned "prodigal like" and speculated about whether the "fatted calf" would be killed. Several months later, under the same headline, the *Louisville Daily Journal* described the case of a son who deserted his Tennessee regiment and returned home to his parents' embrace.³¹ These allusions to prodigality suggest a close link between a son's submission to the Union and to his father's authority.

Fathers appeared to be strict when it came to determining their sons' readiness for parole. One man who had assumed a paternal role in his nephew's life was upset when the young man did not offer a satisfactory apology for his Confederate service. "Had you said in your note that you had been duped, deceived, betrayed into this rebellion, and that you repented," the uncle wrote, "I would have labored for your release." Because he had not, and because he still sided with men who threatened to kill his uncle, the uncle informed him that "you can never have my aid." His nephew had not earned forgiveness.³² Some fathers who were skeptical of their sons' remorse preferred that they remain in prison rather than seek their parole. "I would much sooner see it then [*sic*] to see you in the Rebble army," Henry Whisler wrote his son in 1862. Whisler sympathized with his incarceration but refused to help him because he did not trust his son to return home on his release. Still other fathers viewed imprisonment as a boon to their child's health and well-being. The *Louisville Daily Journal* argued that sons would be well cared for while in the custody of U.S. officials, as they would not experience the cold, hunger, and battlefield dangers that were a part of Confederate service. Even better, prison could act as a deterrent to their rebellious behavior: there "they will not be guilty of the awful crime of . . . attempting to strike down the glorious flag that protected them in their cradles."[33]

Although many rebel sons agreed to "repent" and return home, and were undoubtedly encouraged to do so by the drudgery and danger of war, not all of them accepted the harsh terms on which this prodigal reunion rested. Some declined to refute their Confederate loyalty, or "swallow the dog," as one Tennessee soldier put it, preferring to remain in prison. Thomas Hall of Maryland recoiled at the idea of his father appealing to the Union government for his release. "What—you & my sister go to the Ape as supplicants in my behalf!" he exclaimed after learning that Abraham Lincoln had been consulted about his release. "I would rather spend my days in prison than obtain liberty by such means." Hall and other zealous Confederates like him proposed instead that they be sent back to the Southern army in exchange for the release of a Union soldier from a Confederate prison. An exchange offered the most desirable means by which a soldier could be released from prison, as it allowed him to avoid the insult of having to take an oath to the Union. It was therefore far preferable to a parole. Zeke Clay of Kentucky refused his father's assistance when it became clear that Brutus was seeking a parole rather than an exchange. Zeke argued that it was inconsistent with his "views of honor" to deny him the option of an exchange and that parole as it stood would make him a deserter from the Confederate army—a "brand of disgrace." This should not have been difficult for Brutus to understand, he continued in an appeal to his father's filial concerns, if he took "a father's interest in my welfare."[34]

Brutus Clay, like other fathers who sought paroles for their sons, was forced to reckon with the collision between his son's individual honor and that of his family. Brutus never followed through on an earlier threat of disinheritance and even admitted to his daughter that he could understand Zeke's request. "I would certainly not wish him to do any thing that was dishonorable," he acknowledged, but at the same time he viewed Zeke's parole as honorable. The fact that the U.S. government would allow his son to have his childhood home as his prison showed "greater defference" to him, Brutus reasoned. But more important was the honor that would be his when Brutus stopped his son from again taking up arms against the Union. Zeke would have to return home on those terms—and he eventually did. On his return, Brutus gave

him land and instructed him on earning a livelihood closer to the Clay family
home. Zeke once again had to answer to his father; their father-son conflict
thus ended with Brutus's reassertion of his paternal authority.[35]

All these cases of filial reunion, along with letters of protection and the pro-
vision of food and clothing to prisoners, demonstrate how the bonds of family
duty could facilitate a practical reconciliation of divided families. Families may
have tried to resist the intrusion of public affairs during the war, separating domestic life from politics and the military, but over time, ironically, they found
that they could use this intrusion to permit reconciliation. These reunions
tell a story of how the hardships of war, the concerns of the Union government, and the needs of families all converged in a way that helped dissolve the
borders that separated divided kin. This practical reconciliation, however,
left unanswered questions that would be raised in the postwar period. How
sincere were professed conversions to Union loyalty?[36] And, perhaps more
importantly, to what extent would family duty translate into a more voluntary
and long-standing emotional reconciliation within divided families?

Postwar Reconciliation

The issue of long-term reconciliation became especially meaningful as war-
weariness descended on the divided nation. When Confederate general Jeff
Thompson thanked George Prentice, the Unionist editor of the *Louisville
Daily Journal* and the father of rebel sons, for his assistance while Thompson
was in a Union prison, he expressed hope that such kindness would help pave
the road to future goodwill between the Union and the Confederacy. The
reconciliation of the nation, Thompson explained in February 1864, "must
be by the tendrils of the heart, for the bayonet cannot pin us together." In a
similar vein, during the previous fall a Union man had praised his niece's attempts to remain in touch with her Confederate kin; he hoped that "these old,
tried, erring friends may yet be reclaimed by love when the sword has failed
to bring them back to the Union."[37] Such statements acknowledged the limits
of fighting as a means of settling the conflict between Union and Confederacy.
It was in the realm of emotions, particularly those nurtured in families, that
the real work of reconciliation needed to take place. In other words, reunions
achieved by food, clothing, and paroles were just the beginning.[38]

With the Confederate surrender at Appomattox in April 1865 effectively
ending hostilities, divided families took the first step toward an emotional
reunion by restoring whatever channels of communication had been severed

between them. Men and women who had been forced apart by war now returned to live under one roof; their letters stopped, however, leaving us with little to understand how their reconciliation proceeded. Others who had previously lived apart and had lost contact because of restrictions on travel and mail took advantage of the opportunity to correspond freely with relatives in the absence of censors or other government authorities. Their reunions are more easily examined today. Throughout the immediate postwar period, letters flowed back and forth across the previously divided nation, bringing word of how kinfolk lived and survived during the Civil War. Writers told of the death of family members, of property ruined, and of military honors gained. "I fared well during the war," was how William Evans of Greeneville, Tennessee, opened his first letter to a Union cousin after a three-year lapse in their correspondence.[39] These letters were, by and large, informational, but they also had symbolic meaning. One Union woman explained that the delivery of her Confederate brother's first letter in 1866 "enabled us to realize that the great contest is ended and the same free interchange of expression and sentiment is allowed as in the days preceding our unhappy strife."[40] The recipients of such letters typically expressed gratitude in return. "I thank God for the privilege of again holding correspondence with my kindred," a Confederate wrote his Union father-in-law in August 1865. This man lamented the years that had passed without such contact, but, he continued, "I have just received your letter, & read it with mingled emotions of pleasure & regret."[41]

These exchanges elicited both "pleasure" and "regret" because they inevitably conveyed reminders of what preceded them. Everyone who lived through the war possessed competing emotions derived from their individual war experiences. The conflict left some people drained and scarred psychologically by the death of loved ones, physical destitution, and financial hardship; others were grateful simply for having survived. Some were depressed by the Confederate defeat, others were elated by the Union victory. The challenge became, for all of these people, how to disentangle feelings about one's own war experiences from feelings for relatives on the enemy side. There was no one strategy or method for sorting out these competing emotions — this was unfamiliar territory that required tentative gestures and conscious effort. That is why it is difficult to generalize about how divided families dealt with this problem. Instead, two case studies offer a more in-depth view of how different families embarked on the long-term process of reconciliation. The Halseys of Virginia and New Jersey, already featured in Chapter 3, dealt with colliding emotions while trying to rebuild their material well-being; the Cabell-Ellet clan of Washington, D.C., and Virginia worked through their feelings while reassessing their heritage and familial legacy. The diverse approaches of these two families, which together encompassed all the familiar divisions of fathers and sons, brothers, and husbands and wives, demonstrate how complicated this second layer of reunion — the reconciliation of emotions — could be. At the same time, they reveal that the insulation of their private lives from public affairs, or the isolation of the daily present from the wartime past, continued to offer the only hope for a lasting reunion.

The Halseys spoke openly about their wish that affection would be a reuniting force in the months following Appomattox. Joseph Halsey, a resident of Culpeper, Virginia, received two letters along these lines from family members in New Jersey, one from his father intended "to assure you that my affection for you is not abated by your late erratic course in politics," and the other from Joseph's brother Abraham expressing "how happy I am at being able to renew 'our old remembrances,' to revive our former acquaintance and renew those ties of blood and affection belonging to us as kindred."[42] The Halseys became divided during the war with the enlistment of forty-one-year-old Joseph in the Confederate army. As stated in Chapter 3, twenty years before Joseph had moved from his family's New Jersey home to Virginia, where he married Mildred "Millie" Morton and allied his interests with her father, Jeremiah Morton, a prominent planter, slave trader, and lawyer who served one term in Congress. Joseph built up a thriving estate with his father-in-law and, by the time of the war, was deeply invested in the South's slave economy.[43] He took a great interest in the political debates around him and among his outlets were letters to his family in New Jersey — brothers Samuel, Abraham, and Edmund and father Samuel — with whom he argued the merits of slavery.[44] After Joseph enlisted in the 6th Virginia Cavalry and his brother Edmund in the 15th New Jersey regiment, the Halseys' correspondence consisted only of brief flag-of-truce letters reporting on one another's health and well-being. It was only in the initial postwar months that the Halseys resumed their near-weekly correspondence.

Abraham Halsey had called on his family to "renew" the ties of affection that ideally, as so many brothers had expressed during the war, bound male kin for a lifetime. How to make this happen was a separate question, though, one that was acknowledged by brother Samuel in a letter to Joseph in May 1865. "Never let anything destroy the strong natural fraternal affection that exists between us," Samuel began, words that simultaneously reassured Joseph of the existence of affection while warning him that something still threatened to disrupt their desired harmony. That something, in Samuel's mind, was the war that had left Joseph nearly destitute in battle-scared Virginia. "You must be sadly impoverished. Your farm must be in ruins and you must need aid," he recognized. "I want to help you personally and by solicitation from other members of the family." Samuel knew that, by virtue of its position on the winning side of the war, the New Jersey wing of the family was equipped to help Joseph regain his financial footing. But, Samuel continued, "in order to do this I want you to be more guarded in your communications to them in reference to recent political events. 'Let the dead past bury its dead.' "[45]

Samuel Halsey quoted from the Bible, but his words echoed the sentiments of other letters crossing the previously divided nation. The injunction to "bury" the past and to look only to the future was common in postwar family correspondence, most often in the writings of former Unionists who, as victors in the war, may have felt it their Christian duty to be magnanimous. "Let bye gones [be] bye gones," urged Bethiah McKown, a Missouri mother whose sons had served in the opposing armies, in what became a ubiquitous phrase in the early postwar period. James Yeatman of St. Louis similarly instructed his Confederate brother Henry in Tennessee to "let by gones be by gones," pleading that "the sorrows, trials, & wrongs of the past be forgotten." Union relatives such as these — both close kin and extended family — urged one another not to be "bitter" and to consider the war as a temporary, regrettable phase of their lives that could be easily put behind them and never discussed again. Their letters repeatedly evoked the sentiment described by writers at *Harper's New Monthly Magazine* in December 1865 as a "sober wish that all trace of the difference may disappear as swiftly and as surely as possible." They asked for a reconciliation based on forgetting.[46]

The idea of leaving the past behind is certainly a clichéd response to periods of adversity. But in postwar society, and for decades to come, this rhetoric would assume a powerful force. The "past" became a political issue during Reconstruction, as Radical Republicans intent on "waving the bloody shirt" would recall the past to enact measures to punish the South and to produce social change, while Democrats cited the war as a hurdle to be forgotten in ushering in a reunion of North and South. Others viewed the past as a time of historical importance; writers and newspaper editors published numerous volumes immediately after the war that defined some of the central themes of Civil War history. The "past" was a euphemism for many things, both tangible and intangible, serving different purposes depending on one's present needs. For divided families, the "past" conjured up a range of sentiments, from the lamented memory of a dead relative, to anger over military defeat, to loneliness and sadness after four years of fighting. Families concerned with suppressing these negative feelings and reconnecting on an emotional level found that forgetting, at least in theory, offered a simple solution. A forgotten past was tantamount to a reconciled present.

The desire to suppress the past forced families like the Halseys to articulate what was to be forgotten. Samuel's May 1865 letter to Joseph referred to the past only in terms of "political events," and Joseph's father advised him to "keep yourself as quiet as possible and as free from Politics as possible." The Halseys' focus on "politics" was a general reference to all of the contentious issues surrounding the war. Future letters, however, urged Joseph to avoid particular comments about Northern leaders, the causes of the war, and, especially, slavery ("Never mind the negro now," wrote brother Abraham). The Halseys hoped that by purging "politics" from their conversations, they would avoid the negative feelings associated with it and thus be able to resume the relationships they had enjoyed before the war. "Each feels that he has acted right and each probably has acted as the other would do in the same situation," brother Samuel rationalized in another plea to avoid political talk in the summer of 1865. "It does no good for you to call them abolitionists or they to call you a rebel." The Halseys might never agree on the war, he acknowledged, but that need not matter in the long term. "No political difference will change my personal feelings towards you," Samuel pledged to Joseph, "and what political influence I have you can have the full benefit of." Politics should only have a place in their personal relationship, he argued, when it could serve the ultimate goal of renewing — rather than severing — their attachment.[47]

Soon brother Samuel upheld his offer by suggesting that he use his influence to help Joseph obtain a pardon for his Confederate service. In return, Joseph only had to agree to take an oath of allegiance to the United States, a step resisted by many former Confederates. The oath, much as in wartime, was bound up with several layers of meaning in the postwar period. On a pragmatic level, it allowed white men such as Joseph Halsey to regain their property and political rights at a time when those interests were threatened.[48] But on another level the oath offered a symbolic break with the past and an acknowledgment of the realities of the present — the South had lost, the Union prevailed, and slavery was over. For both of these reasons the New Jersey Halseys urged Joseph throughout 1865 to take the oath and to accept a pardon for his Confederate service. "The sooner you accommodate yourself to the new order of things the better," his father warned sternly in August.[49] The oath would promote the Halseys' goal of forgetting, too, as it would officially erase Joseph's Confederate allegiance and thus eliminate the overt division in their family relationship. The oath, while political in nature, was at the same time an important step in the Halseys' process of forgetting the political past.

The desire to paper over their political differences through silence and oath taking was a significant departure for the Halseys, especially the brothers, who before the war had embraced the intellectual value of debating those differences.[50] But four years of fighting had tainted that kind of debate for this family by revealing the deadly consequences that could arise from prolonged disagreement. The war also, as other Halsey letters suggest, revealed the failings of those who had become too deeply involved in political matters. The war "has caused our statesmen to dwindle into politicians," Joseph's younger brother Edmund declared in 1865. His words evoked a popular insult — "politician" — often used to denote a person who was corrupt or who manipulated public affairs for their own selfish interests. To the New Jersey Halseys, no men personified this corruption more than the Confederacy's Jefferson Davis and Robert E. Lee (whom the elder Samuel once referred to as "Devils incarnate"). "I feel bitterly towards your leaders in treason," brother Samuel Halsey wrote, explaining that in the hands of these men the nation had fallen into ruin.[51] Such statements implied that any animus about the war, or a person's condition after it, ought to be directed toward certain leaders, not toward one another. In this sentiment the Halseys were not alone. In a letter to his son, one Union man contrasted the "miserable ambitions of politicians & would be leaders" with the desires of the "people" for "peace." Another man encouraged his sister to direct her frustration toward the "Radicals" and the "politicians" who had "ruled the government and firesides" during the war.[52] The war, in these writers' views, had exposed the dangerous consequences of politics in American society, making it almost a moral imperative for families to expunge political affairs from their conversations, thus easing the road to reunion.[53]

The New Jersey Halseys suggested a plan for reconciliation that neatly contained the war as "politics," or the work of unscrupulous "politicians," which could be distanced and hopefully forgotten. Their letters in the early postwar years reinforced this idea, with optimistic pronouncements that "the war is almost already forgotten," as Joseph's father wrote in August 1865.[54] They further supported the notion of forgetting with offers of material assistance to Joseph, as brother Samuel had proposed in May 1865, that would help to erase the scars of the past. Joseph's situation in postwar Virginia was indeed precarious as he faced the onerous task of rebuilding his house and property, finding new sources of labor now that he no longer had slaves to perform the work, and reconsidering his entire livelihood. In the previous four years both Union and Confederate troops had occupied his property several times, damaging fences and cropland. Perhaps the worst setback resulted from his father-in-law's ill-advised decision to sell several thousand acres of land, paid for with Confederate money. Devaluation of that currency after the war left Jeremiah Morton nearly penniless, forcing Joseph and his wife Millie to support her parents. Joseph did not hesitate to accept his New Jersey family's offer of help, sending his brother a "memorandum" of the things he needed during the summer of 1865. Over the next six years family members gave him more than $4,300 in loans and gifts of money. Their aid often went beyond direct financial outlays and included advice on buying and selling land, assistance in opening a sawmill, and offers to help Joseph appeal to Congress to authorize the establishment of a post office near his property. Like so many other families, the Halseys described their assistance as a "duty," something that "I choose to do," as brother Samuel wrote, or something done out of a desire to see one's family "prosperous and happy."[55]

But it was precisely this assistance that would undermine the family's efforts to forget the past and suppress their differences. The advice it offered Joseph on how to reestablish his business inevitably digressed into a critique — especially when it involved his shift from slave to free labor. The Halseys not only suggested how to make that transition but also speculated on why it was proving difficult. "Those niggers have made Virginians lazy," brother Samuel declared in one of the harsher assessments. He argued that white Southerners needed to develop "the same energy, enterprise and industry which characterizes the Yankee" to compensate for the loss of slave labor. Joseph's father repeatedly used the same words — "economy, industry and frugality" — to urge Joseph and his compatriots to give their farms a "Northern character" by reducing the size of their holdings to two hundred acres each and thereby reducing the cost of labor. Other New Jersey Halseys went after the "loose way" in which "Virginians" made labor contracts, encouraging Joseph to put labor terms in writing, since, as the elder Samuel explained, "honor is a *very poor thing* in a contract."[56] Here, under the guise of "advice," were direct challenges to two ideals of Southern — and Confederate — society: slavery and honor. The line between advice and criticism proved thin, as the New Jersey Halseys realized their new authority to assert their ideals by virtue of winning the war. At the same time, their pronouncements about the virtue of free labor echoed the antebellum debate over slavery and complicated the Halseys' larger task of forgetting the past.

These statements opened the door to a vigorous, prolonged discussion of slavery. Joseph's replies to the New Jersey clan have not survived, but it is clear from other family letters that he provided a frustrating defense of the institution. "Leave off your unmeasured denunciations of your northern friends as Black Republican abolitionists," his father commanded. "These things are offensive and uncalled for."[57] Joseph's letters seemingly asserted that as an economic system slavery was superior to free labor and had been eliminated only because of the fanaticism of a few abolitionists.[58] His family responded angrily. At the end of 1865 Edmund declared that Joseph's argument was "abominably false as to facts" and filled with "bad logic." Even two and a half years later, Abraham demanded: "How is it that latterly you can neither see or read or hear anything correctly? The late war, its origin, developments, and results are now matters of record and how is it that you cannot read that record more correctly than you do?"[59]

His brothers' references to "facts" and understanding the war "correctly" may have irked Joseph, but only partly for their harsh tone. He also may have objected to what these words revealed about his family's view of reconciliation. The Northern Halseys apparently believed that the war had settled the issues surrounding slavery and the sectional crisis for good. Their acceptance of such a clear-cut outcome to the conflict allowed them to talk about moving on and forgetting the past. Forgetting, then, was less a neutral position than it was a stance loaded with assumptions about the war and its aftermath. Joseph Halsey obviously did not accept these assumptions, particularly about the end of slavery, and therefore could not "forget" the war as easily as his family. This may explain why he did not take the oath to the United States until late 1866.

The Halseys thus had difficulty disconnecting the past — the war, slavery, and its politics — from the present while assisting a destitute family member. And they never entirely succeeded. Letters into the 1870s continued the dispute over the war and Reconstruction, as the brothers shifted their Union and Confederate loyalties to Republican and Democratic Party affiliations. "I dont [sic] like your [Joseph's] continued assaults on the puritan, as you term it, and republican notions of your Northern kin and the almost contemptuous way you speak of them," complained Abraham in 1877, "as though nothing & nobody outside of Virginia & the Democratic party were worthy of any consideration." Such political debates were compounded as new personal issues arose, such as Joseph's refusal to send his children to Northern schools. Joseph also caused a stir among his siblings in 1871, after their father's death, when he asked that his portion of their inherited property be sold for much-needed money. His brothers resisted his attempt to break up the family land for fear it signaled Joseph's renouncement of his "birth right." This family's postwar difficulties stemmed from the fact that the wartime divisions between them—something the Union Halseys wanted to attribute to "politics"—had in some ways deepened and widened after the war. Their differences were based not just on their views on wartime issues but on their disparate experiences of that war that left a father and three brothers prosperous and the fourth brother destitute. The "past" had become too intertwined with everyday financial and material concerns to be neatly separated and forgotten. Yet their desire to put the past behind them was shared by many other Americans in the postwar years.[60]

THE PAST ALSO LOOMED large for divided families dealing with the question of their legacy. Many nineteenth-century Americans were keenly aware of their bloodlines, valuing genealogy and record keeping as an important family duty. Stories of the past were passed down from generation to generation in an effort to keep alive a tradition that would inspire unity and a common pride among kin. In the wake of the Civil War, many families turned to documenting their relatives' experiences in battle. Stories about the wartime heroics of family members were epitomized by Varina Davis's two-volume work about her husband, the Confederate president. Former soldiers also documented their ordeals in memoirs. These accounts gave descendants, both Union and Confederate, something to be proud of and helped ease their memories of those tumultuous four years. This process, though, was not so easily accomplished for divided kin: What should a family do when its wartime legacy included internecine division?[61]

This was an important question for the Ellets of Washington, D.C., and the Cabells of Virginia. On the surface, the Ellets had a proud story to tell about the family's valor during the war. One member, Charles Ellet Jr., gained distinction for lending his engineering skills to the construction of the Union steam ram fleet in the Mississippi and for commanding that fleet as a colonel. Ellet steered the fleet to several victories, including one in June 1862 at Memphis, where he fell mortally wounded on the deck of his flagship, the *Queen of the West*. Ellet received a full military funeral befitting a war hero, with infantry, marines, and a ceremony at Independence Hall in Philadelphia, as well as a number of newspaper tributes to his military service.[62] His wife Elvira and four children received numerous letters of condolence from extended family and friends and were roundly assured of Charles's heroism in the war. Among those tributes were expressions of sympathy from Elvira's kinfolk, the Cabells of Virginia, who sent several of their own members into the Confederate army. All this goodwill failed to assuage Elvira's grief, however; "completely broken down" by her husband's death, she died several weeks after he did.[63] Charles's children took solace in his legacy, with his nineteen-year-old son, Charles Rivers "Charlie" Ellet, serving on the same fleet and his oldest child, twenty-two-year-old Mary, attuned to any victory earned by the steam rams. "My desire for the glory *and* distinction of *that* name is intense," she wrote.[64]

Charles Ellet's legacy of heroism seemed safe and undisturbed by the war's end. Yet within weeks of the South's surrender, some members of the extended family began to question Mary Ellet's professed "intense" loyalty to her father when she made it known that she planned to visit her mother's sister and other Cabell relatives in Virginia in June. Mary had appreciated the family's expressions of condolence during the war, especially when she confronted another loss, the death of her brother Charlie in 1863, and wanted to thank them for their kindness. Mary's paternal uncle, Alfred Ellet, objected heartily to the trip and wrote her a long letter explaining why. "I will not attempt to disguise from you my astonishment, I may indeed say mortification," Alfred began, wasting little time in urging his niece to rethink her decision. He could understand Mary's desire to see her mother's family, calling her affection for her aunt "commendable," but, he argued, "you have allowed your affection to controll your actions." In his view, "it is not the proper time to renew your feelings of intimacy with some of those people," when the hands of her Virginia relatives "are still red with patriots blood." There was an "impropriety" in "too soon forgiving them." More than anything else, though, Alfred believed that the trip would have a detrimental effect on Mary's younger siblings' memory of their father. Cornelia ("Nina") and Willie were vulnerable to the "influence" of former Confederates and might learn to "look lightly upon the crime which made them orphans."[65]

Alfred Ellet's tough language broached the same issue confronted by the Halseys: how to square one's memory of the war — and, in this case, reverence for a Union family member's service — with one's affection for Confederate kin. In contrast to the Halseys, though, Alfred was less willing to see affection as a positive good than as a threat that would overshadow an important part of his family's wartime past. Alfred, who had assumed a paternal role in Mary's life after her parents' deaths, feared that she and her siblings would fall too easily into a relationship with the Cabells in which they would be compelled to forgive, and therefore forget, the indirect role the Virginians played in their parents' deaths. Why Alfred felt so strongly, when other Union men, such as the Halseys, encouraged their kin to forget the past, is unclear. Perhaps it was because he had served alongside Charles on the steam rams and felt a deep, personal need to protect his brother's naval legacy. Moreover, Alfred was not well acquainted with the Virginia Cabells and may not have felt the same personal obligation as blood relatives to be magnanimous. Whatever his motivation, he could not have predicted just how prescient were his warnings about the power of affection. Mary did go to Virginia, and not long after her arrival began a flirtation with her cousin, thirty-one-year-old William Daniel Cabell, a widower living in Nelson County.[66]

By September 1865, after she had returned to Washington, Mary Ellet and her cousin exchanged weekly letters filled with expressions of love. She kept this correspondence secret from the Ellet family, however, for William Cabell represented everything that her uncle despised. Cabell had wholeheartedly supported the South during the war, and, though not serving in the Confederate army himself, he had hired a substitute to take his place and sent several of his slaves to work on fortifications in Richmond. In 1864 he was appointed an impressment agent and for the duration of the hostilities supplied the Confederate army with food and supplies necessary to continue its fight. Cabell's loyalty to the Confederacy stirred mixed feelings in Mary. Part of her eagerly wrote love letters but another part seemed to share her uncle's concerns. She once declared, right after telling William how much she "missed" him, that their illicit romance was "inexpedient" and "wrong."[67] Cabell, for his part, set out to ease her conscience over the next several months by boasting that he had become a fully reconstructed ex-Confederate. He proudly announced his new post as a notary public in Nelson County — "Oh, for the good of my country now!" — and his vote to reunite the Episcopal Church. He also wrote about his trip to Washington to obtain presidential pardons for himself and six friends and family members and complied with Mary's wish (and with Federal law) that he remove the Confederate buttons from his cape. He explained his willingness to do all this by the fact that he was "unmindful of the past."[68]

This former Confederate professed everything that Mary, and her Union uncle, would have wanted, but was he sincere? Cabell, after all, had lost a wife during the war, leaving him with two daughters under five years old. Moreover, according to his own inventory, he had lost $8,355 in damages to a mill, tobacco houses, and other property after Union troops occupied his acreage in March 1865. Emancipation left him without a supply of labor, after the twenty-four male and female slaves he owned were freed, and an 1870 census indicated that he possessed no real or personal property.[69] By all accounts, there was no reason that Cabell's views would differ from those of Joseph Halsey or any other former Confederate who resented what had transpired between North and South. Maybe it was the widower's desire for a wife to care for his young children that encouraged him to appease his Union kin. The fact that Mary was technically a blood relation may have made her more appealing than any other Union woman. Whatever the reason, Cabell was relentless in his campaign to deny his attachment to the Confederate past. "To me there is no longer North, South, East and West but one whole indivisible country," he would declare a year later.[70] Something inside Mary still doubted his sincerity, however. Although she continued to correspond with him regularly, she also referred to his "somewhat self-satisfied assertion that 'you had no prejudices'" against the Union and several times in jest called him "my unprejudiced Friend & Cousin."[71]

Mary Ellet demanded honesty from her cousin. Her words suggest that she could tolerate some degree of pro-Confederate sympathies on his part, that she could understand how these sentiments were a natural result of the war. What seemed to matter more to Mary than his outward expressions of reconstruction were his deeper feelings on the other subject that competed for her attention—preserving the memory of her father, Charles Ellet. She was heartened in February 1866 on receiving a letter from William that, for the first time, aired his thoughts on her father's war activity. Cabell mentioned a profile of Ellet that he had seen in *Harper's New Monthly Magazine* and told Mary how much Virginians respected him: "On several occasions I heard some of our leading & most intelligent men" remark "that the South had much to fear from the accurate knowledge and powerful intellect possessed by Charles Ellet." William hoped that Mary would not be surprised by that statement and asked rhetorically, "Did you ever think for one moment . . . that I was capable of doing less than the *fullest justice* to those who differed with me in opinion"? Pleased by Cabell's reflections, as they both acknowledged his pro-Southern opinions and expressed reverence for her father, Mary forwarded his letter to her Uncle Alfred (who, by this time, was aware of the romance but chose to ignore it).[72] To hear William express that sentiment toward her father no doubt helped allay Mary's conflicting loyalties. By March 1867 Mary Ellet and William Cabell were engaged to be married.

The Ellet family was shocked by the engagement. Mary's other uncle, Edward, also a brother of Charles, called the news "awful intelligence" and told Mary that her paternal grandmother, Mary Israel Ellet, had "serious objections to your marrying a Southern man." The family had suspected for some time that marriage was on the horizon, especially after William made repeated trips to visit Mary in Washington, but formalization of the alliance deeply offended their innermost wishes. Mary's Uncle Edward eventually resigned himself to the news, acknowledging that Mary had a "perfect right to decide this matter to suit yourself exclusively." Her Uncle Alfred at first refused to discuss the engagement, noting only that "I do not approve of the course you have pursued." Within a week he too modified his tone, informing Mary that he would try to attend the wedding and that he was sorry that her grandmother was being "so hostile" about the match. This was, indeed, quite a turnaround for a man who once forbade Mary even to visit her Virginia kin. He explained simply that it was his duty to "accept the inevitable, as the South will the reconstruction act." (The engagement, in fact, took place in the same month that Congress passed the Reconstruction Act, ushering in radical Reconstruction.) Alfred's brother Edward made a similar link between the nation and his family, calling the Ellet-Cabell marriage an "amicable form of 'reconstruction,' which may sanctify and typify, I hope, the much desired union of the North & South."[73]

The uncles' words were not empty rhetoric but suggested instead a conscious effort to reconcile the marriage with their competing war memories. To cast it in the higher terms of national reconstruction was to justify the alliance in a way that was still faithful to their brother's legacy. Indeed, if the marriage could help, even in some small way, to reconstruct the union, then it would be serving the cause for which Charles Ellet had fought. Along these same lines, William Cabell, with his own concerns about appearing to be reconstructed, also embraced the notion that his marriage would serve the larger purpose of reconciling the nation. In the days leading up to the ceremony, he made such allusions in several letters, declaring at one point that "secession is null & void & not in our law books," and for that reason Mary must not "rebel" or back out of their marriage. She objected to being compared with the South, however, forcing William to vow that "I wont [sic] compare *my Mary* to a secessionist again." Cabell then turned his language around and returned Mary to the Union side by declaring that "*submission to Mary & the U.S. Government has become a virtue with me.*" The wedding itself was rife with symbolism of the unification of North and South. The guest list included the names of prominent Union and Confederate officers, with the exception of Robert E. Lee, who Mary crossed off the list in deference to her "conscience." The ceremony took place on Cabell's land in Virginia, and afterward the couple went North for a honeymoon, spending time at Niagara Falls — a place filled with meaning for the Ellets, as it was the site of one of the first bridges built by Mary's father. Mary and William then returned to Virginia, where together they established a boys' school on the Cabell property.[74]

THE STORY OF Mary Ellet and William Cabell, much like that of Joseph Halsey and his New Jersey family, reveal the difficulties encountered by divided families in the process of reunion. In the immediate postwar period, when the fighting had stopped, families such as these turned to the complicated question of how to forge a long-term understanding. They considered what it meant to "reconcile" — what should be expected of individual family members and what should be overlooked? Few people demanded that their kin fully agree on the issues of the war, preferring to forget what had once divided them. Their reconciliation turned instead on a related issue of sentiment, on whether an emotional bond could be as powerful as duty had been. Divided families realized that the biggest hurdles to successful reunion were all of the competing feelings produced by the hostilities between North and South — frustration, resentment, anger, and memory. The war could not be forgotten so easily, and that reality cut against an easy renewal of personal relationships. Both the Halsey and Cabell-Ellet families ultimately demonstrated that family reunions were neither quick nor simple but rather were characterized by long and drawn-out conflicts.

Yet their stories ended differently. The Halseys achieved an uneasy truce, agreeing to move forward while constantly grappling with the divisions that continued to take on new dimensions. But William and Mary Ellet Cabell never reached such a truce with at least one member of the Ellet family, Mary's paternal grandmother. Mary Israel Ellet had always opposed their marriage and continued through the ensuing years to let her views be known. She forbade Mary's younger sister, Nina, from even thinking about marrying a Southerner and asked — through Nina's letters — that Mary return wax miniatures of Mary's great grandfather. She also wrote Mary out of her will and appears never to have spoken to her again. Mrs. Ellet's memoirs, written just before her death in 1870, explain that the estrangement was necessary to up-hold the legacy of her son Charles. "My glorious son's memory is too deeply imbedded in the inmost recesses of my heart to ever call his murderers my friends," she wrote of her granddaughter's marriage to a Confederate sympa-thizer. Consequently, "a partition has been built between my son's children and myself, that time can never pull down." This Ellet could not envision a family that included both a martyred war hero *and* a man who supported those who had killed him. Her family thus was permanently divided.[75]

Most divided families were visibly scarred in the immediate postwar pe-riod. They spoke cautiously in everyday conversations, made mutual decisions to end the regular visits that had been customary before the war, and even filed for divorce. In 1870, for example, Stonewall Jackson's Unionist sister ended her marriage to a man with known Confederate sympathies.[76] Some family members stopped speaking to one another altogether: Union general George H. Thomas reportedly never placated his Confederate sisters and never went home to Virginia to visit them again.[77] Such cases are impossible to count or measure, however, as the break in communication meant that they left no letters documenting their postwar relationship. More commonly seen are those relationships that vacillated between periods of tension and calm. Virginian Lucy Muse Fletcher, who used her diary in 1869 to vent her anger at her Union sister, removed those sections following the sister's first visit later that year. The visit, after years of bitterness, proved to be a "gleam of sunshine," Fletcher reported. Newly determined to forget the past, Fletcher literally erased it from her journal—but she could never, like so many other divided family members, erase the past entirely from her memory.[78]

Reconciliation in the Popular Imagination

The question of remembering—or forgetting—the wartime past reverberated far beyond the walls of individual households. It was central to the nation's attempt to reconcile, as former Unionists and Confederates alike compared their war memories in the process of searching for common ground. The past entered into all facets of Reconstruction—from the practical issues of voting rights, economic assistance, and emancipation to the more emotional dimension of national reunion. Many discussions of the nation's reconcili-ation invoked a central theme: the ordeal of families. Newspaper editors, politicians, and fiction writers again, as they had during the war, gave divided families a metaphoric power in representing the country's tribulations. In the

THE RETURN HOME.

COLUMBIA. "Tell me, Soldier, did you not pass a Wayward Sister of mine on the road?"
RETURNING SOLDIER. "I did. I fetched her a good part of the way myself; but she says
she don't require my services any more now; and here she comes over the hill."

"The Return Home," *Harper's Weekly*, May 20, 1865
(Courtesy of the American Antiquarian Society)

immediate postwar years, from 1865 through 1870, images of divided families
were useful in imagining the reconciliation, rather than the division, of the
nation, and in fostering a reunion culture in which "forgetting" the past was
paramount.[79]

Images of the nation as a reconciled family initially captured the wide-
ranging debate over how quickly — and on what terms — the South should
be readmitted to the Union. An illustration entitled "The Return Home,"
published in *Harper's Weekly*, depicts Reconstruction as a voluntary reunion
of sisters, one from the North and one from the South. The Northern sister,
dressed as Columbia, asks a soldier for help in finding her "wayward sister,"

shown in the background walking down a path toward the United States. This sisterly image suggests a reunion of equals, a natural embrace of horizontal relations, ushered in solely by the bonds of mutual love and affection. Force is no longer needed to bring back the South; as the soldier notes, the Southern sister "don't require my services any more now" but is making her way back to her sister on her own accord.[80] Former Confederate soldier Clarence Prentice, himself the son of a Union father, also turned to siblings as a model of reconciliation that would honor the war service of the defeated. In the 1865 song, "Why Can We Not Be Brothers," Prentice wrote:

> We know that we were rebels,
> We don't deny the name,
> We speak of that which we have done,
> With grief, but not with shame;
> And we never will acknowledge
> That the blood the South has spilt,
> Was shed defending what we deemed
> A cause of wrong and guilt.

The idea of brotherhood inspired Prentice's call for a national reunion based on the mutual respect of two peers, rather than on apology and forgiveness.[81]

In contrast, others found in the sibling image a means of mocking calls for an easy reunion. Artist Thomas Nast's "The Tearful Convention," published in *Harper's Weekly* in September 1866, ridiculed the National Union Convention held the previous summer by supporters of President Andrew Johnson's lenient Reconstruction policies. In the center of the print, Nast, a Republican critical of Johnson, has depicted an actual occurrence at the convention: Governor James L. Orr of South Carolina walking arm-in-arm with General Darius N. Crouch of Massachusetts. Although intended to demonstrate sectional reunion, the gesture becomes in Nast's portrayal a false display of "brotherly affection." Surrounding the pair are images of crying men and animals, most notably a crocodile holding a Confederate towel with tears streaming down its cheeks. Any brotherly sentiment on the South's part, Nast implies, is no more than "crocodile tears," which should be regarded with suspicion.[82]

Other cartoonists who were skeptical of an easy reunion utilized generational imagery to depict a more penitent return of the South. In the January 1866 issue of *Frank Leslie's Illustrated Newspaper*, a tearful boy (or "naughty boy" as he is identified in the image) with the word "South" printed across

"The Tearful Convention," *Harper's Weekly*, September 29, 1866
(Courtesy of the American Antiquarian Society)

NAUGHTY BOY—" *Oh, Uncle, do take this foolscap off me, all the fellows make fun of me so !*"
UNCLE SAM—" *Yes, yes, my boy, as soon as you are good—as soon as you are good.*"

"Naughty Boy and Uncle Sam," *Frank Leslie's Illustrated Newspaper,*
January 13, 1866 (Courtesy of the American Antiquarian Society)

his chest holds a book entitled "Obedience" and asks his Uncle Sam to take
the foolscap off his head. The uncle, who holds a pardon, replies, "Yes, yes,
my boy, as soon as you are good."[83]

   This language of generations, and specifically of father and son, was popular in political speeches, too, in the initial postwar years. Maryland's Governor A. W. Bradford, a Democrat with a rebel son of his own, exhorted a
Baltimore crowd in 1866 to "welcome back the returning prodigal." He urged
his listeners to remember their duty to the "paternal government" and to
seek forgiveness over punishment when dealing with the defeated South.[84]

Bradford's colleague, Tennessee's Republican governor William G. Brownlow, on the other hand, believed that this language was too magnanimous. "It is interesting to note the difference between the Prodigal Son and these returning rebels," Brownlow argued in a speech published in the *Nashville Daily Press* in the fall of 1865. The prodigal son "did not secede," like the Confederates, and, more significantly, the son sincerely repented his sins. "Do rebels, coming home, come repenting of their unparalleled crimes?" Brownlow asked. "Are they not coming back because they are whipped, and 'perish with hunger?'" Frustrated by members of the Tennessee legislature who quoted this parable when advocating the restoration of former Confederates' voting rights, Brownlow demanded more careful scrutiny of Southerners' "repentance" before allowing them to return to the national household.[85]

This imagery of the South's prodigality shows how family language could serve diverse—and conflicting—interests in the postwar period. It was useful to both Democrats and Republicans, former Confederates and former Unionists, precisely because it embodied so richly the dilemmas circumscribing the nation's reunion. Family images did not simply throw a sentimental veil over the war and its aftermath; rather, they captured the practical as well as the emotional dimensions of reconciliation, in which the voluntary bonds of affection worked alongside the more obligatory bonds of duty and obedience to reunite divided Americans. In families like the Halseys and Cabell-Ellets, that affection proved tenuous. Fiction writers, on the other hand, had less difficulty envisioning that affection and offered the most vigorous explorations yet of how forgiveness, repentance, and love could provide lasting reunion. Indeed, stories often associated with the latter part of the century—tales of intersectional marriage or the romantic union of men and women across sectional lines—became widespread in this immediate postwar period.[86]

One such tale was "Rum Creeters Is Women," a short story written by Union war veteran John W. DeForest and published in *Harper's New Monthly Magazine* in March 1867. As we learn in the first sentence, this story revolves around "a girl's heart" that is agitated by "strong and contradictory enthusiasms" during the war. The protagonist, seventeen-year-old Fannie Pendleton, was attending school in Connecticut when she became engaged to Frederick Huntington, a student at Yale College. On the South's secession, Fannie's father compels her to return to their home in Winchester, Virginia, breaking up her romance with Frederick. In Virginia, Fannie endures all the wartime hardships of a Southerner: runaway slaves, worthless investments, the death of her father and brother in battle, and barns on the family property burned by occupying Union troops. By the middle of the war Fannie is desperate for relief and visits the Union provost marshal to seek protection from further destruction. The provost marshal, she discovers with shock, is none other than Frederick Huntington. The sight of her former fiancée is very distressing to Fannie, a proud Southerner who believes in the Confederacy "with enthusiasm, with passion, with anger" and who had sworn off her love for any Yankee. But she cannot "retreat" from the meeting, and Frederick cannot stop "advancing," so without much conversation the two quickly resume their courtship.[87]

The general outline of this story follows other tales of intersectional marriage. A Union man, typically a soldier, falls in love with a Southern woman and, despite the adversities of war, wins her hand in the end. The circumstances surrounding their courtship are almost always discouraging, ranging from disapproving families to wartime deprivations. Nevertheless, the men and women come to realize that "it is better and holier to love than it is to hate," in the words of the narrator in "Rum Creeters," and overcome such adversity. The overpowering force of love is front and center in these stories, marking a departure from the false affection highlighted in wartime seduction and romantic triangle tales. The postwar authors revised the popular saga of Union men and Confederate women, replacing romantic dysfunction with harmony. They may have once departed over whether any deep attachments could prevail beneath the sectional divide, but many now seemed to agree that such loyalties — or affection — did exist. Yet, in this revised version of the romance the power of love is still somewhat mysterious and does not always work smoothly. In "Rum Creeters," Fannie cannot abandon her Southern allegiance and in a moment of weakness betrays Frederick Huntington to Confederate authorities. This leads to his capture by one of Fannie's cousins and then to a skirmish in which Frederick kills the cousin in retaliation. Fannie is distraught but within a year agrees to marry Frederick Huntington anyway. "There was a passion of love in these two young hearts," the narrator explains, "which could make them forgive and ignore the terrific past."[88]

The romantic union thus marked a triumph over the past. At the end of another tale, a Union man vows to "forgive and forget, or remember the past only to make the future redeem it."[89] In other stories writers symbolized the past as a problem to be overcome with the presence of ghosts who trouble the protagonists and with the death — and effective burial of the past — of men and women who threaten to thwart a romantic union.[90] (In "Rum Creeters," Fannie's father, who had forcibly removed her from her fiancée's clutches at the start of the war, dies just before she and her former beau reunite.) These authors shared the same concern with forgetting or putting the past in its proper place that preoccupied families such as the Halseys and the Cabell-Ellets, but they were more successful in burying that past in their fiction. Marriage, more so than other familial relationships, offered them a useful imaginative vehicle. As the *Louisville Daily Journal* explained in May 1865, in an appeal to Northerners and Southerners to literally unite through marriage, romantic unions could build "a strong and beautiful bond of unity, respect, and interest" that could replace "the dreary and morose antagonism" between the two sections. Marriage connoted a fresh start, rather than the resumption of a previously held kin relationship, and implied a more permanent union than had ever before existed between two individuals. This made it an ideal metaphor for a postwar nation that was eager to leave the past behind.[91]

Writers encouraged intersectional marriage by eliminating the extreme contrasts between the two protagonists that had characterized wartime tales of romantic dysfunction. There are no great moral dichotomies between the characters, no villains or victims, no exceptionally good or outrageously evil individuals — although differences are acknowledged by the presence of two genders. In Elizabeth Haven Appleton's "What Five Years Will Do," which appeared in the *Atlantic Monthly* in 1868, a Southern woman is "pretty," "gentle," and "dignified," whereas her father is "noble, considerate, and generous." Her Union suitor — in that he is "wise" and a "model" Christian gentleman — is not very different from her father. Although these individuals are far apart in their sectional allegiances and therefore disagree on the war, their characters, their internal sense of worth and virtue, are fairly similar. The moral contrast between Unionists and Confederates that once drove wartime seduction tales has disappeared, and in its place the authors have offered another dichotomy: politicians versus the people. "I wonder if the politicians who made the war ever think how they are keeping people apart as well as making them miserable," muses the narrator of Appleton's story. The work of the "politicians" is objectionable because "there are no two people in the world better suited to each other" than the Union man and Confederate woman in this tale. Writers like Appleton do not blame one side or the other for the troubles plaguing families and the nation but turn their attention instead, as real families such as the Halseys did, to the legislatures and leaders who started the war. Politicians were an easily identifiable target for any lingering sectional animosities.[92]

Outside the realm of politics, the "people" in these stories do everything they can to undermine the division and antagonism of war. Every account of intersectional marriage contains some act of magnanimity between men and women on opposite sides, a gesture of assistance not unlike the real aid exchanged within divided families during the war. This assistance ranged from Confederate women helping a Union man to escape from prison, to a Union soldier protecting a Confederate woman's home from invasion, to a Union family sending financial aid to a daughter in the South.[93] The inclination to provide help is considered natural and is rarely questioned. As one Confederate woman explains, she was taught as a child "to love thy neighbor as myself, and to do unto others as I would have others do unto me."[94] The aid flowed across both Union and Confederate lines; occasionally, a single act of assistance sparked a romance, thus a deeper bond of love, between a man and a woman. The implication of these gestures is that left alone, unfettered by politicians, people have a natural inclination to be conciliatory and to blur the divisions between them. Or, as John DeForest put it, "Humanity is stronger than politics."[95]

Other authors suggested that more than love or humanity compelled men and women to reach out to one another across the sectional lines. A deep agreement on the war and sectional issues could also facilitate the marriage of men and women on opposite sides. The novel *Sunnybank*, written in 1866 by Marion Harland (Mary Virginia Terhune), centers on the romance of Harry Wilton, a Union soldier, and Elinor Lacy, the daughter in a First Family of Virginia, whose parents are strong Unionists and slaveholders. Theirs is a tale of Northern and Southern Unionists struggling with the obstacles presented by wartime separation as well as with the "flattering lures of specious politicians" who constantly work to pull them apart. Division is imposed on them rather than chosen, and, for that reason, more easily overcome at war's end. Harry and Elinor ultimately marry in a quiet ceremony after Harry vows to "let the dead Past bury its dead," sealing an attachment that had been disrupted only temporarily by the war.[96] The common bond of Unionism, repeated in other stories, served a useful purpose to authors like Harland who were searching for something to reunite the nation. Northerners may have wanted to believe that all Southerners were Unionists at heart, that there was never a deep division of sentiment but rather a superficial and forced division that could be surmounted. In Harland's case, this scenario was also autobiographical. Mary Virginia Terhune—Harland—was born and raised in Virginia by slaveholding parents (her father was a Whig); she married a Northern Presbyterian minister. During the war she supported the Union but remained sympathetic to Virginia, and two of her brothers served in the Confederate army.[97]

In postwar tales of intersectional marriage, white women such as Elinor Lacy were especially important as agents of conciliation. This was in marked contrast to wartime fiction, in which Southern white women had figured centrally precisely because of their ability to irritate, disrupt, and provoke animosity between the sections. In wartime Union fiction, women were prominently seductresses, spies, and smugglers — agents of sectional tension and division — who, in engaging in decidedly unwomanly behavior, fueled the conflict between North and South. But in the postwar embrace of intersectional marriage, these women were less defiant and troublesome, although they often continued to represent the South. They became wives, lovers, and nurturers — rather than corrupters — of affection. They were less dominant and more feminine, easing sectional relations rather than irritating them. Writers thus returned white women to their idealized role in American society, resolving the larger question of reunion, in part, through a resumption of traditional gender roles.

The general outlines of conciliation through marriage were promoted most heavily by Northern writers and editors, who dominated the publishing industry after the war. This is perhaps not surprising given the emphasis that Union writers of wartime fiction had placed on the deep, unbreakable bonds of blood and heritage that existed between the sections. It took only a short imaginative leap for these writers to envision an intersectional marriage between North and South after the war. Former Confederates, who had once rejected the idea that any such ties endured between North and South, found this a harder transition to make. Those who were able to relinquish their earlier viewpoints and incorporate the notion of intersectional marriage in their writing were taken up by Northern publishing outlets, such as *Harper's Weekly* and the *Atlantic Monthly*, making it difficult, at times, to detect the sectional loyalties of the authors of these romances.[98]

Those former Confederates who did not accept the metaphor of reunion through love and rejection of the past sought out their own publishers. The *Southern Magazine*, in Baltimore, one of the few remaining outlets for distinctly Southern writing after the war, published a number of stories in which romance figured centrally — but for different purposes.[99] In these tales, it is the marriage of a Confederate woman and a Confederate man that cements the ties binding members of the former Southern nation. Such stories, which differed little from wartime tales of Confederate family unity, offered a symbolic reinforcement of the emotional solidarity that former Confederates wished for themselves once their hopes for political and economic independence were destroyed.[100] At the same time, though, such postwar fiction shared with intersectional marriage tales the same pattern of triumph over division and difference. The men and women in these Southern stories often possess very different characteristics: in one tale, a rich widow and a less well-to-do teacher marry; in another, the union is between a refugee and someone whose property remained untouched during the war. These characters acknowledge the cleavages exposed in Southern society during the war, but the marriage between them suggests a desire to overcome those divisions and usher in a postwar society in which former Confederates remain united.[101]

POPULAR FICTION thus envisioned an ideal script for reconciliation that real divided families, as well as the nation as a whole, could follow. Scenarios of intersectional marriage, in particular, neatly contained the past — especially ugly "politics" — as something to be forgotten and thus reinforced the boundary between the public world of war and the private arena of family life. Love was free to flourish between Northern men and Southern women, overwhelming the sectional border that once prevented them from marrying. That was, at least, the idealized vision of reunion. The real-life reunions of divided families examined in this chapter — from Union fathers and their repentant Confederate sons, to the Halseys and their slaveholding Virginia brother, to Mary Ellet and her Confederate fiancé — reveal far more difficulty in making that distinction between public affairs and private sentiments.

These families found that on a practical level the war's intervention in their lives could begin to facilitate their reconciliation. Simple concerns about the welfare of family members living in the line of battle helped to obscure resentments about assuming opposing sides in the war. At the same time, government policies, such as prisoner assistance and exchanges, offered formal mechanisms through which families could remain in contact, maintain the sense of duty that had long bound them, and keep some semblance of family ties intact. Yet this same intrusion of war and politics in their intimate lives also proved to be a serious obstacle to a second level of reconciliation — that involving emotions. Once the war ended, and families such as the Halseys and Cabell-Ellets tried to move on with their lives, they found that the war — now referred to as "the past" — could get in the way of resuming their affectionate attachments. The past could not be as neatly boxed up and buried; on the contrary, it lingered to provoke long-lasting tensions, even estrangements, that forever transformed the way some family members related to one another.

These real cases highlight the fiction surrounding the popular imagery of divided families, a fiction that deserves further examination. The imaginative dissolution of the Union-Confederate border by postwar authors was made possible not only by a reinforcement of the boundary between public and private life, but also by a defense of existing social borders in American society. Women were no longer the fierce partisans portrayed in wartime works but loving (and dependent) companions to men. They returned to a subordinate position that depended on stark boundaries between the genders. Racial borders, ostensibly subverted by emancipation and the Confederate surrender, also were significant in postwar intersectional romances. As we will see, African Americans, who once occupied a conflicted position in wartime literature, emerged in less provocative roles in the reunited national family.

Reconciliation and Emancipation

CENTRAL TO Herrick Johnstone's intersectional romance, *Sergeant Slasher; or, The Border Feud* (1865), is a man named only "Moonshine." A slave working as a spy for the rebels, Moonshine rescues Jasper Slasher, a white East Tennessee Unionist held captive by Confederate guerrillas. Moonshine assures Slasher that his loyalties are really with the Union and its fight against slavery, vowing to "never leabe your flag!" Little else is revealed about Moonshine, except that slavery separated him from his mother in Virginia; his ability to serve the Union is most important to the story. A little reconnaissance work enables Moonshine to assist Slasher in another critical way: he arranges for a joyful reunion between the Unionist and his fiancée Daisy Deans, a "lovely wild flower" living with her wealthy Confederate family. Moonshine does not receive any payment for his good deeds, however, as he is shot dead by Confederates in an ensuing battle before he can fully realize his freedom. The Unionists win the battle, and three days later Slasher and Deans are married in a ceremony that might not have been possible without the slave's intervention.[1]

Writers like Johnstone penned their tales of intersectional romance against the backdrop of the principal drama of the Civil War: the emancipation of nearly four million men and women. The destruction of slavery, full of conflict and triumph, was a natural subject for writers who fancied themselves chroniclers of the war and its aftermath. But its portrayal had larger implications. What role should former slaves play in these allegories for the reconciled nation? Slavery had long enabled white Americans to conceive of their nation as a predominantly white one by denying citizenship to black men and women. The end of slavery offered an unprecedented challenge to that national self-image. How would the former slaves and white people relate to one another as citizens? Authors both Union and Confederate thus positioned themselves within the wider national debate on the status of newly freed African Americans as they envisioned what loyalties would bind blacks not only to former Confederates, as in wartime literature, but also to all whites across the reconciled nation.

Herrick Johnstone, a Unionist, chose to depict a short-lived loyalty between Moonshine and Jasper Slasher. Moonshine dies in the middle of battle, leaving open to question how the two men would have interacted after the war. We cannot know Moonshine's postwar prospects or whether he would have reunited with his mother. His attachment to the white Union officer superseded any loyalties to his own family. This was significant in a story of the Civil War, as one of the most striking displays of loyalty in this period was that of former slaves to their own kin. Family division, indeed, was never solely a white phenomenon. Slavery had divided black families in profound ways, and the prospect of freedom created new stresses during and after the war. But, like the white families described in the previous chapter, African Americans largely sought to minimize the damage of division and reunite with long-lost or estranged relatives. Revisiting themes of family division through the experience of the enslaved is thus revealing, and, when viewed alongside the popular literature, suggests how black families' real-life loyalties challenged—and may have hardened—white Americans' self-image as a reunited national family.

African American Families Divided and Reunited

African Americans confronted deep family divisions that, stemming from a lifetime of servitude, were unique but no less complex than those experienced by white families. When they were slaves, they grappled with family division constantly. The slave trade created physical division, wrought by a master's decision to sell human beings and separate them from their families permanently. Masters further divided slave families by inserting themselves in their intimate lives, most drastically by taking slave women as concubines. In addition, all slave families experienced the everyday conflicts and estrangements in the normal course of life.[2] But war intensified another kind of division in the lives of enslaved African Americans, a division over the means and meaning of freedom. As word spread of secession, and of the coming of Union troops, men and women throughout the border slave states were determined to seize the opportunity to liberate themselves. But how should they seize their freedom?

Few disagreed over whether they should be freed or whether they wanted to be free. Rather, the issue centered largely on the *process* of seeking freedom. Did freedom require them to leave the plantation? When and where should they go? How? The answers to these questions appear today in a remarkable collection of correspondence written by freedmen and Union government officials during the war.[3]

Seeking freedom was particularly complex in the border states, where slaves appeared to have various options for liberating themselves but where the dangers of freedom were also evident at every turn. The border states literally marked a border between slavery and freedom, providing a geographic buffer between the free states and the Lower South cotton states, where slavery was most significant in total numbers. The border states also contained the highest percentage of free African Americans, a population that embodied the example and — to the slaveholders' lament — possessed the means of helping slaves to freedom. This was the region where Union troops were especially visible once war came, occupying vast stretches of the Confederate states of Virginia and Tennessee, while drafting men in the Union states of Maryland, Kentucky, Missouri, and Delaware. Here freedom might have seemed attainable to enslaved African Americans by virtue of their proximity to the free states. Instead, however, once Abraham Lincoln issued the Emancipation Proclamation in 1863, his government drew a new border between slavery and freedom, declaring an end to slavery in the Confederate states while leaving the institution untouched in the Union states, whose loyalty it so desperately needed to maintain. Enslaved African Americans in these Union states thus found themselves caught between slavery and freedom in a new way, living in a region of slave states nearly surrounded — to the north and to the south — by the promise of freedom.[4]

U.S. emancipation policy helped to create an unprecedented division in enslaved families, as Union troops began accepting male slaves from the border states as soldiers (in some cases impressing them by force), while expecting their families to remain with their masters. This was, from the Federal perspective, a way to placate Union slaveowners while unburdening themselves of the expense of caring for the families of African American soldiers, as the Union army was already doing in "contraband camps" in the Confederacy. This created a dilemma for enslaved families in the Union border states: Should a man leave for the army and fight for his freedom, or should he remain on the plantation and ride out the war with his kin? The decision to fight thus had serious implications for slave families. As thousands of men left the plantations (indeed, a greater percentage of black soldiers fought from the border states than from other regions), they moved closer to freedom while their wives, children, and other relatives remained in slavery.[5]

Some of these men challenged the Union policy anyway and brought their families with them to army camps. A number of soldiers in Kentucky, for example, who rushed to serve after an initial ban on black enlistment in that state was lifted in 1864, set up tents and temporary housing for their families at Camp Nelson, near Lexington. For a brief time Union officials appeared to tolerate their presence, albeit grudgingly. Yet these informal family camps proved short-lived, which Joseph Miller, a slave attached to the 124th Colored Infantry, learned to his sorrow. In October 1864 Miller had arrived at Camp Nelson with his wife and four children, ranging in age from four to ten. He managed to keep them in his tent for a month, until a guard told him on November 22 that all families had been ordered to leave the camp by the next morning. "The morning was bitter cold. It was freezing hard," Miller wrote a few days later in a sworn statement. "I told him [the guard] that my wife and children had no place to go. . . . He told my wife and family that if they did not get up into the wagon which he had he would shoot the last one of them." His family left. Later that night Miller went searching for his wife and children and found them six miles away in Nicholasville with a large group of other soldiers' families who had also been expelled. Miller and the other soldiers testified that their kinfolk had struggled to keep warm around a fire in a structure variously described as an "old shed" and a "meeting house." They had almost no food and insufficient clothing for the early winter cold. Soon the adverse conditions took their toll on the families. Miller discovered that "my boy was dead," and after walking back to Camp Nelson that night, he returned the next day to dig a grave and bury his son.[6]

The alternative for men like Joseph Miller — leaving their family on the plantation — could be equally agonizing and deadly. The enslaved women and children left behind often became targets for frustrated masters, who, angered by the men's departure, retaliated against their families by withholding rations and medical care or by beating them severely. Patsey Leach of Woodford County, Kentucky, recounted how her master grew especially abusive after her husband left and was mortally wounded in a battle in Virginia. "When my husband was killed my master whipped me severely saying my husband had gone into the army to fight against white folks and he my master would let me know that I was foolish to let my husband go." The master's beating was so severe that blood oozed from the lacerations on Leach's back. She later fled to Lexington, so desperate to run away that she left without four of her children.[7] Such treatment led other wives to turn their frustration on their husbands. Martha Glover, of Mexico, Missouri, wrote her soldier-husband that her masters "abuse me because you went"; they not only refused to care for her children, but constantly "quarrel" and "beat me scandalously." Although the masters were to blame for her treatment, Glover faulted her husband, too: "Oh I never thought you would give me so much trouble as I have got to bear now." His departure left her vulnerable, and she wished he had "staid with me & not gone till I could go with you." She concluded, "You ought not to have left me in the fix I am in."[8]

This letter suggests how freedom, and the choices surrounding the seizure of freedom, could incite conflict within enslaved families. Martha Glover had grown resentful of her husband's departure, as he left her unprotected from her masters' severe beatings and their children "helpless" with only one parent to care for them. His apparent failure to meet her expectations as a husband and father — that they remain together, not necessarily on the plantation, but somewhere, anywhere — was foremost in her mind. Her husband's reply, if there was one, has not survived, but he might have viewed his familial duties differently. Certainly his departure to fight for the Union was at least an indirect service to his family, since a Confederate defeat would guarantee freedom for all slaves — his own family included. Conflicts in the pursuit of freedom were thus exacerbated by slaves' different understandings of themselves as families and of their individual roles within them. What was a man's duty as a husband, father, or son — to fight for their loved ones' freedom over the long term or to ensure their protection and sustenance in the short term?

Or what was a woman's duty? It is possible that Martha Glover's husband disagreed with her decision to stay on the plantation; he may have urged her to leave with him or at least flee somewhere else. As another soldier put it to his wife, "It lays to your own choice to stay or come."[9] But something kept women like Glover on the plantation, something more than the restrictions imposed by Union policy or the tenacious grip of their masters. Glover said that she wished her husband had stayed "till I could go with you" — perhaps she was waiting until she had a secure place to go to, or perhaps something on the plantation, in the slave quarters, kept her there. In other cases, women stayed behind because they feared that escape would jeopardize the health and welfare of their children and elderly kin. Remaining on the plantation was, in their view, necessary to the survival of their families, which these women felt bound to consider as mothers, daughters, and extended kinswomen. Their reluctance to leave was therefore not to be confused with loyalty to the master or mistress. A slave woman might exhibit loyalty by her very presence on the plantation, but it was loyalty to her family. As with men, the question of freedom and how to obtain it could not be considered apart from women's positions in their families.[10]

Freedom thus could divide enslaved families along the lines of gender and generation, paralleling the wartime divisions experienced by white families. As black men took advantage of the opportunity to serve the Union, they left behind wives and children, as well as mothers, fathers, aunts, uncles, and grandparents, in slavery. This division was created in part by Union policy, which, according to the editors of *The Black Military Experience*, "designated black men as the liberators and defenders of black women and children, who, whatever their wartime service, occupied the position of defenseless dependents."[11] Yet, such division also exposed latent tensions between men and women, elders and children, in slave families. Enslaved men, as numerous historians have documented, had been deprived positions of authority in their families and communities by their owners' constant intervention in their lives. Now, by joining the army, these men could derive some satisfaction and authority from earning wages and serving the nation. This new status prompted one man, who managed to persuade Union officials to allow his family to follow him, to write his wife: "You can see I have power." Perhaps his wife was relieved by this declaration of "power"; like Martha Glover, she may have been eager for her husband's protection of his family. Or, if accustomed to what historian Deborah Gray White has termed an "egalitarian" relationship that evolved between enslaved husbands and wives, she may have recoiled at this expression of male dominance. However she responded, this was "power" that, for many enslaved men, was not always reconcilable with the immediate needs and concerns of their families, creating a conflict between men and women over their duties to their families and their duties to the cause of freedom. These tensions were alleviated somewhat in March 1865, one month before the war ended, when a joint resolution of Congress declared that the families of all African American soldiers would be granted their freedom. Yet it was already clear that black loyalty to family and freedom, like white loyalty to family and nation, could become locked in a struggle without an easily identifiable resolution.[12]

This struggle, however, was not as unprecedented in slave families as it had been in divided white families. On a basic level, this was a conflict over how to manage the intrusion of "public" affairs — of politics and war — into family life, an intrusion that had prompted white families to try to protect what had always been, for them, an idealized boundary between public and private. White families, as we have seen, redefined their wartime conflicts as "domestic" affairs, arguing over the degree of filial rebellion in a son's Confederate service or of a father's role in influencing a woman to take a stand that opposed her husband's. Such translations made wartime divisions seem familiar and manageable and, by minimizing the difficult political questions, helped insulate their intimate relations from war. Even when U.S. officials came to view divided families as potentially treasonous, these families argued vigorously that their private relationships were separate from, and had no impact on, the national conflict. Black families in slavery, on the other hand, did not rush to defend a separation between these spheres. Throughout their lives they had found themselves surrounded by "public" pressures, from the slave market and their owners' economic interests, which separated them routinely, to the laws and politics of Southern states that refused to recognize them as families. The war was to some degree a continuation of these pressures, as they had never lived with the same sense of public and private as white families had. Black families therefore did not bring into the war the same defensiveness of the boundary between these spheres; they even accepted the presence of war in their family lives as a necessary — albeit painful — vehicle for achieving their liberation.[13]

This interplay between public and private continued in 1865 with the ratification of the Thirteenth Amendment, which abolished slavery forever and placed reunification at the forefront of ex-slave families' quest for freedom. Throughout the South newly freed men and women set out to find relatives they might not have seen in years and to reunite families long separated by the slave trade. These journeys sometimes lasted months or years, taking family members across state lines and covering hundreds of miles to places where their kin had been last seen or heard from.[14] These were not searches that individuals could easily conduct alone; indeed, many black families turned to the public for help, most notably by placing ads in newspapers seeking information about the whereabouts of their long-lost kin. Residents of Middle Tennessee, for example, inserted short appeals in Nashville's *Colored Tennessean* under the heading "Information Wanted." Armistead Bogle, a veteran of the 44th U.S. Colored Infantry, sought news of his sister, Edmonia Bogle, who had been sold from Tennessee to Texas "years ago." Ben and Flora East, who had not seen their children Polly and George Washington since 1849, offered a $200 reward "to any person who will assist them, or either of them,

to get to Nashville, or get word to us of their whereabouts, if they are alive."
These men and women, like the white divided family members who turned
to newspaper advertising to communicate with one another during the war,
found this very public medium useful. They did not, however, shield their
identities with abbreviations and initials, as the whites had done in their ads.
On the contrary, ex-slaves depended on readers to recognize a name and
become involved in the search for their kin.[15]

The public airing of their private ordeals appears to have helped distinguish the reunions of separated black families from those of divided white
families. But the difference may have lain in their contrasting expectations for
reunion rather than in their actual experiences. Divided white families, as we
have seen, exerted great effort to shelter their private affairs from public view,
but they also came to recognize that their family's welfare was inextricably
linked to the nation's, that the nation's reconstruction depended in part on
the resumption of personal relations like theirs. The public mechanisms of
national reunion and reconstruction therefore could be exploited to bring
their families together as well. Taking advantage of prison policies, they sent
food, clothing, and money to incarcerated relatives; they also used parole
policies to bring enemy kinsmen home. Their enlistment of Union policies
to reunite family members turned out to be little different from the efforts of
former slaves to obtain assistance from the Bureau of Refugees, Freedmen, and
Abandoned Lands — more commonly known as the Freedmen's Bureau.

Established as an instrument of Union control in the South, and an agency
for reconstructing the region's war-torn society and instituting a free labor
system, the Freedmen's Bureau initially played an important role in the reunion of former slave families. Ex-slaves approached the Bureau for assistance
in locating missing kin, in performing marriage ceremonies that would give
legal sanction to relationships previously ignored by the law, and in settling
disputes when a family's reunion triggered conflicts over child custody or
spousal support.[16] Spotswood Rice of St. Louis, Missouri, may have spoken
for others when he expressed confidence in the Bureau's ability to help him
free his daughters from their slave mistress. He believed that the government
that had already freed so many slaves would guarantee their freedom, too.
As he wrote to the mistress, "I have no fears about geting mary out of your
hands[;] this whole Government gives chear to me."[17] For some ex-slaves,
receiving assistance from the Federal government was just compensation for
having served in the Union army. Aaron Oats, a soldier in Virginia, asked the
secretary of war for help in liberating his wife and children from their master in

Kentucky: "And as I am a *Soldier.* willing to loose my life for my Country and the liberty of my fellow man I hope that you will please be So Kind as to attend to this."[18] Former slaves such as Rice and Oats, like white family members, saw the connection between the larger, political goal of reuniting the nation and the liberation of their families from slavery; Abraham Lincoln himself had fused the effort to save the Union by ending slavery when he issued the Emancipation Proclamation back in 1863. The tragedy of the postwar years was that this connection between the public welfare of the nation and the private lives of former slaves did not remain firm in the minds (and actions) of Freedmen's Bureau agents and other government officials. Notoriously underfunded, and staffed at times by people sympathetic to white landowners, the Bureau became of limited help to former slaves and ultimately folded with the demise of Reconstruction.[19]

But reunion was about more than the practicalities of finding and reuniting with lost kinfolk. Ex-slave families, like divided white families, also experienced reconciliation as an emotional process, one involving affection and feelings. White families found this process to be the most difficult part of reconciliation, as they continued to try — but failed — to insulate their private emotions from their very disparate war experiences. They tried to "forget" the past — to let bygones be bygones — but often remained angry with or estranged from family members for years, even if they lived under the same roof. The public world of war could never be shut out of their relationships. Black families grappled with a different past, but they faced a similar challenge in considering how — and whether — to separate that past from their private lives. The lingering scars of bondage had an impact on all of their relationships, from the challenge of becoming reacquainted with relatives long separated, to the absence of family members who were never found, to the enduring memory of rape and assault. The inner, emotional world of former slaves may never be as visible to us as that of divided white families, who left behind numerous letters and diaries. But unquestionably the legacy of slavery and war would continue to torment the emotional lives of freedpeople.[20]

African Americans in the Reunited National Family

It is also not difficult to see the loyalty that animated the reunions of ex-slave families. Regardless of their masters' attempts to keep them apart during slavery and regardless of the fact that emancipation policies may have worked initially to separate kin, the former slaves' searches for one another testify to

the strength and endurance of their family ties. Their fidelity to family was
little different from the loyalty that often kept divided white families from
severing all connections over the course of the war. Yet it was very different
from the way in which some of those white families, and the novelists whose
works they read, chose to imagine the loyalties of black people.

During the war white Northern and Southern authors had disagreed over
whether kinship connections bound white and black people, whether real
blood ties or the figurative bonds of the "family black and white" united
blacks and whites. Confederates celebrated master-slave affection, whereas
Unionists emphasized an antagonism between the two that often stemmed
from real blood ties. But by the late 1860s and early 1870s, a distinguishing
feature of this collective fiction was the drift of writers from both sections toward similar conceptions of loyalty. As Southern writers joined their Northern
counterparts in depicting revived affections binding whites across sectional
lines, Northerners came to embrace a more traditionally Southern conception
of black loyalty. In these postwar tales of intersectional marriage and family
reunion, African Americans are subordinate and less troublesome to whites,
often more loyal to whites than to members of their own race. "I don't want
to be free," exclaimed a black woman in a story that recycled the motif of the
loyal slave. The author of another tale assured readers that "freedom has
had little effect on them." Former slaves "are perfectly satisfied," this author
continued, "and as faithful as the generations before them." Such loyalty to
whites, even after emancipation, entitled black men and women to a place
in the national family, these stories suggested, a place that was central but
subordinate to the "marriage" of North and South.[21]

African Americans became the facilitators of sectional reunion in postwar fiction. For example, in John DeForest's "Rum Creeters Is Women," a
slave urges a suffering Confederate woman to seek help from the local Union
provost marshal, who, it turns out, is her estranged fiancée. The slave's encouragement is pivotal in forever reuniting this Union man and Confederate
woman.[22] Similarly, in J. M. Smythe's Southern novel, *Mary Clifton: A Tale
of the Late War* (1865), a slave man gives a Union man flowers to include in
his correspondence with a Confederate woman. In a Northern tale, a slave
provides key evidence to help a Union soldier arrest two thieves — an act that
endears him to a Confederate woman. And in another Northern story, a slave
informs a Union soldier of a death in a Confederate woman's family, news that
compels the soldier to visit the woman and rekindle an estranged romance.[23]
In all of these stories, enslaved African Americans provide crucial advice or

information, or perform a pivotal act, that makes possible a romance and eventual marriage between a Union man and a Confederate woman.

At other times slaves simply provide loyal companionship that helps whites survive the war—and remain alive and well—so they may be reunited with loved ones when it is over. Jane G. Austin, a native of Massachusetts, offered this scenario in *Dora Darling: The Daughter of the Regiment* (1865). Set in western Virginia, a border state "full of divided households," this novel follows the ordeal of twelve-year-old Dora Darley, the daughter of a white, slaveholding family who finds herself caught between her Union mother and her father and brother who serve in the Confederate army. Feeling distraught and isolated by her family's division, Dora takes solace in the companionship of the male slave Picter, who, despite being freed by Dora's mother at the onset of war, does not abandon the Darley family. Picter initially leaves to serve as a cook in an Ohio regiment, but, on seeing Dora again soon afterward, remains by her side for the duration of the war. There is "perfect harmony" between the former slave and Dora, as Dora takes on nursing duties in the regiment and relies on Picter for assistance. This story is at once antislavery—Dora's mother declares her hatred for slavery on freeing Picter—but still reluctant to envision a place for Picter in wartime society that is separate from his white family. His dedication to that family, in fact, is a virtue, as Picter helps Dora secure the release of her brother after his capture by the Ohio regiment and assists her in her travels north, where the Darley siblings reunite with their long-lost Northern aunt. Although this story does not end in a marriage, thanks to the support of the loyal Picter, Dora is able to reunite with her Confederate brother as well as to reconcile her Virginia and Massachusetts kin.[24]

African Americans are a part of these stories of national reunion, but only as slaves, as willing and loyal enablers of the reconciliation of white people. They make reunion possible, but they are not reunited themselves. Their welfare, their future, and their freedom—so central to the war itself—are all subordinated to the reconciliation of white Americans. In *Dora Darling*, we never know what happens to Picter, such as where he finds employment after the war and whether he starts his own family. Other tales do not feature African Americans at all. The national family imagined in all of these stories is predominantly white, as African Americans are connected to, but not an equal part of, this national family at war with itself. This trend is less pronounced but still evident in the works of more racially progressive writers. In 1865 Epes Sargent, a white Northern novelist whose stories were among the most sympathetic to blacks during the war, wrote "Strategy at the Fireside." Here, a slave's death provides a wake-up call to a Confederate woman about the evils of Southern society and motivates her to seek out and marry a Union man. Sargent does not go so far as to romanticize the Confederacy or slavery, but the slave is still the pivot around which the story turns, making possible—but not entirely participating in—the reunion of North and South.[25]

Such characterizations essentially "whitewashed" the past, to borrow the words of historian Nina Silber, allowing white Americans to forget the contentiousness surrounding emancipation and black freedom. Both Silber and historian David Blight have documented how the literature of the late nineteenth century—especially of the 1880s and 1890s—emphasized sectional reunion at the expense of black progress, consigning African Americans to positions of servility, subordination, and, most commonly, the familiar role of the loyal slave. As Blight puts it, "How better to forget a war about slavery than to have faithful slaves play the mediators of white folks' reunion?" What is striking about this scenario in the fiction of the immediate postwar period examined here is that it appeared earlier than often assumed, coinciding with, rather than resulting from, Reconstruction. The speed with which Northern writers joined their Southern counterparts in endorsing these portrayals of black Americans as early as the 1860s and 1870s underscores the anxieties that white Americans experienced as nearly four million African Americans had their freedom guaranteed by the Thirteenth Amendment in 1865. Black liberation clearly challenged the racial hierarchy so long reinforced by slavery—and so long relied on by white Americans, Northern as well as Southern.[26]

In the postwar literature of the 1860s and 1870s, shifting characterizations of African Americans and especially individuals of mixed race most clearly reflect these emerging fears. No longer are the blacks in Northern stories celebrated for acts of revenge against white kin, as they were during the war, but instead are viewed as suspicious—and dangerous—people. Edmund Kirke (James Roberts Gilmore) offered this new perspective in *Among the Guerrillas* (1866). This novel features Robert, the son of a slave woman and her white master, a prominent Virginian named "the Captain." Robert grew up a "privileged" slave but did not learn until later in life that his master was also his father. This fact, along with the knowledge that his master-father had sold his mother to be a gambler's mistress, stirs intense feelings of revenge in Robert, who, when war comes, vows to meet the Captain in battle "and strike, at one blow, for my mother and my people!" After several attempts to stab and shoot his father, Robert finally succeeds in a skirmish that takes place, appropriately, on the grounds of his father's plantation. The narrator does not praise Robert for killing a Confederate; instead, he is pronounced "insane" and a "murderer," as if only illness or a mental lapse can account for the slave's resentment of his white father. In the postwar world of healing and sectional reconciliation, black revenge against the white South is no longer cause for celebration.[27]

Revenge was exactly how some whites characterized blacks' postwar embrace of freedom. After serving in large numbers in the Union army, literally battling their former masters, African Americans now began to mobilize politically. Within their communities, leaders emerged to hold rallies and voting drives, and generally assert their voices in Reconstruction politics. This political activity, which led to officeholding for hundreds of black men during Reconstruction, and which occurred at the same time that blacks assumed control over their families and religious lives, struck some white Americans as nothing more than an undeserved punishment for slavery. Black men wielded power, or threatened to wield power, over their former masters, a reversal in Southern politics that for some whites — in North and South alike — threatened a smooth reconciliation of the divided nation. Certainly there were white Americans, namely Radical Republicans, who supported black progress wholeheartedly. But others did not, and their ambivalence, which eventually prevailed in the demise of Reconstruction, is evident in early postwar fiction. Kirke dramatizes this ambivalence in *Among the Guerrillas*, in part by choosing a mulatto as his major character. Indeed, men of mixed-race parentage comprised a significant portion of black political leaders immediately after the war.[28]

Kirke's story evinces little of the sympathy for mixed-race people that appeared in Northern wartime stories of divided interracial families. The blood ties that once inspired fascination and intrigue now are merely tragic. Near the end of his novel, Kirke, who made many trips to the South before and during the war, offers the dire conclusion that it is the mixed-race man and woman who will one day be conquered, since "it is not desirable that the mulatto should live." This judgment echoes a popular mythology about mixed-race people in the postwar period and especially in late-nineteenth-century America: that mulattoes were mentally, physically, and biologically inferior and destined only for death. "Abundant observation has shown," Kirke writes, "that after three or four generations of breeding in-and-in, the mulatto becomes enfeebled, and dies out, as the mule dies, stamping his image on none of his species." It was a myth that brought a measure of comfort to white Americans: the image of the dying, or "tragic," mulatto, as authors of fiction imagined them, soothed fears that the nation's racial borders — no longer protected by slavery — could be permanently subverted by mixed-race people. It also reinforced the simultaneous tendency to reinscribe the division between white and black as white Americans attempted to close the distance between North and South.[29]

This concern with drawing lines between white and black in the newly reunited national family encouraged other writers to depict just the opposite: a mixed-race person who is not only healthy and vibrant, but also possesses the blood ties necessary to redeem former slaves. In the illustration " 'Uncle Tom' and His Grandchild," displayed prominently on the cover of *Harper's Weekly* in November 1866, a mixed-race girl teaches her black grandfather how to read. A short paragraph accompanying the image explains that the plantation scene tells "at the same time a very sad and a very hopeful story." The grandfather is "a pure negro" whose inability to read reflects one of the injustices of slavery. Yet the girl, who possesses "far more of 'Southern chivalry' in her veins than of negro blood" and who has attended school, now helps her grandfather — an act that "spoke of a new era for the negro race." But it was a "new era" only for a man named "Uncle Tom," recalling the central character in Harriet Beecher Stowe's best-selling novel of 1852 whose personality had been exaggerated in dramatic renditions as loyal to white people. It is also only a "new era" when a mostly white person takes charge of educating her black kin. White blood, the illustration suggests, civilizes black people — a point that clearly distinguished between black and white by emphasizing the superiority of white blood.[30]

Various representations of lamented, or tragic, people of color persisted throughout white writers' tales of the nation's reunion. African Americans are loyal to the national family, some authors go further to suggest, in part because of their failure to establish a viable life of their own after freedom. They are either helpless or conniving, unintelligent or dangerous, but all are unable to meet the challenges of emancipation. Some cannot or refuse to find work, others go hungry, while still others, most commonly, fail in the central pursuit of freedom for so many former slaves after the war: cementing the bonds of their own families. In a story set in Maryland, a black man's drunkenness prevents him from having a stable marriage and he is forced to continue living with his white employers — just as he did as a slave. In Helen W. Pierson's "Chip," published in *Harper's New Monthly Magazine* in July 1865, a slave woman called "Milly Mo" flees a plantation. On finding it difficult to carry her crying infant, however, she is forced to choose whether to continue her flight to freedom or to return home and care for her child. She decides to pursue the

"'Uncle Tom' and His Grandchild," *Harper's Weekly*, November 3, 1866
(Courtesy of the American Antiquarian Society)

former course, abandoning her baby by the roadside; a white Union soldier later comes upon the infant and rescues him. The infant, "Chip," or as the narrator describes him, "that little waif, cast so utterly adrift," is then taken to the North and raised in a happy home by the soldier and his fiancée. The message of this tale is clear: the slave woman is selfish and cowardly, unwilling to care for her child, and it takes a white father figure to ensure a future for the black child. According to these works, kinship with white Americans—that

TESTING THE QUESTION.

MRS. RANDOLPHUS (*a descendant of* POCAHONTAS, *and former owner of many slaves*). "Here, Uncle TOM, go down to the Tavern and tell your master I want him."

UNCLE TOM. "No, I won't. I ain't your Uncle or your Arnty any more: I'SE YOUR EKLE" (equal)!

"Testing the Question," *Harper's Weekly*, August 12, 1865
(Courtesy of the American Antiquarian Society)

is, a kinship based on continued dependency — is in the best interest of newly freed slaves, as well in the best interest of reuniting North and South.[31]

Such a formulation of dependent kinship in the national family shows how much the Southern view of blacks and black rights — once characterized by condescending references to the plantation "family black and white" — had come to dominate in the immediate postwar period. But this perspective did not go unchallenged. "Testing the Question," an image that appeared in *Harper's Weekly* in August 1865 and was likely drawn by a white artist, offers a more ambiguous portrait of kinship between whites and blacks. The African American man in the picture rejects the patronizing labels of "Uncle" and "Arnty" used by masters to refer to slaves, as well as the loyalties that supposedly existed beneath those labels. That he is an "Uncle Tom" who renounces this stereotype so forthrightly to a Virginia plantation mistress is even more meaningful. At the same time, however, because his grammar is weak and his desire to be "ekle" must be translated to "equal," the reader is left to wonder if he has the intellectual capacity to be truly "equal."[32]

African American leaders rejected the formulation of an unequal and dependent kinship between the races more unequivocally. "Was it . . . because we were not really human that we have not been recognized as a member of the nation's family?" Henry Turner, a minister, asked in frustration at an Emancipation Day celebration in 1866. In demanding the political, economic, and social rights of the newly freed people, leaders such as Turner did not repudiate the language of family. Rather, former slave and abolitionist Frederick Douglass, one of the nation's most skilled orators, had long advocated for blacks "the most full and complete adoption in the great national family of America." In this speech, delivered in 1863, Douglass equated membership in the "national family" with obtaining a position of equality, a point he reinforced by calling for "one great law of Liberty, Equality and fraternity for all Americans without respect to color" — a reference to a motto popular in the French Revolution, one that stressed the familial relationship of brotherhood to imagine a nation of equals.[33]

Other black leaders looked to Christianity to conceive of a national family in which equality, rather than dependency, was paramount. In January 1865, near the end of the war, a group of "American Citizens of African Descent" petitioned the Union Convention of Tennessee, claiming "to be men belonging to the great human family, descended from one great God . . . who bestowed on all races and tribes the priceless right of freedom." That family was one in which God was the father, a father who made no "degrading distinction against his children, because of their color." Likewise, Alabama blacks comprising Mobile's National Lincoln Association appealed to the Alabama State Constitutional Convention in September 1865, describing themselves as "part of the family of this great republic, and a part of that family . . . created by the same Almighty Being with whom there is no discrimination on the part of cast [*sic*] or color."[34] These men imagined the national family on a spiritual level, one created by God and thus one that did not make distinctions by color or create the dependencies envisioned by postwar white writers. In this way they drew on Christianity to subvert the language of family used so readily by whites to justify black subordination in the postwar period.

SUCH WORDS MAY have been powerful, but nothing exposed the fallacy of the postwar white imagination more than the actions of African Americans themselves. As white writers produced their stories of white reunion and black subordination, newly emancipated men and women fought against their dependence at every turn, not only by creating their own schools and churches and negotiating labor contracts, but also by seeking out and reuniting with their families. Former slaves clearly demonstrated that their families were not as dysfunctional as white authors imagined and could come together again without the paternalistic intervention of white people.

Emancipation thus widened the gap between the reality and the imagery of postwar family reconciliation. Reflecting more than simple creative license, that gap highlights the significant force of racism that would sustain the nation's racial borders and impede social justice for decades to come. It especially indicates white fear of the progress made by newly freed African Americans, progress evident, in part, in the reunification of their families. The loyalty that drew black families together could not go unnoticed by white Americans. It was a threat in that it demonstrated a measure of freedom from subservience to whites. Yet to ignore that loyalty and, instead, to visualize a national family that emphasized blacks' loyalty to white Americans, to the detriment of their own families' welfare, was to offer an imaginative bulwark against black independence. The reunion of white Northerners and Southerners came first, while blacks remained dependent, subordinate members of that family, with race and slavery receding into the background.[35] Here the push toward forgetting the past proved successful, for the selective historical memory of the Civil War as a battle fought within a loving national family only endured and strengthened as the century progressed.

Epilogue

DIVIDED FAMILIES had evolved in the popular imagination since Abraham Lincoln's dire prediction in 1858 that a "house divided" could not stand. No longer seen as tragic, they emerged from the war and immediate postwar period as something to be celebrated, models of reunion and enduring loyalty rather than hatred and division. With each passing year, it seemed, Americans maintained their attachment to this image with vigor, as other voices joined fiction writers in embracing divided families. Among them were Southerners claiming to have been Union sympathizers during the war in an effort to win compensation for destroyed property from the U.S. Southern Claims Commission in the 1870s. Some of these claimants openly acknowledged the division within their families as a means of testifying to their loyalty: a willingness to depart from Confederate family members was proof of their firm devotion to the Union. Family division became almost a badge of honor. Later in that decade and beyond, the authors of anecdote books, a genre of Civil War writing that professed to offer "true" accounts of the war, presented — among other tales of divided families — stories of battlefield encounters between brothers as examples of the "heroic" and "thrilling" nature of war.[1]

Veterans' magazines that surfaced in later decades, such as the *Confederate Veteran* and the *Blue and Gray*, perhaps did the most to associate family division with honor and heroism. *Blue and Gray*, for instance, published an 1893 poem by Union veteran Matthew H. Peters entitled "My Brother and I," that recounted Peters's and his Confederate brother's simultaneous wounding in battle:

> Both of us fought for what we thought right,
> But of duty each took a different view;
> Both of us entered the perilous fight
> And did our duty as patriots do —
> But he wore the gray and I wore the blue.

Both brothers were motivated by "duty," the poem states, and thus they shared a common bond that transcended their divided national loyalties. Neither was wrong, neither deserved punishment; instead, the two men could reunite with a common pride in their wartime service. Such sentiments were echoed in photographs of blue and gray veterans standing side by side, equally honored, at what were sometimes termed "fraternal" reunions.[2]

There were always voices that dissented from this celebration of family division. Mark Twain poked fun at the pretensions of a war of "brother against brother" in his 1868 short story, "The Siamese Twins." Fascinated with the real-life conjoined twins, Chang and Eng, Twain wrote a fictional tale in which he put Chang on the Confederate side and Eng on the Union. Both fight in their respective armies and, at the Battle of Seven Oaks, take one another prisoner. The twins are then exchanged for each other, but Chang the Confederate, later convicted of "disobedience of orders," is again imprisoned. His brother Eng, though "entirely innocent," "felt obliged to share his [brother's] imprisonment." As a "just reward of faithfulness" to his brother, however, Union officials agree to release the two men. Leaving unstated the anatomical connection that, of course, forced the men to be faithful to one another, Twain mocked the claims of Northerners and Southerners that a more voluntary, deep-seated affection would rise again to reconcile Americans on both sides of the sectional divide.[3]

Ambrose Bierce went even further to challenge the sentimentality of national reunion with his own brand of realism in the 1880s and 1890s. His stories of divided families are dark and violent and end not with reconciliation, but often with the death of one family member at the hands of another. In "A Horseman in the Sky" (1891), a Union son shoots his Confederate father; in "Three and One Are One" (1908), a son leaves his Confederate home to join the Union army, only to learn later that Federal troops shot and killed his entire family. A Union veteran with few illusions about the bravery or heroism of soldiers at war, Bierce found in divided families a subject better suited to highlighting the traumas experienced by fighting men. Especially jarring is his story entitled "The Affair at Coulter's Notch" (1889), which depicts a Union officer named Coulter choosing duty to his army over that to his family when he agrees to begin firing a cannon at his own house. Coulter's gunfire eventually kills his Confederate-sympathizing wife and their infant child. In this and other tales, Bierce did not gloss over violence with the paeans to bravery seen in other works of Civil War fiction. Instead, he described a wife's blood-soaked hair, as well as the severing of an infant's foot — images to counteract the popular celebrations of sectional reunification.[4]

Yet the momentum behind the celebratory culture of family division overwhelmed these dissenting voices well into the twentieth century. Even today, Americans continue to invoke family division almost as a source of pride. Throughout the research for this book, in fact, I was struck by the number of people who declared, "My ancestors were divided too!" Their stories were often fascinating but rarely led me to tangible letters, diaries, or other documentation of their division. I heard the same thing from my own family members, who told me that two of our ancestors, brothers from Missouri, may have enlisted as soldiers on opposing sides of the war. In fact, a closer look at this story persuaded me that the two men apparently fought in the same Union regiment. Clearly a vibrant oral tradition of Civil War family division exists in American culture and has allowed the history of divided families to reverberate into the present. Some of these stories are likely true, others are probably exaggerated or even false. Still, the tendency to claim division raises lingering questions: Why, in the absence of substantive proof, do so many people still want to claim family division for themselves? Why, after Abraham Lincoln initially held up the "house divided" as a tragedy to be avoided, and after real divided families agonized about their conflicts during the war, would subsequent generations embrace, even brag about, their own divided houses?

Any answers to these questions must consider the various layers of meaning that have surrounded divided families, layers that undoubtedly have changed, and have been added to, over time. For some Americans, the compelling scenario of division in one's family may allow them to feel more connected to the authentic experience of war. To be divided suggests that one's ancestors did not sit on the sidelines as passive spectators but instead must have been deeply devoted to their principles if they were so willing to split from their kin. And, as literature and documentaries have come to revere the Civil War as a triumphant event, a transformative fight for justice and freedom, it is no surprise that many Americans today would desire a personal connection to it. Family divisions are thus intriguing not as obscure, private quarrels, but as conflicts deeply embedded in the central drama of the war.[5]

Indeed, the families featured in this book grappled with the fundamental question of loyalty: What drove midcentury Americans to take opposing sides and kill one another in war? Families slaveholding and nonslaveholding, prominent and obscure, spanning territory from Missouri to Maryland, from

Delaware to Virginia, all confronted this basic question when they learned of relatives whose national loyalty fell on the other side of the sectional divide. Confusion and anger often followed, as people realized that the very institution long revered as a model for national unity had failed to remain united. Family loyalty had proven weak, fueling a domestic crisis that both fed and embodied the larger national crisis. Divided families demonstrated that Civil War loyalties were not clear-cut, not easily determined, and not always easily sustained — but, as a result, almost always complex. This is especially significant given that these families lived in the border states, where the battle for the hearts and minds of the people decisively affected the outcome of the war. Yet it may be that the enduring fascination with these families stems as much from what they have obscured as from what they have exposed.

Members of divided families — as well as those who wrote about them — sought to repair the strained ligaments of family loyalty by reinforcing protective boundaries around their domestic lives. To varying degrees they distanced their domestic conflict from the larger national conflict by minimizing their political differences, viewing those differences instead through the more familiar lens of generation, gender, and kinship. This translation — or domestication — of their wartime divisions may not have been embraced wholeheartedly by all, but nonetheless it offered these family members a measure of protection by reinscribing borders between their public and private lives. This translation was more difficult to achieve in reality than in the imagination, however, as real families struggled to mend the lingering scars of war while writers of fiction romanticized the nation's conflict as a family quarrel easily resolved by the latent bonds of love and affection. This simplified story of a national family division and reunion allowed Americans to obscure the very things that pulled them apart, to move beyond the violence and death that Ambrose Bierce lamented so greatly, or the status and equality of former slaves that Frederick Douglass urged Americans to remember.

The divided family image thus grew more resonant as a metaphor for the nation as it became distanced from the reality of war. Its simplicity is likely part of its appeal, as with any metaphor, making it easier for Americans then and now to understand and embrace a war that touched so many deep nerves in American society. The history of divided families in the border region, however, offers a simultaneously complex view of the Civil War. More than two armies fighting over a political border, it was an event in which an entire population called into question how its members would relate to one another across many social borders: generation, gender, and race. These families show

how all-encompassing the war was, crossing, most profoundly, the idealized border between public and private life around which so many Americans sought to structure their lives. Divided families, in all their forms, thus endure today as complex yet simple, full of meaning but also easily comprehended. And that may be the point. The ability to capture so much, particularly about a war that continues to excite such curiosity and yet be easily understood, may explain why divided families have resonated in American popular culture for so long — and will likely continue to do so in the future.

Appendix

A NOTE ON NUMBERS AND SOURCES

WHILE CONDUCTING this research, I was often asked: "How many divided families were there?" "More than you might think," I often responded to what was—and still is—a difficult question to answer. Because no survey or special census of divided families was conducted during the war, there is no way to count them with any precision. Moreover, if there had been such a source, it is doubtful that all families would have owned up to their division. Even estimates are difficult to make.

Divided families do appear in a variety of other primary sources from the war. Their words and perspectives are clearest in the manuscript papers (diaries and letters) that some of them left behind. For that reason, the portions of this book that analyze individual families in the greatest depth (especially Chapters 1, 2, and 3) are based primarily on the 166 families represented by manuscript papers (see table).

I have provided additional data about this sample of families in endnotes throughout the book. Cross-checking the manuscript papers against the U.S. population census revealed distinct patterns regarding who these families were, such as their household composition, wealth, age, and slave ownership. Not all of the families with manuscript papers could be found in the census, however, so at times smaller samples are presented in the endnotes.

The larger sample of 166 still represents only a fraction of the total number of divided families encountered while researching this book. Newspapers offer glimpses of others, but, as I suggest in the text, it is often difficult to distinguish fact from fiction. For this reason, I have not counted these other families and instead have examined the rumors for their commentary on the phenomenon of family division. Still other sources, such as government documents, give more reliable information on divided families, and in my analysis of them (especially in Chapter 4), I offer additional data on the number of divided families represented. Government sources also provide evidence of divided African American families, but as their divisions are even harder to document

Family Division Recorded in Manuscripts, by State

State*	Generational	Marital	Brothers	Sisters	Brother-Sister	Total
Delaware	2	1	—	1	—	4
Kentucky	28	7	27	1	2	65
Maryland	4	4	5	—	1	14
Missouri	3	4	6	—	—	13
Tennessee	9	7	6	—	—	22
Virginia	2	5	5	4	6	22
West Virginia	4	4	1	1	—	10
Washington, D.C.	—	2	—	—	—	2
Other**	3	6	5	—	—	14
Total	55	40	55	7	9	166

* "State" refers to the primary place of residence, although in some cases, especially that of siblings, the family members occupied two residences in different states. In those cases, the family is classified according to the state in which its members once lived together.

** "Other" refers to cases in which the family once lived together outside the border region, but during the war at least one member lived in a border state.

and count with any precision (as discussed in Chapter 7), I have not included them in this larger sample, either.

In the absence of perfect data, I also have taken seriously the constantly repeated "thousands" and "hundreds" by border state residents in referring to the number of divided families in their states or the nation as a whole. Such statements, I believe, indicate a far greater number of divided families than were ever documented in manuscript sources.

Notes

Abbreviations

DPA   Delaware Public Archives, Dover
Duke   Rare Book, Manuscript, and Special Collections Library, Duke
       University, Durham, North Carolina
Emory Special Collections and Archives, Robert W. Woodruff Library,
       Emory University, Atlanta
FDS   Fort Delaware Society Collection, Delaware City
FHS   The Filson Historical Society, Louisville, Kentucky
Hagley Hagley Museum and Library, Wilmington, Delaware
HSD   Historical Society of Delaware, Wilmington
LC   Library of Congress, Washington, D.C.
MC   Museum of the Confederacy, Richmond
MDHS   Maryland Historical Society, Baltimore
MHS   Missouri Historical Society, St. Louis
NA   National Archives, Washington, D.C., and College Park, Maryland
OR   U.S. War Department. *The War of the Rebellion: A Compilation of
       the Official Records of the Union and Confederate Armies.* 128 vols.
       Washington, D.C.: GPO, 1880–1901. *OR* citations take the following
       form: volume number:page number. Unless otherwise indicated,
       citations are from series 1.
PCA   Philadelphia City Archives, Philadelphia
SHC   Southern Historical Collection, University of North Carolina,
       Chapel Hill
TSLA   Tennessee State Library and Archives, Nashville
UKY   Margaret I. King Library, University of Kentucky, Lexington
UVA   Albert and Shirley Small Special Collections Library, University of
       Virginia, Charlottesville
VHS   Virginia Historical Society, Richmond
WHMC   Western Historical Manuscript Collection, University of Missouri,
       Columbia
WKU   Kentucky Library, Western Kentucky University, Bowling Green

Introduction

1. On the family metaphor in contexts outside of the American Civil War, see, e.g., Lynn Hunt, *Family Romance*; Petrone, "Family, Masculinity"; and Castigliola, "Nuclear Family." On the family metaphor in the American Revolutionary and post-Revolutionary periods, see Fliegelman, *Prodigals and Pilgrims*, and Anne C. Norton, *Alternative Americas*.

2. Scholars who have considered the divided family image as part of larger studies of the Civil War include Forgie, *Patricide*; Mitchell, *Vacant Chair*; Anne C. Norton, *Alternative Americas*; Dicker, "Home Repair"; and Christine Anne Bell, "Family Conflict." These studies explore the family metaphor mainly from the standpoint of literary, psychological, or cultural analysis. My book departs from them by grounding its examination of divided family imagery in the social reality of actual divided families, looking at the resonances and interconnections between the two.

3. The novels and films dealing with divided families are too numerous to list here, although a recent documentary on divided families is *Divided Houses: Families Split by War*, A&E Television Network, 1999. The few scholarly treatments of actual divided families have emerged only recently. See Clinton, *Tara Revisited*, 53–57, and *Fannie Kemble's Civil Wars*; McPherson, *For Cause and Comrades*, 14–15; Stephen W. Berry, *All That Makes a Man*, 200–218; Judith Lee Hunt, " 'High with Courage' "; and Inscoe and McKinney, "Highland Houses Divided." Two published diaries have been marketed specifically as sources on family division. See Chadwick, *Brother against Brother*, and Johnston, *"Him on the One Side and Me on the Other."* All of these scholarly works tend to deal with a few individual families; none offer the comprehensive study of family division as a more widespread phenomenon that is presented here.

4. Kirkland, *Pictorial Book of Anecdotes*, 529–30; Garrison, *Unusual Persons*, 151. For other examples from anecdote books, see Vickers, *Under Both Flags*, 138; Member of the G.A.R., *Picket Line*, 70–71; Moore, *Civil War in Song*, 76, 132, 347; and Greene, *Thrilling Stories*, 86–92, 175–76.

5. See, e.g., Fellman, *The Making of Robert E. Lee*, 85; Farwell, *Stonewall*, 424, 455, 489; and Kirwan, *John J. Crittenden*, 446–48.

6. Maria I. Knott to Sallie Knott, December 25, 1861, Knott Collection, WKU; William Daniel Jr. to Sister, April 23, 1861, Cabell-Ellet Family Papers, UVA.

7. "What Secession Has Done," *Missouri Statesman*, October 4, 1861. Scholars have found that divided families existed in other parts of the country, too, especially in places with a significant presence of both Unionists and Confederates. Three such places were northern Alabama, northern Georgia, and western North Carolina, all parts of the Confederate states with significant Unionist populations. See Inscoe and McKinney, "Highland Houses Divided." There also were divided families in cities along the coast, such as Charleston and Philadelphia, as merchant families moved north and south and intermarried. See Judith Lee Hunt, " 'High with Courage.' " Still, at the time of the war, newspaper reports and other commentaries usually cited the border region as the home of divided families.

8. "What Constitutes the South," *Richmond Enquirer*, November 28, 1862. These

various terms for the border region appear everywhere — in newspapers, private letters, and speeches. See, e.g., George H. Reese, *Proceedings of the Virginia State Convention*, 2:82, 103, 4:19, and "The Geographical Situation," *Louisville Daily Journal*, November 13, 1861. Except for Edward Conrad Smith's *Borderland*, only recently have scholars of the Civil War and the nineteenth century focused on the border as a distinct region. The most detailed examples are Edward L. Ayers's *In the Presence of Mine Enemies* and the related digital archive by Ayers et al., "The Valley of the Shadow," <http://valley. vcdh.virginia.edu>, both of which document the everyday lives of Virginians and Pennsylvanians on either side of the Union-Confederate border. William W. Freehling (*The South vs. the South*) considers how residents of this region had unique perspectives on the Civil War from people farther south, as does Daniel Crofts (*Reluctant Confederates*). In addition, a volume edited by Joan Cashin (*The War Was You and Me*) devotes an entire section to "The Border Regions" as a place distinct from "The North" and "The South." One reason for the relative lack of attention to the border region may be that historians have disagreed on its boundaries. For example, James McPherson (*Battle Cry of Freedom*, 284) restricts the area to the Union slaveholding states of Missouri, Kentucky, Maryland, and Delaware; Edward Conrad Smith (*Borderland*) excluded Maryland and Delaware; and others include Ohio, Illinois, Indiana, and Pennsylvania. My definition keeps the Union-Confederate line more directly in view: the states examined in this book represent those located immediately north and south of the wartime border.

9. Joseph C. Breckinridge to Robert J. Breckinridge, February 23, 1862, container 220, Breckinridge Family Papers, LC (quotation). A number of studies have documented these internal political divisions in individual states, including Harrison, *Civil War in Kentucky*, 1-13; Fellman, *Inside War*; McPherson, *Battle Cry of Freedom*, 276-307; Freehling, *The South vs. the South*; Blair, *Virginia's Private War*; Groce, *Mountain Rebels*; Fisher, *War at Every Door*; and Ash, *Middle Tennessee Society*. See also Crofts, *Reluctant Confederates*.

10. On the specific — and mutually supportive — relationship of family and national loyalty, see David Potter's seminal article, "The Historian's Use of Nationalism and Vice Versa." For similar, and more recent, perspectives, see Anthony D. Smith, *Nationalism and Modernism*, 202-8, and Chatterjee, *The Nation and Its Fragments*.

11. Divided families reveal how Civil War Americans grappled with the question that has intrigued modern historians for years: To what extent did ideology motivate citizens North and South to take up arms for their respective causes? For an overview of this debate on why Americans fought, see Mitchell, " 'Not the General but the Soldier.' " For works that lean toward ideology as a primary motivator, see Jimerson, *Private Civil War*; Mitchell, *Civil War Soldiers*; McPherson, *For Cause and Comrades*; and Glatthaar, *March to the Sea*. For those who give more weight to factors such as masculinity, courage, and family, see Linderman, *Embattled Courage*, and Stephen W. Berry, *All That Makes a Man*. Whereas the above scholarship tends to focus on soldiers, this study is also very much concerned with the motivations of civilians, men and women alike.

12. This dialogue revealed by divided families adds to a rapidly growing body of literature on familial relations in the Civil War era. A recent overview is Clinton, *Southern Families at War*. See also Mitchell, *Vacant Chair*, and Rable, "Hearth, Home, and

Family." Studies that deal specifically with gender have been more numerous, although more so for the South than for the North. See Clinton, *Tara Revisited*; Clinton and Silber, *Divided Houses*; Faust, *Mothers of Invention*; Rable, *Civil Wars*; Whites, *Crisis in Gender*; Edwards, *Gendered Strife*; Leonard, *Yankee Women*; Attie, *Patriotic Toil*; Sizer, *Political Work*; Stephen W. Berry, *All That Makes a Man*; Bercaw, *Gendered Freedoms*; Bleser and Gordon, *Intimate Strategies*; and Campbell, *When Sherman Marched North*. The theme of generations has been less studied in Civil War scholarship, however. See Anne C. Rose, *Victorian America*, 162–83, and Carmichael, "Last Generation."

13. Historians generally agree that this nuclear, or "modern," family emerged by the late eighteenth and early nineteenth centuries. For an overview, see Hareven, "History of the Family," 120–21; Ryan, *Cradle of the Middle Class*; and Mintz and Kellogg, *Domestic Revolutions*, 43–65. See also Fliegelman, *Prodigals and Pilgrims*; Anne C. Rose, *Victorian America*, 145–92; Mintz, *Prison of Expectations*; Degler, *At Odds*; and Grossberg, *Governing the Hearth*. Although the emergence of this family ideal was perhaps clearest among the Northern white, urban middle class, the extent to which it influenced Southerners has been the subject of some debate among historians. Plantation slavery required an assertion of patriarchal authority on the part of masters that ran counter to this modern family ideal. At the same time, there is evidence that Southerners also aspired to the small, inward-looking, loving family even if it was difficult to achieve. An important study of how republican political values and evangelical religion fostered this family ideal in the South is Lewis, *Pursuit of Happiness*. For the importance of love and emotion to otherwise patriarchal Southern men, see Stephen W. Berry, *All That Makes a Man*. For a comparative study of Northern and Southern wartime marriages that also found similarity in family practices, see Bleser and Gordon, *Intimate Strategies*, xx–xxi. For related studies of nuclear families — and the nuclear family ideal — in the South, see Censer, *North Carolina Planters*; Jabour, *Marriage in the Early Republic*; Burton, *In My Father's House*; Lyerly, "Tale of Two Patriarchs"; and Kilbride, "Class, Region, and Memory." Cashin ("Structure of Antebellum Planter Families") points out that a minority of planter families ever achieved this ideal. I believe it is important to distinguish between the *ideal* of the modern, nuclear family and the *reality* experienced by wartime border-state residents. As this study will show, Southern men and women in the region were strongly attached to the nuclear family model — or to their individual interpretation of that model — even if it eluded them. Moreover, that attachment was pivotal to the way in which they both understood and reconciled their wartime divisions.

14. My attention to the relationship between public and private is influenced by a rich and pervasive literature — from policy studies, to political history, to feminist theory — that examines the connection between these spheres. Much of this scholarship, especially the conceptualization of the "public sphere," has been influenced, in turn, by the ideas of Jürgen Habermas, who defined the bourgeois "public sphere" as the space that emerged between the state and the private family in the eighteenth century, a separate region of political association where public opinion could be formed and expressed (including, but not limited to, salons, taverns, and literary clubs). See Habermas, *Struc-*

tural Transformation, esp. 1–26. For useful discussions of Habermas's work and its application to historical studies, see Eley, "Nations, Publics"; Weintraub, "Theory and Politics of the Public/Private Distinction"; and Landes, *Women and the Public Sphere*, 1–13. A significant shortcoming of some early historical studies of public and private was the tendency to take the ideology of separation between the spheres as reality and to overlook the far more complex relationship between them. A wide-ranging assortment of recent works have addressed this shortcoming by emphasizing the interconnections of public and private throughout U.S. history. Historians of gender in the nineteenth century, for example, have demonstrated how an acknowledgment of such linkages (and a redefinition of what is "political") can deepen our view of women's influence in society at large. See, e.g., Kerber, "Separate Spheres"; Lewis, "Republican Wife"; McCurry, "Two Faces of Republicanism"; Edwards, *Gendered Strife*, 5–6; and Cott, *Public Vows*. Historians of political culture have also begun to rethink early national political behavior by connecting questions of private character to campaigns and party politics. See Cogan, "Reynolds Affair"; Basch, "Marriage, Morals, and Politics"; Freeman, "Slander, Poison"; and Trees, *Founding Fathers*.

15. Gary Gallagher (*Confederate War*, esp. 8–9) has made an explicit case for integrating homefront and battlefield. See also Paludan, "What Did the Winners Win?" Drew Gilpin Faust's *Mothers of Invention* and George Rable's *Civil Wars* are representative studies that emphasize how homefront stress could undermine the Confederacy's military progress. Reid Mitchell's *Vacant Chair* and Stephen W. Berry's *All That Makes a Man* likewise demonstrate how family ties could shape a soldier's outlook on the war. Other recent studies that successfully integrate homefront and battlefield include Campbell, *When Sherman Marched North*; Cashin, *War Was You and Me*; Bleser and Gordon, *Intimate Strategies*; and Ayers, *In the Presence of Mine Enemies*.

16. My interest in how divided families used the terms "public" and "private" follows the lead of historians such as Linda Kerber ("Separate Spheres"), who termed the ideology of separate spheres "a rhetorical construction that responded to a changing social and economic reality." Here I am concerned with the way in which that rhetoric intensified in response to the specific threat of war and thus the way in which the war's intrusion reinforced midcentury Americans' attachment to the ideal of the private nuclear family. Other historians have made similar arguments about the war's reinforcement of traditional domestic models. See, e.g., Faust, *Mothers of Invention*, and Anne C. Rose, *Victorian America*. One could argue that this domestic ideology has resonated more strongly in U.S. history during and after national crises, particularly wars. Another clear example is the celebration of the nuclear family following World War II and during the Cold War. See, e.g., May, *Homeward Bound*.

17. Benedict Anderson, *Imagined Communities*, esp. 1–7. Eric Hobsbawm similarly focuses on the cultural construction of nationalism, pointing out that "invented traditions" have served as a unifying force for diverse populations. Hobsbawm, Introduction to Hobsbawm and Ranger's *Invention of Tradition*, 1–14. These theories of nationalism have influenced historians worldwide — especially those who study the United States in the nineteenth century. See, e.g., Waldstreicher, *In the Midst of Perpetual Fetes*; Lawson,

Patriot Fires, 4; and O'Leary, *To Die For*, 4. I join these authors in viewing nineteenth-century America as an "imagined community," but here I look specifically at the role of family in influencing the meaning and shape of that "community."

18. Autobiography of John Adams, June 2, 1778, in Butterfield, *Diary and Autobi-ography*, 4:123. On the family's dual role as a private incubator of public (republican) values in the early to mid-nineteenth century, see Kerber, *Women of the Republic*; Lewis, "Republican Wife"; Mary Beth Norton, *Liberty's Daughters*; Fliegelman, *Prodigals and Pilgrims*; and Grossberg, *Governing the Hearth*, 6–9. Jürgen Habermas, despite imply-ing a sharp distinction between public and private in his theory of the "public sphere," also acknowledges another "public" role of the family by pointing out that in the family individuals learn the knowledge and reason that they will bring into the public sphere. See Habermas, "The Bourgeois Family and the Institutionalization of a Privateness Oriented to an Audience," *Structural Transformation*, 43–51. Another useful analysis of this duality in a European context is Saglia, "'O My Mother Spain!'" Here I am in-terested in how this ideological duality challenged divided families' efforts to separate and distance their personal affairs from the public stress of war.

19. Metaphors were—and still are—important to American political and social thought because they offer an entire conceptual system for joining complex questions, simplifying some issues while ignoring others. Metaphors are most powerful when they can be easily grasped by a wide range of people. As Anne Norton (*Alternative Americas*, 11) has argued, metaphors are necessary when "nationality is inchoate, nascent, or in flux," offering clarity where it does not otherwise exist. The metaphor of family pro-vided that clarity as an easily identifiable symbol for diverse Americans of the bonds of duty and affection that were to unite the new nation. For useful general analyses of the metaphor, see Lakoff and Johnson, *Metaphors We Live By*; Edelman, *Politics as Symbolic Action*; and Geertz, "Ideology as a Cultural System." On the specific linkage between the family metaphor and national identity, see Anthony D. Smith, *National Identity*, esp. 78–79. On this linkage in the U.S. context, see esp. Fliegelman, *Prodigals and Pilgrims*; Jensen, "British Voices"; Lewis, "Republican Wife"; Yazawa, *From Colonies to Commonwealth*; and Jordan, "'Old Worlds' in 'New Circumstances.'"

20. I am grateful to Reid Mitchell for his insights on the popularity of the divided family metaphor in wartime. To some extent, I agree with the ideas of two historians who have previously explored the family metaphor in the Civil War. George Forgie (*Patricide*, 18) and Anne Norton (*Alternative Americas*, 266) attribute the resonance of this metaphor at least in part to a crisis in family, to a perceived sense of "loss" or "decay" of the family in the first half of the nineteenth century. Neither examine these feelings in depth, however, although Forgie argues that the perception of crisis stemmed from the very privatization and isolation of the nuclear family that left some Americans longing for its traditional form. This encouraged a preoccupation with family imagery in wartime. True, a family crisis is significant here, but the crisis I see is specifically one of loyalty—of the bonds of duty, affection, and companionship—that some Americans may have found threatened before the war and especially by the war itself. This crisis, in fact, fed into the nation's own crisis of loyalty in wartime—giving new meaning to

the imaginative links between them. In tracing these intersecting family and national crises, I am influenced by the work of Lynn Hunt (*Family Romance*) and Jay Fliegelman (*Prodigals and Pilgrims*) who, in their analyses of the family metaphor in the French and American Revolutions respectively, argue that its power was rooted in a larger cultural revolt against patriarchy. I am also swayed by Hunt's view of family not as a static, fixed symbol or "modal social experience," but as an "imaginative construct of power relations" (196).

21. Nina Silber (*Romance of Reunion*) and David Blight (*Race and Reunion*) have provided the most comprehensive studies of how Americans constructed a "whitewashed" memory of the Civil War to ease the process of sectional reconciliation. Both scholars see this memory of the war peaking in the late nineteenth century. As Chapter 7 will explain, however, it is possible to find the origins of this memory earlier — in the war and its aftermath — in the use of the family metaphor to tell the story of sectional division and reunion.

22. "The Home and the Flag," *Harper's New Monthly Magazine* (April 1863): 667.

23. George H. Reese, *Proceedings of the Virginia State Convention*, 2:42, 393, 601, 4:116; [Untitled], *Daily Richmond Enquirer*, December 3, 1861; [Untitled], *Louisville Daily Journal*, November 15, 1861; [Untitled], *Southern Field and Fireside*, September 12, 1863; [Untitled], *Harper's New Monthly Magazine* (May 1862): 807. For more on the father-son imagery, see Forgie, *Patricide*. On the general inclination to draw on the legacy of the Revolution and the Founding Fathers to substantiate one's position during secession, see Rubin, "Seventy-six and Sixty-one," and Wallach, *Obedient Sons*, 151–62.

Chapter One

1. Henry Stone to Mother and Father, February 13, 1863, Henry Stone to Father, September 7, 1863, and Henry Stone to Mother and Father, December 5, 1863, Stone Collection, FHS.

2. I have found that the Union father–Confederate son division (over 100 cases) was far more common than the Confederate father–Union son division (only 3 cases). Of the more than 100 cases identified in this study, 55 have surviving manuscript papers.

3. Josie Underwood Diary, February 9, 1861, WKU; "Letters of a Father No. 1," *Louisville Daily Journal*, September 9, 1861. For a similar observation, see Adjutant General Lorenzo Thomas to Union Secretary of War Simon Cameron, quoted in Harrison, *Civil War in Kentucky*, 15. William W. Freehling (*The South vs. the South*, 57) observes this same Union father–Confederate son trend. A different take on this type of border-state family conflict is Joseph Glatthaar's "Duty, Country, Race," a study of a Union father and a Union son initially at odds over race and slavery. According to genealogical records in the Underwood family papers, Josie Underwood was born in 1840 and would have been twenty-one when the war began. Census records, however, list her age as sixteen in 1861. Genealogical Clippings, Henry L. Underwood Collection, WKU; U.S. Census, Population Schedule: Kentucky, 1860.

4. On the generational divide in the South, see Barney, *Secessionist Impulse*, 61–88, and Carmichael, "Last Generation."

5. Samuel Halsey to Joseph J. Halsey, July 23, 1857, Morton-Halsey Family Papers, UVA.

6. John J. Crittenden to George Crittenden, April 30, 1861, John J. Crittenden Letters, FHS. For other fathers who tried to deter their sons from joining the Confederate forces, see "Lincoln, Sumner, & Corwin: Reminiscences of Interviews with Charles Sumner, President Abraham Lincoln, and Judge Thomas Corwin," by John Cox Underwood, n.d., 3, Underwood Collection, WKU, and Samuel Kennard Letters, MHS.

7. [Untitled], *Louisville Daily Journal*, September 19, 1862. On the political socialization process in families, see McCormick, *Party Period*, 164; Rable, *Confederate Republic*, 178; and esp. Jean Baker, *Affairs of Party*, 22, 29–70.

8. Matthew Page Andrews to Anna Robinson, May 7, July 28, 1861, and Charles Wesley Andrews to Matthew Page Andrews, May 27, 1861, Charles Wesley Andrews Papers, Duke. In a similar case of paternal pressure, a Confederate son named John Denney told a friend that "if it hadn't been for his father he would have been in the southern army long ago." Conversation described in Lyd[ia] Moor to Brother, July 5, 1864, Moor-Naudain Collection, DPA. On the peer pressures compelling men to fight anyway, see McPherson, *For Cause and Comrades*, 88–89, and Rotundo, "Boy Culture."

9. On conscription laws, see McPherson, *Battle Cry of Freedom*, 427–31, 492–94; Paludan, *People's Contest*, 189–90; and Thomas, *Confederate Nation*, 152–55.

10. Henry Stone to Father, February 13, 1863, Stone Collection, FHS.

11. Letters of Matthew and Charles Andrews, Charles Wesley Andrews Papers, Duke.

12. Ann Clay to Brutus J. Clay, September 25, 1861, Clay Family Papers, UKY.

13. Ezekiel Clay to Family, September 24, 1861, ibid.

14. Ann Clay to Brutus Clay, September 25, 1861, and Brutus Clay to Ann Clay, October 14, 1862, ibid.

15. For an example of paternal anger, see William Preston Johnston to Rosa Johnston (wife), September 18, 1861, William Preston Johnston Papers, FHS. A related discussion of volunteering for Confederate service as a sign of coming of age can be found in Mitchell, *Vacant Chair*, 3–18.

16. Wyatt-Brown, *Southern Honor*, 117–98 (quotation, 170). On the endurance of patriarchal authority, see also Cashin, *Family Venture*, 32–52, and Kett, *Rites of Passage*, 45. For additional works on the conflicted relationship between fathers and sons, see Mintz, *Prison of Expectations*, esp. 59–101; Anne C. Rose, *Victorian America*, 68–108, 166–68; Ryan, *Cradle of the Middle Class*, 32; and Oakes, *Ruling Race*, 69–71. On the emergence of affectionate child rearing, see Rotundo, "American Fatherhood"; Griswold, *Fatherhood in America*, 11–30; Frank, *Life with Father*, 23–51; and Fliegelman, *Prodigals and Pilgrims*.

17. "Letters of a Father, No. 1" and "Letters of a Father, No. 2," *Louisville Daily Journal*, September 9, 20, 1861.

18. Barney, *Secessionist Impulse*, 61–88, and "Towards the Civil War." Though

Barney's works deal with the Deep South, a similar dynamic was evident in the border states.

19. William Sydnor Thomson to Warner Alexander Thomson, March 24, 1861, Warner Alexander Thomson to William Sydnor Thomson, March 17, 1861, William Sydnor Thomson Papers, Emory. I am grateful to Peter Carmichael for bringing this collection to my attention. See also John J. Crittenden Papers, UKY, and John Kempshall Papers, TSLA. The census records include 39 of the 55 families with surviving papers identified in this study; of those 39, 31 (or 79 percent) had rebel sons living in their fathers' household in 1860. U.S. Census, Population Schedule: Delaware, Kentucky, Maryland, Missouri, Tennessee, and Virginia, 1860.

20. S. F. Gano to Brutus J. Clay, March 29, 1864, Clay Family Papers, UKY; [Untitled], *Louisville Daily Journal*, October 23, 1861.

21. For an extended discussion of the "confidence man," see Halttunen, *Confidence Men*, chap. 1.

22. Reflecting how seriously some border-state residents took the threat of confidence men, Howard Smith, charged by Robert J. Breckinridge with influencing his son William to become a Confederate, offered a vigorous defense: "I heard, with much surprise, that you were censuring me for the connexion of your son William with the 'Confederate Army.' Nothing could be more unjust to me. I say to you on the integrity of a gentleman and a Christian that I am entirely guiltless of even *attempting* to influence your son on that subject." Smith, whom Breckinridge had previously called "the most offensive disloyal man in the neighborhood," admitted to having William over for dinner but called the evening *"purely social."* D. Howard Smith to Robert J. Breckinridge, July 25, 1862. See also Robert J. Breckinridge to William C. P. Breckinridge, July 15, 1862, William C. P. Breckinridge to Robert J. Breckinridge, July 15, 1862, and W. L. Breckinridge to William C. P. Breckinridge, May 3, 1862, containers 224–25, Breckinridge Family Papers, LC. For a similar case, see C. L. Field to Brutus J. Clay, May 24, 1861, Clay Family Papers, UKY.

23. John H. Morgan, "Kentuckians!," July 15, 1862, in Breckinridge Family Papers, LC; C. Alice Ready Diary, March 8, 1862, SHC; "Errant Youth," *Louisville Daily Journal*, September 26, 1861; Henry Stone to James Stone, September 3, 1863, Stone Collection, FHS; Creek, "Memoirs of Mrs. E. B. Patterson," 351. The estimate of the number of sons who followed Morgan is taken from a combined count of the following sources: manuscript collections of Union families in which sons served with Morgan; letters written by Union fathers to their Kentucky congressmen complaining of Morgan's influence; and newspaper accounts of service in Morgan's cavalry. See the 1862 issues of the *Louisville Daily Journal* and the *Nashville Daily Press*, and the letters from fathers to Congressman Brutus J. Clay, Clay Family Papers, UKY. On Morgan's appeal, see McPherson, *Battle Cry of Freedom*, 514, and Ramage, *Rebel Raider*, 1–7, 65–70, 100–101. On the desire for adventure as a motivator of enlistment for military service, see McPherson, *For Cause and Comrades*, 26–28, and Wiley, *Life of Johnny Reb*, 17.

24. Will S. Richart to Brutus J. Clay, January 22, 1864, A. H. Calvin to Brutus J. Clay, January 16, 1864, John [Leer?] to Brutus J. Clay, February 18, 1864, and James Hanagan

to Brutus J. Clay, March 29, 1864, Clay Family Papers, UKY; Henry Stone to Mother, January 4, 1864, Stone Collection, FHS.

25. Charles Wesley Andrews to Sarah Andrews, June 1, 1861, Charles Wesley Andrews Papers, Duke; Louisa Brown Pearl Diary, TSLA.

26. Adeline L. Lawton to Alexander J. Lawton, June 8, 1861, Alexander R. Lawton Papers, SHC; Bethiah McKown to John D. McKown, April 17, June 4, 1863, John D. McKown Papers, WHMC. On the civic education provided by mothers, see the discussion of "republican motherhood" in Kerber, *Women of the Republic*, 283. For mothers' influence on Civil War soldiers, see Mitchell, *Vacant Chair*, xi–xiv, 86–87.

27. Henry Stone to Father and Mother, December 5, 1863, Henry Stone to Father, February 5, 1864, Stone Collection, FHS.

28. William Thomson to Warner Thomson, February [?], 1861, William Sydnor Thomson Papers, Emory.

29. Ezekiel Clay to Family, September 24, 1861, Clay Family Papers, UKY; Henry Stone to Father, December 29, 1862, July 21, 1863, Stone Collection, FHS; Matthew Page Andrews to Anna Robinson, March 10, 1861, Charles Wesley Andrews Family Papers, Duke; Samuel Kennard to Parents, March 12, 1862, Samuel Kennard Letters, MHS. On why soldiers fought, see McPherson, *For Cause and Comrades*; Wiley, *Life of Johnny Reb*, chap. 1; Jimerson, *Private Civil War*; Mitchell, *Civil War Soldiers*; Stephen W. Berry, *All That Makes a Man*; and Linderman, *Embattled Courage*.

30. C. W. Andrews to Matthew Page Andrews, May 21, 1861, Charles Wesley Andrews Papers, Duke. Of the 39 families located in the census, 33 (or 84 percent) were slave-owners. U.S. Census, Population and Slave Schedules: Delaware, Kentucky, Maryland, Missouri, Tennessee, and Virginia, 1860. For more on the proslavery thought of Union men such as these fathers, see Inscoe and McKinney, *Heart of Confederate Appalachia*, chap. 4.

31. Robert J. Breckinridge to William C. P. Breckinridge, July 16, 1862, Breckinridge Family Papers, LC. Census records indicate that in 1860 Robert Breckinridge owned seventeen slaves and John J. Crittenden owned nine. U.S. Census, Population and Slave Schedules: Boyle and Franklin Counties, Ky., 1860, 154, 490. On the link between slavery and manly independence, see Cashin, *Family Venture*, 34.

32. Brutus Clay to Ann Clay, October 14, 1862, and Ann Clay to Brutus Clay, September 10, 1862, Clay Family Papers, UKY. See also William Sydnor Thomson Papers, Emory. On disinheritance practices among Southern planters, see Cashin, "According to His Wish." A case of disinheritance is described in Mrs. John Lawrence to Caroline Bedinger, [?] 14, 1862, Bedinger-Dandridge Family Papers, Duke.

33. On the importance of letters in sustaining parent-child relationships, see Stowe, *Intimacy and Power*, 144–47, and Marten, "Fatherhood in the Confederacy."

34. Warner Alexander Thomson Diary, May 29, 1864, Warner Thomson to William Sydnor Thomson, December 3, 1860, and William Sydnor Thomson to Josephine Thomson, July 27, 1864, William Sydnor Thomson Papers, Emory. Warner Thomson owned five slaves in 1860. U.S. Census, Population and Slave Schedules: Jefferson County, Va., 1860, 164. For another discussion of the Thomson family, see Stephen W. Berry, *All That Makes a Man*, 169–71.

35. William Sydnor Thomson to Josephine Thomson, July 27, 1864, William Sydnor Thomson Papers, Emory.

36. Warner Alexander Thomson Diary, February 19, 1863, William Sydnor Thomson Papers, Emory. Warner Thomson's awkward avoidance of William was fairly typical of Union fathers when caught between the competing impulses of paternal authority and affection for their sons. In another example, Samuel Starling, a slaveholding Kentuckian and a second lieutenant in the Union army, withheld letters from his Confederate son, George, as a punishment but then took on the unique responsibility of meeting with, counseling, and pardoning young Confederate soldiers who deserted to Union lines. These encounters were apparently emotional at times, with men breaking down in gratitude for Starling's willingness to pardon them, leading one of Starling's superiors to chide him "for being too easily moved by stories of grief or professions of repentance." George Starling never benefited from his father's magnanimity but may have nonetheless inspired him to reach out to other Confederate soldiers. Helping these men may have offered Starling a vicarious means of aiding his own son — and assuaging any feelings of guilt over their estrangement — without undermining the stern, paternal authority he felt necessary to reinforce by cutting off contact with his son. Samuel Starling to Daughters, October 10, November 14, 15, December 6, 1862, March 7, 1863, and George Starling to "My Dear Father," May 25, 1864, Lewis-Starling Collection, WKU.

37. William Sydnor Thomson to Josephine Thomson, July 27, 1864, and Josephine Thomson to William Sydnor Thomson, August [?], 1864, William Sydnor Thomson Papers, Emory.

38. William C. P. Breckinridge to "My Dear Pa," March 8, 1864, Robert J. Breckinridge to Issa Breckinridge, March 31, 1864, Issa Breckinridge to Robert J. Breckinridge, n.d., Issa Breckinridge to William C. P. Breckinridge, April 2, 1864, and William C. P. Breckinridge to Issa Breckinridge, July 7, 1864, container 233, Breckinridge Family Papers, LC.

39. Exactly how far the South's honor culture extended is difficult to determine, although the border-state families considered here clearly embraced its tenets. For more on family honor, see Anne C. Rose, *Victorian America*, 182–83, and Wyatt-Brown, *Southern Honor*, 132–33. On the intersection of private life and public reputation in antebellum America, see Basch, "Marriage, Morals, and Politics," and Cogan, "Reynolds Affair."

40. "John J. Crittenden," *Louisville Daily Journal*, March 10, 1864; Crofts, *Reluctant Confederates*, 17; Kirwan, *John J. Crittenden*, vii. Crittenden is best known for his work in the Senate, where he served through the end of 1860. In June 1861 he won a seat in the U.S. House of Representatives.

41. John J. Crittenden to George Crittenden, April 30, 1861, John J. Crittenden Letters, FHS; [Untitled], *Louisville Daily Journal*, May 5, 1862; "Mr. Crittenden's Position," *Daily Missouri Democrat*, June 21, 1861; "The Rebel General Crittenden," *Smyrna Times*, January 30, 1862.

42. John J. Crittenden to George D. Prentice, May 8, 1862, John J. Crittenden Letters, FHS.

43. Ibid. For an overview of the literature on separate spheres, see Kerber, "Separate Spheres."

44. [Untitled], *Louisville Daily Journal*, March 26, 1862; [Untitled], *Richmond Enquirer*, June 18, 1861. For an overview of Prentice's politics, see Prichard, "Champion of the Union."

45. "George D. Prentice and His Son," *Daily Missouri Democrat*, October 4, 1862 (reprinted from *Cincinnati Commercial*); "Letter from George D. Prentice," *Daily Missouri Democrat*, October 8, 1862 (reprinted from *Cincinnati Commercial*); [Untitled], *Daily Missouri Democrat*, October 3, 1862 (reprinted from *Cincinnati Gazette*); "George D. Prentice in Memory of His Rebel Son," *Missouri Statesman*, December 12, 1862 (also printed in *Daily Missouri Democrat*, October 11, 1862).

46. "William Courtland Prentice: A Brief Sketch," *Louisville Daily Journal*, October 10, 1862 (reprinted as "George D. Prentice in Memory of his Rebel Son," *Missouri Statesman*, December 12, 1862). On mourning as a private affair, see Halttunen, *Confidence Men*, chap. 5.

47. For how religious beliefs motivated others to publish similar funeral narratives during the war, see Faust, "Civil War Soldier."

48. "A Note from Geo. D. Prentice — Reply to a Slander," *Missouri Statesman*, March 27, 1863 (also published in *Daily Missouri Democrat*, March 20, 1863); "Parson Brownlow on George D. Prentice — A Withering Expose of a Copperhead," *Daily Missouri Democrat*, November 16, 1864. Prentice's pride in his newspaper's political influence is reflected in a remark he once made to Abraham Lincoln: "Without it [the *Louisville Daily Journal*], Kentucky could not have been kept in the Union." Prentice to Lincoln, November 16, 1861, George D. Prentice Papers, UKY. See a related article, "Capture of a Son of George D. Prentice," *Washington Evening Star*, April 1, 1863.

49. [Untitled], *Louisville Daily Journal*, March 11, 1862.

50. Ibid. On the Southern veneration of bloodlines, see Wyatt-Brown, *Southern Honor*, 118–25; Carmichael, "Last Generation," 128–30; and Taylor, *Cavalier and Yankee*, esp. chap. 4. For more on the backgrounds of Davis and Stephens, see William C. Davis, *Jefferson Davis*, and Schott, *Alexander H. Stephens*.

51. "One of Jeff. Davis's Children in Wisconsin," July 23, 1863, *Daily Missouri Democrat* (reprinted from *Oshkosh [Wis.] Northwestern*); also published in *Frank Leslie's Illustrated Newspaper*, August 8, 1863, 311; [Untitled], *Louisville Daily Journal*, June 18, 1865. For more on Davis's alleged offspring, see "The Divided Interracial Family" in Chapter 5. For his early military career and encounters with Indians in the Northwest, see Cooper, *Jefferson Davis*, 43–55.

52. "The Representative Characters of Ex-Vice President and Rev. Dr. Breckinridge Compared," *Louisville Daily Journal*, December 25, 1861 (quotations); [Untitled], *Louisville Daily Journal*, October 26, 1863, and "Arrest of Jas. B. Clay," *Smyrna Times*, October 10, 1861 (the Clays); "Jefferson's Descendants," *Nashville Daily Press*, November 21, 1863. "Did the writing of a patriotic song entitle the writer's posterity to immunity in treason and adultery?" the *Louisville Daily Journal* (August 19, 1861 [untitled]) asked hypothetically of Francis Scott Key. The articles discussing the Breckinridges are numerous, including at least six that appeared in the *Louisville Daily Journal* alone during the war years and five in the *Missouri Statesman*.

Chapter Two

1. Bergner, *Legislative Record*, 879–80.

2. Ibid.

3. Ibid. Norma Basch (*Framing American Divorce*, 52–57) notes that the 1838 Pennsylvania Constitution stripped the legislature of concurrent jurisdiction with the courts in divorce cases. After that, only cases "that did not fit the statutory slots" were brought before the legislature. In the Hopkins case, political differences provided the special circumstance requiring legislative action.

4. For examples of press coverage in the Hopkins case, see "Disloyalty a Plea for Divorce—Singular Case," *Daily Missouri Democrat*, March 28, 1862, and [Untitled], *Louisville Daily Journal*, March 29, 1862.

5. William Glasgow Jr. to Sarah Glasgow, February 14, 1864, William Carr Lane Papers, MHS. For another example of divorce on the grounds of divided Civil War loyalties, see "Eccentric Divorce Case," *Daily Missouri Democrat*, November 24, 1863.

6. For a marriage triggered by a Northern man's relocation in the South, see Morton-Halsey Family Papers, UVA. For examples of Northern women who traveled South to teach and ended up marrying Southern men, see Emily Howe Dupuy Papers, VHS, and "A Union Woman in South Carolina," *New York Herald*, March 19, 1865. On relationships developed at resorts, see, e.g., [Untitled], *Louisville Daily Journal*, April 23, 1861. On geographically extended families, see Samuella Hart Curd Diary, VHS, and Clay Family Papers, UKY.

7. Bergner, *Legislative Record*, 879, 881.

8. Ibid., 881.

9. Ibid., 881–82.

10. Ibid., 882–83.

11. Although historians of the North and South alike generally agree that over the course of the century fathers backed away from supervising their daughters' courtship and marriage, lingering attachments still persisted and created conflict. For a discussion of this phenomenon, see Frank, *Life with Father*, 169–70. See also Anne C. Rose, *Victorian America*, 166, 181; Laas, "'A Good Wife'"; Clinton, *Plantation Mistress*, 44; and Wyatt-Brown, *Southern Honor*, 272–73.

12. In dismissing Catherine's petition, one state senator said that "I am not satisfied by the evidence before the committee and the Senate that it is a case in which this body should adjudicate." Instead, it appeared to him to be a matter of desertion—brought on by Hopkins's trip to Virginia—which therefore belonged in the courts. Bergner, *Legislative Record*, 880–84. The Hopkins divorce was finally decreed on April 29, 1865, just weeks after the war ended. Pennsylvania Common Pleas Court, Divorce Docket, 1865, 232, PCA. For the conflicting roles of the courts and legislatures in divorces, see Basch, *Framing American Divorce*, esp. chap. 2.

13. Jeb Stuart to Flora Cooke Stuart, November 24, December 1, 4, 11, 12, 1861, Stuart Papers, Emory. Flora eventually agreed to change her son's name but asked her husband to keep the reason for the change a secret—and he agreed. The Stuart family's division

was well known. Lucy Muse Fletcher called it "the most dreadful feature of this war." Fletcher Diary, June 16, 1862, Duke.

14. Josie Underwood Diary, April 17, January 1, 1861, WKU. For an extended discussion of a family's political socialization, see Jean Baker, *Affairs of Party*, 27–42.

15. Data on 38 of the 40 women studied in this chapter were compiled from both census and manuscript sources. Of these 38, 27 (or 69 percent) were under age twenty-eight in 1860. Almost the same percentage (25 of 38, or 64 percent) had been married less than ten years. U.S. Census, Population Schedule: Delaware, Kentucky, Maryland, Missouri, Tennessee, and Virginia, 1860.

16. At least 22 of the 38 women with data available (or 58 percent) were childless in 1860. This figure may have decreased by the start of the Civil War, since there was at least a one-year lag between the time these data were collected and the war began. U.S. Census, Population Schedule: Delaware, Kentucky, Maryland, Missouri, Tennessee, and Virginia, 1860.

17. Jno. Lawrence to Carolina Lawrence Bedinger, December 22, 1860, Bedinger-Dandridge Family Papers, Duke. For a Tennessee father who had more success in persuading his daughter to leave her enemy husband, see Sarah Kennedy to "My Dear Husband," December 29, 1862, Kennedy Papers, TSLA.

18. This father, John F. Henry, wrote: "The claims of wife and children would weigh in the balance with me much more than all the ambitious pollitichans in the world." Henry to N. T. Jackson, June 7, 1861, in McKee, "Reflections of an East Tennessee Unionist." Another father who resorted to deception—including feigning illness—to encourage his daughter to leave her husband is described in Maria McGregor (Campbell) Smith, "Narrative of My Blockade Running," n.d., Smith Papers, VHS. Another Union father went directly to Confederate officials to seek his son-in-law's discharge (over his daughter's protest). Martha M. Jones to W. L. Buford, December 21, 1862, Jones Family Papers, FHS. For similar cases, see James A. Bayard Jr. to Benomi Lockwood, September 1, 1861, folder 7, Bayard Letters, HSD; Mary Y. K. Smith to "Hay," October 1, 1861, Smith Papers, UVA.

19. William Eames to "Dearest Mary," July 9, 1862, Eames Papers, TSLA; "An Affecting Incident of the War," *Daily Missouri Democrat*, September 23, 1861.

20. Cassius Clay to Brutus J. Clay, January 3, 1864, Clay Family Papers, UKY. Martha explained her political switch as partly motivated by a sincere ideological shift, but also by her desire to "perform my duty to my husband." She elaborated: "If I endorse Lincoln's administration, I am encouraging . . . those who are trying to destroy & shot [*sic*] my property, taking my liberties from me, trying to hang my husband & degrade my children." Martha Clay Davenport to Ann Clay, June 7, September 21, 1861, Clay Family Papers, UKY.

21. Josie Underwood Diary, July 2, 1861, WKU; Anne Lane to Sarah Lane Glasgow, April 26, 1863, William Carr Lane Papers, MHS. For a similar case in which a woman chose neutrality, see George M. Anderson, "Civil War Courtship."

22. Mary Macgill to Charles Macgill, November 5, 1861, Charles Macgill Papers, Duke.

23. Matthew Page Andrews to Anna Robinson, November 18, 1860, Charles Wesley

Andrews Papers, Duke. In the meantime, Matthew asked her: "Cant you find one [fabric] with Virginia & Southern rights on it?" In the course of later discussions, however, he somehow became satisfied that Anna had not become too politically independent. The two married in July 1861, without inviting her Unionist relatives, in what Andrews termed "a secessionist military wedding." Andrews to Robinson, March 10, August 22, 1861, ibid.

24. Evidence of women independently seeking and absorbing information about war politics abounds throughout the diaries and letters examined for this study. See, e.g., Josie Underwood Diary, January 4, 8, 1861, WKU, and Letters of Sarah Glasgow and Anne Lane in William Carr Lane Papers, MHS. For the political content of antebellum fiction, see Varon, *We Mean to Be Counted*, 103–24.

25. Benjamin Buckner to Helen Martin, April 18, 1861, February 24, 1862, Buckner Papers, UKY. Buckner's age determined from U.S. Census, Population Schedule: Clark County, Ky., 1860, reel 362, p. 823.

26. This view of political behavior extended back to the Revolution and was fundamental to republican thought. For a discussion of how these ideas lingered into the middle of the nineteenth century, see Rable, *Confederate Republic*, 6–19, and Jean Baker, *Affairs of Party*, 115–17.

27. Benjamin Buckner to Helen Martin, January 8, 1862, Buckner Papers, UKY. Historians across the period from the Revolution to the Civil War have examined popular beliefs that a woman's public or political role was to grow out of her partnership with her husband. Linda Kerber (*Women of the Republic*, chap. 4) found that even when tempted by property interests to side differently from Tory husbands in the Revolution, women still almost always sided with their spouses. Elizabeth Varon (*We Mean to Be Counted*, esp. chap. 3) has suggested that in antebellum Virginia a woman's accepted role as moral authority in the home extended to providing her husband with support on political matters. Other historians have shown that a woman's very alliance with her husband could offer her a public role as a model for political and social relations outside of the household. See, e.g., Lewis, "Republican Wife," and McCurry, "Two Faces of Republicanism." Two works on Civil War women that illustrate this partnership at work are Bleser and Gordon, *Intimate Strategies*, and Faust, *Mothers of Invention*.

28. Catherine Allgor (*Parlor Politics*, 125–27, 139, 147–89) argues that in the early national context, these responsibilities could be rationalized as a service to their husband's — and family's — interest, which, in turn, gave women license to act in politically assertive ways.

29. For an exhaustive study of the importance of respectful, loving companionship to husbands and wives, see Anya Jabour's *Marriage in the Early Republic*. For other works that highlight the increasing importance of affection in marriage by midcentury, see Censer, *North Carolina Planters*; Lystra, *Searching the Heart*; Anne C. Rose, *Victorian America*; and Mintz, *Prison of Expectations*. In the Civil War context, see Stephen W. Berry, *All That Makes a Man*.

30. Benjamin Buckner to Helen Martin, January 8, 1862, Buckner Papers, UKY.

31. Benjamin Buckner to Helen Martin, December 19, 1861, March 15, June 5, August 10, 1862, ibid. Buckner exemplified a proslavery Unionism not uncommon in the border

states — and already seen in the views of the Union fathers described in Chapter 1. He once explained his decision to side with the Union despite his proslavery views: "I think it better to fight for that side, which has heretofore given us peace prosperity and happiness, than for that which only promises us [lawless?] violence and commercial ruin" (Buckner to Martin, June 5, 1862).

32. See Chapter 4 for an extended discussion of this type of assistance.

33. "Arrest of Mrs. Phillips," *Daily Missouri Democrat*, August 30, 1861. See also Journal of Eugenia Phillips, August 23, 29, 30, 1861, Philip Phillips Papers, LC, and Jacobs, "Eugenia Levy Phillips," 23–26. Eugenia wrote of her letter writing: "If an ardent attachment to the land of my birth and the expression of deepest sympathy with my relatives and friends in the South, constitute treason — then I am indeed a traitor" (Journal, August 30, 1861). In August 1861 she was arrested for treason but was released three weeks later. She and her husband later moved to Alabama for the duration of the war. "Arrest of Mrs. Phillips," *Daily Missouri Democrat*, August 30, 1861; "More Petticoat Rebels," *Louisville Daily Journal*, August 27, 1861 (reprinted from *New York Times*). See Philip Phillips's account of the arrest in "The Imprisonment of the Hon. P. Phillips and Family at Washington," *Louisville Daily Courier*, October 25, 1861. A similar case is recounted in "Arrest of Mrs. Senator Gwin — Another Infamous Outrage," *Louisville Daily Courier*, August 27, 1861.

34. [Untitled], *Louisville Daily Journal*, July 21, 1862.

35. For a general discussion of family honor, see Wyatt-Brown, *Southern Honor*, 132–33. On the importance of honor to Civil War soldiers in particular, see McPherson, *For Cause and Comrades*.

36. Green Clay to Brutus J. Clay, November 30, 1863, Clay Family Papers, UKY (Kentucky Union officer). The Lincolns' story is discussed in depth in Chapter 4. The headlines over these newspaper articles alone indicate the scrutiny endured by Lincoln: "Mrs. President Lincoln's Sister," *Chambersburg (Pa.) Valley Spirit*, April 6, 1864, from Ayers et al., "The Valley of the Shadow," <http://valley.vcdh.virginia.edu>; "Mrs. Lincoln's Rebel Brother," *Louisville Daily Journal*, April 13, 1864; "Lincoln's Sister-in-Law," *Daily Missouri Democrat*, February 21, 1861; "Old Abe's Kentucky Relatives," *Daily Missouri Democrat*, October 7, 1861.

37. Story retold in Joseph Cabell Breckinridge to Robert J. Breckinridge, January 9, 1861, Breckinridge Family Papers, LC.

38. Bethiah P. McKown to "My Dear Son," June 4, 1863, in Goodrich, "Civil War Letters," 357–58.

39. [Untitled], *Nashville Daily Press*, April 25, 1863; "Jeff Thompson's Family," *Louisville Daily Journal*, October 23, 1861. Thompson was not the only husband who resorted to insulting his wife's mental capacity in response to her divergent views on the war. West Virginian Warner Thomson, an ardent Unionist, observed in his diary that his wife's judgment in supporting the Confederacy was "like that of poor weak men." Warner Alexander Thomson Diary, August 10, 1864, Emory.

40. Benjamin Buckner to Helen Martin, January 8, March 15, 1862, Buckner Papers, UKY.

41. Anya Jabour (*Marriage in the Early Republic*, chap. 3) illustrates how the conflict

between love and duty played out in the marriage of Elizabeth and William Wirt of Virginia earlier in the century.

42. Benjamin Buckner to Helen Martin, March 15, May 11, August 28, November 5, 22, December 2, 1862, Buckner Papers, UKY. Buckner's resignation was rejected initially but, according to his pension record, eventually granted in April 1863. He was honorably discharged that month, and "private business" is listed in the paperwork as the accepted "cause" of his resignation. Invalid Pension Application of Benjamin F. Buckner, January 28, 1898, Application 203852, Certificate 966944, and Widow's Pension Application of Helen M. Buckner, July 22, 1901, Application 745474, Certificate 520999, both in Pension Application Files, NA.

43. Quoted in Josie Underwood Diary, January 6, 1861, WKU. Todd remained in the Union army after the war and was promoted to major in 1867. Cullum, *Biographical Register*, 307.

44. The U.S. Army included procedures for accepting the resignations of officers — but not of enlisted soldiers — in its 1861 regulations. See *Revised United States Army Regulations of 1861*, 12. The same was true in the Confederate army regulations, which were adapted from those of the U.S. Army. See *Regulations for the Army of the Confederate States*, 3. On conscription laws in general, see McPherson, *Battle Cry of Freedom*, 427–31, 492–94; Paludan, *People's Contest*, 189–90; Blair, *Virginia's Private War*, 103–4, 126–27; and Thomas, *Confederate Nation*, 152–55.

45. Green Clay to Brutus J. Clay, November 30, 1863, Clay Family Papers, UKY (Holmbergs' story); Joseph Willard to Mr. E. R. Ford, February 28, 1864, Willard Family Papers, LC.

46. "Letters from Richmond," *Charleston Mercury*, March 9, 1863.

47. "A Yankee Girl Converts a Rebel Surgeon and Marries Him," *Louisville Daily Journal*, July 6, 1863. For other examples, see "A Romance of the War," *Memphis Argus* (reprinted in *Louisville Daily Journal*, October 18, 1864), and "Love and Disloyalty: A True Tale," *Nashville Daily Press*, May 21, 1863. On women who joined the army, see, e.g., "The Female Lieutenant," *Staunton Spectator*, September 22, 1863, and "Another Bold Soldier Girl," *Louisville Daily Journal*, May 5, 1863.

48. "Mrs. Lee," *Daily Missouri Democrat*, June 26, 1862 (published previously in *Newark Advertiser*). Such questioning of Mrs. Lee's loyalty likely had little connection with reality. Lee biographer Emory Thomas ("Lee Marriage," xiii, 32–48) has written that not only was Mary Custis Lee a "fiercely partisan Confederate," but her loyalty had helped influence Lee to side with the South.

49. "The Families of Southern Men at the North," *Louisville Daily Journal*, July 18, 1861; [Untitled], *Louisville Daily Courier*, July 19, 1861; [Untitled], *Nashville Daily Press*, April 26, 1864.

50. [Untitled], *Louisville Daily Journal*, July 10, 18, 1863. For other examples, see [Untitled], *Louisville Daily Journal*, September 16, 1861, and [Untitled], *Nashville Daily Press*, August 14, 1863.

51. "Mrs. Stonewall Jackson," *Missouri Statesman*, September 12, 1862; "Rev. Geo. Junkin, D.D.," *Frank Leslie's Illustrated Newspaper*, September 20, 1862, 406. On the Jackson-Morrison marriage and, in particular, on Anna Morrison's staunch support

of his service, see Gardner, "'Sweet Solace to My Lonely Heart,'" and "A Message to Stonewall Jackson from His Father-in-Law, Who Resides in Brooklyn, NY," *Daily Missouri Democrat*, April 16, 1863. For a similar article, see "The Rebel General Stonewall Jackson," *Harper's Weekly*, March 14, 1863, 174–75. On the Junkin-Jackson relationship, see Robertson, *Stonewall Jackson*, 208–13, 233, and Royster, *Destructive War*, 67–68.

52. Case of Mrs. E. K. Baldwin, Register of Arrests for Disloyalty, 1:18, NA.

53. "Deputation of Rebels' Wives," *Louisville Daily Journal*, May 21, 1863; General Order No. 66, *OR* 23:328, 340.

54. "A Touching Story," *Nashville Daily Press*, December 25, 1863.

55. On family and family protection as a reason why men fought, see McPherson, *For Cause and Comrades*, 95–97; Stephen W. Berry, *All That Makes a Man*, esp. 191; and Mitchell, *Vacant Chair*.

56. Josie Underwood Diary, November 9, 1861, WKU.

57. Ibid., September 30, 1861. On popular views of love, see Lystra, *Searching the Heart*, chap. 2.

58. Matthew Page Andrews to Anna Andrews, August 22, 1861, Charles Wesley Andrews Papers, Duke.

59. Confederate William C. P. Breckinridge told his wife that Union soldiers in Tennessee "insult every woman. . . . Several Federals headed by an officer went into the bed chamber of two highly respectable ladies & made them dress in their presence[,] in the mean while using the most vulgar & obscene language. These are but specimens of their savage brutality." William Breckinridge to Issa Breckinridge, February 11, 1863, containers 779–80, Breckinridge Family Papers, LC. On the fear of occupying Union troops, see Ash, *Middle Tennessee Society*, 87–88, 144–46, and *When the Yankees Came*, 147. On Confederate guerrillas, see Fellman, *Inside War*, chap. 2, and Faust, *Mothers of Invention*, 200. On the specific threat and prevalence of sexual assaults, see Mitchell, *Vacant Chair*, 103–10, and Royster, *Destructive War*, 23.

60. "Marrying 'For the War,'" *Daily Missouri Democrat*, July 18, 1863; "Marrying and Settling Soldiers," *Nashville Daily Press*, February 4, 1864. For more on this phenomenon, see "The News of the War," *Charleston Mercury*, June 4, 1862 (from a report by a correspondent of the *Lynchburg Republican*). See also "The War—An Affecting Incident," *Smyrna Times*, August 1, 1861.

61. "Converting Lady Rebels," *Missouri Statesman*, April 29, 1864; "An Apology versus a Marriage," *Nashville Daily Press*, May 10, 1864.

62. Reminiscences of the Civil War, 1914, 249, Sarah Jane Full Hill Papers, LC (quotation); Faust, *Mothers of Invention*, chap. 9; Simkins and Patton, *Women of the Confederacy*, 58–64; Durham, *Nashville*, 90.

63. Josie Underwood Diary, September 30, October 14, 22, December 8, 1861, WKU.

64. Simkins and Patton, *Women of the Confederacy*, 59 (quotation). Occupied regions, which gave these men and women time to become acquainted, were perhaps unique in fostering these relationships. In other areas, particularly those where Union soldiers passed through only briefly, it is more likely that initial antagonisms never gave way to

familiarity and romance. For more hostile relations between Confederate women and Union men, see Faust, *Mothers of Invention*, chap. 9; Rable, "Missing in Action"; Fellman, *Inside War*, chap. 2; Simkins and Patton, *Women of the Confederacy*, 58–64; Ash, *When the Yankees Came*, 69–70; Durham, *Nashville*, 90; and Campbell, *When Sherman Marched North*. Some of these studies refer to, but do not elaborate on, more friendly encounters between Union men and Confederate women. For a more in-depth discussion of less hostile relations, see Clinton, *Tara Revisited*, 83–84. On women who took in Union soldiers as boarders, see Faust, *Mothers of Invention*, 206, and Mary Starling to Samuel Starling, July 12, 1863, Lewis-Starling Collection, WKU.

65. See "A Touching Incident," *Daily Missouri Democrat*, September 24, 1864, and Clinton, *Tara Revisited*, 83–84. For other humanitarian aid, see William Barnard to Mother, November 17, 1861, S. G. Barnard Letters, SHC; Josie Underwood Diary, September 30, 1861, WKU.

66. "An Apology versus a Marriage," *Nashville Daily Press*, May 10, 1864.

67. "Love and Loyalty—Chapter Third," *Missouri Statesman*, February 17, 1865. Information about the women imprisoned for political reasons can be found in Register of Arrests for Disloyalty, vols. 1–2, NA. For the perspective of one woman imprisoned in St. Louis, see Eleanor Ann King Diary, WHMC.

68. For an extended discussion of Boyd's career, see Faust, *Mothers of Invention*, 214–19. Her relationship with her captor is also discussed in "The Husband of Belle Boyd," *Louisville Daily Journal*, December 13, 1864, and "Marriage of the Notorious Belle Boyd," *Nashville Daily Press*, September 13, 1864.

69. Antonia Ford to Joseph C. Willard, December 31, 1863, Willard Family Papers, LC.

70. Aide-de-Camp Proclamation signed by Jeb Stuart, October 7, 1861, Willard Family Papers, LC; "A Female Aid-de-Camp," *Southern Field and Fireside*, April 4, 1863, 112 (reports of Ford's arrest); "General Stuart's New Aid," *Harper's Weekly*, April 4, 1863; "Miss Antonia J. Ford in the Old Capitol," *Baltimore Sun*, September 18, 1863; [Untitled], *Louisville Daily Journal*, September 26, 1863; "Females Sent South," *Washington Evening Star*, May 14, 1863; "Antonia J. Ford in the Old Capitol," *Washington Evening Star*, September 16, 1863. Union officials had little doubt about Ford's role in the raid that led to the capture of Union general Edwin H. Stoughton in March 1863; the head of the U.S. Secret Service, L. C. Baker, dispatched a female detective to go undercover and solicit a confession from Ford, which she provided. Baker to Secretary E. M. Stanton, March 17, 1863, reprinted in L. C. Baker, *History of the United States Secret Service*, 170–73. Confederate Jeb Stuart, however, immediately set about trying to clear Ford of the charges on the basis of her "innocence." Stuart to John Singleton Mosby, March 25, 1863, Willard Family Papers, LC. Although none of the newspaper accounts or Ford's own letters refer to this, Union Provost Marshal records reveal that Ford's father, Edward R. Ford, may have been arrested for espionage around the same time. An "E. R. Ford" is listed with eight other Fairfax County, Va., men who were apprehended in March 1863 and sent to Old Capitol prison in Washington, D.C. Case no. 4486, microfilm roll 16, Union Provost Marshal's File, NA.

71. Joseph C. Willard Diary, August 24, 1862, and Antonia Ford to Willard, Decem-

ber 31, 1863, Willard Family Papers, LC. Here I am more concerned with the Ford-Willard relationship than with Ford's spying career, which has already received scholarly treatment. See Leonard, *All the Daring of the Soldier*, 45–50; Kane, *Spies*, 169–75; and Kinchen, *Women Who Spied*, 43–50.

72. Antonia Ford to Joseph C. Willard, February 22 (quotation), 29, 1864, Willard Family Papers, LC. Ford reported that other women around her praised Willard for being "so *handsome* and so exceedingly gentlemanly," and on hearing this she herself "felt proud that *my darling* should be held in such estimation by the best of Virginians" (Ford to Willard, February 29, 1864).

73. Antonia Ford to Joseph C. Willard, February 26, 1864, ibid. References in family papers suggest that Ford took the oath to the Union at the end of September 1863.

74. Antonia Ford to Joseph C. Willard, December 31, 1863, February 29, 1864, Willard Family Papers, LC.

75. It is unclear why Willard divorced his first wife, although some letters include vague hints: for example, Ford once referred to Willard having "been sinned against deeply" by his first wife. Antonia Ford to Julia Ford (mother), [?], 1864, Mrs. Willard to Joseph Willard, May 10, 1863, and Joseph C. Willard Diary, August 2, 24, 1862, Willard Family Papers, LC. See also "Decree of Divorce," *Washington Evening Star*, March 2, 1864.

76. Ben Ogle Tayloe to Joseph Willard, March 23, 1863, March 6, 1864, Willard Family Papers, LC; L. C. Baker, *History of the United States Secret Service*, 170. Both Joseph Willard and Antonia's father, Edward R. Ford, had substantial wealth. In 1860 Willard possessed $162,000 in real and personal property, and Ford, a farmer, merchant, and boardinghouse keeper, $29,000. U.S. Census, Population Schedule: Fairfax County, Va., 1860, roll 1343, p. 41, and Washington, D.C., roll 102, p. 233.

77. Joseph Willard to E. R. Ford, February 28, 1864. For more family discussion of Willard's resignation, see Antonia Ford to Willard, February 28, 1864, Willard Family Papers, LC.

78. District of Columbia Marriage Certificate, March 10, 1864, and Antonia Ford to Julia Ford (mother), [?], 1864, October 10, 1864, Willard Family Papers, LC. The marriage was announced in the *National Intelligencer*, March 11, 1864, and *Washington Evening Star*, March 15, 1864. Ford and Willard went on to have a son, Joseph Edward Willard, who served as lieutenant governor of Virginia from 1902 to 1906.

79. George Neville to Nellie Newman, February 8, 1864, Neville-Newman Correspondence, UVA; Fletcher Diary, August 30, 1865, Duke; [Untitled], *Southern Field and Fireside*, January 30, 1864, 4. See also "Wanted — Husbands and Wives," *Southern Field and Fireside*, February 25, 1865, 4. Reid Mitchell (*Vacant Chair*, 71–75) notes that Union soldiers also could be characterized as desperate for women's companionship after spending time away from home in the company of all-male regiments.

80. "I'm in Want of a Beau," *Missouri Statesman*, January 15, 1864; "Marrying 'For the War,'" *Daily Missouri Democrat*, April 18, 1863; "A Petition to the Missouri Legislature Favoring Polygamy," *Louisville Daily Journal*, February 17, 1864.

81. [Untitled], *Louisville Daily Journal*, August 17, 1861.

82. On the reactions of Union soldiers to Confederate women, see Ash, *Middle Tennessee Society*, 145, and *When the Yankees Came*, 42–44; Royster, *Destructive War*, 20, 86–87; and "Converting Lady Rebels," *Missouri Statesman*, April 29, 1864.

83. For an assessment of the consequences of the Nashville occupation, see McPherson, *Battle Cry of Freedom*, 402–3. See also Ash, *Middle Tennessee Society*, 85.

84. *Louisville Daily Journal*, April 5, 1862, and Columbus *Daily Ohio State Journal*, April 10, 1862, both quoted in Durham, *Nashville*, 88.

85. See Durham, *Nashville*, 89.

86. [Untitled], *Louisville Daily Journal*, April 1, 7, 1862.

87. "A Rebel Girl on Union," *Missouri Statesman*, June 23, 1865. The letter is dated January 29, 1865. For more on intersectional romance during the Nashville occupation, see Simkins and Patton, *Women of the Confederacy*, 61–62.

88. Gates Thruston to Mother, March 3, 1865, Thruston Papers, FHS. Joseph C. Willard was advised by a close friend that Virginia women could only be "conquered" if men such as themselves "take to our hearts the wayward sisters." Ben Ogle Tayloe to Willard, March 23, 1863, Willard Family Papers, LC. On newspaper accounts of actual marriages in Nashville, see Durham, *Nashville*, 188, 265–66. On Thruston's wedding, see Rowena Webster Memoir, n.d., Jill Knight Garrett Collection, TSLA.

89. The *Democrat* (February 28, 1863) referred to Sutherland as "Edward," but it was "Edwin Sutherland" who commanded the *Queen of the West*. Reaction to the Sutherland-Harris marriage was less enthusiastic outside the newspaper. The marriage, like others across sectional lines, also made Sutherland's Union loyalty suspect. A naval comrade observed that the union "boded no good for the Captain," as his commander, Alfred Ellet, later issued an order restricting Sutherland's bride's time on the ship in the event that she was a spy. See Hearn, *Ellet's Brigade*, 120–23. (Ironically, Ellet's own niece later married a Confederate. See Chapter 6.) A similar case is recounted in "A Bit of War Romance," *Louisville Daily Courier*, November 12, 1861.

90. [Untitled], *Louisville Daily Journal*, July 17, 1862.

91. Quoted in Mary Starling to Anna Starling, August 4, 1864, Lewis-Starling Collection, WKU. Sometimes Union soldiers complained, rather than boasted, of being Southern women's best protectors. From his vantage point in St. Louis in April 1862, Major General Henry Halleck wrote: "Nearly all the secessionists of this State who have entered the rebel service have left their wives and daughters to the care of the Federal troops. There is scarcely a single instance where this confidence has been abused by us. But what return have these ladies made for this protection? In many cases they have acted as spies and informers for the enemy and have been most loud-mouthed in their abuse of our cause and most insulting in their conduct towards those who support it." Men like Halleck resented instances in which their "protection" did not translate into gratitude or even Union loyalty. Halleck to William M. McPherson, Esq., April 3, 1862, *OR* 8:657–58.

92. Women gradually became "political," historians of women North and South traditionally argue, when they carried domestic concerns nurtured in the household into public campaigns and organizations. Women looked outward from their vantage point

as wives and mothers and saw politics outside of their households; it was a decidedly "public" activity. Matthews, *Rise of Public Woman*, 9; Kierner, *Beyond the Household*, 1–8; Varon, *We Mean to Be Counted*, 1–9; Ryan, *Women in Public*, 1–19.

93. Lizette Woodworth Reese, *Victorian Village*, 83; also quoted in Bardaglio, "On the Border," 321.

Chapter Three

1. [Untitled], *Louisville Daily Journal*, November 15, 1862.

2. This chapter is largely based on 71 cases of divided siblings. In 19 of the 31 cases (or 61 percent) for which the relevant data are available, a father was dead, and in 16 cases (52 percent) a mother had died. The number of cases in which both parents were dead was 14 (45 percent). (In the remaining cases, the parents were either both alive or their status was unclear.) The death of parents eliminated the potentially volatile conflict of generations and made more visible the fissures between brothers and sisters. That is, siblings focused more directly on divisions with one another after a parent, with whom they might also have come into conflict, died. This also explains why my sample of divided siblings is as old as it is. U.S. Census, Population Schedule: Delaware, Kentucky, Maryland, Missouri, Tennessee, and Virginia, 1860.

3. Rotundo, *American Manhood*, 31–55. For a similar discussion of the early years of Southern men, see Wyatt-Brown, *Southern Honor*, 149–74. One of the only extended studies of blood brother relationships in nineteenth-century America, Lorri Glover's *All Our Relations*, finds little to no evidence of sibling rivalries or struggles. In contrast, I see competition even in the most mundane behavior.

4. For examples of these boyhood political games, see Josie Underwood Diary, March 10, June 20, 1861, WKU, and Anne Lane to Sarah Glasgow, August 30, [1863?], William Carr Lane Papers, MHS. For political game playing among young children, see Marten, *Children's Civil War*, 148–86.

5. Samuel Halsey (brother) to Joseph Halsey, August 24, 1856, Morton-Halsey Family Papers, UVA.

6. Samuel Halsey (brother) to Joseph Halsey, February 25, 1858, ibid.

7. Edmund Halsey to Joseph Halsey, January 18, 1857, ibid.

8. Samuel Halsey (father) to Joseph Halsey, October 18, 1857, ibid.

9. Edmund Halsey to Joseph Halsey, September 15, 1856, ibid.

10. Edmund Halsey to Joseph Halsey, January 18, 1857, ibid.

11. Edmund Halsey to Joseph Halsey, September 15, 1856, ibid.

12. Samuel Halsey (brother) to Joseph Halsey, August 24, 1856, ibid.

13. William Cooper to Matthew D. Cooper, October 12, 1856, Cooper Family Papers, TSLA.

14. George William Brown to George C. Shattuck, February 21, 1862, Brown Collection, MDHS.

15. On brotherly love, see Rotundo, *American Manhood*, 39; Wyatt-Brown, *Southern Honor*, 165; Glover, *All Our Relations*, 42–43; Richards, "Passing the Love of Women,"

93; and Stowe, *Intimacy and Power*. Affection may have been even more overt when the brothers' parents were dead. See also Atkins, *We Grew Up Together*, 109.

16. Samuel Halsey (brother) to Joseph Halsey, September 3, 1857, November 19, 1862, Morton-Halsey Family Papers, UVA.

17. Valentine Stone to Henry Stone, October 12, 1862, Stone Collection, FHS; Joseph Cabell Breckinridge to Robert J. Breckinridge, August 7, 1862, Breckinridge Family Papers, container 225, LC.

18. Jabez Pratt to John Pratt, April 20, 1861, and John Pratt to Jabez Pratt, April 24, 1861, Jabez D. and John C. Pratt Letters, MDHS.

19. Jabez Pratt to John Pratt, April 27, 1861, ibid.

20. Jabez Pratt to John Pratt, May 1, 1861, ibid.

21. See "From Baltimore," *Boston Daily Journal*, April 26, 1861.

22. Jabez Pratt to John Pratt, May 3, 1861, Jabez D. and John C. Pratt Letters, MDHS.

23. John Pratt to Jabez Pratt, May 6, [?], 1861, ibid.

24. Charles Henry Lee to "Bro," April 16, 1861, Edmund Jennings Lee II Papers, Duke. Older brothers beyond military age sometimes took comfort in knowing that their differences would not play out in direct combat. Josie Underwood of Kentucky recorded a conversation between her fifty-two-year-old father and his brother Henry: "Today Pa said, 'It is hard brother that we are not younger men.' Uncle Henry said 'Maybe it is best for us we are not, Warner.' I am quite sure the dear old man was thinking he would be in the Rebel army and he knew Pa's loyalty to the Union could not be shaken." Josie Underwood Diary, August 1, 1861, WKU.

25. William B. Whiting to John Crittenden, December 8, 1860, reel 12, and James W. Bacon to John Crittenden, July 14, 1861, reel 13, John J. Crittenden Papers, LC.

26. See "Romantic Triangle Stories" in Chapter 5.

27. For examples of fratricide unrelated to the war, see *Louisville Daily Journal*: "Terrible Fratricide," April 2, 1861; "Distressing Fratricide," April 17, 1861; and "Melancholy Affair," April 23, 1861.

28. On how fratricide figured in wartime literature, see "Romantic Triangle Stories" in Chapter 5. For an analysis of fratricide in the literature of the American Revolution, see Forgie, *Patricide*, 201–50.

29. Willie Tavenner to Bettie Withers, December 11, 1860, Cabell Tavenner and Alexander Scott Withers Papers, Duke. A recent study of nineteenth-century sibling relations also finds little consideration of birth order among brothers and sisters. See Glover, *All Our Relations*, 28. For an overview of theories on birth order and children, see Sulloway, *Born to Rebel*. See also Bank and Kahn, *Sibling Bond*, 6–7, 55–56, and Merrell, *Accidental Bond*, 223–30.

30. Samuel Halsey (brother) to Joseph Halsey, May 16, 1861, Morton-Halsey Family Papers, UVA; Henry Stone to Father, December 29, 1862, Stone Collection, FHS.

31. One Union soldier sought to resign in April 1861 to avoid "brother being arraigned against brother" but found that his commanding officer was no longer accepting resignations. Lydia T. Lawrence to Brother Henry, April 24, 1861, Brasher-Lawrence Family

Papers, SHC. On conscription laws, see McPherson, *Battle Cry of Freedom*, 427–31, 492–94; Paludan, *People's Contest*, 189–90; and Thomas, *Confederate Nation*, 152–55. In its 1861 regulations the U.S. Army included procedures for accepting the resignations of officers, but not of enlisted soldiers. *Revised United States Army Regulations of 1861*, 12.

32. On the connection between masculinity and Civil War enlistment, see, e.g., McPherson, *For Cause and Comrades*, 25–26; Linderman, *Embattled Courage*; and Stephen W. Berry, *All That Makes a Man*. During legislative sessions several Confederate congressmen launched into tirades against "skulkers." See Proceedings of the Confederate Congress, January 21, 1863, 47:173–75.

33. Alfred Mordecai to George Mordecai, January 20, 1861, and W. Hardee to Alfred Mordecai, March 4, 1861, Alfred Mordecai Papers, LC.

34. Alfred Mordecai to Samuel Mordecai, March 17, 1861, ibid.

35. This language of military brotherhood was pervasive in newspapers, letters, and other wartime writings. See McPherson, *For Cause and Comrades*, 85–89.

36. Alfred Mordecai to Lieutenant Colonel J. W. Ripley, May 2, 1861, Alfred Mordecai Papers, LC.

37. George Mordecai to Alfred Mordecai, April 16, May 5, 1861, and Ellen Mordecai to Alfred Mordecai, May 28, 1861, ibid.

38. J. E. [Berlin?] to Alfred Mordecai, May 5, 1861, [?] Maynadier to Alfred Mordecai, May 6, 1861, and J. W. Jones to Alfred Mordecai, May 8, 1861, ibid.

39. Alfred Mordecai to Samuel Mordecai, June 2, 1861, ibid.

40. "The Resignation of Major Mordecai," *Troy Daily Times*, May 9, 1861, clipping in ibid. See also "Major Mordecai," *Troy Daily News*, May 8, 1861, clipping in ibid.

41. Alfred Mordecai to Samuel Mordecai, June 2, 1861, ibid.

42. Data on military service are available for 46 of the 55 cases of divided brothers examined in this chapter. In 35 of those 46 cases (76 percent), the two brothers served in opposing armies. In 6 cases (13 percent), neither brother served, and in 5 cases (11 percent), only one brother served.

43. Dyer and Moore, *Tennessee Civil War Veterans Questionnaires*, 1266–68.

44. "Franklin County Rebel Killed," *Franklin Repository*, June 29, 1864, from Ayers et al., "The Valley of the Shadow," <http://valley.vcdh.virginia.edu>; James Proctor Knott to Maria I. Knott, August 4, 1861, Knott Collection, WKU.

45. William F. Cooper to His Brothers, May 31, 1861, Cooper Family Papers, TSLA.

46. Joseph Crider to William Crider, October 2, 1862, Joseph Crider Letters, WHMC.

47. James Welsh to John Welsh, June 2, 1861, in Bean, "House Divided," 401. A similar sentiment is conveyed in Ly[dia] Moor to Brother, July 5, 1864, Moor-Naudain Collection, DPA.

48. Melvin Dwinnell to Parents, August 6, 1861, in Bailey, "Letters of . . . Dwinnell," 199.

49. See ibid.; Charles Chase to Henry Chase, July 30, 1861, Charles Monroe Chase Papers, WHMC; and "The Situation," *New York Herald*, November 14, 1861.

50. Melvin Dwinnell to Parents, August 6, 1861, in Bailey, "Letters of . . . Dwinnell," 199.

51. Matthew Page Andrews to Anna Andrews, July 28, 1861, Charles Wesley Andrews Papers, Duke.

52. [Untitled], *Louisville Daily Journal*, July 25, 1862.

53. On the importance of exhibiting courage, see Linderman, *Embattled Courage*, and McPherson, *For Cause and Comrades*, 77–78.

54. "Brother against Brother," *Daily Missouri Democrat*, December 9, 1861; "Brother Shoots Brother," *Nashville Daily Press*, September 10, 1864; "Brother's Blood," *Louisville Daily Journal*, March 12, 1865.

55. "Old Battery, Stono River, SC," *New York Herald*, June 17, 1862; "Headquarters First Division Missouri State Guard," *New York Herald*, November 29, 1861; "An Incident of the War," *Richmond Enquirer*, October 8, 1861. For similar stories, see "An Incident of the War," *Daily Missouri Republican*, April 3, 1864; [Untitled], *Smyrna Times*, October 10, 1861; "Singular Meeting of Two Brothers after a Battle," *Schenectady Weekly Republican*, August 30, 1861; and "An Affecting Incident of the Late Battle — Singular Meeting of Brothers after Seven Years' Absence — Both Wounded," *Louisville Daily Courier*, August 19, 1861.

56. [Untitled], *Louisville Daily Journal*, October 10, 1861. This article, which implicitly condones revenge and violence, reflects a popular journalistic tendency of "urging on and vicariously reliving the war's violence," in the words of Charles Royster (*Destructive War*, 240).

57. "Horrors of Civil War," *Louisville Daily Journal*, February 25, 1862, reprinted in "Horrors of Cival [*sic*] War," *Missouri Statesman*, March 14, 1862.

58. [Untitled], *Louisville Daily Journal*, April 18, 1862.

59. "Brother against Brother," *Daily Richmond Examiner*, July 30, 1863.

60. "Incidents of the Late Battle of Lebanon," *Louisville Daily Journal*, May 14, 1862 (reprinted from *Nashville Union*). For a similar story, see "An Affecting Scene," *Missouri Statesman*, June 20, 1862.

61. "Singular Episode of the War," *Missouri Statesman*, February 12, 1864 (also printed in "A Singular Episode of the War," *Nashville Daily Press*, February 8, 1864). For a similar story, see "The Details of the Fight near Winchester," *Valley Spirit*, April 2, 1862, from Ayers et al., "The Valley of the Shadow," <http://valley.vcdh.virginia.edu>.

62. "At South Mountain," *Harper's Weekly*, October 25, 1862, 674.

63. "Scenes on the Battlefield," *New York Herald*, December 22, 1864.

64. "An Incident of the War — Two College Mates Colonels in Opposing Armies," February 26, 1865, *Louisville Daily Journal* (also printed in *Nashville Daily Press*, February 16, 1865).

65. Mitchell, *Civil War Soldiers*, 24–55; Linderman, *Embattled Courage*, 65–71. See also Royster, *Destructive War*, 318. Reports of real-life sibling encounters in private letters and diaries also support some of the themes in the newspaper stories. Two accounts of brothers having one another arrested, for example, appear in James B. and B. P. McKown to "My Dear Son," July 27, 1862, in Goodrich, "Civil War Letters," 250–52, and Arrest Record of Jerome R. Barber, Register of Arrests for Disloyalty, 1:11–12, NA.

Walt Whitman took note of two Maryland brothers he met in a hospital who had both fought at Petersburg, had both been mortally wounded there, had both been sent to the same hospital, and had both eventually died from their wounds. Basler, *Walt Whitman's Memoranda*, 53.

66. See "Wartime Reunion" in Chapter 6. For examples of brothers' assistance, see James Yeatman to General Sherman, April 6, 1864, Yeatman-Polk Family Papers, TSLA; Bennett, "Burke's Civil War Journal," 288; Charles C. Tucker to E. H. Smith, Esq., April 5, 1862, Hubbard Smith Papers, FHS; and Oliver A. Sandusky to Abraham Lincoln, January 21, 1865, Sandusky Petition, WHMC.

67. Lewis Merrill to Major Caldwell, September 2, 1862, *OR*, ser. 2, 4:480–81.

68. Arthur [?] to Percy Luck, July 29, 1863, Percy Frere Luck Papers, LC.

69. "Brother against Brother," *Frank Leslie's Illustrated Newspaper*, May 24, 1862, 94.

70. "Headquarters First Division Missouri State Guard," *New York Herald*, November 29, 1861.

71. Kirshner, *Class of 1861*, 75 (DuPont-Browne); Patterson, *Rebels from West Point*, 27 (Lee-Kearny). Edward Chauncey Marshall (*Are the West Point Graduates Loyal?*, 7) estimated that three-quarters (623 of 820) of West Point graduates still serving in the military in 1861 fought for the Union, and the other quarter (197) served the Confederacy. For other examples of intersectional fraternity—including a Union officer's participation in a Confederate wedding—see the memoir of Morris Schaff, an 1862 graduate of West Point, in Schaff, *Spirit of Old West Point*, 36, 56–57, 99–100, 132–34, 169–70, 175–77, 179–81.

72. "Friends and Foes," *Philadelphia Inquirer*, February 25, 1862. Similar criticism is described in Williams, "Attack upon West Point." Grant and Buckner did remember their position as "foes" during the Union's capture of Fort Donelson in February 1862 and exchanged a terse set of letters negotiating the surrender of Confederate forces at the fort. A hint of their previous friendship surfaced in the letters, however, when Grant agreed to allow some of Buckner's men to move outside the lines to bury their dead. See Grant, *Personal Memoirs*, 310–15.

73. W. J. Clift to Thomas [?], May 30, 1862, Camp Chase Papers, VHS.

74. William T. Sherman to Thomas Hunton, August 24, 1862, in Berlin et al., *Free at Last*, 69.

75. The most influential work on women's friendship is still Carroll Smith-Rosenberg's "The Female World of Love and Ritual." See also Cott, *Bonds of Womanhood*, 160–96, and Buza, "'Pledges of Our Love.'" On blood sisters, see Glover, *All Our Relations*. Politics was not foreign to women's relationships; in fact, such friendships and sisterly bonds sometimes formed the basis for networks of women's public reform and political activities in the antebellum period. Political agreement, rather than difference, however, tended to animate these efforts. For women's political activities in the early national and antebellum border states, see Allgor, *Parlor Politics*, and Varon, *We Mean to Be Counted*.

76. Emma Read Berry to Harriet Read, March 9, 1861, Read Family Papers, VHS.

77. [L. or S. P. Cornwall?] to Carrie Lawrence Bedinger (sister), June 26, 1862, Bedinger-Dandridge Family Papers, Duke.

78. Josie Underwood Diary, October 9, 1861, WKU.

79. Alice to "Cousins," August 23, 1863, Lizzie C. Gilmore Papers, WHMC.

80. Sarah Bibb to Mary Starling, April 17, 1862, Lewis-Starling Collection, WKU.

81. Harriet Archer Williams to Lewis Williams, February 9, October 17, 1864, Archer-Mitchell-Stump-Williams Papers, MDHS.

82. Sophie DuPont to Samuel F. DuPont, May 16, 1862, DuPont Family Papers, Hagley.

83. Agnes Babb to John Babb Jr., July 20, August 10, 1862, May 26, June 13, 1863, John D. Babb Family Papers, Emory.

84. Josie Underwood Diary, August 31, 1862, WKU.

85. Harriet Archer Williams to Lewis Williams, February 9, 1864, Archer-Mitchell-Stump-Williams Papers, MDHS.

86. Emma Read Berry to Harriet Read, March 9, 1861, Read Family Papers, VHS.

87. Josie Underwood Diary, June 13, 1861, WKU.

88. Ibid., February 10, 1861.

89. Anna Dupuy to Alicia Boyleston, August 10, 1861, Emily Howe Dupuy Papers, VHS. Later that year Anna left Virginia to live with family in Massachusetts.

90. Josie Underwood Diary, September 15, 1861, WKU.

91. Ibid., August 1, 1861.

92. Alice [?] to Bettie Withers, August 16, 1861, Cabell Tavenner and Alexander Scott Withers Papers, Duke.

93. C. Alice Ready Diary, March 20, 1862, SHC.

94. Letter quoted in Sophie DuPont to Samuel F. DuPont, April 20, 1862, DuPont Family Papers, Hagley.

95. "A Spirited Fight between Two Girls at Church," *Nashville Daily Press*, August 23, 1864 (reprinted from *St. Joseph Herald*, July 29, 1864); also printed as "An Amusing Affair in Gentry," *Daily Missouri Democrat*, August 3, 1864.

96. Ellen Coolidge to Benjamin Randolph, February 6, 1861, Trist-Burke Family Papers, UVA.

97. Mary Davis to Brother, May 25, 1861, Rebecca Dorsey Davis Papers, MDHS.

98. Martha M. Tipton Diary, September 1, 1863, TSLA.

99. "Mr. and Mrs. Hussbar," *Southern Literary Messenger*, November–December 1862, 674.

100. Lorri Glover (*All Our Relations*) argues for this egalitarian view of brother-sister relations. For other studies of sibling relationships, see Atkins, *We Grew Up Together*; Stowe, *Intimacy and Power*, 187; Degler, *At Odds*, 158; Censer, *North Carolina Planters*, 21–24; and Mintz, *Prison of Expectations*, 148–51.

101. Maria I. Knott to "My Dear Children," September 26, 1861, Knott Collection, WKU.

102. Mary Davis to Brother, May 25, 1861, Rebecca Dorsey Davis Papers, MDHS.

103. "The Yankee General Thomas," *Staunton Spectator*, October 27, 1863, from

Ayers et al., "The Valley of the Shadow," <http://valley.vcdh.virginia.edu>; Cleaves, *Rock of Chickamauga*, 3–7.

104. Mary Davis to Brother, May 25, 1861, Rebecca Dorsey Davis Papers, MDHS.

105. Jackson, for his part, still honored his sister when he named a daughter born in 1862 "Julia Laura Jackson," although his death a year later precluded any reunion with her. On the Jackson-Arnold relationship, see esp. Robertson, *Stonewall Jackson*, 7–15, 38–39, 80, 90, 102 ("closest confidante"), 157, 207–9, 233, 690–91, 760, and Royster, *Destructive War*, 46–47, 218–19. See also the letters exchanged between the two siblings in Stonewall Jackson Papers, <www.vmi.edu/archives/Jackson/tjjpaprs.html>. Newspapers circulated rumors about the Jackson-Arnold relationship during the war. In one paper it was said that Arnold was "not very popular with the friends of her deceased brother." According to another rumor, which appeared in Union papers: "Mrs. Arnold of Beverly, Va., says of Stonewall Jackson, her brother, that although it was with agony she said it, he had lived too long with the treasonable enemies of the best Government that God ever gave man." It was also alleged that "she seemed very much depressed, but said that she would rather know that he was dead than to have him a leader in the rebel army." Such reports offered little additional details about the relationship but instead seemed most fascinated that such a brother-sister split had occurred at all. See [Untitled], *Louisville Daily Journal*, June 8, 1864 (reprinted as "Stonewall Jackson's Sister a Loyal Woman," June 15, 1864, *Nashville Daily Press*); [Untitled], *Franklin Repository*, July 8, 1863, from Ayers et al., "Valley of the Shadow," <http://valley.vcdh.virginia.edu>; [Untitled], *Missouri Statesman*, November 13, 1863.

106. Josie Underwood Diary, February 5, August 25, 1861, WKU. Mary Ellet, of Washington, D.C., did not have to deal with her brother's resignation — he fought for the Union, which she supported too — but she still urged her brother to fight proudly and uphold the family name. "You must be a worthy son of him whose fame you are bravely striving to support, in all ways, as well as those of mere worldly success. Anxious as I am about your personal safety . . . I cannot feel sorry that you are so placed as to bear your share in what may be done by 'the Ellets.'" Mary Ellet to Charlie Ellet, August 21, 1862, Cabell-Ellet Family Papers, UVA. A similar case was reported in [Untitled], *Washington Evening Star*, July 23, 1863.

107. Josie Underwood Diary, August 25, 1861, WKU.

108. Ibid., July 22, 1862.

109. Ibid., August 8, 1862.

Chapter Four

1. Martha Davenport to Ann Clay, March 27, 1862, Clay Family Papers, UKY.

2. Samuel Halsey (father) to Joseph Halsey, April 19, 1861, Morton-Halsey Family Papers, UVA. See also J. N. Lawrence to Caroline Bedinger, October 5, 1863, Bedinger-Dandridge Family Papers, Duke.

3. Mary Ellet to Charlie Ellet, August 28, 1862, Cabell-Ellet Family Papers, UVA.

4. On leaving boarding school, see Ambrose J. Erwin to Secretary Seward, February 3, 1862; on leaving an asylum, see J. W. Norwood to Dr. B. Robinson, January 10,

1862. For examples of family members desiring to cross the lines for medical care, see Alexander Henry to Secretary Seward, October 8, 1861, and Colonel E. D. Townsend to Secretary Seward, December 27, 1861. For subsistence and financial support, see A. S. Pennington to Secretary Seward, December 12, 1861. All of these letters are in Letters Requesting Passes to Visit the South, NA. See also William Daniel Jr. to "My Dear Sister," May 10, 1861, Cabell-Ellet Family Papers, UVA.

5. James A. Seddon to Jefferson Davis, January 11, 1865, *OR*, ser. 4, 3:1015; General Order 56, Assistant Adjutant General S. Williams, December 19, 1861, *OR* 5:689-95. For other discussions of the pass system, see Radley, *Rebel Watchdog*, 74-101; Neely, *Southern Rights*, 2-6; and Coulter, *Confederate States*, 395.

6. Southern slaves were required to obtain passes from their masters in a system that monitored (and tried to prevent) runaways. One white Missourian noticed the resemblance between this and the wartime pass system when she complained about having to obtain a pass "like any other darkie." Sallie Knott to Mother, July 2, 1861, Knott Collection, WKU. Confederates had more reason than Union citizens to complain about the burden of passes: in the South, all travel, even within Confederate lines, required a pass, whereas in the Union only travel across the military border called for a pass. Yet, as Mark Neely (*Southern Rights*, 5-6) points out, these complaints did not translate into formal pressure to change the system.

7. J. B. Jones, *War Clerk's Diary*, 1:102, 2:77, 102.

8. In this study, 375 Union pass applications were found and examined. Because I uncovered very few pass applications to the Confederate government, they are not analyzed in depth here. Union applications for travel to the South are available in Letters Requesting Passes to Visit the South, NA. The State Department initially assumed control of the pass system (and civilian arrests for disloyalty) until the War Department took over after 1862. On the State Department and its disloyalty investigations, see Neely, *Fate of Liberty*, 19-31. Applications to the Union for passes to travel to the North (reflecting a new Federal requirement after 1863 that travelers receive permission to enter the Union as well as to leave it) are located in Letters Received Applying for Passes to Enter Union Territory, NA. The Confederate passes are scattered throughout the voluminous collection, Letters Received, Confederate Secretary of War, NA. Other records of pass applications to travel within the Confederacy are available in Records of the Passport Office, NA.

9. R. J. Walker to Secretary Seward (via Mrs. Gwin), November 2, 1861, Letters Requesting Passes to Visit the South, NA.

10. P. F. Spencer to Secretary Seward, January 23, 1862, Francis French to Seward, January 18, 1862, Sisters of Visitation to Seward (via Mrs. Douglas), February 5, 1862, and D. H. Craig to Seward, January 21, 1862, ibid.

11. James Monroe Heiskell to Secretary Seward, December 31, 1861, and Mrs. John Foule to Seward, February 7, 1862, ibid. Another woman wrote Secretary Stanton that "I am a daughter of your old friend Chief Justice Gibson." Margaritta G. McClure to Stanton, January 7, 1864, ibid.

12. W. G. Freeman to Secretary Seward, January 27, 1862, ibid.

13. Of the 375 Union pass applications examined in this study, 277 were for family

visits; 59 were initiated out of a concern for property, 12 solely for health, and 27 for other reasons. John C. McGowan to Secretary Seward, December 13, 1861, ibid.

14. William Bayne to Hon. James F. Simmons, January 29, 1862, and Selectman of Northfield to Secretary Seward, January 20, 1862, ibid.

15. George W. Cullum to Mary Wagner Faulkner, December 30, 1863, Faulkner Family Papers, VHS. Article III, Section 3, of the Constitution states: "Treason against the United States, shall consist only in levying War against them, or in adhering to their Enemies, giving them Aid and Comfort." *We the People: The Constitution of the United States of America* (Washington, D.C.: National Archives and Records Administration, n.d.), 14.

16. Selectman of Northfield to Secretary Seward, January 20, 1862, Letters Requesting Passes to Visit the South, NA.

17. James Humphrey to Secretary Seward, December 23, 1861, ibid.

18. On civilian arrests for disloyalty to the Union, see Neely, *Fate of Liberty*, 138.

19. Charles A. Mott to Secretary Seward, November 18, 1862, Letters Requesting Passes to Visit the South, NA.

20. J. Benthall to George McClellan, January 22, 1862, William Pennington to Secretary Seward, December 11, 1861, Mrs. W. M. Given to Seward, January 24, 1862, P. W. Derham to Seward, February 8, 1862, Edward Purcell to Secretary Cameron, November 12, 1861, and Mrs. J. Sheppard to Seward, February 25, 1862, Letters Requesting Passes to Visit the South, NA. Of the 242 applications examined for gender, 195 were written by women.

21. For women's wartime activities, see Chapter 2. See also Faust, *Mothers of Invention*, 214–19, 221, and Clinton, *Tara Revisited*, 89–97.

22. See "Attempting to Pass to the Enemy — Arrest of the Guilty Parties," *Richmond Enquirer*, March 28, 1864, and "Female Spies," *New York Tribune*, January 21, 1862. In 1863 the *Nashville Daily Press* lampooned the efforts of disloyal women to obtain passes from the Union in the following dialogue between a Union officer and a "good-looking female" with a "seductive smile" who wished to leave Nashville:

> "Lieutenant Osgood — Madame, do you recognize the right and authority of the Constitution and laws of the United States?
> Lady — Yes, sir, I recognize the Constitution.
> Lieutenant Osgood — That is not the question. Do you or do you not consider the United States the only and true Government to which you are accountable?
> Lady — Why, we have a Confederate Government and I suppose when that is fully established, Nashville will be under that rule.
> Lieutenant Osgood — Well, madame, once and for all, are you loyal to Abe Lincoln's Government, as it has been is now, and ever shall be?
> Angry Lady — What! Loyal to that nasty, ni — er stealing puppy, Lincoln!"

The woman did not receive her pass. "Incidents of the War," *Nashville Daily Press*, May 26, 1863.

23. Henry W. Halleck to Major General Foster, September 23, 1864, *OR*, ser. 2, 7:866. "No More Passes to Ladies," *New York Tribune*, January 4, 1862. On June 8, 1863, in

an effort to limit women's ability to smuggle, Judge Advocate L. C. Turner ordered that women could not travel with more than "one trunk or package of female wearing apparel, weighing not over one hundred pounds and subject to inspection." "Official: Order in Relation to Passes," *Washington Evening Star*, June 11, 1863.

24. Only 103 of the 375 applications studied here received clear answers from the Federal government. Of those, 95 were denied and 8 were approved. In contrast, all of the 10 applications to the Confederate government examined here were approved. However, this sample is too small to determine whether the data indicate a difference in the two governments' willingness to let men and women travel across the lines. But one Confederate official, War Department clerk J. B. Jones, later complained that various Southern provost marshals and even one assistant secretary of war were too free in their issuance of passes — particularly to friends and patrons. Jones, *War Clerk's Diary*, 1:105, 320, 2:77–78, 93, 102.

25. One man writing in support of Eliza Carrington of Kentucky insisted that her application be delayed because she wanted to travel toward the Shenandoah Valley. He knew that troops were headed in the same direction, and it was not the "proper time" to issue her a pass. Edward Bates to General E. C. Carrington, September 23, 1864, Preston Family Papers, VHS.

26. Juliana Gardiner to Secretary Seward, January 25, 1862, NA. Tyler's rampant secessionism was remembered by fellow first lady Mary Lincoln, who criticized her request for a presidential widow's pension in 1879. Lincoln complained that Tyler was "so bitter against our cause during the War" and during those four years was "so fearful a Secessionist." Jean Baker, *Mary Todd Lincoln*, 361. It is possible that Gardiner made the trip to Virginia without a pass. A collection of correspondence between Gardiner and her daughter contains an eleven-month gap in 1862, suggesting that they might have been together. See ser. 3, film 1666, reel 3, John Tyler Papers, LC.

27. Mrs. Esther A. Tiffany to Secretary Seward, January 30, 1862, Letters Requesting Passes to Visit the South, NA.

28. Jean Baker, *Mary Todd Lincoln*, 226.

29. "A Premium Uniform," *Daily Richmond Examiner*, March 2, 1862 (reprinted in *Memphis Daily Appeal*, March 5, 1864).

30. See, e.g., "A Premium Uniform," *Daily Missouri Democrat*, and "A Premium Uniform," *Missouri Statesman*, March 18, 1864; "Aid and Comfort for the Enemy," *New York Tribune*, March 28, 1864; "Disloyal Relations," *Daily Missouri Republican*, April 7, 1864 (reprinted from *Chicago Post*); and "The Story about Mrs. White," *Washington Evening Star*, April 28, 1864.

31. According to biographical accounts, only one of Mary Lincoln's eight half siblings, Margaret Todd Kellogg, supported the Union. All eight were the children of Mary's father, Robert Smith Todd, and his second wife, Elizabeth (Betsy) Humphreys, whereas Mary was the daughter of Todd's first wife, Eliza Parker. For more on the Todd family, see Jean Baker, *Mary Todd Lincoln*, esp. 3–73, 222–26; Townsend, *Lincoln*, 27–73; Squires, "Lincoln's Todd In-Laws"; Emilie Helm, "Todd Family," 69–96; and Stephen W. Berry, *All That Makes a Man*, 200–218.

32. On the Confederate Todds and their movements before Martha White's trip, see

"Lincoln's Sister-in-Law," *Daily Missouri Democrat*, February 21, 1861 (reprinted from *Columbus [Ga.] Times*); "Old Abe's Kentucky Relatives," *Daily Missouri Democrat*, October 7, 1861 (reprinted from *Cincinnati Commercial*); [Untitled], *Daily Missouri Democrat*, October 29, 1862 (reprinted from *Atlanta Confederacy*); [Untitled], *Daily Missouri Democrat*, November 26, 1863; "Important from the South," *New York Herald*, January 18, 1862; "Interesting from New Orleans," *New York Herald*, March 8, 1863; [Untitled], *Frank Leslie's Illustrated Newspaper*, December 12, 1863, 178; "Mrs. Lincoln's Mother," *Staunton Spectator*, November 17, 1863, from Ayers et al., "Valley of the Shadow," <http://valley.vcdh.virginia.edu>; [Untitled], *Louisville Daily Journal*, August 2, 1861, October 13, 1863; "Mrs. Lincoln's Brother Killed," *Smyrna Times*, August 28, 1862; and "Personal," *Washington Evening Star*, November 19, 1863.

33. On these previous scandals, see Rothman, *Notorious*, chap. 1; Cogan, "Reynolds Affair"; and Basch, "Marriage, Morals, and Politics."

34. See "Marriage" in Chapter 2.

35. This incident has been discussed briefly in biographical treatments of the Lincolns. But most of these accounts take either the newspaper reports or subsequent memoirs at face value, whereas my interest is in unraveling how the story was told over time, how and why it changed, and why it became so powerful in Northern society. For previous accounts, see Jean Baker, *Mary Todd Lincoln*, 226; Squires, "Lincoln's Todd In-Laws," 126; Townsend, *Lincoln*, 317; and Randall, *Mary Lincoln*, 343–44.

36. "Aid and Comfort for the Enemy," *New York Tribune*, March 28, 1864.

37. "Mrs. Lincoln's Sister Gone South," *National Intelligencer*, March 29, 1864.

38. On the passes issued to Emilie Todd Helm and Elizabeth Todd, see Lyman B. Todd to Abraham Lincoln, October 31, 1863, and Lincoln to "To Whom it May Concern," December 14, 1863, "The Abraham Lincoln Papers at the Library of Congress," <http://www.memory.loc.gov>. Other Todds who sought favors from Lincoln include Mary's half sister Katherine Todd, who asked for an exchange for General W. N. R. Beall, and half sister Margaret Todd Kellogg, who sought aid in the release of a political prisoner. See Katherine Todd to Lincoln, September 5, 1864, and Margaret Todd Kellogg to Lincoln, September 5, 1864, in "The Abraham Lincoln Papers," ibid. In another case, Lincoln approved the return of furniture to a Kentucky woman whose husband was in the Confederate army. He did require some indication of the woman's Union loyalty, however, and asked that she "not live with him [her husband] again" after receiving her furniture. "Memorandum for Mrs. Hunt," April 11, 1864, in Nicolay and Hay, *Complete Works of Abraham Lincoln*, 10:72–73. For other examples from the same volume, see Lincoln to B. F. Butler, February 26, 1864, p. 20, and Lincoln to Officer in Command, Knoxville, Tenn., March 2, 1864, p. 28. Lincoln also made arrangements to provide a pass for Kentuckian Margaret Preston, explaining that he did so on behalf of his wife's "early and strong friendship" with her. Lincoln to Mrs. Margaret Preston, August 21, 1863, in Katherine Helm, *Mary, Wife of Lincoln*, 214.

39. For an overview of the 1864 electoral season, see Paludan, *People's Contest*, 231–52. On Greeley's efforts to find a replacement for Lincoln on the Republican ticket, see Harper, *Lincoln and the Press*, 309–14, and Donald, *Lincoln*, 525.

40. "Mrs. Lincoln's Sister," *New York Herald*, April 2, 1864. This story was reprinted

in the *Nashville Daily Press*, April 18, 1864, in an article that chastised other newspapers for the "misrepresentations and bogus news which are so freely circulated." See also "Mrs. Lincoln and the Blockade," *Daily Missouri Republican*, April 24, 1864.

41. On Bennett, see Mott, *American Journalism*, 348–50. The Lincolns were grateful for Bennett's support; Mary Lincoln once wrote him "with feelings of more than ordinary gratitude" for his "kind support and consideration" when the press began to question her loyalty to the Union because of her Southern family. Mary Lincoln to James Gordon Bennett, October 25, 1861, in Turner and Turner, *Mary Todd Lincoln*, 111. Bennett had most recently defended her in "The First Lady of the White House in the Newspapers," *New York Herald*, October 21, 1861. Other examples of Bennett's editorial defenses of the Lincoln family include "Satanic Abolitionists and the President's Family," January 7, 1862, and "The Latest Washington Excitement," February 5, 1862, *New York Herald*.

42. "Mrs. President Lincoln's Sister," *New York World*, April 1, 1864 (reprinted in *Nashville Daily Press*, April 9, 1864); "Mrs. President Lincoln's Sister," *Valley Spirit*, April 6, 1864, from Ayers et al., "Valley of the Shadow," <http://valley.vcdh.virginia.edu>.

43. See Chapter 2. For studies that examine white women as the political supporters of the men in their lives, especially their husbands, see Varon, *We Mean to Be Counted*, esp. chap. 3; Kerber, *Women of the Republic*, chap. 4; Lewis, "Republican Wife"; and, in the specific context of the Civil War, Bleser and Gordon, *Intimate Strategies*.

44. "Disloyal Relations," *Daily Missouri Republican*, April 7, 1864.

45. See "Marriage" in Chapter 2.

46. For more on Butler in New Orleans, see Faust, *Mothers of Invention*, 207–13, and Clinton, *Tara Revisited*, 98–99. On the Northern myth of the "rebel girl," see Silber, "Northern Myth."

47. [Untitled], *Louisville Daily Journal*, October 13, 1863; [Untitled], *Valley Spirit*, March 9, 1864, from Ayers et al., "Valley of the Shadow," <http://valley.vcdh.virginia.edu>; Jean Baker, *Mary Todd Lincoln*, 226.

48. For example, O. Stewart, a soldier in the 3rd Michigan who was recovering from wounds in a Washington, D.C., hospital, sent Lincoln a clipping of the copperhead version of the White story from the *Detroit Free Press* and wrote, "I dont beleive our President would do that pleese Answer." Stewart to Lincoln, April 27, 1864, "Abraham Lincoln Papers" <http://www.memory.loc.gov>.

49. This was quite an admission from a man known by Southerners as "Beast Butler" for treating women as anything but ladies while in New Orleans. John G. Nicolay to Benjamin F. Butler, April 19, 1864, Butler to Nicolay, April 21, 1864, ibid. Butler ended his letter to Nicolay on a sympathetic note: "I cannot believe the President has been much annoyed by this foolish story. If he has, it is because [he] has not been pounded in that way as much as I have and got hardened."

50. "The Story about Mrs. White," *New York Tribune*, April 27, 1864. This headline identified Martha as a wife, rather than a sister-in-law of the president—a less damaging role from the Lincolns' point of view. Why did Lincoln and Nicolay choose the *Tribune*, the first Northern newspaper to take the Martha White story seriously? Possibly because the *Tribune* had the widest circulation (300,000) of all Northern papers. Harper, *Lincoln*

and the Press, 101. Moreover, why did Greeley agree to assist Lincoln in refuting the allegations about Martha White? The editor explained to Nicolay privately: "I want to publish all the truth I can get and as few falsehoods as possible." Greeley had become exasperated by the way the White story had traveled since it first appeared in his paper and especially by the fact that "the Copperhead papers," his rivals, had quoted his original story "to sustain assertions never made through our columns." John G. Nicolay to Horace Greeley, April 25, 1864, Greeley to Nicolay, April 26, 1864, "Abraham Lincoln Papers," <http://www.memory.loc.gov>.

51. John G. Nicolay to Benjamin F. Butler, April 28, 1864, "Abraham Lincoln Papers," <http://www.memory.loc.gov>.

52. The *World* did not recant its story, although it later faced a two-day suspension of operations by the Union government for another unsubstantiated anti-Lincoln article. Mott, *American Journalism*, 350–52.

53. Martha Todd White to Abraham Lincoln, December 19, 1863, Mrs. S. B. French to Lincoln, April 20, 1864, and White to Lincoln, March 14, 1865, "Abraham Lincoln Papers," <http://www.memory.loc.gov>. The real Martha Todd White may not have been easy to pin down, and this could explain why she continued to intrigue Todd and Lincoln family members, as well as historians, years after the war. New accounts of her Northern trip in 1864 reappeared in postwar writings, the most unique provided in 1928 by one of Mary Lincoln's nieces, Katherine Helm (the daughter of Confederate half sister Emilie Todd Helm). "The true story is this," Helm began her biography, *Mary, Wife of Lincoln* (181–83). According to Helm, White was innocent of the smuggling charge; rather she was the victim of Baltimore friends who concealed a Confederate uniform and sword — intended for none other than Robert E. Lee — in her trunks without her knowledge. White did not see them until she arrived in Virginia (to her "mortification"). Immediately seeking "wise council" about what to do, she went to see President Jefferson Davis. Davis advised her to send the uniform on to Lee but promised to write a personal letter to Lincoln himself, "with whom he had for many years been on pleasant terms." White took the letter to Washington, and Lincoln read it and reacted to the incident "good-naturedly." Helm's telling of the story smoothed over all the difficulties with innocence, ladylike behavior, the chivalry of two men protecting a woman's reputation, and, most importantly after the war, a uniting of the two presidents over the issue. White now was an agent of sectional reconciliation, bringing the two presidents together through a common bond. As other members of the Todd and Lincoln families published memoirs, and historians wrote their own accounts of the war, the White story appeared with new details. Most of these agreed that White had smuggled something — "quinine" was most popular — but they also made sure to claim that the Lincolns knew nothing of her activities (a version that protected the loyalty of both sides of the family). Unlike the wartime newspaper accounts, these postwar works focused on Mary Lincoln — and on defending her Union loyalty — rather than on her husband. Perhaps in the postwar period it was no longer necessary to defend the loyalty of the martyred president. See Elizabeth Todd Grimsley, "Six Months in the White House," 43–44; Townsend, *Lincoln*, 317; and Jean Baker, *Mary Todd Lincoln*, 226.

54. S. C. Hayes to Secretary Seward, January 18, 1862, Miscellaneous Letters and Newspapers, NA.

55. See Martha McDonald Diary, December 17, 1861, Charles B. France Papers, WHMC; Henry Stone to Father, September 22, 1862, Stone Collection, FHS; and Josie Underwood Diary, January 2, 10, 1862, WKU.

56. Maria McGregor (Campbell) Smith, "Narrative of My Blockade Running," n.d., Smith Papers, VHS.

57. Millie Halsey to Joseph Halsey, June 20, 21, 27, 1864, Morton-Halsey Family Papers, UVA.

58. Joseph Halsey to Millie Halsey, July 4, 1864, ibid.

59. Millie Halsey to Joseph Halsey, July 12, 1864, ibid.

60. Drew Gilpin Faust (*Mothers of Invention*, 115–20) suggests that this was true for most families that had members serving in the army. See also Rable, "Hearth, Home, and Family," and Marten, "Fatherhood in the Confederacy." Union fathers, as discussed in Chapter 1, withheld letters to punish their rebellious offspring, testifying again to their value.

61. Alice Hawes to Samuel Horace Hawes, November 11, 1861, Katherine Heath Hawes Papers, VHS.

62. Martha Bouldin to Ellie Ellet, November 30, 1861, Cabell-Ellet Family Papers, UVA.

63. Fowler, *Unmailable*, 43; Shenfield, *Special Postal Routes*, 5; Platt Dickenson to Sister, June 8, 1861, Dickenson Letters, SHC; Samuel Horace Hawes Diary, July 13, 1861, Katherine Heath Hawes Papers, VHS. On the "paper blockade," see Fannie to Uncle David, August 6, 1861, Miscellaneous Letters and Newspapers, NA.

64. Union and Confederate flag-of-truce regulations were nearly identical. For the Union version, see John A. Dix to Hon. E. M. Stanton, May 15, 1863, *OR*, ser. 2, 5:616; Memorandum Order, August 10, 1861, *OR*, ser. 2, 1:639; and "How to Send Letters South," *Louisville Daily Journal*, November 17, 1863. For Confederate regulations, see Shenfield, *Special Postal Routes*, 32–38; and *Daily Richmond Examiner*, May 18, 1863, in Dietz, *Postal Service of the Confederate States*, 329. Civil War censors may have been guided in part by earlier instances of mail censorship during the sectional crisis. The most significant was an 1835 controversy over the sending of antislavery pamphlets to the South by abolitionists in the North, which resulted in the censorship of Northern mail by some Southern post offices. See Fowler, *Unmailable*, 21–41. Rumors of censorship also surfaced in the aftermath of John Brown's raid in 1859. At the end of the year a man in Canada writing to his son in Kentucky noted that he had heard that postal authorities were opening letters "in case the parties corresponding may have some connection with the unfortunate affair at Harpers Ferry." William Clark to James Clark, December 29, 1859, Clark-Strater-Watson Family, FHS.

65. Fowler, *Unmailable*, 44; A. V. Colburn to Brigadier General A. Porter, August 7, 1861, *OR*, ser. 2, 2:40; John A. Dix to Richard H. Dana Jr., October 5, 1862, *OR*, ser. 2, 4:599; Charles Wesley Andrews to Sarah Andrews, November 7, 1861, Charles Wesley Andrews Papers, Duke. On sympathetic clerks, see John A. Dix to Hon. E. M. Stanton,

May 15, 1863, *OR*, ser. 2, 5:616. On the general delays of flag-of-truce mail, see Mary M. Stockton Terry Diary, August 5, 1864, VHS, and Mary Josephine Withers Owen to Jennet Withers Tavenner, February 9, 1864, Cabell Tavenner and Alexander Scott Withers Papers, Duke. The Union commander at Fortress Monroe noted in 1862 that the "majority" of letters were rejected (Dix to Dana, October 5, 1862).

66. Fanny Lawrence to Hannah Lawrence, March 15, 1863, Brasher-Lawrence Family Papers, SHC; Sallie Knott to Mother, September 19, 1861, Knott Collection, WKU; Anne Lane to Sarah Glasgow, September 6, 1862, William Carr Lane Papers, MHS; Yates Levy to Phillip Phillips, July 28, 1864, Phillip Phillips Papers, LC.

67. Chas. O. Wood to Lieutenant Colonel M. Burke, October 22, 1861, *OR*, ser. 2, 2:782. Two collections of rejected letters still exist at the National Archives: Intercepted Letters, Record Group 109, entry 189, includes letters seized by Confederates, and Miscellaneous Letters and Newspapers contains those confiscated by the Union inspectors. From these two collections and letters that were published in the *OR*, I have gathered thirty-four intercepted letters—a small portion of the total seized. It is likely that some letters were returned to the senders and have not been preserved as a separate collection. At least one correspondent noted that his letters were returned to him in November 1861. Samuel Halsey to Joseph Halsey, November 19, 1861, Morton-Halsey Family Papers, UVA. Many other letters were probably destroyed.

68. An 1861 Union order stated only that letters "be confined to family and domestic affairs." Memorandum Order, August 10, 1861, *OR*, ser. 2, 1:639. An 1863 article in the *Louisville Daily Journal* also noted that any letter must "relate to merely personal and domestic matters." "How to Send Letters South," *Louisville Daily Journal*, November 17, 1863. The *Daily Richmond Examiner* similarly told its Confederate readers to keep their letters focused on "purely domestic matters." *Daily Richmond Examiner*, May 18, 1863, in Dietz, *Postal Service of the Confederate States*, 329. None of these orders or articles defined the term "domestic."

69. [?] to Lizzie Winston, November 26, 1862, Winston-Jones Family Papers, FHS.

70. Issa Breckinridge to William C. P. Breckinridge, January 11, 1863, Breckinridge Family Papers, containers 779–780, LC; George Bedinger to Virginia Bedinger, April 29, 1862, Bedinger-Dandridge Family Papers, Duke (a "cod-fish eater" was a derogatory term for a New Englander); Matthew Page Andrews to Mother, February 2, 1862, Charles Wesley Andrews Family Papers, Duke; Adeline L. Robert to Alexander J. Lawton, August 5, 1865, Alexander R. Lawton Papers, SHC. Adeline Robert expressed concern that mail censorship would continue after the war.

71. "From a Sister in Augusta to Her Brother in New York," *New York Tribune*, December 26, 1863; "Important from Rebeldom," *New York Herald*, February 29, 1864 (reprinted in *Daily Missouri Republican*, March 4, 1864); "Capture of a Rebel Mail," *Daily Missouri Republican*, May 29, 1864.

72. Memorandum Order, August 10, 1861, *OR*, ser. 2, 1:639.

73. Anne Lane to Sarah Glasgow, September 6, 1862, William Carr Lane Papers, MHS. For an overview of popular expectations about privacy, see, e.g., Lewis, *Pursuit*

of Happiness; Degler, *At Odds*, 53–54; and Stephen W. Berry, *All That Makes a Man*, 115.

74. Henry Clay Yeatman to Wife, November 30, 1862, Polk-Yeatman Family Papers, SHC.

75. Thomas W. Hall to Mother, September 15, 1862, Hall Correspondence, MDHS.

76. Josephine Withers Owen to Jannet Withers Tavenner, February 9, 1864, Cabell Tavenner and Alexander Scott Withers Collection, Duke.

77. Henry Stone to Parents, August 3, [n.d.], Stone Collection, FHS; Inslee Deaderick to Charlie Deaderick (brother), February [?], 1865, Deaderick Family Letters, FDS.

78. Julia Gardiner Tyler to Mother, April 20, 1861, John Tyler Papers, LC; James Proctor Knott to Maria I. Knott, August 4, 1861, Knott Collection, WKU.

79. Alice Hawes to Samuel Hawes (brother), November 11, 1861, Katherine Heath Hawes Papers, VHS.

80. "Letters for the North," *Daily Richmond Examiner*, January 7, 1863.

81. Smith and Cooper, *Union Woman*, 87. According to one of her neighbors, this made Henrietta Morgan "very angry."

82. Julia Read to Harriet Sublett Berry, May 13, 1861, Read Family Papers, VHS.

83. Thomas Hall to Father, September 9, 1862, Hall Correspondence, MDHS.

84. Mary Ellet Diary, June 15, 1861, Cabell-Ellet Family Papers, UVA.

85. William Daniel Jr. to Ellie Ellet, December 10, 1861, ibid.

86. On military officials, see Charles Wesley Andrews to Wife, November 29, 1861, Charles Wesley Andrews Papers, Duke. On postmasters, see Smith and Cooper, *Union Woman*, 108, and L. C. Baker to Secretary of State, October 10, 1861, *OR*, ser. 2, 1:600. On the Knights of the Golden Circle, see Testimony of Green B. Smith, August 2, 1864, *OR*, ser. 2, 7:648. For evidence of other men of prominence involved in mail smuggling, see William Daniel Jr. to Mary Ellet, August 31, 1862, Daniel to Ellie Ellet, December 10, 1861, and Mary Ellet Diary, June 12, 1861, Cabell-Ellet Family Papers, UVA.

87. Jeb Stuart to Flora Stuart, December 6, 1861, Stuart Papers, Emory. Robert J. Breckinridge, a prominent Kentucky minister and former member of the legislature, also engaged in mail smuggling. See Mary Davis to Breckinridge, February 18, 1862, Breckinridge Family Papers, container 218, LC. For another example, see Buford Twyman to John J. Crittenden, May 5, 1862, reel 14, Crittenden Papers, LC.

88. W. Hoffman to Hon. Montgomery Blair, November 11, 1863, *OR*, ser. 2, 6:501; B. P. Wells to Captain D. G. Swaim, October 19, 1863, *OR* 30:484.

89. "Confinement of a Female Spy," *New York Tribune*, January 1, 1862; "Attempted Release of Mrs. Greenhow," *New York Tribune*, January 1, 1862.

90. "Communication with the Rebels," *New York Tribune*, January 6, 1862.

91. F. A. Dick to Colonel W. Hoffman, March 5, 1863, *OR*, ser. 2, 5:320–21.

92. For examples, see case files of Mrs. Rachel Mayer and Mrs. E. K. Baldwin, Register of Arrests for Disloyalty, 1:18, 191, NA; "Female Spy—Mrs. Patterson Allan—Treason Confessed," *New York Herald*, July 27, 1863 (originally published in *Richmond Enquirer*, July 20, 1863); "Letters to the South Intercepted—The Writers to be Sent Beyond

the Federal Lines," *Baltimore Sun*, October 1, 1863; "Female Rebel Sentenced to the Penitentiary," *Baltimore Sun*, May 9, 1864; and [Untitled], *Smyrna Times*, August 29, 1861.

93. See Greenhow Papers, NA; Greenhow Letter, Records concerning the Conduct and Loyalty of Certain Union Officers, NA; Register of Arrests for Disloyalty, 1:289, NA; "Rose O'Neal Greenhow Papers," <http://scriptorium.lib.duke.edu/gree>.

94. John McNeil to Major General Schofield, July 25, 1863, *OR*, ser. 2, 6:148; Secretary Seward to Hon. Montgomery Blair, December 19, 1861, *OR*, ser. 2, 2:179; Smith and Cooper, *Union Woman*, 108; "Baltimore Rebel Correspondence," *New York Tribune*, December 30, 1861; "Rebel Letters Seized," *New York Tribune*, December 2, 1861; "Mail and Merchandise for the Rebels," *New York Tribune*, December 27, 1861; L. C. Baker to Hon. Secretary of State, October 10, 1861, *OR*, ser. 2, 1:600.

95. *OR*, ser. 2, 2:862–68. Investigators had more luck targeting mail smuggling in the confined space of a river than they did on open land. Frances Peter, of Lexington, Ky., noted the frustration of Union officials who knew that mail left that city for the South every night but "have not yet been able to find who takes it." Peter speculated that it was simply too easy for smugglers to leave without being noticed by the military, since "it would be almost impossible to surround Lex with guards." Smith and Cooper, *Union Woman*, 82.

96. J. B. Jones, *War Clerk's Diary*, 1:93.

97. E. N. Thurston to [?], July 17, 1861, Miscellaneous Letters and Newspapers, NA.

98. Samuel Pierce Hawes to Samuel Horace Hawes, June 27, 1861, Katherine Heath Hawes Papers, VHS. George Miles, a Richmond tobacco manufacturer, wrote to the Union secretary of war after his arrest that "I know nothing of the contents" of the letters found on him during a trip North. George Miles to Hon. Simon Cameron, *OR*, ser. 2, 2:533–34.

99. Emma to Mother, November 27, 1861, Miscellaneous Letters and Newspapers, NA; Matthew Page Andrews to Mother, May 29, 1861, Charles Wesley Andrews Papers, Duke; Proctor Knott to Maria Knott (mother), August 4, 1861, Knott Collection, WKU. "Remember all you hear is through the North," a Richmond woman cautioned her aunt. "You cannot depend on the truth in their reports." [?] to Aunt, September 26, 1861, Miscellaneous Letters and Newspapers, NA.

100. See, e.g., Martha Bouldin to Mary Ellet, [?], 1862, Cabell-Ellet Family Papers, UVA.

101. Mary Ellet to Charlie Ellet (brother), July 13, 1863, ibid.

102. W. E. Simms to Brutus J. Clay, November 1, 1863, Clay Family Papers, UKY.

103. *Richmond Enquirer*, May 27, February 23, January 15, 1864.

104. Over two thousand family advertisements is a conservative estimate. I counted 2,261 different ads in the *Richmond Enquirer* and the *New York Daily News* between January 1864 and January 1865. Some ads appeared as many as five days in a row on the advice of the *Daily News* editors. The count of 2,261 does not include several columns of ads that were obscured by poor microfilm copy or ads published in issues that are miss-

ing, nor does it include any ads written by obvious prisoners of war to their families (who shared their national loyalties). On instructions for placing ads, see *Richmond Enquirer*, September 23, 1864. These ads are also briefly described in Coulter, *Confederates States*, 129.

105. *Richmond Enquirer*, October 11, 1864.

106. *Richmond Enquirer*, February 16, 19, 1864.

107. The $2.00 charge also covered the cost of printing the reply that appeared in the *Daily News. Richmond Enquirer*, September 23, April 26, May 6, 1864.

108. *Richmond Enquirer*, April 26, 1864.

109. J. Holt to Hon. E. M. Stanton, January 20, 1865, *OR*, ser. 3, 4:1064–68.

110. Ibid.

111. Ibid.; E. D. Townsend to Major General John A. Dix, January 22, 1865, *OR*, ser. 3, 4:1064. I have found no evidence that the Confederate government commented publicly on the personal ads. Judge Holt later presided at the trials of the Lincoln assassination conspirators and was criticized for letting his zeal get in the way of guaranteeing the defendants a fair trial. On Holt's background, see Neely, *Fate of Liberty*, 162, and Koerting, "For Law and Order." (I am grateful to Kenneth Williams for bringing the latter article to my attention). See also Leonard, *Lincoln's Avengers*, esp. 12–31. On Holt's other wartime investigations, see Joseph Holt Papers, LC, and *Richmond Enquirer*, April 26, August 16, September 23, October 11, 1864.

112. "Self-Betrayal of the Public Press," January 26, 1865, "Our Personals," January 26, 1865, "The Circulation of the New York News," January 28, 1865, and "Suppression of the 'Personals' of the New York News," January 30, 1865, all in *New York Daily News*. On Benjamin Wood and the *New York Daily News*, see Mott, *American Journalism*, 352–53.

113. "Suppression of the 'Personals' of the New York News," January 30, 1865, "Mr. Holt and Our 'Personals,'" February 8, 1865, "Warring on Women and Families," January 27, 1865, and "The Suppressed Personals: The Government War on Family Ties," January 31, 1865, all in *New York Daily News*.

114. "The Suppression of the Personals in the New York Daily News," February 23, 1865 (reprinted from *London Times*), "The Suppressed Personals," January 31, 1865, "The Excluded Personals," January 27, 1865, and "No More Personals," February 3, 1865 (reprinted from *Richmond Whig*, January 31, 1865), all in *New York Daily News*; [Untitled], *Richmond Enquirer*, February 8, 1865.

Chapter Five

1. Delphine P. Baker, *Solon*.

2. Fairfax, *Elopement*, vi; Fahs, *Imagined Civil War*, 25. Wartime fiction grew out of an antebellum tradition in which writers told stories for the greater purposes of social and political commentary. On "cultural work," see Jane Tompkins, *Sensational Designs*. See also Davidson, *Revolution and the Word*; Baym, *Women's Fiction*; and Barnes, *States of Sympathy*. For works that deal specifically with the agenda of war-related fiction,

see Faust, *Mothers of Invention*, 153–78; Fahs, *Imagined Civil War*; Moss, *Domestic Novelists*; Varon, *We Mean to Be Counted*; Sizer, *Political Work*; Young, *Disarming the Nation*; Diffley, *Where My Heart Is Turning*; and Dicker, "Home Repair."

3. Of the 37 Civil War novels (1861–65) I have located and read, 32 deal with divided family themes. I arrived at these figures through a compilation of several bibliographies of Civil War novels: Lively, *Fiction Fights*; Menendez, *Civil War Novels*; Rebecca Washington Smith, "The Civil War and Its Aftermath in American Fiction"; and Wright, *American Fiction*. The rare book collection card catalog at the Library of Congress was helpful as well. I have also found 43 short stories published in literary journals and newspapers dealing specifically with divided family themes, suggesting that division was a predominant focus of short stories as well. I therefore depart from Kathleen Diffley's (*Where My Heart Is Turning*, 22) finding that there are "very few instances of divided families in popular war stories."

4. On sentimentality, see Anne C. Rose, *Victorian America*, esp. 145–92; Douglas, *Feminization of American Culture*, 254–56; Branch, *Sentimental Years*, vii–viii; and Halttunen, *Confidence Men*, xiv. On sentimental fiction, see Jane Tompkins, *Sensational Designs*; Moss, *Domestic Novelists*; and Baym, *Women's Fiction*.

5. Kelso, *Stars and Bars*, v–vi; Delphine P. Baker, *Solon*, cover. Richard Shuster makes note of a similar trend toward "truth" and realism in "American Civil War Novels to 1880." An interesting discussion of the desire to depict truth and "history" among authors of Civil War fiction can be found in Stephen Cushman's *Bloody Promenade*, 207–29. On the general demand for realism as a vicarious experience of war, see Royster, *Destructive War*, 232–95.

6. Nearly three-quarters of the novels and short stories considered here were set in the states along the border, especially Kentucky and Virginia. Other scholars who note the prevalence of border states as a setting for war novels include Fahs, *Imagined Civil War*, 233–34; Diffley, *Where My Heart Is Turning*; Young, *Disarming the Nation*, 17; Appleby, "Reconciliation and the Northern Novelist," 125–26; Olpin, "Missouri and the Civil War Novel"; and Thompson, "War between the States in the Kentucky Novel." The authors of the stories examined here were, by and large, natives of the border region and often made reference to the influence of their surroundings on their writing. Sallie J. Hancock (*Etna Vandemir*, 5), of Kentucky, explained that she wrote her novel after "dwelling in the very midst of 'battles and sieges' of a fratricidal war, seeing daily, households divided." Robert A. Lively's (*Fiction Fights*, 26–28) survey of Civil War novels published during and after the war found that most authors were from the Upper South and Middle States.

7. As early as 1833 tales of marriages between Northerners and Southerners appeared in popular fiction. These stories generally turned on the "conversion" of a man or a woman from one section to the other, which resulted in a romantic union. See Moss, *Domestic Novelists*, 78–82, and Varon, *We Mean to Be Counted*, 105. The few scholars who mention the presence of intersectional romance in wartime novels are Lively, *Fiction Fights*, 57–58; Fahs, "Feminized Civil War," 1493–94; Menendez, *Civil War Novels*, ix; and Diffley, *Where My Heart Is Turning*, 62–76. (In her survey of wartime literary journals, Kathleen Diffley [77–79] also detects the theme of romantic "failure.")

On similar imagery in wartime art, see Christine Anne Bell, "Family Conflict." More common are studies of intersectional romance in the postwar years. See Buck, *Road to Reunion*; Censer, "Reimagining the North-South Reunion"; Appleby, "Reconciliation and the Northern Novelist," 118–19; and Silber, *Romance of Reunion*, 39–65.

8. "Love and Disloyalty," *Nashville Daily Press*, May 21, 1863.

9. McCabe, *Aid-de-Camp*.

10. The most extensive work on the image of seduction is Karen Halttunen's *Confidence Men*. Other overviews of seduction as a literary motif include Davidson, *Revolution and the Word*, 98–108, and Jane Tompkins, *Sensational Designs*, 84–85.

11. For studies of the use of seduction to depict republican fears, see Lewis, "Republican Wife"; Fliegelman, *Prodigals and Pilgrims*, 83–88; Barnes, *States of Sympathy*, chap. 1; and Halttunen, *Confidence Men*, chap. 1.

12. The voluminous body of work on the secession crisis highlights these conspiratorial fears, including Gienapp, "Political System," 92–93, and Holt, *Political Crisis*, 238–44.

13. On efforts to explain border-state loyalties, see Chapters 1 and 2.

14. "The Border State Bugbear," *Daily Missouri Democrat*, November 12, 1862. The *Southern Literary Messenger* ("Editor's Table," February 1861) railed against the "despotism" to which border states were subjected during the secession crisis: "Men of the Border States! will you submit to this? Sons of Maryland and Virginia! the chains are already on your limbs! Will you sit quietly until they are riveted?"

15. "Love and Disloyalty," *Nashville Daily Press*, May 21, 1863. Smuggling is depicted in "How a Federal Major Became Enamored with a Texan Widow — A Romantic Story," *Nashville Daily Press*, September 30, 1863. Spying is the goal of the Confederate seductress in "Trapped," *Harper's Weekly*, February 22, 1864, 126. And a story of a woman who sought her release from prison is "War and Romance," *Daily Missouri Democrat*, February 28, 1863.

16. Stories in which Union men attempt to seduce Southern women with promises of marriage include "Sad Affair — Love, Desertion, and Suicide," *Louisville Democrat* (reprinted in *Nashville Daily Press*, October 5, 1865), and "A Country Girl Seduced by a U.S. Officer," *Daily Missouri Democrat*, November 21, 1861. In both tales the narrator reveals that the Union seducers intended to sell the women into prostitution.

17. McCabe, *Aid-de-Camp*, 53–54. Other descriptions of seducers are from "All for Love — A Federal Officer Seduced," *Missouri Statesman*, February 13, 1863, and "War and Romance," *Daily Missouri Democrat*, February 28, 1863.

18. The quest for sincerity at a time of expansion and social anonymity is described in Halttunen, *Confidence Men*, chap. 2.

19. An example of this sort of question was Kentuckian Marie Handy's query, "How do Uncle Williams Sons stand, with North or South?" that she directed to her father two months after the war began. Handy to Robert J. Breckinridge, June 24, 1861, Breckinridge Family Papers, LC.

20. Accounts of men and women attempting to travel between the Union and the Confederacy during the war are rife with stories of downplaying or hiding one's loyalty in order to be allowed across the border — see Chapter 4. In his study of Civil War Mis-

souri, Michael Fellman (*Inside War*, 49) also addresses the prevalence of "survival lying" or the covering up of one's political loyalty for protective purposes. John Inscoe and Gordon McKinney describe this same pattern for southern Appalachia in "Highland Houses Divided."

21. "Love and Disloyalty," *Nashville Daily Press*, May 21, 1863.

22. "A Sad Case of Seduction," *Daily Missouri Democrat*, November 23, 1864, and *Louisville Daily Journal*, November 28, 1864.

23. Sarah Jane Full Hill, "Reminiscences of the Civil War," 249, manuscript, Hill Papers, LC. Drew Gilpin Faust (*Mothers of Invention*, 214–19) makes a related point about the fact that gender provided women with a layer of protection from Yankee aggression. For more on the encounters of Union men and Confederate women, see "Courtship" in Chapter 2.

24. "All for Love — A Federal Officer Seduced," *Missouri Statesman*, February 13, 1863; "War and Romance," *Daily Missouri Democrat*, February 28, 1863; "How a Federal Major Became Enamored with a Texas Widow," *Nashville Daily Press*, September 30, 1863.

25. "How a Federal Major Became Enamored with a Texas Widow," *Nashville Daily Press*, September 30, 1863; "Love and Disloyalty," *Nashville Daily Press*, May 21, 1863; "Trapped," *Harper's Weekly*, February 22, 1864, 126; "Sad Affair — Love, Desertion, Suicide," *Louisville Democrat* (as reprinted in *Nashville Daily Press*, October 5, 1865); Connelly, *Elopement*; "Adventures of a Young Lady in the Army," *Magnolia Weekly*, June 27, 1863, 215; and "The Female Lieutenant," *Staunton Spectator*, September 22, 1863, from "The Valley of the Shadow," <http://valley.vcdh.virginia.edu>. The idea of "passionlessness" as a moral ideal for women is described in Cott, "Passionlessness."

26. For this interconnection between women and national stability during the antebellum period, see Lewis, "Republican Wife," and Basch, "Marriage, Morals, and Politics."

27. "Converting Lady Rebels," *Missouri Statesman*, April 29, 1864; [Untitled], *Louisville Daily Journal*, August 5, 1862; "She-Secessionists," *Smyrna Times*, September 11, 1862. In a letter to her husband, Delawarean Sophie DuPont complained that Southern women bore some responsibility for raising sons who supported secession: "This thought saddens & discourages me most of all — that my own sex — whom God created for good & gentle deeds, to be the softeners of men's rougher nature, the *peace makers*, should in this fearful national strife have been from the beginning the fomenters of violence." Sophie DuPont to Samuel Francis DuPont, May 28, 1862, DuPont Family Papers, Hagley. See also Royster, *Destructive War*, 20, 86–87. On how this view took on mythical proportions, see Silber, "Northern Myth"; Buck, *Road to Reunion*; Moss, *Domestic Novelists*, 78–82; and Censer, "Reimagining the North-South Reunion."

28. McCabe, *Aid-de-Camp*, 53–54.

29. On love and affection, see Lystra, *Searching the Heart*. On the greater political significance of affection, see Lewis, "Republican Wife."

30. "A New York Colonel and a Virginia Girl," *Louisville Daily Journal*, July 2, 1863 ("conquered"); Gates Thruston to Mother, March 3, 1865, Gates Phillips Thruston

Letters, FHS ("subjugated"). For another perspective on sexuality in Civil War fiction, or what Alice Fahs calls the "sexually charged war," see Fahs, *Imagined Civil War*, 225–55.

31. See Jeffords, "Commentary," 91–96.

32. "Love and Disloyalty," *Nashville Daily Press*, May 21, 1863; McCabe, *Aid-de-Camp*. Another story in which a Confederate man shoots a Union seducer dead is Herrington, *Captain's Bride*. In Alex. St. Clair Abrams's *Trials of the Soldier's Wife*, the Union seducer is executed by Confederate officials acting at the behest of the Southern lover.

33. Kenneth Greenberg (*Honor and Slavery*, chap. 4) emphasizes the importance of confronting death as a test of a man's honor.

34. McCabe, *The Guerrillas*. For announcements of the play, see *Richmond Enquirer*, December 23, 1862, and *Daily Richmond Examiner*, December 22–29, 1862.

35. "Christmas at the Varieties," *Daily Richmond Examiner*, December 23, 1862; Watson, "Confederate Drama," 110. The play's author, twenty-one-year-old Richmond native James Dabney McCabe Jr., received high praise and within a year became the editor of a new Southern journal, the *Magnolia Weekly*. He later admitted, however, that this production was one of his "literary sins." Fife, "Theater in the Confederacy," 246a. See also Waal, "First Confederate Drama," 459. Despite the title of this article, *The Guerrillas* was not the first original Confederate drama. The first may have been John Hill Hewitt's *The Scouts; or, The Plains of Manassas*, produced on November 18, 1861. Watson, "Confederate Drama," 104, 109.

36. "'The Guerrillas' at the Varieties," *Daily Richmond Examiner*, December 27, 1862. The *Southern Illustrated News*, however, took the author to task for not getting all his facts straight, such as Robert E. Lee's correct rank at the beginning of the war. "The Southern people are *making history* now," the reviewer declared, and "our Southern play-writers should be faithful chroniclers of the times in which we live." *Southern Illustrated News*, January 3, 1863, 8, quoted in Fife, "Theater in the Confederacy," 248.

37. See, e.g., "On the Kentucky Border," *Harper's Weekly*, February 1, 1862, 70–71.

38. "'The Guerrillas' at the Varieties," *Daily Richmond Examiner*, December 27, 1862.

39. For stories that feature orphan women, see "Brothers in Arms," *Harper's Weekly*, January 10, 1863, 30–31; Wood, *Fort Lafayette*; Remick, *Millicent Halford*; "The Tory's Revenge," *Magnolia Weekly*, October 17, 1863, 17–19; and Herrington, *Captain's Bride*. For portrayals of women as objects of male infatuation, see "On the Kentucky Border," *Harper's Weekly*, February 1, 1862, 70–71, and "Curious Story of a Photograph," *Daily Missouri Democrat*, August 16, 1864.

40. *The Rivals* was first serialized in the *Southern Illustrated News* in 1864 under the title, "The Rivals: A Tale of the Chickahominy," appearing on April 16 (125–27), 23 (133–35), 30 (141–43), and May 7 (149–51). It was then compiled and published as a novel. See Haw, *The Rivals*. On the prize won by this story, see "The $1,000 Prize Romance," *Southern Illustrated News*, March 12, 1864, 84. For other romantic triangle stories see "Brothers in Arms," *Harper's Weekly*, January 10, 1863, 30–31; Remick,

Millicent Halford; Bartlett, *Clarimonde*; and "The Two Generals: A Christmas Story of the War," *Harper's Weekly*, January 2, 1864, 6–7.

41. Forgie, *Patricide*, 16 (Webster); "Let Us Be Friends," *Harper's Weekly*, March 30, 1861, 195 (poet). For more on the idea of political fraternity, see Anne C. Norton, *Alternative Americas*, 136, 144–46.

42. Haw, *The Rivals*, 16.

43. Rotundo, *American Manhood*, 84–99. See also "Brothers in Conflict" in Chapter 3.

44. [Untitled], *Daily Richmond Examiner*, January 22, 1864.

45. Anonymous, "Strategy," *American Mail-Bag*, 235–45. On manhood and military enlistment, see Mitchell, *Vacant Chair*, 11–12; McPherson, *For Cause and Comrades*, 22–29; and Stephen W. Berry, *All That Makes a Man*. A Confederate example is McCabe, *The Guerrillas*, 30.

46. "The Two Generals: A Christmas Story of the War," *Harper's Weekly*, January 2, 1864, 6–7; [Untitled], *Louisville Daily Journal*, September 8, 1862; "Disfederation of the States," *Southern Literary Messenger*, February 1861, 118–19. Anne C. Norton (*Alternative Americas*, 267) also takes note of the biblical allusions to fraternity in political discourse and argues that these allusions admitted no disparities between "brothers." In contrast, I see the biblical allusions as an attempt to draw very clear disparities.

47. "The Tory's Revenge: A Tale of the Shenandoah," *Magnolia Weekly*, October 17, 1863, 17–19.

48. Royster, *Destructive War*. George Fredrickson (*Inner Civil War*, 80–84) makes a similar point.

49. Here I depart from Anne C. Rose (*Victorian American*, 237), who argues that Civil War writers had a tendency to "subsume evidence of ill fortune."

50. Charles Royster (*Destructive War*, 232–95) argues for this "vicarious" war.

51. Herrington, *Captain's Bride*, 22–23. The advertisement appears in the back of this volume.

52. Haw, *The Rivals*, 54–56; "The Tory's Revenge," *Magnolia Weekly*, October 17, 1863; Bartlett, *Clarimonde*, 78–79.

53. "On the Kentucky Border," *Harper's Weekly*, February 1, 1862, 70–71.

54. Austin, *Dora Darling*, 251.

55. "Reciprocal Affection," *Louisville Daily Journal*, April 28, 1862; "Letter from Kentucky," *Missouri Statesman*, November 1, 1861.

56. "A Touching Scene," *Nashville Daily Press*, May 15, 1863. This notion was reinforced by Union fiction that portrayed intersectional romances that culminated in marriage. See, e.g., Delphine P. Baker, *Solon*; "A Southerner's Courtship," *Harper's Weekly*, July 23, 1864, 474–75; "A Yankee Girl Converts a Rebel Surgeon and Marries Him," *Louisville Daily Journal*, July 6, 1863; Kelso, *Stars and Bars*; and Anonymous, "Love and Duty," *American Mail-Bag*, 209–17.

57. "Events of the Day," *Southern Field and Fireside*, April 4, 1863, 112; "The Broken Tie," *Southern Illustrated News*, March 7, 1863, 4; "Editor's Table," *Southern Literary Messenger*, September 1863, 573; [Untitled], *Daily Richmond Examiner*, April 2, 1864.

58. "The True Question: A Contest for the Supremacy of Race, as between the Saxon Puritan of the North, and the Norman of the South," *Southern Literary Messenger*, July 1861, 19–27; Dr. Stuart, "The Anglo-Saxon Mania," *Southern Literary Messenger*, November–December 1863, 667–88. See also William C. Davis, *Look Away!*, 20–21, 40–42. For an extended study of popular beliefs in the distinct civilizations — and races — of North and South, see Taylor, *Cavalier and Yankee*.

59. "Kitty's Southern Relations," *Magnolia Weekly*, January 28, 1865 (1–2), February 4, 1865 (1–2). For a typical story of Confederate-Confederate romance, see Herrington's *Deserter's Daughter*.

60. McCabe, *The Guerrillas*, 17–19, 24–25, 42–44; "Christmas at the Varieties," *Daily Richmond Examiner*, December 23, 1862. Such "devotion" is also a central feature of Alex St. Clair Abrams's *Trials of the Soldier's Wife* (26–27), which frequently refers to a slave woman named Elsy as a "faithful negress" and a "faithful slave" who "shed bitter tears" when separated from her mistress.

61. Genovese, "'Our Family, White and Black,'" 87. A related but different model of paternalistic race relations was also evident in the writings of white Northern soldiers. See Mitchell, *Vacant Chair*, 55–69.

62. George Starling to Father, Samuel Starling, May 19, 1864, Lewis-Starling Collection, WKU.

63. Rowena Webster Memoir, 15, Jill Knight Garrett Collection, TSLA.

64. Litwack, *Been in the Storm So Long*, 17–18.

65. "The Old Mammy's Lament for Her Young Master," *Southern Literary Messenger*, November–December 1863, 732–33.

66. Haw, *The Rivals*, 52. Such images of alleged slave loyalty would endure in Southern culture well into the twentieth century. See Blight, *Race and Reunion*, 286–88, and Savage, *Standing Soldiers, Kneeling Slaves*, 155–58.

67. Although the Emancipation Proclamation directly affected only the Confederate states in the border region, slaves in the Union border states seized the opportunity provided by the policy to emancipate themselves. On slavery and wartime emancipation in the border states, see Berlin et al., *Wartime Genesis of Free Labor*, 63, 72, 371–73, 481–82, 489, 625–34; Fields, *Slavery and Freedom*, 100–102, 118; and Howard, *Black Liberation*.

68. Genovese, *Roll, Jordan, Roll*, 97–140; Litwack, *Been in the Storm So Long*, 300–328; Weiner, *Mistresses and Slaves*, 168–69; Robert J. Breckinridge, "Negroes of Dr. R. J. Breckinridge at Camp Nelson, up to July 20, 1864," E. B. Miles to Breckinridge, April 12, 1864, "Memorandum," May 14, 1864, and Jacob Warren to Breckinridge, May 13, 1864, all in Breckinridge Family Papers, LC. For an extended discussion of emancipation, see Chapter 7.

69. C. Graham, M.D., to President Andrew Johnson, July 24, 1865, in Berlin et al., *Free at Last*, 408–16. See also Elizabeth Minor to President Lincoln, July 1864, and E. H. Green to the Secretary of War, March 14, 1865, both in Berlin, Reidy, and Rowland, *Black Military Experience*, 265, 272–73; Mrs. Silliman to "Brother," n.d., Silliman Letters, WHMC.

70. "Ought Predatory Invaders to Be Made Prisoners," *Charleston Mercury*, June 27,

1862; "The War in Mississippi," *Charleston Mercury*, April 25, 1863. See also Litwack, *Been in the Storm So Long*, 157.

71. Fairfax, *Elopement*. Connelly was born in Pennsylvania in 1837, lived in Washington, D.C., and London, and became a journalist and playwright before her death in 1904. Oscar Fay Adams, *Dictionary of American Authors*, 133. In the preface to *The Elopement* (xi), she explains her concern with countering "the false views of the social worth of the Confederates" distributed by Northern fiction writers.

72. Fairfax, *Elopement*. Alice Fahs (*Imagined Civil War*, 190) has argued that the absence of interracial sex (or mulattoes) in Confederate literature helped maintain "the fiction that no such sexual or social relations existed."

73. Studies of interracial sex and families in the antebellum South include Rothman, *Notorious*; Hodes, *White Women, Black Men*; Clinton, *Tara Revisited*, 35–37; Schwartz, *Born in Bondage*, 44–46; and Williamson, *New People*.

74. [Untitled], *Frank Leslie's Illustrated Newspaper*, November 18, 1865, 131.

75. The Lee-Custis-Syphax relationship was complex. Mrs. Lee (Mary Anna Randolph Custis Lee) was raised at Arlington House, a large plantation in Virginia, which, during her childhood, was home to at least sixty slaves, all owned by her father, George Washington Park Custis, the stepson of George Washington. Custis, according to contemporary and modern accounts, fathered a child with Airy Carter, one of his slaves. That child was Maria Carter, who later married Charles Syphax and had ten children with him, including William Syphax. Custis later freed Maria Carter Syphax and the children, who all grew up at Arlington as freed people; some of them later went to nearby Washington, D.C., to be educated and employed. Thus, Mrs. Lee would have been a half sister to Maria Carter Syphax, rather than to Charles Syphax, and thus a half aunt to the Syphaxes' son William, who worked in Washington. See "Washington Custis Head of 16 Syphax Families," *Washington Afro-American*, February 12, 2000, from the files of Arlington House, the Robert E. Lee Memorial, Arlington, Va.; Preston, "William Syphax"; Syphax, "William Syphax — Community Leader"; Abbott, "Land of Maria Syphax." Thanks to Karen Kinzey of Arlington House for bringing this material to my attention, and to Joshua Rothman for sharing his insights on the Lee-Syphax family. For more on Mrs. Lee's childhood at Arlington, see Coulling, *Lee Girls*. Similar stories about Southerners who were not so well known are "Desertion and Miscegenation," *Daily Missouri Republican*, May 5, 1864, and "A Woman's Adventures," *Smyrna Times*, August 15, 1861.

76. "Jeff Davis's Son in the National Service," *Louisville Daily Journal*, February 9, 1864; "Miscegenation by Jeff. Davis," *Daily Missouri Democrat*, April 27, 1864 (reprinted from *Boston Journal*); "Jeff Davis's Son in the Federal Service," *Daily Missouri Democrat*, February 3, 1864 (reprinted from *London Star*). For other rumors about Davis, see "Widening the Breach" in Chapter 1.

77. "Miscegenation by Jeff. Davis," *Daily Missouri Democrat*, April 27, 1864; "Jeff Davis's Son in the Federal Service," *Daily Missouri Democrat*, February 3, 1864.

78. On the emergence of miscegenation as a highly charged political issue during the war, see Hodes, "Wartime Dialogues on Illicit Sex," 230–42.

79. "Davisegination," *Franklin Repository and Transcript*, June 22, 1864, from Ayers et al., "Valley of the Shadow," <http://valley.vcdh.virginia.edu>. Some aspects of the Davis stories do ring true. The slave woman most frequently mentioned as the mother of Davis's son was named Eliza — and both Jefferson Davis and his brother Joseph owned a slave called Eliza. See Crist et al., *Papers of Jefferson Davis*, 235, 393. Also, one of Joseph Davis's slaves did serve as an officer's steward on the ship identified in one story as Purser Davis's ship, the *Carondelet*. That slave, Thornton Montgomery, and his family had found protection during the war with Admiral David D. Porter of the Union navy. Moreover, Montgomery's brother Isaiah served as Porter's cabin boy and personal assistant. See Hermann, *Pursuit of a Dream*, 40–43. I am grateful to Lynda Lasswell Crist (*Papers of Jefferson Davis*) for sharing her insights on the Davis-Montgomery-Porter connection.

80. "My Boy Ben," *Harper's Weekly*, October 29, 1864, 695.

81. Narrative of Nannie Eaves, in Rawick, *American Slave*, 61.

82. Martha Clay Davenport to Brutus Clay, June 11, 1863, Clay Family Papers, UKY.

83. Louisa May Alcott, "The Brothers," *Atlantic Monthly*, November 1863, 584–95. For another story of black revenge — in this case, the killing of a slave trader — see Warren, *Old Peggy Boggs*. The idea of black revenge against white masters was not new to nineteenth-century fiction. Prior to the war antiabolitionist writers popularized this theme, depicting horrific black violence against whites as a way of demeaning blacks as savage, dishonorable people. It appears that in wartime fiction, however, black violence and revenge had been transformed into a positive good for white Northerners, as violent slaves could serve the interests of the Union against the Confederacy. On the rebellious slave in antiabolitionist fiction, see Roth, "Rebels and Martyrs," 91–109. For the Northern embrace of black violence against whites in wartime fiction, see Fahs, *Imagined Civil War*, 169–81. The wartime stories I discuss here are a specific subset of all these depictions of black violence, as they focus solely on revenge against white kin, rather than on whites generally, thus intensifying racial conflict with patricide or fratricide. These stories prefigured what have been termed "avenging mulatto" stories, that is, tales of mixed-race people who kill their white kin, that would become popular later in the century in works such as Mark Twain's. See Gillman, "The Mulatto."

84. For further discussion of "The Brothers," see also Sizer, *Political Work*, 156–57; Fahs, *Imagined Civil War*, 171–72; Diffley, *Where My Heart Is Turning*, 34–39; and Young, *Disarming the Nation*, 94–96.

85. Burnett, *Incidents of the War*, 107–13.

86. Gutman, *Black Family*, 390–93; Howard, *Black Liberation*, 123.

87. [Untitled], *Frank Leslie's Illustrated Newspaper*, November 18, 1865, 131. Another case did not require an appeal by a slave to elicit the help and sympathy of Union officials. A provost marshal in northeastern Missouri informed his superior that on one plantation a master's sons forced slaves to leave after "the old man began to show signs of recognizing five of his servants as half brothers & sisters to his children lawfully begotten." He reported this with the hope that the Union army would force rebels like these to take

care of their "helpless negroes." John Tyler to Superior, January 12, 1865, in Berlin et al., *Free At Last*, 378–79.

88. Quoted in Gutman, *Black Family*, 388.

Chapter Six

1. Nina Silber (*Romance of Reunion*, chap. 2) and Anne Sarah Rubin ("Redefining the South," 346–97) make a similar distinction between practical and emotional forms of reconciliation between the Union and the Confederacy.

2. Other historians have seen something similar. In *Rehearsal for Reconstruction*, Willie Lee Rose documented a wartime reconstruction process in the South Carolina Sea Islands. Eric Foner (*Reconstruction*, 35–51) describes how the border states responded to Lincoln's 1863 Proclamation of Amnesty and Reconstruction.

3. Childers, "Virginian's Dilemma," 184.

4. For examples of monetary aid, see Josie Underwood Diary, March 1, 1862, WKU, and "Union Feeling at the South," *Missouri Statesman*, February 28, 1862. For offers of shelter, see Chapter 4.

5. James Yeatman to General Sherman, April 6, 1864, Yeatman-Polk Collection, TSLA.

6. Such exemptions do not appear in Union or Confederate army regulations, suggesting that these requests were not official policy but, rather, solely up to the discretion of individual commanding officers. For similar examples, see Ellen Wilkins Tompkins, "Colonel's Lady," 387–89, and David F. Boyd to William T. Sherman, April 7, 1864, Boyd Papers, SHC.

7. "Dr. R. J. Breckinridge," *Louisville Daily Journal*, October 13, 1862; William C. P. Breckinridge to Robert J. Breckinridge, October 27, 1862, Breckinridge Family Papers, LC.

8. Ann Clay to Brutus J. Clay, April 17, August 19, September 17, 24, 1862, and Brutus J. Clay to Ann Clay, October 14, 1862, Clay Family Papers, UKY.

9. Confederate army regulations, adopted from the U.S. Army code, officially condoned the conveyance of aid to Union men in Southern prisons. I have found little evidence of this assistance in practice, however, suggesting that individual Confederate prison officials were less likely to accept and distribute items provided by families than their Union counterparts. This difference could be attributed to the Union's more efficient prison bureaucracy. Indeed, as Reid Mitchell ("'Our Prison System'") found, Union officials were not necessarily more humane, just more competent. See *Regulations for the Army of the Confederate States*, 73–74.

10. On Union policy regarding prisoners, see Circular, Office of the Commissary General of Prisoners, April 20, 1864, *OR*, ser. 2, 7:72–75; Circular No. 4, Office of the Commissary General of Prisoners, August 10, 1864, *OR*, ser. 2, 7:573; Noah Walker & Co. to Commander of Post, Elmira, N.Y., August 22, 1864, *OR*, ser. 2, 7:677; and Colonel W. Hoffman to Lieutenant Colonel S. Eastman, September 8, 1864, *OR*, ser. 2, 7:787. See also Minor H. McLain, "Military Prison at Fort Warren," 39–40, T. R. Walker,

"Rock Island Prison Barracks," 51, and Edward T. Downer, "Johnson's Island," 101, all in Hesseltine, *Civil War Prisons*, 46–50.

11. Mary "Fanny" Warren to Fred Warren, March 17, 1863, and William Warren to Fred Warren, March 22, 1863, Edward J. Warren Papers, SHC.

12. [Moncure?] Robinson to Bennett Taylor, December 22, 1864, Taylor Papers, UVA; and Mary M. Stockton Terry Diary, September 13, 1864, VHS. For more on popular views of prison life, see Linderman, *Embattled Courage*, 236, and Julia Hunt to Fanny Brashear, October 20, 1864, Brasher-Lawrence Family Papers, SHC. For other examples of prison aid, see the Fort Delaware Society for an excellent collection of prisoners' letters, including Stuart Family Papers, James Perry Letters, Ward Papers, Goldsborough Family Letters, and the Deaderick Family Letters. See also J. P. Pryor to Sister, December 19, 1864, Joseph Pryor Fuller Letters, SHC; Arthur H. Edey to Mrs. Batelle, August 27, 1864, and Hiram C. Reid to Mrs. Batelle, December 1, 1864, Finney Family Papers, VHS; Letters between Susannah "Low" Eleanor Dorsey and George B. Clarke (cousin), Dorsey Family Papers, MHS; and Virginia Trist to Martha Burke, August [?], 1863, Trist-Burke Family Papers, UVA.

13. Robert J. Breckinridge to Mr. and Mrs. Lincoln, July 25, 1864, Breckinridge to Edward Carrington, August 16, 1864, and Passes signed by Abraham Lincoln, July 23, October 18, 1864, all in Preston Family Papers, VHS; Eliza Carrington to Robert J. Breckinridge, August 22, 1864, and Edward C. Carrington to Breckinridge, August 23, 1864, Breckinridge Family Papers, LC.

14. A. C. T. [Anne Campbell Thomas] to Sir [J. C. R. Taylor], August 1, 1863, Bennett Taylor Papers, UVA. For another example of reciprocal family aid, see Frederick Shriver to Henry Shriver, July 12, 1863, Shriver Family Papers, MDHS.

15. Courtney Pickett to Mrs. Batelle, January 8, 1864, Finney Family Papers, VHS.

16. Colonel Hoffman to Lieutenant Colonel S. Eastman, September 8, 1864, *OR*, ser. 2, 7:787.

17. Rebecca Davis Diary, August 13, 1864, Davis Papers, MDHS. Soldiers also "discovered" relatives in the course of battle. In Kentucky, Confederate Henry Stone saw "a man who was grandson to Ensibius Stone. Kinfolks I guess." Henry Stone to Parents, June 30, 1863, Stone Collection, FHS.

18. Matthew Page Andrews to Anna Robinson Andrews, July 28, August 6, 8, 23, October 25, 1861, Charles Wesley Andrews Papers, Duke. For similar examples, see Sidney Clay to Brutus J. Clay, May 6, 1864, Clay Family Papers, UKY; ASW to Eugene [?], July 25, 1862, Fort Delaware Collection (#99.036), FDS.

19. James Perry to "My Dear Cousin," April 10, 1865, Fort Delaware Collection (FIC 100), FDS; Inslee Deaderick to Mother, November 16, 1864, Deaderick Family Letters, Fort Delaware Collection (#92.019.2), FDS.

20. C. M. Killian to Cousin, November 21, 1864, Fort Delaware Collection (#01.012), FDS. A Confederate soldier imprisoned at Fort Warren in Boston was "surprised and delighted" to receive letters and a box of cakes from his family. George Barnard to Charles Barnard, November 18, 1861, S. G. Barnard Letters, SHC. A contemporary in Camp Chase, Ohio, boasted that his brothers in Iowa "send me almost anything I

want." Anything that could alleviate prison conditions was appreciated. W. C. Criner to Hennie (wife), April 20, 1862, Camp Chase Papers, VHS

21. John W. Warren to Ed Warren, January 29, 1865, Edward J. Warren Papers, SHC; William Thomson to Josephine Thomson, December 8, 1863, William Sydnor Thomson Papers, Emory.

22. William Thomson to Josephine Thomson, December 8, 1863, July 27, 1864, ibid.

23. Phineas Savery to Mother-in-Law, September 7, 1866, Savery Papers, Duke.

24. Warner Thomson Diary, October 25, 1864, William Sydnor Thomson Papers, Emory. Another Union man wrote his imprisoned son: "If I were you, rather than remain I'd take the oath, if permitted, & come home. Return to loyalty, home, & love." W. J. Clift to Thomas, May 30, 1862, Camp Chase Papers, VHS.

25. See Oath to the United States, June 25, 1865, Samuel Kennard Papers, MHS.

26. Colonel W. Hoffman to Brigadier General A. Schoepf, August 4, 1863, and Colonel Hoffman to Major General W. S. Rosecrans, August 7, 1863, *OR*, ser. 2, 6:175, 186.

27. The government policies considered in this chapter are in direct contrast to the official restrictions on travel and mail, discussed in Chapter 4, which ostensibly kept divided families apart. But there was no real contradiction between these policies. Limits on travel and mail addressed—and discouraged—family reunions *across* the lines, whereas prisoner aid and parole policies addressed—and encouraged—family reunions *within* Union lines. In both cases, government policies dealing with families were shaped by the strategic interests of the Union. For petitions from these families, see Camp Chase Papers, VHS, and Brutus J. Clay Series, Clay Family Papers, UKY. See also Goldsborough Family Papers, FDS.

28. [Untitled], *Nashville Daily Press*, August 28, 1863.

29. See letters in Brutus J. Clay Series, Clay Family Papers, UKY.

30. Will S. Richart to Brutus J. Clay, January 22, 1864, Allen Kiser to Clay, February 20, 1864, M. E. Glover to Abraham Lincoln, February 28, 1864, and A. H. Calvin to Clay, January 16, 1864, all in ibid.

31. George Starling to Mary, December 22, 1862, Lewis-Starling Papers, WKU; "Return of a Prodigal Son," *Missouri Statesman*, December 13, 1861; "Return of a Prodigal Son," *Louisville Daily Journal*, February 28, 1862.

32. "Letter from a Rebel Prisoner to His Loyal Uncle—The Uncle's Reply," *Daily Missouri Democrat*, April 18, 1862.

33. Henry Whisler to Son, June 5, 1862, Camp Chase Papers, VHS; [Untitled], *Louisville Daily Journal*, February 20, 1862. A similar view was expressed in Timothy Ward to Anderson J. Ward, October 28, 1864, Ward Papers, Fort Delaware Collection (#94.032), FDS.

34. John Kempshall Memoirs, 5, Kempshall Papers, TSLA; Thomas Hall to Father, November 3, 1862, Hall Correspondence, MDHS; Ezekiel Clay to Father, January 18, 24, 1865, Clay Family Papers, UKY.

35. Brutus Clay to Martha Clay Davenport, January 21, 1865, Clay Family Papers, UKY. For another view of father-son relations at war's end, one that stresses the challenge to paternal authority created by the conflict, see Mitchell, *Vacant Chair*, 115–26.

36. The reluctance with which Zeke Clay and other sons accepted their paroles naturally raised questions about how sincere and meaningful were their oaths of allegiance. The *Missouri Statesman* disdainfully called one paroled prisoner "the pretended Union man." "What Is Loyalty?," *Missouri Statesman*, April 22, 1864. Other newspapers also began to explore the meaning of the oath to the United States. See, e.g., "Loyalty—What Is It?," *Nashville Daily Press*, March 29, 1865; "Spurious Loyalty," *Border Times*, May 14, 1864; and "Who Are Loyal?," *Louisville Daily Journal*, February 12, 1863.

37. "A Sensible Expression," *Louisville Daily Journal*, February 10, 1864 (reprinted from *Buffalo Courier*) (Thompson); Alfred Ellet to Mary Ellet, September 12, 1863, Cabell-Ellet Family Papers, UVA. Thompson apparently received aid from several sources while incarcerated at Fort Delaware. For example, a man named Captain Ahl was thanked by James [Oakes?] of Boston for his "gentlemanlike kindness and courtesy to Genl. M. Jeff Thompson, now a prisoner of war, at Fort Delaware." James [Oakes?] to Captain Ahl, April 9, 1864, James Oakes Letters, Fort Delaware Collection (#01.012), FDS.

38. My attention to feelings is influenced by two works that argue for the powerful influence of emotions in American history. For an overview of the subject, see Stearns and Lewis, *Emotional History*. For an in-depth study of how emotion, and in particular, love, could influence the Civil War (and a soldier's motivation to serve in the war), see Stephen W. Berry, *All That Makes a Man*.

39. William Evans to Mary Ann, August 31, 1866, Mary Ann Covington Wilson Letters, SHC.

40. Jennie [Warren?] to Edward J. Warren, April 4, 1866, Warren Papers, SHC.

41. Joseph Roberts to Alexander J. Lawton, August 15, 1865, Lawton Papers, SHC. "You cannot imagine . . . how glad I was to receive your letter," Unionist Abraham Halsey similarly wrote his Confederate brother Joseph in Virginia. Abraham Halsey to Joseph Halsey, March 26, 1866, Morton-Halsey Family Papers, UVA.

42. Samuel Halsey (father) to Joseph Halsey, August 17, 1865, and Abraham Halsey to Joseph Halsey, March 26, 1866, Morton-Halsey Family Papers, UVA.

43. The exact number of slaves owned by Joseph Halsey cannot be determined from his papers; he also fails to appear in the 1860 slave census schedules for Culpeper County, Va. But one clue emerges from a list of slaves in his father-in-law's—and business partner's—papers. This list indicates that in October 1860 the family owned at least 84 slaves (36 men, 48 women). "List of Virginia Slaves," 1860, Morton-Halsey Family Papers, UVA.

44. For an in-depth discussion of these letters, see Chapter 3. Joseph initially opposed secession, preferring a constitutional amendment protecting slavery that could stave off war, but eventually threw his support behind the Confederacy. See "Secession Not the Remedy," Letter to Newspaper Editor, December 21, 1860, and "Constitutional Amendments," Letter to Newspaper Editors, January 14, 1861, both in Morton-Halsey Family Papers, UVA. Joseph's brothers and father, meanwhile, tended to be Republican, but "conservative Republican[s]" as brother Samuel put it, with varying views on slavery. Samuel Halsey (brother) to Joseph Halsey, March 23, 1861, ibid.

45. Samuel Halsey (brother) to Joseph Halsey, May 21, 1865, ibid.

46. Bethiah McKown to "My Dear Son," June 12, 1865, John D. McKown Papers, WHMC; James Yeatman to Henry Yeatman, May 27, 1865, Yeatman-Polk Collection, TSLA; "Editor's Easy Chair," *Harper's New Monthly Magazine*, December 1865, 121. For another example, see "A Sensible Southerner," *Louisville Daily Journal*, May 18, 1865.

47. Samuel Halsey (father) to Joseph Halsey, May 8, 1865, Abraham Halsey to Joseph Halsey, August 20, 1868, Samuel Halsey (brother) to Joseph Halsey, July 19, 1865, Morton-Halsey Family Papers, UVA.

48. The postwar oath administered by President Andrew Johnson in May 1865 required former participants in the Confederate cause to pledge their loyalty to the Union and their support for emancipation. To do so would ensure the restoration of an individual's rights to own property and to vote. For more on postwar pardons and oaths, see Foner, *Reconstruction*, 183, 190–91, and Rubin, "Redefining the South," 346–57.

49. Samuel Halsey (father) to Joseph Halsey, October 17, 1865, Samuel Halsey (brother) to Joseph Halsey, November 4, 1865, and Samuel Halsey (father) to Joseph Halsey, August 17, 1865, Morton-Halsey Family Papers, UVA.

50. See Chapter 3, "Brothers in Conflict."

51. Edmund Halsey to Joseph Halsey, May 24, 1865, Samuel Halsey (father) to Joseph Halsey, August 17, 1865, and Samuel Halsey (brother) to Joseph Halsey, May 1, 1865, Morton-Halsey Family Papers, UVA.

52. Warner Thomson to William Thomson, April 11, 1866, William Sydnor Thomson Papers, Emory; J. P. Pryor to Sister, August 17, 1867, Joseph Pryor Fuller Papers, SHC. A similar distinction was made as early as 1862 in Sophie DuPont to Samuel F. DuPont, May 4, 1862, DuPont Family Papers, Hagley.

53. This prefigured a larger trend in the 1870s of citizens' disillusionment with their popularly elected leaders and Reconstruction policies. In her study of reunion culture, Nina Silber (*Romance of Reunion*, 45) found that "an increasing number [of Americans] were becoming convinced that American politics were not equipped to handle the challenges of Reconstruction, that the system led only to chaos, confusion, and corruption." See also Wiebe, *Search for Order*, 5–7, and Foner, *Reconstruction*, 488–99.

54. Samuel Halsey (father) to Joseph Halsey, August 17, 1865, Morton-Halsey Family Papers, UVA.

55. Samuel Halsey (brother) to Joseph Halsey, July 3, 12, 19, 28, August 6, October 20, November 4, December 27, 30, 1865, Samuel Halsey (father) to Joseph Halsey, October 17, 1865, February 19, May 8, October 11, 1866, March 22, 1867, August 20, 1869, February 12, 1871, and Edmund Halsey to Joseph Halsey, February 28, 1866, all in ibid. On the establishment of a post office, see Joseph Halsey to Hon. John Hill, December 30, 1868, ibid.

56. Samuel Halsey (brother) to Joseph Halsey, November 22, 1866, February 21, 1867, and Samuel Halsey (father) to Joseph Halsey, May 25, 1867, February 11, 1869, March 26, 1870, ibid.

57. Samuel Halsey (father) to Joseph Halsey, August 17, 1865, ibid.

58. This is evident in part from his family's letters and also from letters that Joseph wrote to other Virginians. In one he expressed the wish that the Supreme Court would

strike down emancipation as unconstitutional. Joseph Halsey to "Sir," April 22, 1867, ibid.

59. Edmund Halsey to Joseph Halsey, December 17, 1865, Abraham Halsey to Joseph Halsey, August 20, 1868, ibid.

60. Abraham Halsey to Joseph Halsey, February 10, 1877, ibid. In 1873 Samuel wrote Joseph that selling a portion of their inherited property was "so contrary to what father would have approved of or done if living and so much like giving away your birth right." Edmund Halsey to Joseph Halsey, n.d., and September 15, 1871, and Samuel Halsey (brother) to Joseph Halsey, October 4, 1871, January 5, 1873, ibid.

61. William C. Davis, *Jefferson Davis*. For other women who wrote tributes to their husbands' wartime service, see essays on Anna Jackson, LaSalle Pickett, and Libbie Custer in Bleser and Gordon, *Intimate Strategies*, 49–68, 69–86, 178–98.

62. Ellet's daughter Mary discussed her happiness at seeing a tribute to her late father in a Newark, N.J., newspaper. Mary Ellet to Charlie Ellet, July 8, 1863, Cabell-Ellet Family Papers, UVA. For more on Charles Ellet, his war service, and death, see Hearn, *Ellet's Brigade*.

63. Mary Ellet to Nina Ellet, June 21, 1862, Cabell-Ellet Family Papers, UVA. It is unclear what killed Elvira; her brother-in-law, Edward Ellet, later wrote that she died "of a broken heart occasioned by the sad loss of her husband." Genealogical Files, document dated October 5, 1897, ibid.

64. Mary Ellet to Charlie Ellet, August 21, 1863, ibid. After one such victory in April 1863, Mary wrote to her brother, "Does it not almost seem like a tribute of Providence to our noble Father that every service of importance or daring on the Mississippi should have been performed by *his* boats, *his* son—*his* family?" Mary Ellet to Charlie Ellet, April 4, 1863, ibid.

65. Alfred Ellet to Mary Ellet, July 13, 1865, ibid.

66. William Cabell to Mary Ellet, August 9, 19, 26, 28, 1865, ibid.

67. Mary Ellet to William Cabell, September 10, 1865, ibid.

68. William Cabell to Mary Ellet, September 14, October 6, November 24, 26, December 9, 18, 1865, February 3, 1866, and Mary Ellet to William Cabell, November 28, December 10, 1865, ibid.

69. "Estimate of Property Lost by William D. Cabell on the 8th, 9th, & 10th Mar. 1865 by & during the Presence of the Enemy," n.d., ibid. On Cabell's slaveholding, see U.S. Census, Population and Slave Schedules: Nelson County, Va., 1860, 55; on Cabell's post-war position, see U.S. Census, Population Schedule: Nelson County, Va., 1870, 117.

70. William Cabell to Mary Ellet, February 10, 1867, Cabell-Ellet Family Papers, UVA.

71. Mary Ellet to William Cabell, January 17, March 22, 1866, ibid.

72. John S. C. Abbot, "Heroic Deeds of Heroic Men: Charles Ellet and His Naval Steam Rams," *Harper's New Monthly Magazine*, February 1866, 295–312; William Cabell to Mary Ellet, February 15, 1866, and Alfred Ellet to Mary Ellet, March 29, September 9, 1866, Cabell-Ellet Family Papers, UVA.

73. Edward Ellet to Mary Ellet, March 28, 1867, and Alfred Ellet to Mary Ellet, March 30, April 7, 1867, Cabell-Ellet Family Papers, UVA.

74. William Cabell to Mary Ellet, May 10, 12, June 1, 1867, and Mary Ellet to William Cabell, June 30, 1867, Cabell-Ellet Family Papers, UVA; "Norwood School" advertisement, *Charlottesville Chronicle*, July 4, 1867.

75. Nina Ellet to Mary Ellet Cabell, March 19, 1868, February 15, 28, 1869, and Mary Israel Ellet Reminiscence, May 1870, typescript, Cabell-Ellet Family Papers, UVA.

76. On the care taken to talk in a neutral and unprovocative manner, see Alfred Mordecai to Sara Ann Mordecai, November 8, 1865, and Alfred Mordecai to Ellen Mordecai, November 10, 1865, Alfred Mordecai Papers, LC; Emma Read Berry to Harriet Read Berry, May 13, 1865, Read Family Papers, VHS; W. A. Durant to Henry Slack, August 1, 1866, Slack Family Papers, SHC. On breaks in visiting, see Emma Read Berry to Harriet Read Berry, July 3, 1865, Read Family Papers, VHS. Laura Jackson Arnold and Jonathan Arnold, residents of West Virginia, were married in 1844 but became estranged during the Civil War. Records from their 1870 divorce suggest that their divided politics played a role in the split. Laura was a Unionist known to nurse sick and wounded Union soldiers; Jonathan, a Democrat with Confederate sympathies, was once arrested by Union authorities on the charge of "disloyalty" and sent to Camp Chase, Ohio. It was rumored at the time — and during the divorce — that Laura might have used her ties to Union officials to have her husband arrested. She was also said to have had an affair with a Union soldier. See Castel, "Arnold vs. Arnold."

77. Cleaves, *Rock of Chickamauga*, 5. Thomas's 1881 memoir, written by a close friend, fails to mention the sisters at all. Instead, in a passage intended to demonstrate his devotion to the Union, Thomas apparently once stated: "If these ties can only be preserved on the condition of my abandonment of the government for which my forefathers fought, bled, and died, then let them be severed." No remorse about his estranged relatives appears in the memoir. Richard W. Johnson, *Memoir of . . . George H. Thomas*, 246.

78. Three pages of Fletcher's diary for 1869 were cut out, leaving as the next page a testimonial by Fletcher to how important her sister's love was to her. Fletcher Diary, September 1869 – September 1870, Duke.

79. According to Nina Silber (*Romance of Reunion*, 4), in the North, "forgetfulness, not memory, appears to be the dominant theme in the reunion culture." Forgetting would also become a feature of what David Blight (*Race and Reunion*, 255–99) has termed the "reconciliationist" vision of Civil War memory. Both authors emphasize that this culture of forgetting peaked in the 1880s and 1890s. Here I am more interested in tracing the roots of this culture in the immediate postwar period.

80. "The Return Home," *Harper's Weekly*, May 20, 1865, 320.

81. Clarence Prentice, *Why Can We Not Be Brothers, We Know That We Were Rebels* (Louisville, Ky.: D. P. Faulds, 1865), in "Historic American Sheet Music," <http://scriptorium.lib.duke.edu/sheetmusic>, Duke.

82. "The Tearful Convention," *Harper's Weekly*, September 29, 1866, 617.

83. [Untitled], *Frank Leslie's Illustrated Newspaper*, January 13, 1866, 272.

84. Governor A. W. Bradford, "Address," [?], 1866, Bradford Papers, MDHS. Newspapers across the border states also published overtures to the "returning prodigals" throughout the 1860s. See, e.g., "Duty of the Returning Prodigals," *Nashville Daily Press*, May 26, 1865.

85. "Gov. Brownlow's Message," *Nashville Daily Press*, October 3, 1865.

86. Other historians have discussed the intersectional marriage motif in postwar writings, but most suggest that it became popular in the 1880s and 1890s, along with the rise of "Lost Cause" sentiment. Nina Silber, for example, argues that "in the early postwar period, stories depicting the close, emotional bonding of northerners and southerners were extremely rare." Silber, *Romance of Reunion*, 39–65 (quotation, 40). See also Buck, *Road to Reunion*, 230–32; Moss, *Domestic Novelists*, 78–82; Censer, "Reimagining the North-South Reunion"; Blight, *Race and Reunion*, 151, 216–17; and Diffley, *Where My Heart Is Turning*, 180–81. In contrast, my research suggests that the intersectional marriage scenario was popular even in the 1860s and was an outgrowth of wartime tales of romantic dysfunction. Reid Mitchell (*Vacant Chair*, 126–33) similarly takes note of the early emergence of intersectional marriage stories.

87. John W. DeForest, "Rum Creeters Is Women," *Harper's New Monthly Magazine*, March 1867, 484–91. DeForest is better known for *Miss Ravenel's Conversion from Secession to Loyalty* (1867), a similar work utilizing the intersectional marriage theme set in New Orleans.

88. DeForest, "Rum Creeters Is Women," 484–91.

89. Maria J. McIntosh, "Olive Raymond's Story," *Appleton's Journal*, August 14, 1869, 610–14.

90. For stories that feature ghosts, see, e.g., Lizzie W. Champney, "'Ministerin' Meally," *Appleton's Journal*, December 1876, 538–43; Will Wallace Harney, "How Captain Ascott Floored the Ghost," *Atlantic Monthly*, August 1877, 207–25; and Harland, *Sunnybank*.

91. "One Good Effect of the War," *Louisville Daily Journal*, May 20, 1865. Nina Silber (*Romance of Reunion*, 63–64, 95–116) also points out that marriage was a "new" relationship, "freed from the burdens of the familial past" (p. 63), and therefore ideal for depicting a postwar reunion.

92. Elizabeth Haven Appleton, "What Five Years Will Do," *Atlantic Monthly*, November 1868, 525–43.

93. For women helping men to escape from prison, see, e.g., William H. Morris, "Betrayed and Rescued," *Frank Leslie's Illustrated Newspaper*, November 11, 1865, 123, and E. G. R., "The Escaped Spy: A Story of the Late War," *Frank Leslie's Illustrated Newspaper*, August 5, 1865, 309–10. On the protection of a woman's home, see John W. DeForest, "Rum Creeters Is Women," *Harper's New Monthly Magazine*, March 1867, 484–91, and Elizabeth Haven Appleton, "What Five Years Will Do," *Atlantic Monthly*, November 1868, 525–43. On sending aid to Southern families, see Maria J. McIntosh, "Olive Raymond's Story," *Appleton's Journal*, August 14, 1869, 610–14, and William Wirt Sikes, "Absalom Mather," *Harper's New Monthly Magazine*, September 1866, 463–70.

94. Strebor, *Home Scenes*, 21.

95. DeForest, "Rum Creeters Is Women," 486. Nina Silber (*Romance of Reunion*, 46–55) observes a tendency in postwar reunion culture to "depoliticize" the subject of reconciliation and emphasize instead "the sentimental language of reunion."

96. Harland, *Sunnybank*, 58, 404. For similar marriages, see, e.g., Hannah Muller,

"Waiting for Sherman's Army," *Frank Leslie's Illustrated Newspaper*, November 25, 1865, 149–50; Helen W. Pierson, "Queen's Good Work," *Harper's New Monthly Magazine*, May 1866, 772–78; and Epes Sargent, "Strategy at the Fireside," *Atlantic Monthly*, August 1865, 151–67. For Northern interest in themes of Southern Unionism in fiction, see Lively, *Fiction Fights*, 55–56.

97. For more on Terhune, see Moss, *Domestic Novelists*, 194–221. Another author of a similar postwar marriage tale, Maria J. McIntosh, also balanced her Southern roots with her marriage to a Northern man. See McIntosh, "Olive Raymond's Story," *Appleton's Journal*, August 14, 1869, 610–14. For more on McIntosh, see Moss, *Domestic Novelists*, 88–100.

98. For Northern publishers' embrace of conciliatory Southern writing, see Buck, *Road to Reunion*, 225.

99. On the demise of Southern literary journals after the war, see Mott, *American Journalism*, 89, 113, 200. Some of these journals that ceased to exist by 1866 included the *Southern Illustrated News*, *Magnolia Weekly*, and *Southern Field and Fireside*.

100. For Confederates' postwar hopes, see Rubin, "Redefining the South."

101. For examples of these stories, see Caroline Marsdale, "Cousin Jack," *Southern Magazine*, December 1873, 712–19, and Clara Marshall, "The Refugees," *Southern Magazine*, September 1873, 356–65. For studies of the internal divisions in Southern society during the war, see Escott, *After Secession*; Freehling, *The South vs. the South*; and Faust, *Mothers of Invention*.

Chapter Seven

1. Johnstone, *Sergeant Slasher*, 28, 8.

2. The vast literature on slave families focuses largely on the extent to which their intimate relations were disrupted by the stress and trauma of enslavement. For an early interpretation that emphasized the destruction of black family life, see Elkins, *Slavery*. For subsequent studies of the stability of slave family life, particularly in nuclear families, see Gutman, *Black Family*; Genovese, *Roll, Jordan, Roll*; White, *Ar'n't I a Woman?*; and Blassingame, *Slave Community*. Recent works have emphasized more complex slave family structures that emerged to adapt to the stresses of slavery. See Malone, *Sweet Chariot*; Stevenson, *Life in Black and White*; and Penningroth, *Claims of Kinfolk*.

3. This chapter draws from oral histories, private manuscript papers, and especially a collection of documents generated largely by the interactions of enslaved men and women with the Federal government (especially the War Department and the Freedmen's Bureau) both during and after the war. This vast collection is held by the National Archives, but parts of it have been collected and published in the multivolume series, *Freedom: A Documentary History of Emancipation, 1861–1867*, edited by the Freedmen and Southern Society Project at the University of Maryland.

4. The Emancipation Proclamation also exempted Tennessee and Union-occupied regions of Virginia and Louisiana. See Berlin et al., *Slaves No More*, 120–21.

5. This dilemma of enslaved families was particularly acute in Kentucky, where a greater percentage of black men of military age enlisted during the war — 57 percent —

than from any other Southern state. But it was also of grave concern to husbands and wives who had lived together; for many more previously separated by their masters, this wartime problem was not as severe. On the unique pressures facing enslaved families in the border states, see Berlin et al., *Free at Last*, 463; Berlin et al., *Wartime Genesis*, 63, 489, 634; Berlin, Reidy, and Rowland, *Black Military Experience*, 195–96; and Berlin and Rowland, *Families and Freedom*, 22, 95–96. On the general process of wartime emancipation, see Berlin et al., *Slaves No More*, and Litwack, *Been in the Storm So Long*, chaps. 1–4. On the way in which the dilemma of whether to leave or stay on the plantation played out in the Deep South, see Campbell, *When Sherman Marched North*, 45–50.

6. Sworn Statement of Joseph Miller, November 26, 1864, in Berlin et al., *Free at Last*, 493–95. For similar cases, see Affidavits of John Higgins, November 28, 1864 (686-87), and John Vetter, Agent of the American Missionary Association, December 16, 1864 (689–90), in Berlin et al., *Wartime Genesis*; and Sworn Statement of John Burnside, December 15, 1864, in Berlin et al., *Free at Last*, 393–95.

7. Deposition of Patsey Leach, March 25, 1865, in Berlin et al., *Free at Last*, 400–401. For other cases of abuse inflicted on the families left behind, see Ann [?] to "My Dear Husband," January 19, 1864, in ibid., 360–61; D. M. Sells to Brigade Commander, February 6, 1865, in Berlin and Rowland, *Families and Freedom*, 107–10; and Affidavit of Clarissa Burdett, March 27, 1865, in Berlin et al., *Destruction of Slavery*. For an overview of the plight of these families, see Berlin, Reidy, and Rowland, *Black Military Experience*, 657–59.

8. Martha Glover to "My Dear Husband," December 30, 1863, in Berlin et al., *Free at Last*, 463–64.

9. Sam Bowmen to Wife, May 10, 1864, in Berlin et al., *Destruction of Slavery*, 484.

10. On the decision of women to remain on plantations or to run away, see Weiner, *Mistresses and Slaves*, 175–79, 183; Kelita Suit to Commander, Middle Department and 8th Army Corps, December 25, 1864, in Berlin et al., *Destruction of Slavery*, 391; Fields, *Slavery and Freedom*, 119; and Berlin and Rowland, *Families and Freedom*, 22–31. On the general connection between family and the process of seeking freedom, see Berlin and Rowland, *Families and Freedom*, and Bercaw, *Gendered Freedoms*, 102.

11. Berlin, Reidy, and Rowland, *Black Military Experience*, 30.

12. Sam Bowmen to Wife, May 10, 1864, in Berlin et al., *Destruction of Slavery*, 484. Maryland and Missouri abolished slavery by January 1865, thus eliminating outright the division between slavery and freedom for families in those states. See Berlin et al., *Slaves No More*, 67. Here I join Dylan C. Penningroth (*Claims of Kinfolk*, esp. 187–92) in calling attention to what he terms "internal diversity and conflict" in slave families, rather than assuming unity among African Americans. On gender relations in black families during slavery and emancipation, see White, *Ar'n't I a Woman?*; Stevenson, *Life in Black and White*; Schwalm, *Hard Fight*; Stanley, *From Bondage to Contract*; Edwards, *Gendered Strife*; Berlin and Rowland, *Families and Freedom*; Berlin et al., *Slaves No More*, 228; and Penningroth, *Claims of Kinfolk*, esp. 163–86. One study that emphasizes the diverse ways in which black families adjusted their gender relations to freedom is Bercaw, *Gendered Freedoms*, esp. 99–116.

13. Nancy Bercaw (*Gendered Freedoms*, 104–5) offers a different view of public and

private, suggesting that some black families sought privacy as a component of their freedom and independence. For another important discussion of public and private in the context of black family life, see Edwards, *Gendered Strife*, 145–83.

14. For a general context on the reunions of enslaved families after emancipation, see Litwack, *Been in the Storm So Long*, chap. 5; Foner, *Reconstruction*, 82–84; and Hahn, *Nation under Our Feet*, 165–70.

15. *Colored Tennessean*, July 18, 1866, October 14, 1865. For an extended analysis of ads like these, see Michael Johnson, "Looking for Lost Kin."

16. Examples of family assistance provided by the Freedmen's Bureau can be found throughout Berlin and Rowland, *Families and Freedom*. See also Schwalm, *Hard Fight*, 234–68; Foner, *Reconstruction*, 87–88; Stanley, *From Bondage to Contract*, 36–59; and Penningroth, *Claims of Kinfolk*, 167–68, 181.

17. Spotswood Rice to [Slaveowner], September 3, 1864, in Berlin and Rowland, *Families and Freedom*, 196–97. Adam Woods of Louisville, Ky., also enlisted the help of the Bureau when, after serving in the Union army, he learned that his brother had died, leaving behind three orphaned sons. The sons still remained in the possession of their master in 1867, prompting Woods to seek assistance in obtaining legal custody of the boys. It is unclear whether Woods succeeded; he may have run into some difficulty, given that after the war Southern states passed apprenticeship laws legally binding orphans to white landowners as laborers. Statement of Adam Woods, November 11, 1867, in Berlin and Rowland, *Families and Freedom*, 228–30.

18. Aaron Oats to Secretary of War, January 26, 1865, in Berlin and Rowland, *Families and Freedom*, 160.

19. On the career of the Freedmen's Bureau and the politics surrounding it, see Foner, *Reconstruction*.

20. David Blight (*Race and Reunion*, 311–19) has most recently examined African Americans' postwar memory of slavery and demonstrated how remembrance of this past was fraught with feelings of agony and shame. This created a major challenge: how to deal with the burden of the past while keeping it alive and answering the call of men like Frederick Douglass, who urged African Americans to counter white Americans' tendency to "forget" in the interest of national reconciliation.

21. Strebor, *Home Scenes*, 66; L. V., "My Sister-in-Law," *Southern Magazine*, October 1875, 483.

22. John W. DeForest, "Rum Creeters Is Women," *Harper's New Monthly Magazine*, March 1867, 484–91.

23. Smythe, *Mary Clifton*; J. O. Culver, "Robbed of Half a Million," *Harper's New Monthly Magazine*, October 1866, 634–42; Elizabeth Haven Appleton, "What Five Years Will Do," *Atlantic Monthly*, November 1868, 525–43.

24. Austin, *Dora Darling*. For similar examples of slaves' loyal companionship in North-South reunion tales, see Harland, *Sunnybank*, and William Wirt Sikes, "Absalom Mather," *Harper's New Monthly Magazine*, September 1866, 463–70.

25. Epes Sargent, "Strategy at the Fireside," *Atlantic Monthly*, August 1865, 151–67. For Sargent's wartime writing, see Fahs, *Imagined Civil War*, 192–93.

26. Studies that date the emergence of the "whitewashed" reunion to the 1880s and after include Blight, *Race and Reunion*, chap. 7 (quotation, 225); Silber, *Romance of Reunion*, chap. 5; and Young, *Disarming the Nation*, 195. Two other studies of postwar fiction have argued that the tendency to obscure race and slavery had its roots in the immediate postwar (and even wartime) period. In her study of wartime fiction, Alice Fahs (*Imagined Civil War*, 154) suggests that Northern writers during the war "offered only a circumscribed vision of how freedmen and freedwomen became part of a new national family." And Lyde Cullen Sizer (*Political Work*, 231, 244), who studied the appearance of miscegenation tales in postwar Northern writing, likewise finds that early stories helped "erase" the "racial problems of Reconstruction."

27. Kirke, *Among the Guerrillas*. Similarly, in Alouette's *Angeline: The Octaroon*, a dime novel written in 1865, the main character is a mixed-race slave, referred to only as "Quadroon," who sets off a chain of tragic events after switching at birth the black and white daughters of her master. The quadroon's swap was an act of revenge against the master and his white wife, but rather than celebrated as a subversion of slavery, in this story it is a "cruel" cause of "distress and suffering."

28. On mixed-race black leaders, see Foner, *Reconstruction*, 100–101. Richard Schuster ("Civil War Novels," 248) also reads Kirke's *Among the Guerrillas* as "an allegorical argument against the wrong sort of vindictive Reconstruction." For an overview of black politics during Reconstruction, see Hahn, *Nation under Our Feet*, esp. chaps. 3–5.

29. Kirke (Gilmore), *Among the Guerrillas*, 280–85. Born in Boston, James R. Gilmore maintained many ties with the South during his lifetime, beginning with his profitable shipping firm that did business with Southern cotton planters and culminating with his work as a peace emissary who visited Richmond to meet with President Jefferson Davis in 1864. Gilmore maintained a "love/hate" relationship with the South, according to one scholar, in which he spoke out strongly against slavery but at the same time sympathized with the white Southerners with whom he was acquainted. On Gilmore, see Miles, "James Roberts Gilmore"; Hart, *Manual of American Literature*, 479–89; and Schuster, "Civil War Novels," 209–19. On the mythology surrounding mulattoes in the late nineteenth century, see Williamson, *New People*, 94–97. The "tragic mulatto" theme had been used by antislavery writers before the war to depict the tragedy that emerged from slavery. See Kinney, *Amalgamation!*, 55–104.

30. "'Uncle Tom' and His Grandchild," *Harper's Weekly*, November 3, 1866, 689–90. Lyde Cullen Sizer (*Political Work*, chap. 8) has examined a similar theme in postwar miscegenation tales that do not end in the death of a mixed-race person but instead describe the marriage of white and black people as a process that will redeem and civilize African Americans. These stories similarly reinscribe divisions between blackness and whiteness and emphasize the superiority of the latter. On the Uncle Tom character's portrayal in dramatic renditions of Stowe's novel (or "Tom Shows"), see Railton, "Uncle Tom's Cabin and American Culture," <http://www.iath.virginia.edu/utc>.

31. Olive A. Wadsworth, "Our Phil," *Atlantic Monthly*, November 1869, 560–70; Helen W. Pierson, "Chip," *Harper's New Monthly Magazine*, July 1865, 254–58. Similar stories include Nora Perry, "Mrs. F's Waiting Maid," *Harper's New Monthly Magazine*,

June 1867, 74–79, and Helen W. Pierson, "Queen's Good Work," *Harper's New Monthly Magazine*, May 1866, 772–78.

32. "Testing the Question," *Harper's Weekly*, August 12, 1865, 512.

33. Gutman, *Black Family*, 388 (Turner); "The Present and Future of the Colored Race in America: An Address Delivered in Brooklyn, New York, on 15 May 1863," in Blassingame, *Frederick Douglass Papers*, 572. David Blight has demonstrated that Douglass's claim to membership in the figurative "national family" emerged only with the onset of the Civil War. "In 1852," Blight writes, "Douglass had disclaimed any part of the fathers' inheritance and, although dearly wishing it were otherwise, felt no attachment to the Fourth of July. In 1862, however, in the midst of the sectional war he had hoped for, the revolutionary fathers became his own." Blight, *Frederick Douglass' Civil War*, 75–77, 99 (quotation, 77).

34. Gutman, *Black Family*, 388; Petition of American Citizens of African Descent to the Union Convention of Tennessee, January 9, 1865, in Berlin et al., *Free at Last*, 497–505.

35. By the 1890s black writers would counter these white depictions by increasingly emphasizing themes of black family loyalty and reunion in their stories of the war and emancipation. See Young, *Disarming the Nation*, 200–211.

Epilogue

1. In his claim to the U.S. Southern Claims Commission, Daniel J. Good of Rockingham County, Va., asserted: "I had a brother who was a rebel. He volunteered and was as strong a rebel as I was a union man. After the rebels were whipped he cleared out and went to Texas. I tried to persuade him not to volunteer but he would go. I did not aid him in any way." According to this statement, Good appears to have been a stalwart Unionist, doing what he could to discourage his brother from enlisting in the Confederate service. The commission apparently agreed, for it approved his claim. Many other claimants also were found to have been loyal to the Union despite having Confederates in the family. I examined the approved claims of five counties — Davidson and Washington in Tennessee, Rockingham and Frederick in Virginia, and Jefferson County in West Virginia. Of 151 claims approved, 34 (or 23 percent) noted that the petitioners had Confederate kin. Claim of Daniel J. Good, #21843, Records of Accounting Officers of the Department of the Treasury, NA. For examples of anecdote books, see Vickers, *Under Both Flags*, 138; Member of the G.A.R., *Picket Line*, 70–71; Moore, *Civil War in Song*, 76, 132, 347; and Greene, *Thrilling Stories*, 86–92, 175–76.

2. Matthew H. Peters, "My Brother and I," *Blue and Gray: The Patriotic American Magazine*, June 1893, 468. See also "A Fraternal Gathering after the War," *Confederate Veteran*, September–October 1932, 1. For an extended discussion of veterans' publications, reunions, and the general sentiment of "blue-gray fraternalism," see Blight, *Race and Reunion*, 198–210.

3. Twain, "The Siamese Twins," *Writings*, 248–53.

4. For these stories, as well as an insightful introduction to Bierce's wartime fiction, see Duncan and Klooster, *Phantoms*.

5. For a fascinating analysis of recent interpretations of the war, see Ayers, "Worrying about the Civil War." For another exploration of why Americans today — especially descendants of Confederates — seek an attachment to the Civil War, see Horwitz, *Confederates in the Attic*.

Bibliography

Primary Sources

MANUSCRIPT SOURCES

Delaware Public Archives, Dover
  Bell Collection
  LaMotte Collection
  Moor-Naudain Collection, Small Manuscripts
Rare Book, Manuscript, and Special Collections Library, Duke University,
    Durham, North Carolina
  Charles Wesley Andrews Papers
  Bacon Family Papers
  Bedinger-Dandridge Family Papers
  Lois Wright Richardson Davis Papers
  Lucy Muse Walton Fletcher Diary
  Ann Henshaw Gardiner Papers
  Henry Wager Halleck Papers
  Edmund Jennings Lee II Papers
  Charles Macgill Papers
  Purviance Family Papers
  James Ramsey Papers
  Phineas Messenger Savery Papers
  Laura Stebbins Papers
  Charles Steedman Papers
  Cabell Tavenner and Alexander Scott Withers Papers
  Samuel Yates Papers
Special Collections and Archives, Robert W. Woodruff Library, Emory University,
    Atlanta
  John D. Babb Family Papers
  James Ewell Brown "Jeb" Stuart Papers
  Warner Alexander Thomson Diary
  William Sydnor Thomson Papers
  Bettie Tindall Papers

The Filson Historical Society, Louisville, Kentucky
  Stephen Barker Collection
  Robert J. Breckinridge Letters
  Helm Bruce Collection
  Stephen Burbridge Papers
  J. W. Calvert Letter
  Clark-Strater-Watson Family Papers
  Josephine Covington Letter
  John J. Crittenden Letters
  Grigsby Family Papers
  Sylvann P. Hathaway Collection
  William Preston Johnston Papers
  Jones Family Papers
  Robert E. Lee Letters
  Mary Todd Lincoln Letter
  Humphrey Marshall Papers
  Marshall Family Papers
  George D. Prentice Papers
  Preston Family Papers
  David Putnam Letter
  Hubbard Smith Papers
  Stone Collection
  Gates Phillips Thruston Papers
  Winston-Jones Family Papers
Fort Delaware Society, Delaware City
  Deaderick Family Letters
  Goldsborough Family Letters
  C. M. Killian Letter
  Captain J. R. McMichael Papers
  James Oakes Letter
  James Perry Letters
  Stuart Family Papers
  Ward Papers
Hagley Museum and Library, Wilmington, Delaware
  DuPont Family Papers
Historical Society of Delaware, Wilmington
  James A. Bayard Jr. Letters
Kentucky Library, Western Kentucky University, Bowling Green
  Knott Collection
  Lewis-Starling Collection
  Henry L. Underwood Collection
  Johanna Louisa "Josie" Underwood Diary
  Underwood Collection

Library of Congress, Washington, D.C.
  Jasper N. Barritt Papers
  Breckinridge Family Papers
  John J. Crittenden Papers
  Simon Palmer Gillet Papers
  Sarah Jane Full Hill Papers
  Joseph Holt Papers
  Percy Frere Luck Papers
  Alfred Mordecai Papers
  Philip Phillips Papers
  John Tyler Papers
  Cadmus Marcellus Wilcox Papers
  Willard Family Papers
Margaret I. King Library, University of Kentucky, Lexington
  Breckinridge Family Papers
  Benjamin Buckner Papers
  Clay Family Papers
  John J. Crittenden Papers
  George D. Prentice Papers
  Letters to Clarence Prentice
  Mary E. Vanmeter Diary
Maryland Historical Society, Baltimore
  Anonymous Letter from Northern to Southern Cousin
  Archer-Mitchell-Stump-Williams Papers
  Governor A. W. Bradford Papers
  George William Brown Collection
  Brune-Randall Family Papers
  Rebecca Dorsey Davis Papers
  Thomas W. Hall Correspondence
  Mayer-Clarke Papers
  Jabez D. and John C. Pratt Letters
  Shriver Family Papers
Missouri Historical Society, St. Louis
  Beauregard Family Papers
  Blow Family Papers
  Dorsey Family Papers
  Fannie Echard Letter, Civil War Collection
  Corinne Steele Hall Papers
  Samuel Kennard Letters, Civil War Collection
  William Carr Lane Papers
  George E. Leighton Collection
  Lucy Thurman Letters, Civil War Collection
Museum of the Confederacy, Richmond
  Janet Henderson Weaver Randolph Papers

Kate Mason Rowland Papers
Frances Dunbar Ruggles Papers
Sullivan Family Papers
National Archives, Washington, D.C., and College Park, Maryland
　Rose Greenhow Papers, Records of the Department of State, Civil War Papers,
　　Record Group 59, Entry 986
　Intercepted Letters, Record Group 109, Entry 189
　Letters Received, Confederate Secretary of War, Record Group 109, M-437
　Letters Received Applying for Passes to Enter Union Territory, Records of the
　　Office of the Secretary of War, Record Group 107, Entry 54
　Letters Requesting Passes to Visit the South, Records of the Department of State,
　　Record Group 59, Entry 968
　Miscellaneous Letters and Newspapers Relating to the Civil War, 1861–65,
　　Records of the Department of State, Record Group 59, Entry 984
　Pension Application Files Based on Service in the Civil War and Spanish-
　　American War, Records of the Department of Veterans Affairs, Record Group 15
　Records of Accounting Officers of the Department of the Treasury, Records of
　　the Land, Files, and Miscellaneous Division, Settled Case Files Approved by
　　the Southern Claims Commission, 1871–80, Record Group 217, Entry 732
　Records concerning the Conduct and Loyalty of Certain Union Officers, Civilian
　　Employees of the War Department, and U.S. Citizens during the Civil War,
　　Records of the Office of the Secretary of War, Record Group 107, Entry 68
　Records concerning Travel Passes, Records of the Office of the Secretary of War,
　　Record Group 107, Entry 56
　Records of the Passport Office at Richmond, 1861–65, Record Group 109,
　　Entry 10
　Register of Arrests for Disloyalty, Records of the Department of State, Record
　　Group 59, Entry 958
　Union Provost Marshal's File of Two or More Name Papers Relating to Citizens,
　　Record Group 109, M-416
Philadelphia City Archives, Philadelphia
　Pennsylvania Common Pleas Court, Divorce Docket, 1865
Southern Historical Collection, University of North Carolina, Chapel Hill
　Mary Ann Albinson Letters, Confederate Papers
　S. G. Barnard Letters
　David F. Boyd Papers
　Brasher-Lawrence Family Papers
　Platt K. Dickenson Letters
　Joseph Pryor Fuller Letters
　Gordon Family Papers
　John Wilson Hines Letters
　Alexander R. Lawton Papers
　James Isaac Metts Papers
　Nathaniel Middleton Papers

Polk-Yeatman Family Papers
C. Alice Ready Diary
Slack Family Papers
Edward J. Warren Papers
Mary Ann Covington Wilson Letters
Tennessee State Library and Archives, Nashville
Lila Tennessee Blackburn Letters
Cooper Family Papers
William Driver Papers
William Eames Papers
J. Fancher Diary
L. Virginia French Diary
Jill Knight Garrett Collection
Margaret Griffis Diary
John Kempshall Papers
Sarah Kennedy Papers, Civil War Collection
Curtis McDowell Papers
Sam C. Mitchell Letters
Hugh G. Moore Papers
Louisa Brown Pearl Diary
Martha M. Tipton Diary
George W. Wynne Papers
Yeatman-Polk Family Papers
Albert and Shirley Small Special Collections Library, University of Virginia,
    Charlottesville
Cabell-Ellet Family Papers
Houston and Willson Family Papers
Morton-Halsey Family Papers
Neville-Newman Correspondence
Mary Y. K. Smith Papers
Bennett Taylor Papers
Trist-Burke Family Papers
Virginia Historical Society, Richmond
Arthur Lee Brent Papers
Camp Chase Papers
Robert Young Conrad Papers
Cooke Family Papers
Samuella Hart Curd Diary
Emily Howe Dupuy Papers
Faulkner Family Papers
Finney Family Papers
Katherine Heath Hawes Papers
Samuel Horace Hawes Diary
Lee Family Papers

Lomax Family Papers
Elizabeth Virginia Lomax Diary
Pegram Family
Preston Family Papers
Read Family Papers
Maria McGregor (Campbell) Smith Papers
Stephen Spurlock Letter
Mary M. Stockton Terry Diary
John R. Thompson Papers
John G. Webb Papers
Fanny Churchill Braxton Young Papers
Western Historical Manuscript Collection, University of Missouri, Columbia
Alley-Brewer Family Letters
Charles Monroe Chase Papers
Joseph Crider Letters
Arretta Davidson Letters
Charles B. France Papers
Lizzie C. Gilmore Papers
Jacob J. Hayden Letter
Eleanor Ann King Correspondence and Diary
Lesieur Family Letters
Martha McDonald Diary
John D. McKown Papers
Monroe County Provost Marshal Papers
Patton-Scott Family Papers
Mary Ream Letter
Richard Huston Ryall Letters
Oliver A. Sandusky Petition
Silliman Letters
Robert W. Wells Papers

NEWSPAPERS AND LITERARY JOURNALS

Appleton's Journal
Atlantic Monthly
Baltimore American
Baltimore Morning Sun
Blue and Gray: The Patriotic American Magazine
Border Times (Weston, Mo.)
Boston Daily Journal
Chambersburg (Pa.) Valley Spirit
Charleston Mercury
Charlottesville Chronicle
Colored Tennessean

Confederate Veteran
Daily Missouri Democrat (St. Louis)
Daily Missouri Republican (St. Louis)
Daily Richmond Examiner
Delaware Republican
Frank Leslie's Illustrated Newspaper
Franklin (Pa.) Repository and Transcript
Galaxy
Harper's New Monthly Magazine
Harper's Weekly
Jefferson County (Mo.) Herald
Louisville Daily Courier
Louisville Daily Journal
Magnolia Weekly
Memphis Daily Appeal
Missouri Statesman (Columbia)
Nashville Daily Press
National Intelligencer
New York Daily News
New York Herald
New York Tribune
New York World
Philadelphia Inquirer
Richmond Enquirer
Smyrna (Del.) Times
Southern Field and Fireside
Southern Illustrated News
Southern Literary Messenger
Southern Magazine
Southern Record of News, History, and Literature
Staunton (Va.) Spectator
Washington Evening Star

PUBLISHED NOVELS

Abrams, Alex. St. Clair. *The Trials of the Soldier's Wife: A Tale of the Second American Revolution.* Atlanta: Intelligencer Steam Power Presses, 1864.

Alouette. *Angeline: The Octaroon.* Dawley's Ten-Penny Novel No. 12. New York: T. R. Dawley, Publisher for the Million, 1865.

Anonymous. *At Anchor: A Story of Our Civil War.* New York: Appleton, 1865.

Austin, Jane G. *Dora Darling: The Daughter of the Regiment.* Boston: J. E. Tilton and Co., 1865.

Baker, Delphine P. *Solon; or, The Rebellion of '61: A Domestic and Political Tragedy.* Chicago: S. P. Rounds, 1862.

Baker, William Mumford. *Inside: A Chronicle of Secession*. New York: Harper and Brothers, 1866.

Bartlett, Napier. *Clarimonde: A Tale of New Orleans Life and of the Present War*. Richmond: M. A. Malsby, 1863.

Bell, Alfreda E. *The Rebel Cousins*. Philadelphia: Barclay and Co., 1864.

Bradshaw, Wesley. *The Angel of the Battlefield: A Tale of the Rebellion*. New York: American News Co., 1865.

Browne, Junius Henry. *Four Years in Secessia: Adventures within and beyond Union Lines*. Chicago: O. D. Case and Co., 1865.

Buntline, Ned. *The Battle of Hate*. New York: Frederic A. Brady, 1865.

Child, Lydia Maria. *A Romance of the Republic*. Boston: Ticknor and Fields, 1867.

Clemens, Jeremiah. *Tobias Wilson: A Tale of the Great Rebellion*. Philadelphia: Lippincott, 1865.

Cooke, John Esten. *Surry of the Eagle's Nest; or, The Memoirs of a Staff-Officer Serving in Virginia*. New York: Bunce and Huntington, 1866.

Cross, Jane T. H. *Duncan Adair; or, Captured in Escaping: A Story of One of Morgan's Men*. Macon, Ga.: Burke, Boykin, and Co., 1864.

DeForest, John William. *Miss Ravenel's Conversion from Secession to Loyalty*. New York: Harper and Brothers, 1867.

Edgeville, Edward. *Castine*. Raleigh: William B. Smith and Co., 1865.

Fairfax, L. (Connelly, Celia Logan). *The Elopement: A Tale of the Confederate States of America*. London: William Freeman, 1863.

Ford, Sallie Rochester. *Raids and Romance of Morgan and His Men*. Mobile ed., 1864. Reprint, New York: Charles B. Richardson, 1866.

Haco, Dion. *Sue Munday*. N.p.: Dawley's Camp and Fireside Library, No. 6, 1865.

Hancock, Sallie J. *Etna Vandemir: A Romance of Kentucky*. New York: Cutter, Tower and Co., 1863.

Harland, Marion (Mary Virginia Terhune). *Sunnybank*. New York: Sheldon and Co., 1866.

Haw, Mary Jane. *The Rivals: A Chickahominy Story*. Richmond: Ayres and Wade, 1864.

Herrington, W. D. *The Captain's Bride: A Tale of the War*. Raleigh: William B. Smith, 1864.

———. *The Deserter's Daughter*. Raleigh: Wm. B. Smith and Co., 1865.

Hiatt, James M. *The Test of Loyalty*. Indianapolis: Merrill and Smith, 1864.

Holmes, Mary Jane. *Hugh Worthington*. New York: Carleton, 1865.

Howe, Mary Ann. *The Rival Volunteers; or, The Black Plume Rifles*. New York: John Bradburn, 1864.

Johnstone, Herrick. *Sergeant Slasher; or, The Border Feud: A Romance of the Tennessee Mountains*. New York: American News Co., 1865.

Jones, Buehring. *The Sunny Land; or, Prison Prose and Poetry*. Baltimore: Innes, 1868.

Kelso, Isaac. *The Stars and Bars; or, The Reign of Terror in Missouri*. Boston: A. Williams and Co., 1864.

Kirke, Edmund (James Roberts Gilmore). *Among the Guerrillas*. New York: Carleton, 1866.

———. *Among the Pines; or, South in Secession Time*. New York: Charles T. Evans, 1862.

———. *My Southern Friends*. New York: Carleton, 1863.

———. *On the Border*. Boston: Lee and Shephard, 1867.

Longstreet, Abby Buchanan. *Remy St. Remy; or, The Boy in Blue*. New York: James O'Kane, 1866.

Mathews, Joanna H. *Guy Hamilton*. New York: American News Co., 1866.

McCabe, James Dabney, Jr. *The Aid-de-Camp: A Romance of the War*. Richmond: W. A. J. Smith, 1863.

———. *The Guerrillas: An Original Domestic Drama*. Richmond: West and Johnston, 1863.

A Member of the N. O. Washington Artillery. *Clarimonde: Tale of New Orleans Life, and of the Present War*. Richmond: M. A. Malsby, 1863.

Morford, Henry. *The Days of Shoddy: A Novel of the Great Rebellion in 1861*. Philadelphia: Peterson, 1863.

———. *Shoulder-Straps: A Novel of New York and the Army, 1862*. Philadelphia: Peterson, 1863.

Newbrough, J. B. *The Fall of Fort Sumter; or, Love and War in 1860–61*. New York: Brady, 1867.

Nichols, George Ward. *The Sanctuary: A Story of the Civil War*. New York: Harper, 1866.

Peck, Ellen. *Renshawe: A Novel*. New York: Carleton, 1867.

Remick, Martha. *Millicent Halford: A Tale of the Dark Days of Kentucky*. Boston: A. Williams and Co., 1865.

Russell, Charles Wells. *Roebuck: A Novel*. New York: H. Taylor and Co., 1868.

Sargent, Epes. *Peculiar: A Tale of the Great Transition*. New York: Carleton, 1864.

Smythe, J. M. *Mary Clifton: A Tale of the Late War*. Augusta, Ga.: 1865.

Spencer, Mrs. Bella Zilfa. *Tried and True; or, Love and Loyalty: A Story of the Great Rebellion*. Springfield, Mass.: W. J. Holland, 1866.

Strebor, Eiggam (Maggie Roberts). *Home Scenes during the Rebellion*. New York: Trow and Son, 1875.

Swain, Martha. *Mara: A Romance of the War*. Selma, Ala.: Mississippian Steam Book and Job Office, 1864.

Trowbridge, John T. *The Drummer Boy*. Boston: Tilton, 1863.

Warren, J. Thomas. *Old Peggy Boggs; or, Nick Whiffles in the War*. New York: Frank Starr, 1865.

Wood, Benjamin. *Fort Lafayette; or, Love and Secession*. New York: Carleton, 1862.

PUBLISHED GOVERNMENT RECORDS

Bergner, George, ed. *The Legislative Record: Containing the Debates and Proceedings of the Pennsylvania Legislature for the Session of 1862*. City of Harrisburg: Printed at the 'Telegraph' Book and Job Office, 1862.

Proceedings of the Confederate Congress. House of Representatives. *Southern Historical Society Papers*. Vol. 47. Wilmington, N.C.: Broadfoot Publishing Co., 1991.

Reese, George H., ed. *Proceedings of the Virginia State Convention of 1861*. Vols. 2, 4. Richmond: Virginia State Library, 1965.

Regulations for the Army of the Confederate States, 1863. Revised and Enlarged with a New and Copious Index. Second and Only Correct Edition. Richmond, Virginia: J. W. Randolph, 1863.

Revised United States Army Regulations of 1861. Washington, D.C.: GPO, 1863.

U.S. Census. Population and Slave Schedules: Delaware, Kentucky, Maryland, Missouri, Tennessee, Virginia, Washington, D.C., 1860, 1870.

U.S. War Department. *The War of the Rebellion: A Compilation of the Official Records of the Union and Confederate Armies*. 128 vols. Washington, D.C.: GPO, 1880–1901.

We the People: The Constitution of the United States of America. Washington, D.C.: National Archives and Records Administration, n.d.

OTHER PUBLISHED PRIMARY SOURCES

Anderson, George M., ed. "The Civil War Courtship of Richard Mortimer Williams and Rose Anderson of Rockville." *Maryland Historical Magazine* 80 (Summer 1985): 119–38.

Anonymous. *The American Mail-Bag; or Tales of the War*. London: Ward and Lock, 1863.

Bailey, Virginia Griffin, ed. "Letters of Melvin Dwinnell: Yankee Rebel." *Georgia Historical Quarterly* 47 (1963): 193–203.

Baker, L. C. *History of the United States Secret Service*. Philadelphia: L. C. Baker, 1867.

Basler, Roy P., ed. *Walt Whitman's Memoranda during the War [and] Death of Abraham Lincoln*. Bloomington: Indiana University Press, 1962.

Bean, W. G., ed. "A House Divided: The Civil War Letters of a Virginia Family." *Virginia Magazine of History and Biography* 59 (October 1951): 397–422.

Bennett, Pamela J., ed. "Curtis R. Burke's Civil War Journal," *Indiana Magazine of History* 65 (1969): 283–329.

Berlin, Ira, Barbara J. Fields, Thavolia Glymph, Joseph P. Reidy, and Leslie S. Rowland, eds. *The Destruction of Slavery*. Ser. 1, vol. 1, of *Freedom: A Documentary History of Emancipation, 1861–1867*. Cambridge: Cambridge University Press, 1985.

Berlin, Ira, Steven F. Miller, Joseph P. Reidy, and Leslie S. Rowland, eds. *The Wartime Genesis of Free Labor: The Upper South*. Ser. 1, vol. 2, of *Freedom: A Documentary History of Emancipation, 1861–1867*. Cambridge: Cambridge University Press, 1993.

Berlin, Ira, Joseph P. Reidy, and Leslie S. Rowland, eds. *The Black Military Experience*. Ser. 2 of *Freedom: A Documentary History of Emancipation, 1861–1867*. Cambridge: Cambridge University Press, 1982.

Berlin, Ira, and Leslie S. Rowland, eds. *Families and Freedom: A Documentary History of African-American Kinship in the Civil War Era*. New York: The New Press, 1997.

Berlin, Ira, Barbara J. Fields, Steven F. Miller, Joseph P. Reidy, and Leslie S. Rowland, eds. *Free at Last: A Documentary History of Slavery, Freedom, and the Civil War*. New York: Free Press, 1992.

Berlin, Ira, Barbara J. Fields, Steven F. Miller, Joseph P. Reidy, and Leslie S. Rowland. *Slaves No More: Three Essays on Emancipation and the Civil War*. Cambridge: Cambridge University Press, 1992.

Berry, Mary Clay. *Voices from the Century Before: The Odyssey of a Nineteenth-Century Kentucky Family*. New York: Arcade Publishing, 1997.

Bohemian. *War Songs of the South*. Richmond: West and Johnston, 1862.

Burnett, Alfred. *Incidents of the War: Humorous, Pathetic, and Descriptive*. Cincinnati: Rickey and Carroll, 1863.

Butterfield, L. H., ed. *Diary and Autobiography of John Adams*. Vol. 4. Cambridge, Mass.: Belknap Press, 1961.

Chadwick, Bruce, ed. *Brother against Brother: The Lost Civil War Diary of Lt. Edmund Halsey*. Secaucus, N.J.: Birch Lane Press, 1997.

Childers, William C., ed. "A Virginian's Dilemma: The Civil War Diary of Isaac Noyes Smith." *West Virginia History* 27 (January 1966): 173–200.

Creek, Christian Ashby, ed. "Memoirs of Mrs. E. B. Patterson: A Perspective on Danville during the Civil War." *Register of the Kentucky Historical Society* (Autumn 1994): 347–99.

Crist, Lynda Lasswell, Mary Seaton Dix, and Kenneth H. Williams. *The Papers of Jefferson Davis*. Vol. 9. Baton Rouge: Louisiana State University Press, 1997.

Cullum, George W. *Biographical Register of the Officers and Graduates of the U.S. Military Academy at West Point, N.Y.* Vol. 2. New York: D. Van Nostrand, 1868.

Darrin, Charles V., ed. "Your Truly Attached Friend, Mary Lincoln." *Journal of the Illinois State Historical Society* 44 (Spring 1951): 7–25.

Davis, Varina. *Jefferson Davis: Ex-President of the Confederate States of America*. 2 vols. New York: Belford Co., 1890.

Donald, David Herbert. *Lincoln at Home: Two Glimpses of Abraham Lincoln's Family Life*. New York: Simon and Schuster, 1999.

Duncan, Russell, and David J. Klooster, eds. *Phantoms of a Blood-Stained Period: The Complete Civil War Writings of Ambrose Bierce*. Amherst: University of Massachusetts Press, 2002.

Durham, Walter T. "Civil War Letters to Wynnewood." *Tennessee Historical Quarterly* 34 (Spring 1975): 32–47.

Dyer, Gustavus W., and John Trotwood Moore, eds. *The Tennessee Civil War Veterans Questionnaires*. Easley, S.C.: Southern Historical Press, 1985.

Garrison, Webb. *Unusual Persons of the Civil War*. Fredericksburg, Va.: Sergeant Kirkland's Museum, 1996.

Goodrich, James W., ed. "The Civil War Letters of Bethiah Pyatt McKown." *Missouri Historical Review* 67 (January–April 1973): 227–52, 351–70.

Grant, U. S. *Personal Memoirs of U. S. Grant*. Vol. 1. New York: Charles L. Webster and Co., 1885.

Greene, Charles S. *Thrilling Stories of the Great Rebellion: Comprising Heroic Adventures and Hairbreadth Escapes of Soldiers, Scouts, Spies, and Refugees*. Philadelphia: John E. Potter, 1866.

Grimsley, Elizabeth Todd. "Six Months in the White House." *Journal of the Illinois State Historical Society* 19 (April–July 1926): 43–73.

Helm, Emilie. "Todd Family." *Kittochtinny Magazine* (January 1905): 69–96.

Hoobler, James A., ed. "The Civil War Diary of Louisa Brown Pearl." *Tennessee Historical Quarterly* 38 (Fall 1979): 308–21.

Johnson, Richard W. *Memoir of Major-General George H. Thomas*. Philadelphia: J. B. Lippincott and Co., 1881.

Johnston, Jr., Terry A. *"Him on the One Side and Me on the Other": The Civil War Letters of Alexander Campbell, 79th New York Infantry Regiment and James Campbell, 1st South Carolina Battalion*. Columbia: University of South Carolina Press, 1999.

Jones, J. B. *A Rebel War Clerk's Diary*. Vols. 1, 2. New York: Old Hickory Bookshop, 1935.

Kirkland, Frazar. *The Pictorial Book of Anecdotes of the Rebellion; or, the Funny and Pathetic Side of the War*. Chicago: Henry S. Stebbins, 1887.

Marshall, Edward Chauncey. *Are the West Point Graduates Loyal?* New York: D. Van Nostrand, 1862.

McKee, James W., Jr. ed. "Reflections of an East Tennessee Unionist." *Tennessee Historical Quarterly* 33 (Winter 1974): 433–35.

A Member of the G.A.R. *The Picket Line and Camp Fire Stories: A Collection of War Anecdotes Both Grave and Gay*. New York: Hurst and Co., Publishers, n.d.

Moore, Frank. *The Civil War in Song and Story, 1860–1865*. New York: P. F. Collier, 1889.

Nicolay, John G., and John Hay, eds. *Complete Works of Abraham Lincoln*. Vol. 10. New York: Lamb Publishing Co., 1905.

Rawick, George P., ed. *The American Slave: A Composite Autobiography*. Vol. 16, Kansas, Kentucky, Maryland, Ohio, Virginia, and Tennessee Narratives. Westport, Conn.: Greenwood Publishing Co., 1972.

Reese, Lizette Woodworth. *A Victorian Village: Reminiscences of Other Days*. Farrar and Rinehart, 1929.

Reynolds, Arlene, ed. *The Civil War Memories of Elizabeth Bacon Custer: Reconstructed from Her Diaries and Notes*. Austin: University of Texas Press, 1994.

Rosenbloom, Joseph R., ed. "Rebecca Gratz: Example of Conflicting Sectional Loyalties during the Civil War." *Filson Club Historical Quarterly* 35 (January 1961): 5–10.

Schaff, Morris. *The Spirit of Old West Point, 1858–1862*. Boston: Houghton Mifflin, 1907.

Smith, John David, and William Cooper Jr., eds. *A Union Woman in Civil War Kentucky: The Diary of Frances Peter*. Lexington: University Press of Kentucky, 2000.

Tompkins, Ellen Wilkins, ed. "The Colonel's Lady: Some Letters of Ellen Wilkins Tompkins, July–December 1861." *Virginia Magazine of History and Biography* 69 (October 1961): 387–89.

Twain, Mark, and Charles Dudley Warner.*Writings of Mark Twain*. Vol. 19. New York: Harper and Brothers, 1899–1910.

Vickers, George M. *Under Both Flags: A Panorama of the Great Civil War as Represented in Story, Anecdote, Adventure and the Romance of Reality*. Richmond: B. F. Johnson Publishing, 1896.

Virginia Girl. *A Southern Song: Address to Her Maryland Lover by a Virginian Girl*. Richmond: N.p., 1861.

WEBSITE SOURCES

Ayers, Edward L., et al. "The Valley of the Shadow: Two Communities in the American Civil War." Virginia Center for Digital History, University of Virginia, <http://valley.vcdh.virginia.edu>.

"Rose O'Neal Greenhow Papers: An On-Line Archival Collection." Rare Book, Manuscript, and Special Collections Library, Duke University, <http://scriptorium.lib.duke.edu/gree>.

"Historic American Sheet Music." Rare Book, Manuscript, and Special Collections Library, Duke University, <http://scriptorium.lib.duke.edu/sheetmusic>.

"Stonewall Jackson Papers." Virginia Military Institute Archives, MS Acc. # 00102, <http://www.vmi.edu/archives/Jackson/tjjpaprs.html>.

"The Abraham Lincoln Papers at the Library of Congress." American Memory Collection, Library of Congress, <http://www.memory.loc.gov>.

Plake, Kate. "The Southern Husband Outwitted by His Union Wife." 1867. Documenting the American South, University of North Carolina at Chapel Hill, <http://metalab.unc.edu/docsouth/plake>.

Railton, Stephen. "Uncle Tom's Cabin and American Culture: A Multi-Media Archive." University of Virginia, <http://www.iath.virginia.edu/utc>.

Secondary Sources

BOOKS AND ARTICLES

Aaron, Daniel. *The Unwritten War: American Writers and the Civil War*. New York: Knopf, 1973.

Abbott, Dorothea E. "The Land of Maria Syphax and the Abbey Mausoleum," *Arlington Historical Magazine* 7 (October 1984): 42–44.

Adams, Oscar Fay. *A Dictionary of American Authors*. 4th ed. Boston: Houghton Mifflin, 1901.

Allan, Graham A. *A Sociology of Friendship and Kinship*. London: George Allen and Unwin, 1979.

Allgor, Catherine. *Parlor Politics: In Which the Ladies of Washington Help Build a City and a Government.* Charlottesville: University Press of Virginia, 2000.

Anderson, Benedict. *Imagined Communities: Reflections on the Origins and Spread of Nationalism.* Rev. ed. London: Verso, 1991.

Anderson, Galusha. *The Story of a Border City during the Civil War.* Boston: Little, Brown, 1908.

Appleby, Joyce. "Reconciliation and the Northern Novelist, 1865–1880." *Civil War History* 10 (June 1964): 117–29.

Ash, Stephen V. *Middle Tennessee Society Transformed, 1860–1870: War and Peace in the Upper South.* Baton Rouge: Louisiana State University Press, 1988.

———. *When the Yankees Came: Conflict and Chaos in the Occupied South, 1861–1865.* Chapel Hill: University of North Carolina Press, 1995.

Atkins, Annette. *We Grew Up Together: Brothers and Sisters in Nineteenth-Century America.* Urbana: University of Illinois Press, 2001.

Attie, Jeanie. *Patriotic Toil: Northern Women and the Civil War.* Ithaca, N.Y.: Cornell University Press, 1998.

Ayers, Edward L. *In the Presence of Mine Enemies: War in the Heart of America, 1859–1863.* New York: Norton, 2003.

———. "Worrying about the Civil War." In *Moral Problems in American Life: New Perspectives on Cultural History*, edited by Karen Halttunen and Lewis Perry, 144–65. Ithaca, N.Y.: Cornell University Press, 1998.

Baker, Jean. *Affairs of Party: The Political Culture of Northern Democrats in the Mid-Nineteenth Century.* Ithaca, N.Y.: Cornell University Press, 1983.

———. *Mary Todd Lincoln: A Biography.* New York: Norton, 1987.

Bank, Stephen P., and Michael D. Kahn. *The Sibling Bond.* New York: Basic Books, 1997.

Bardaglio, Peter W. "On the Border: White Children and the Politics of War in Maryland." In *The War Was You and Me: Civilians in the American Civil War*, edited by Joan E. Cashin, 313–31. Princeton, N.J.: Princeton University Press, 2002.

———. *Reconstructing the Household: Families, Sex, and the Law in the Nineteenth-Century South.* Chapel Hill: University of North Carolina Press, 1995.

Barnes, Elizabeth. *States of Sympathy: Seduction and Democracy in the American Novel.* New York: Columbia University Press, 1997.

Barney, William. *The Secessionist Impulse: Alabama and Mississippi in 1860.* Princeton, N.J.: Princeton University Press, 1974.

———. "Towards the Civil War: The Dynamics of Change in a Black Belt County." In *Class, Conflict, and Consensus: Antebellum Community Studies*, edited by Orville Vernon Burton and Robert C. McMath Jr., 146–72. Westport, Conn.: Greenwood Press, 1982.

Basch, Norma. *Framing American Divorce: From the Revolutionary Generation to the Victorians.* Berkeley: University of California Press, 1999.

———. "Marriage, Morals, and Politics in the Election of 1828." *Journal of American History* 80 (December 1993): 890–918.

Baym, Nina. *American Women Writers and the Work of History, 1790–1860.* New Brunswick, N.J.: Rutgers University Press, 1995.

———. *Women's Fiction: A Guide to Novels by and about Women in America.* Ithaca, N.Y.: Cornell University Press, 1978.

Bercaw, Nancy. *Gendered Freedoms: Race, Rights, and the Politics of Household in the Delta, 1861–1875.* Gainesville: University Press of Florida, 2003.

Berry, Stephen W., II. *All That Makes a Man: Love and Ambition in the Civil War South.* New York: Oxford University Press, 2003.

Blair, William. *Virginia's Private War: Feeding Body and Soul in the Confederacy, 1861–1865.* New York: Oxford University Press, 1998.

Blassingame, John. *The Slave Community: Plantation Life in the Antebellum South.* New York: Oxford University Press, 1972.

———, ed. *The Frederick Douglass Papers.* Series 1, *Speeches, Debates, and Interviews.* Vol. 3, *1855–1863.* New Haven: Yale University Press, 1985.

Bleser, Carol, ed. *In Joy and in Sorrow: Women, Family, and Marriage in the Victorian South.* New York: Oxford University Press, 1991.

Bleser, Carol K., and Lesley J. Gordon, eds. *Intimate Strategies of the Civil War: Military Commanders and Their Wives.* New York: Oxford University Press, 2001.

Blight, David. *Frederick Douglass' Civil War: Keeping Faith in Jubilee.* Baton Rouge: Louisiana State University Press, 1989.

———. *Race and Reunion: The Civil War in American Memory.* Cambridge: Belknap Press of Harvard University Press, 2001.

Branch, E. Douglas. *The Sentimental Years, 1836–1860.* New York: Hill and Wang, 1934.

Buck, Paul. *The Road to Reunion.* Boston: Little, Brown, 1937.

Burke, W. J., and Will D. Howe. *American Authors and Books: 1640 to the Present Day.* New York: Crown Publishers, Inc., 1972.

Burton, Orville Vernon. *In My Father's House Are Many Mansions: Family and Community in Edgefield, South Carolina.* Chapel Hill: University of North Carolina Press, 1985.

Buza, Melinda A. "'Pledges of Our Love': Friendship, Love, and Marriage among the Virginia Gentry." In *The Edge of the South: Life in Nineteenth-Century Virginia,* edited by Edward L. Ayers and John C. Willis, 9–36. Charlottesville: University Press of Virginia, 1991.

Campbell, Jacqueline Glass. *When Sherman Marched North from the Sea: Resistance on the Confederate Homefront.* Chapel Hill: University of North Carolina Press, 2003.

Carnes, Mark C., and Clyde Griffen. *Meanings for Manhood: Constructions of Masculinity in Victorian America.* Chicago: University of Chicago Press, 1990.

Carroll, Rosemary F. "A Plantation Teacher's Perceptions of the Impending Crisis." *Southern Studies: An Interdisciplinary Journal of the South* 18 (Fall 1979): 339–50.

Carson, William Glasgow Bruce. "Anne Ewing Lane." *Bulletin of the Missouri Historical Society* 21 (January 1965): 87–99.

——. "Secesh." *Bulletin of the Missouri Historical Society* 23 (January 1967): 119–46.
Cashin, Joan. "According to His Wish and Desire: Female Kin and Female Slaves in Planter Wills." In *Women of the American South: A Multicultural Reader*, edited by Christie Anne Farnham, 100–104. New York: New York University Press, 1997.
——. *A Family Venture: Men and Women on the Southern Frontier*. New York: Oxford University Press, 1991.
——. "The Structure of Antebellum Planter Families: 'The Ties That Bound Us Was Strong.'" *Journal of Southern History* 56 (February 1990): 55–70.
——, ed. *The War Was You and Me: Civilians in the American Civil War*. Princeton, N.J.: Princeton University Press, 2002.
Castel, Albert. "Arnold vs. Arnold: The Strange and Hitherto Untold Story of the Divorce of Stonewall Jackson's Sister." *Blue and Gray Magazine* 12 (October 1994): 28–36.
Castigliola, Frank. "The Nuclear Family: Tropes of Gender and Pathology in the Western Alliance." *Diplomatic History* 21 (Spring 1997): 163–83.
Censer, Jane Turner. *North Carolina Planters and Their Children, 1800–1860*. Baton Rouge: Louisiana State University Press, 1984.
——. "Reimagining the North-South Reunion: Southern Women Novelists and the Intersectional Romance, 1876–1900." *Southern Cultures* 5 (Summer 1999): 64–91.
Chase, Karen, and Michael Levenson. *The Spectacle of Intimacy: A Public Life for the Victorian Family*. Princeton, N.J.: Princeton University Press, 2000.
Chatterjee, Partha. *The Nation and Its Fragments: Colonial and Post Colonial Histories*. Princeton, N.J.: Princeton University Press, 1993.
Cleaves, Freeman. *Rock of Chickamauga: The Life of General George H. Thomas*. Norman: University of Oklahoma Press, 1948.
Clinton, Catherine. *Fannie Kemble's Civil Wars: The Story of America's Most Unlikely Abolitionist*. New York: Simon and Schuster, 2000.
——. *The Plantation Mistress: Woman's World in the Old South*. New York: Pantheon Books, 1982.
——. *Tara Revisited: Women, War, and the Plantation Legend*. New York: Abbeville Press, 1995.
——, ed. *Southern Families at War: Loyalty and Conflict in the Civil War South*. New York: Oxford University Press, 2000.
Clinton, Catherine, and Nina Silber, eds. *Divided Houses: Gender and the Civil War*. New York: Oxford University Press, Paperback ed., 1992.
Cogan, Jacob Katz. "The Reynolds Affair and the Politics of Character." *Journal of the Early Republic* 16 (Fall 1996): 389–417.
Congleton, Betty Carolyn. "George D. Prentice: Nineteenth-Century Southern Editor." *Register of the Kentucky Historical Society* 65 (April 1967): 94–119.
Cooke, Miriam, and Angela Woollacott, eds. *Gendering War Talk*. Princeton, N.J.: Princeton University Press, 1993.
Coontz, Stephanie. *The Social Origins of Private Life: A History of American Families, 1600–1900*. London: Verso, 1988.

Cooper, William J., Jr. *Jefferson Davis: American*. New York: Knopf, 2000.

Cott, Nancy. *The Bonds of Womanhood: 'Woman's Sphere' in New England, 1780–1835*. New Haven: Yale University Press, 1977.

———. "Passionlessness: An Interpretation of Victorian Sexual Ideology, 1790–1850." In *A Heritage of Her Own: Toward a New Social History of American Women*, edited by Nancy Cott and Elizabeth Pleck, 162–81. New York: Simon and Schuster, 1979.

———. *Public Vows: A History of Marriage and the Nation*. Cambridge: Harvard University Press, 2000.

Coulling, Mary P. *The Lee Girls*. Winston-Salem, N.C.: John F. Blair, 1987.

Coulter, E. Merton. *The Civil War and Readjustment in Kentucky*. Chapel Hill: University of North Carolina Press, 1926.

———. *The Confederate States of America, 1861–1865*. Baton Rouge: Louisiana State University Press, 1950.

Crocker, Helen B. "A War Divides Green River Country." *Register of the Kentucky Historical Society* 70 (October 1972): 295–311.

Crofts, Daniel. *Reluctant Confederates: Upper South Unionists in the Secession Crisis*. Chapel Hill: University of North Carolina Press, 1989.

Cushman, Stephen. *Bloody Promenade: Reflections on a Civil War Battle*. Charlottesville: University of Virginia Press, 1999.

Davidson, Cathy. *Revolution and the Word: The Rise of the Novel in America*. New York: Oxford University Press, 1986.

Davis, William C. *Jefferson Davis: The Man and His Hour*. New York: HarperCollins, 1991.

———. *Look Away! A History of the Confederate States of America*. New York: Free Press, 2002.

Degler, Carl. *At Odds: Women and the Family in America from the Revolution to the Present*. New York: Oxford University Press, 1980.

Dietz, August. *The Postal Service of the Confederate States of America*. Richmond: Dietz Printing Co., 1929.

Diffley, Kathleen. *Where My Heart Is Turning Ever: Civil War Stories and Constitutional Reform, 1861–1876*. Athens: University of Georgia Press, 1992.

Donald, David Herbert. *Lincoln*. New York: Simon and Schuster, 1995.

Douglas, Ann. *The Feminization of American Culture*. New York: Doubleday, 1988.

Durham, Walter T. *Nashville, the Occupied City: The First Seventeen Months—February 16, 1862, to June 30, 1863*. Nashville: Tennessee Historical Society, 1985.

Edelman, Murray. *Politics as Symbolic Action: Mass Arousal and Quiescence*. Chicago: Markaham Publishing Co., 1971.

Edwards, Laura F. *Gendered Strife and Confusion: The Political Culture of Reconstruction*. Urbana: University of Illinois Press, 1997.

Eley, Geoff. "Nations, Publics, and Political Cultures: Placing Habermas in the Nineteenth Century." In *Culture/Power/History: A Reader in Contemporary Social Theory*, edited by Nicholas B. Dirks, Geoff Eley, and Sherry B. Ortner, 297–335. Princeton: Princeton University Press, 1994.

Elkins, Stanley. *Slavery: A Problem in American Institutional and Intellectual Life.*
3rd ed. Chicago: University of Chicago Press, 1976.

Escott, Paul. *After Secession: Jefferson Davis and the Failure of Confederate National-ism.* Baton Rouge: Louisiana State University Press, 1978.

Fahs, Alice. "The Feminized Civil War: Gender, Northern Popular Literature, and
the Memory of the War, 1861–1900." *Journal of American History* 85 (March
1999): 1461–94.

———. *The Imagined Civil War: Popular Literature of the North and South,
1861–1865.* Chapel Hill: University of North Carolina Press, 2001.

Farwell, Byron. *Stonewall: A Biography of General Thomas J. Jackson.* New York:
Norton, 1992.

Faust, Drew Gilpin. "The Civil War Soldier and the Art of Dying." *Journal of South-ern History* 67 (February 2001): 3–38.

———. *Mothers of Invention: Women of the Slaveholding South in the American Civil
War.* Chapel Hill: University of North Carolina Press, 1996.

Fellman, Michael. *Inside War: The Guerrilla Conflict in Missouri during the Ameri-can Civil War.* New York: Oxford University Press, 1989.

———. *The Making of Robert E. Lee.* New York: Random House, 2000.

Fields, Barbara Jeanne. *Slavery and Freedom on the Middle Ground: Maryland during
the Nineteenth Century.* New Haven: Yale University Press, 1985.

Fisher, Noel. *War at Every Door: Partisan Politics and Guerrilla Violence in East
Tennessee, 1860–1869.* Chapel Hill: University of North Carolina Press, 1997.

Fliegelman, Jay. *Prodigals and Pilgrims: The American Revolution against Patriar-chal Authority, 1750–1800.* Cambridge: Cambridge University Press, 1982.

Foner, Eric. *Reconstruction: America's Unfinished Revolution, 1863–1877.* New York:
Harper and Row, 1988.

Forgie, George B. *Patricide in the House Divided: A Psychological Interpretation of
Lincoln and His Age.* New York: Norton, 1979.

Fowler, Dorothy Ganfield. *Unmailable: Congress and the Post Office.* Athens: Univer-sity of Georgia Press, 1977.

Frank, Stephen. *Life with Father: Parenthood and Masculinity in the Nineteenth-Century American North.* Baltimore: Johns Hopkins University Press, 1998.

Fredrickson, George. *The Inner Civil War: Northern Intellectuals and the Crisis of
the Union.* New York: Harper and Row, 1965.

Freehling, William W. *The South vs. the South: How Anti-Confederate Southerners
Shaped the Course of the War.* New York: Oxford University Press, 2001.

Freeman, Joanne. "Slander, Poison, Whispers, and Fame: Jefferson's 'Anas' and Polit-ical Gossip in the Early Republic." *Journal of the Early Republic* 15 (1995): 25–57.

Gallagher, Gary. *The Confederate War.* Cambridge: Harvard University Press, 1997.

———. "Homefront and Battlefield: Some Recent Literature Relating to Virginia and
the Confederacy." *Virginia Magazine of History and Biography* 98 (April 1990):
135–68.

Gardner, Sarah E. "'A Sweet Solace to My Lonely Heart': 'Stonewall' and Mary Anna

Jackson and the Civil War." In *Intimate Strategies of the Civil War*, edited by Carol K. Bleser and Lesley J. Gordon, 49–68. New York: Oxford University Press, 2001.

Gatell, Frank Otto. "The Slaveholder and the Abolitionist: Binding Up a Family's Wounds." *Journal of Southern History* 27 (August 1961): 368–91.

Geertz, Clifford. "Ideology as a Cultural System." *The Interpretation of Cultures*. New York: Basic Books, 1973.

Genovese, Eugene. "'Our Family, White and Black': Family and Household in the Southern Slaveholders' World View." In *In Joy and in Sorrow: Women, Family, and Marriage in the Victorian South*, edited by Carol Bleser, 69–87. New York: Oxford University Press, 1991.

———. *Roll, Jordan, Roll: The World the Slaves Made*. New York: Vintage Books, 1976.

Gienapp, William E. "The Political System and the Coming of the Civil War." In *Why the Civil War Came*, edited by Gabor Borritt, 92–93. New York: Oxford University Press, 1996.

Gillman, Susan. "The Mulatto: Tragic or Triumphant? The Nineteenth-Century Race Melodrama." In *The Culture of Sentiment: Race, Gender, and Sentimentality in Nineteenth-Century America*, edited by Shirley Samuels, 221–43. New York: Oxford University Press, 1992.

Glatthaar, Joseph T. "Duty, Country, Race, and Party: The Evans Family of Ohio." In *The War Was You and Me: Civilians in the American Civil War*, edited by Joan Cashin, 332–57. Princeton, N.J.: Princeton University Press, 2002.

———. *The March to the Sea and Beyond: Sherman's Troops in the Savannah and Carolinas Campaigns*. New York: New York University Press, 1985.

Glover, Lorri. *All Our Relations: Blood Ties and Emotional Bonds among the Early South Carolina Gentry*. Baltimore: Johns Hopkins University Press, 2000.

Greenberg, Kenneth. *Honor and Slavery: Lies, Duels, Noses, Masks, Dressing as a Woman, Gifts, Strangers, Humanitarianism, Death, Slave Rebellions, the Pro-slavery Argument, Baseball, Hunting, Gambling in the Old South*. Princeton, N.J.: Princeton University Press, 1996.

Grimsley, Mark. *The Hard Hand of War: Union Military Policy toward Southern Civilians, 1861–1865*. Cambridge: Cambridge University Press, 1995.

Griswold, Robert E. *Fatherhood in America: A History*. New York: Basic Books, 1993.

Groce, Todd. *Mountain Rebels: East Tennessee Confederates and the Civil War, 1860–1870*. Knoxville: University of Tennessee Press, 1999.

Grossberg, Michael. *Governing the Hearth: Law and the Family in Nineteenth-Century America*. Chapel Hill: University of North Carolina Press, 1985.

Gutman, Herbert G. *The Black Family in Slavery and Freedom, 1750–1925*. New York: Vintage Books, 1976.

Habermas, Jürgen. *The Structural Transformation of the Public Sphere: An Inquiry into a Category of Bourgeois Society*. Translated by Thomas Burger. Cambridge: MIT Press, 1989.

Hahn, Steven. *A Nation under Our Feet: Black Political Struggles in the Rural South from Slavery to the Great Migration*. Cambridge: Belknap Press of Harvard University Press, 2003.

Halttunen, Karen. *Confidence Men and Painted Women: A Study of Middle-Class Culture in America*. New Haven: Yale University Press, 1982.

Hareven, Tamara K. "The History of the Family and the Complexity of Social Change," *American Historical Review* 96 (February 1991): 95–124.

Harper, Robert S. *Lincoln and the Press*. New York: McGraw-Hill, 1951.

Harrison, Lowell H. *The Civil War in Kentucky*. Lexington: University Press of Kentucky, 1975.

———. "The Civil War in Kentucky: Some Persistent Questions." *Register of the Kentucky Historical Society* 76 (January 1978): 1–5.

Hart, John Seely. *A Manual of American Literature*. New York: Johnson Reprint Corp., 1969.

Hearn, Chester G. *Ellet's Brigade: The Strangest Outfit of All*. Baton Rouge: Louisiana State University Press, 2000.

Helm, Katherine. *The True Story of Mary, Wife of Lincoln*. New York: Harper, 1928.

Hermann, Janet Sharp. *The Pursuit of a Dream*. New York: Oxford University Press, 1981.

Hesseltine, William B. *Civil War Prisons: A Study in War Psychology*. Columbus: Ohio State University Press, 1930.

———. ed. *Civil War Prisons*. Kent State University Press, 1962.

Hobsbawm, Eric, and Terence Ranger, eds. *The Invention of Tradition*. Cambridge: Cambridge University Press, 1992.

Hodes, Martha. "Wartime Dialogues on Illicit Sex: White Women and Black Men." In *Divided Houses: Gender and the Civil War*, edited by Catherine Clinton and Nina Silber, 230–42. New York: Oxford University Press, 1992.

———. *White Women, Black Men: Illicit Sex in the Nineteenth-Century South*. New Haven: Yale University Press, 1997.

Holt, Michael F. *The Political Crisis of the 1850s*. New York: Norton, 1978.

Horwitz, Tony. *Confederates in the Attic: Dispatches from the Unfinished Civil War*. New York: Pantheon, 1998.

Howard, Victor B. *Black Liberation in Kentucky: Emancipation and Freedom, 1862–1864*. Lexington: University Press of Kentucky, 1983.

Hubbell, John T., and James W. Geary. *Biographical Dictionary of the Union: Northern Leaders of the Civil War*. Westport, Conn.: Greenwood Press, 1995.

Hunt, Judith Lee. "'High with Courage and Hope': The Middleton Family's Civil War." In *Southern Families at War: Loyalty and Conflict in the Civil War South*, edited by Catherine Clinton, 101–18. New York: Oxford University Press, 2000.

Hunt, Lynn. *The Family Romance of the French Revolution*. Berkeley: University of California Press, 1992.

Inscoe, John C., and Gordon B. McKinney. *The Heart of Confederate Appalachia: Western North Carolina in the Civil War*. Chapel Hill: University of North Carolina Press, 2000.

———. "Highland Houses Divided: Family Deceptions, Diversions, and Divisions in Southern Appalachia's Inner Civil War." In *Enemies of the Country: New Perspectives on Unionists in the Civil War South*, edited by John C. Inscoe and Robert C. Kenzer, 54–72. Athens: University of Georgia Press, 2001.

Inscoe, John C., and Robert C. Kenzer, eds. *Enemies of the Country: New Perspectives on Unionists in the Civil War South*. Athens: University of Georgia Press, 2001.

Jabour, Anya. "Male Friendship and Masculinity in the Early National South: William Wirt and His Friends." *Journal of the Early Republic* 20 (Spring 2000): 83–111.

———. *Marriage in the Early Republic: Elizabeth and William Wirt and the Companionate Ideal*. Baltimore: Johns Hopkins University Press, 1998.

Jacobs, Joanna. "Eugenia Levy Phillips vs. the United States of America." *Alabama Heritage* 50 (Fall 1998): 22–29.

Jeffords, Susan. "Commentary: Culture and National Identity in U.S. Foreign Policy." *Diplomatic History* 18 (Winter 1994): 91–96.

Jensen, J. Vernon. "British Voices on the Eve of the American Revolution: Trapped by the Family Metaphor." *Quarterly Journal of Speech* 63 (February 1977): 43–50.

Jimerson, Randall C. *The Private Civil War: Popular Thought during the Sectional Conflict*. Baton Rouge: Louisiana State University Press, 1988.

Johnson, Michael. "Looking for Lost Kin: Efforts to Reunite Freed Families after Emancipation." In *Southern Families at War: Loyalty and Conflict in the Civil War South*, edited by Catherine Clinton, 15–34. New York: Oxford University Press, 2000.

Jones, Anne Goodwyn. *Tomorrow Is Another Day: The Woman Writer in the South, 1859–1936*. Baton Rouge: Louisiana State University Press, 1981.

Jordan, Cynthia. "'Old Worlds' in 'New Circumstances': Language and Leadership in Post-Revolutionary America." *American Quarterly* 40 (December 1988): 491–513.

Kane, Harnett T. *Spies for the Blue and Gray*. New York: Hanover House, 1954.

Kerber, Linda. "Separate Spheres, Female Worlds, Woman's Place: The Rhetoric of Women's History." *Journal of American History* 75 (June 1988): 9–39.

———. *Women of the Republic: Intellect and Ideology in Revolutionary America*. New York: Norton, 1980.

Kett, Joseph F. *Rites of Passage: Adolescence in America, 1790-Present*. New York: Basic Books, 1977.

Kierner, Cynthia A. *Beyond the Household: Women's Place in the Early South*. Ithaca, N.Y.: Cornell University Press, 1998.

Kilbride, Daniel. "Class, Region, and Memory in a South Carolina–Philadelphia Marriage." *Journal of Family History* 28 (October 2003): 540–60.

Kinchen, Oscar A. *Women Who Spied for the Blue and Gray*. Philadelphia: Dorrance and Co., 1972.

Kinney, James. *Amalgamation! Race, Sex, and Rhetoric in the Nineteenth-Century American Novel*. Westport, Conn.: Greenwood Press, 1985.

Kirshner, Ralph. *The Class of 1861: Custer, Ames, and Their Classmates after West Point*. Carbondale: Southern Illinois University Press, 1999.

Kirwan, Albert D. *John J. Crittenden: The Struggle for the Union*. Lexington: University of Kentucky Press, 1962.

Klotter, James C. *The Breckinridges of Kentucky, 1760–1981*. Lexington: University Press of Kentucky, 1986.

Koerting, Gayla. "For Law and Order: Joseph Holt, the Civil War, and the Judge Advocate General's Department," *Register of the Kentucky Historical Society* 97 (Winter 1999): 1–25.

Kunstling, Frances Williams. "The Cooper Family Papers — A Bibliographic Note," *Tennessee Historical Quarterly* 28 (Summer 1969): 197–205.

Laas, Virginia Jeans. " 'A Good Wife, the Best Friend in the World': The Marriage of Elizabeth Blair and S. Phillips Lee." In *Intimate Strategies of the Civil War: Military Commanders and Their Wives*, edited by Carol K. Bleser and Lesley J. Gordon, 225–42. New York: Oxford University Press, 2001.

Lakoff, George, and Mark Johnson. *Metaphors We Live By*. Chicago: University of Chicago Press, 1980.

Landes, Joan B. *Women and the Public Sphere in the Age of the French Revolution*. Ithaca, N.Y.: Cornell University Press, 1988.

Lawson, Melinda. *Patriot Fires: Forging a New American Nationalism in the Civil War North*. Lawrence: University Press of Kansas, 2002.

Leonard, Elizabeth D. *All the Daring of the Soldier: Women of the Civil War Armies*. New York: Norton, 1999.

———. *Lincoln's Avengers: Justice, Revenge, and Reunion after the Civil War*. New York: Norton, 2004.

———. *Yankee Women: Gender Battles in the Civil War*. New York: Norton, 1994.

Lewis, Jan. *The Pursuit of Happiness: Family and Values in Jefferson's Virginia*. Cambridge: Cambridge University Press, 1983.

———. "The Republican Wife: Virtue and Seduction in the Early Republic." *William and Mary Quarterly* 44 (October 1987): 689–721.

Linderman, Gerald. *Embattled Courage: The Experience of Combat in the American Civil War*. New York: Free Press, 1987.

Litwack, Leon F. *Been in the Storm So Long: The Aftermath of Slavery*. New York: Knopf, 1979.

Lively, Robert A. *Fiction Fights the Civil War: An Unfinished Chapter in the Literary History of the American People*. Chapel Hill: University of North Carolina Press, 1957.

Lufkin, Charles L. "Divided Loyalties: Sectionalism in Civil War McNairy County, Tennessee." *Tennessee Historical Quarterly* 47 (Fall 1988): 169–77.

Lyerly, Cynthia Lynn. "A Tale of Two Patriarchs; or, How a Eunuch and a Wife Created a Family in the Church." *Journal of Family History* 28 (October 2003): 490–509.

Lystra, Karen. *Searching the Heart: Women, Men, and Romantic Love in Nineteenth-Century America*. New York: Oxford University Press, 1989.

Malone, Ann Patton. *Sweet Chariot: Slave Family and Household Structure in
    Nineteenth-Century Louisiana*. Chapel Hill: University of North Carolina Press,
    1992.

Marten, James. *The Children's Civil War*. Chapel Hill: University of North Carolina
    Press, 1998.

——. "Fatherhood in the Confederacy: Southern Soldiers and Their Children."
    Journal of Southern History 63 (May 1997): 269–92.

Masur, Louis P., ed. *'Real War Will Never Get in the Books': Selections from Writers
    during the Civil War*. New York: Oxford University Press, 1993.

Matthews, Glenna. *The Rise of Public Woman: Woman's Power and Woman's Place
    in the United States, 1630–1970*. New York: Oxford University Press, 1992.

May, Elaine Tyler. *Homeward Bound: American Families in the Cold War Era*. New
    York: Basic Books, 1990.

McCormick, Richard L. *The Party Period and Public Policy: American Politics from
    the Age of Jackson to the Progressive Era*. New York: Oxford University Press, 1986.

McCurry, Stephanie. "The Two Faces of Republicanism: Gender and Proslavery
    Politics in Antebellum South Carolina." *Journal of American History* 78 (March
    1992): 1245–64.

McDonough, James L. "Tennessee and the Civil War." *Tennessee Historical Quar-
    terly* 54 (Fall 1995): 190–209.

McMurtry, R. Gerald. *Ben Hardin Helm: 'Rebel' Brother-in-Law of Abraham Lincoln*
    Chicago: Civil War Round Table, 1943.

McPherson, James M. *Battle Cry of Freedom: The Civil War Era*. New York: Ballen-
    tine Books, 1988.

——. *For Cause and Comrades: Why Men Fought in the Civil War*. New York: Ox-
    ford University Press, 1997.

——. *Is Blood Thicker Than Water? Crises of Nationalism in the Modern World*.
    New York: Vintage Books, 1998.

McPherson, James M., and William J. Cooper Jr., eds. *Writing the Civil War: The
    Quest to Understand*. Columbia: University of South Carolina Press, 1998.

Menendez, Albert J. *Civil War Novels: An Annotated Bibliography*. New York: Gar-
    land Publishing, 1986.

Merrell, Susan Scarf. *The Accidental Bond: The Power of Sibling Relationships*. New
    York: Times Books, 1995.

Messmer, Charles. "Louisville during the Civil War." *Filson Club Historical Quar-
    terly* 52 (April 1978): 210–13.

Miles, Vernon G. "James Roberts Gilmore." In *American National Biography*, edited
    by John A. Garraty and Mark C. Carnes, 68–69. New York: Oxford University
    Press, 1999.

Mintz, Steven. *A Prison of Expectations: The Family in Victorian Culture*. New York:
    New York University Press, 1983.

Mintz, Steven, and Susan Kellogg. *Domestic Revolutions: A Social History of Ameri-
    can Family Life*. New York: Free Press, 1988.

Mitchell, Reid. *Civil War Soldiers*. New York: Viking, 1988.

———. "'Not the General but the Soldier': The Study of Civil War Soldiers." In *Writing the Civil War: The Quest to Understand*, edited by James M. McPherson and William J. Cooper Jr., 81–95. Columbia, SC: University of South Carolina Press, 1998.

———. "'Our Prison System, Supposing We Had Any': The Confederate and Union Prison Systems." In *On the Road to Total War: The American Civil War and the German Wars of Unification, 1861–1871*, edited by Stig Förster and Jörg Nagler, 565–86. Cambridge: German Historical Institute and Cambridge University Press, 1997.

———. *The Vacant Chair: The Northern Soldier Leaves Home*. New York: Oxford University Press, 1993.

Moss, Elizabeth. *Domestic Novelists of the Old South: Defenders of Southern Culture.* Baton Rouge: Louisiana State University Press, 1992.

Mott, Frank Luther. *American Journalism: A History of Newspapers in the United States through 250 Years, 1690 to 1940*. New York: Macmillan, 1941.

———. *A History of American Magazines*. Cambridge: Harvard University Press, 4th printing, 1970.

Neely, Mark Jr. *The Fate of Liberty: Abraham Lincoln and Civil Liberties*. New York: Oxford University Press, 1991.

———. *Southern Rights: Political Prisoners and the Myth of Confederate Constitutionalism*. Charlottesville: University Press of Virginia, 1999.

Noe, Kenneth W., and Shannon H. Wilson, eds. *The Civil War in Appalachia: Collected Essays*. Knoxville: University of Tennessee Press, 1997.

Norton, Anne C. *Alternative Americas: A Reading of Antebellum Popular Culture*. Chicago: University of Chicago Press, 1986.

Norton, Mary Beth. *Liberty's Daughters: The Revolutionary Experience of American Women, 1750–1800*. Boston: Little Brown, 1980.

Oakes, James. *The Ruling Race: A History of American Slaveholders*. New York: Vintage Books, 1983.

O'Leary, Cecilia Elizabeth. *To Die For: The Paradox of American Patriotism*. Princeton, N.J.: Princeton University Press, 1999.

Olpin, Larry. "Missouri and the Civil War Novel." *Missouri Historical Review* 85 (October 1990): 1–20.

Owsley, Harriet Chappell. "Peace and the Presidential Election of 1864." *Tennessee Historical Quarterly* 18 (March 1959): 3–19.

Paludan, Phillip Shaw. *A People's Contest: The Union and the Civil War, 1861–1865.* 2nd ed. Lawrence: University Press of Kansas, 1996.

———. "What Did the Winners Win? The Social and Economic History of the North during the Civil War." In *Writing the Civil War: The Quest to Understand*, edited by James M. McPherson and William J. Cooper Jr., 174–200. Columbia: University of South Carolina Press, 1998.

Patterson, Gerard A. *Rebels from West Point*. New York: Doubleday, 1987.

Penningroth, Dylan C. *The Claims of Kinfolk: African American Property and Com-*

munity in the Nineteenth-Century South. Chapel Hill: University of North Carolina Press, 2003.

Petrone, Karen. "Family, Masculinity, and Heroism in Russian War Posters of the First World War." In *Borderlines: Gender and Identities in War and Peace, 1870–1930*, edited by Billie Melman, 95–120. New York: Routledge, 1998.

Potter, David. "The Historian's Use of Nationalism and Vice Versa." *American Historical Review* 67 (July 1962): 924–50.

Preston, E. Delorus, Jr. "William Syphax: A Pioneer in Negro Education in the District of Columbia." *Journal of Negro History* 20 (October 1935): 450–55.

Rable, George. *Civil Wars: Women and the Crisis of Southern Nationalism*. Urbana: University of Illinois Press, 1989.

———. *The Confederate Republic: A Revolution against Politics*. Chapel Hill: University of North Carolina Press, 1994.

———. "Hearth, Home, and Family in the Fredericksburg Campaign." In *The War Was You and Me: Civilians in the American Civil War*, edited by Joan Cashin, 85–111. Princeton, N.J.: Princeton University Press, 2002.

———. "Missing in Action: Women of the Confederacy." In *Divided Houses: Gender and the Civil War*, edited by Catherine Clinton and Nina Silber, 134–46. New York: Oxford University Press, 1992.

Radley, Kenneth. *Rebel Watchdog: The Confederate States Army Provost Guard*. Baton Rouge: Louisiana State University Press, 1989.

Ramage, James A. *Rebel Raider: The Life of General John Hunt Morgan*. Lexington: University Press of Kentucky, 1986.

Randall, Ruth Painter. *Mary Lincoln: Biography of a Marriage*. Boston: Little, Brown, 1953.

Richards, Jeffrey. "Passing the Love of Women." In *Manliness and Morality: Middle-Class Masculinity in Britain and America, 1800–1940*, edited by J. A. Managan and James Walvin, 92–122. New York: St. Martin's Press, 1987.

Robertson, James I., Jr. *Stonewall Jackson: The Man, the Soldier, the Legend*. New York: Macmillan, 1997.

Rose, Anne C. *Victorian America and the Civil War*. Cambridge: Cambridge University Press, Paperback ed., 1994.

Rose, Willie Lee. *Rehearsal for Reconstruction: The Port Royal Experiment*. New York: Vintage Books, 1964.

Rothert, Otto A. *A History of Muhlenberg County*. Louisville, Ky.: John P. Morton and Co., 1913.

Rothman, Joshua D. *Notorious in the Neighborhood: Sex and Families across the Color Line in Virginia, 1787–1861*. Chapel Hill: University of North Carolina Press, 2003.

Rotundo, E. Anthony. "American Fatherhood: A Historical Perspective." *American Behavioral Scientist* 29 (September/October 1985): 7–13.

———. *American Manhood: Transformations in Masculinity from the Revolution to the Modern Era*. New York: Basic Books, 1993.

————. "Boy Culture: Middle-Class Boyhood in Nineteenth-Century America." In *Meanings for Manhood: Constructions of Masculinity in Victorian America*, edited by Mark C. Carnes and Clyde Griffen, 15–33. Chicago: University of Chicago Press, 1990.

Royster, Charles. *The Destructive War: William Tecumseh Sherman, Stonewall Jackson, and the Americans*. New York: Knopf, 1991.

Rubin, Anne Sarah. "Seventy-six and Sixty-one: Confederates Remember the American Revolution." In *Where These Memories Grow: History, Memory, and Southern Identity*, edited by Fitzhugh Brundage, 85–106. Chapel Hill: University of North Carolina Press, 2000.

Ryan, Mary P. *Cradle of the Middle Class: The Family in Oneida County, New York, 1790–1865*. New York: Cambridge University Press, 1981.

————. *Women in Public: Between Banners and Ballots, 1825–1880*. Baltimore: Johns Hopkins University Press, 1990.

Saglia, Diego. "'O My Mother Spain!': The Peninsular War, Family Matters, and the Practice of Romantic Nation-Writing." *ELH* 65 (1998): 368.

Samuels, Shirley. *The Culture of Sentiment: Race, Gender, and Sentimentality in Nineteenth-Century America*. New York: Oxford University Press, 1992.

Savage, Kirk. *Standing Soldiers, Kneeling Slaves: Race, War, and Monument in Nineteenth-Century America*. Princeton, N.J.: Princeton University Press, 1997.

Schott, Thomas Edwin. *Alexander H. Stephens of Georgia: A Biography*. Baton Rouge: Louisiana State University Press, 1988.

Schwalm, Leslie. *A Hard Fight for We: Women's Transition from Slavery to Freedom in South Carolina*. Urbana: University of Illinois Press, 1997.

Schwartz, Marie Jenkins. *Born in Bondage: Growing Up Enslaved in the Antebellum South*. Cambridge: Harvard University Press, 2000.

Scott, Joan W. "Gender: A Useful Category of Historical Analysis." *American Historical Review* 91 (December 1986): 1053–75.

Shaler, Nathaniel Southgate. *Kentucky: A Pioneer Commonwealth*. New York: AMS Press, 1973.

Shenfield, Lawrence W. *Confederate States of America: The Special Postal Routes*. New York: Collectors Club, 1961.

Silber, Nina. "The Northern Myth of the Rebel Girl." In *Women of the American South: A Multicultural Reader*, edited by Christie Anne Farnham, 120–31. New York: New York University Press, 1997.

————. *The Romance of Reunion: Northerners and the South, 1865–1900*. Chapel Hill: University of North Carolina Press, 1993.

Simkins, Frances Butler, and James Welch Patton. *The Women of the Confederacy*. Richmond: Garrett and Massie, Inc., 1936.

Sizer, Lyde Cullen. *The Political Work of Northern Women Writers and the Civil War, 1850–1872*. Chapel Hill: University of North Carolina Press, 2000.

Smith, Anthony D. *National Identity*. Reno: University of Nevada Press, 1991.

————. *Nationalism and Modernism: A Critical Survey of Recent Theories of Nations and Nationalism*. New York: Routledge, 1998.

Smith, Edward Conrad. *The Borderland in the Civil War*. New York: Macmillan, 1927.

Smith-Rosenberg, Carroll. "The Female World of Love and Ritual: Relations between Women in Nineteenth-Century America." In *The American Family in Social-Historical Perspective*, edited by Michael Gordon, 334–58. 2nd ed. New York: St. Martin's Press, 1978.

Squires, J. Duane. "Lincoln's Todd In-Laws." *Lincoln Herald* (Fall 1967): 121–28.

Stanley, Amy Dru. *From Bondage to Contract: Wage Labor, Marriage, and the Market in the Age of Slave Emancipation*. Cambridge: Cambridge University Press, 1998.

Stearns, Peter N., and Jan Lewis, eds. *An Emotional History of the United States*. New York: New York University Press, 1998.

Stevenson, Brenda E. *Life in Black and White: Family and Community in the Slave South*. New York: Oxford University Press, 1996.

Stowe, Steven M. *Intimacy and Power in the Old South: Ritual and the Lives of Planters*. Baltimore: Johns Hopkins University Press, 1987.

Sulloway, Frank J. *Born to Rebel: Birth Order, Family Dynamics, and Creative Lives*. New York: Pantheon Books, 1996.

Sutherland, Daniel E. *Seasons of War: The Ordeal of a Confederate Community, 1861–1865*. New York: Free Press, 1995.

———. ed. *Guerrillas, Unionists, and Violence on the Confederate Home Front*. Fayetteville: University of Arkansas Press, 1999.

Syphax, Evelyn Reid. "William Syphax—Community Leader." *Arlington Historical Magazine* 6 (October 1977): 42–44.

Taylor, William R. *Cavalier and Yankee: The Old South and American National Character*. Cambridge: Harvard University Press, 1979.

Tebbel, John. *The Creation of an Industry, 1630–1865*. Vol. 1 of *A History of Book Publishing in the United States*. New York: R. R. Bowker, 1972.

Thomas, Emory. *The Confederate Nation, 1861–1865*. New York: Harper and Row, 1979.

———. "The Lee Marriage." In *Intimate Strategies of the Civil War*, edited by Carol K. Bleser and Lesley J. Gordon, 32–48. New York: Oxford University Press, 2001.

Thompson, Lawrence S. "The War between the States in the Kentucky Novel." *Register of the Kentucky Historical Society* 50 (January 1952): 26–34.

Tompkins, Jane. *Sensational Designs: The Cultural Work of American Fiction, 1790–1860*. New York: Oxford University Press, 1985.

Townsend, William H. *Lincoln and the Bluegrass: Slavery and Civil War in Kentucky*. Lexington: University of Kentucky Press, 1955.

Trees, Andrew S. *The Founding Fathers and the Politics of Character*. Princeton, N.J.: Princeton University Press, 2003.

Turner, Justin G., and Linda Levitt Turner, eds. *Mary Todd Lincoln: Her Life and Letters*. New York: Knopf, 1972.

Turner, Martha. "The Cause of Union in East Tennessee." *Tennessee Historical Quarterly* 40 (Winter 1981): 366–80.

Varon, Elizabeth. *We Mean to Be Counted: White Women and Politics in Antebellum Virginia*. Chapel Hill: University of North Carolina Press, 1998.

Vinovskis, Maris A. *Toward a Social History of the American Civil War: Exploratory Essays*. Cambridge: Cambridge University Press, 1991.

Waal, Carla. "The First Confederate Drama: The Guerrillas." *Virginia Magazine of History and Biography* 70 (October 1962): 459–67.

Waldstreicher, David. *In the Midst of Perpetual Fetes: The Making of American Nationalism, 1776–1820*. Chapel Hill: University of North Carolina Press, 1997.

Wallach, Glenn. *Obedient Sons: The Discourse of Youth and Generations in American Culture, 1630–1860*. Amherst: University of Massachusetts Press, 1997.

Watson, Charles S. "Confederate Drama: The Plays of John Hill Hewitt and James Dabney McCabe." *Southern Literary Journal* 21 (Spring 1989): 100–112.

Waugh, John C. *The Class of 1846: From West Point to Appomattox: Stonewall Jackson, George McClellan, and Their Brothers*. New York: Warner Books, 1994.

Weil, Rachel. *Political Passions: Gender, the Family, and Political Argument in England, 1680–1714*. New York: Manchester University Press, 1999.

Weiner, Marli F. *Mistresses and Slaves: Plantation Women in South Carolina, 1830–1880*. Urbana: University of Illinois Press, 1998.

Weintraub, Jeff. "The Theory and Politics of the Public/Private Distinction." In *Public and Private in Thought and Practice: Perspectives on a Grand Dichotomy*, edited by Jeff Weintraub and Krishan Kumar, 1–42. Chicago: University of Chicago Press, 1997.

White, Deborah Gray. *Ar'n't I a Woman? Female Slaves in the Plantation South*. Rev. ed. New York: Norton, 1999.

Whites, Lee Ann. *The Civil War as a Crisis in Gender: Augusta, Georgia, 1860–1890*. Athens: University of Georgia Press, 1995.

Wiebe, Robert. *The Search for Order, 1877–1920*. New York: Hill and Wang, 1967.

Wiley, Bell Irvin. *The Life of Johnny Reb: The Common Soldier of the Confederacy*. Baton Rouge: Louisiana State University Press, 1978.

Williams, Harry. "The Attack upon West Point during the Civil War." *Mississippi Valley Historical Review* 25 (March 1939): 491–504.

Williamson, Joel. *New People: Miscegenation and Mulattoes in the United States*. New York: Free Press, 1980.

Wilson, Edmund. *Patriotic Gore: Studies in the Literature of the American Civil War*. New York: Oxford University Press, 1962.

Wright, Lyle H. *American Fiction, 1851–1875: Cumulative Index of the Microfilm Collection*. New Haven: Research Publications, 1974.

Wyatt-Brown, Bertram. *Southern Honor: Ethics and Behavior in the Old South*. New York: Oxford University Press, 1982.

Yazawa, Melvin. *From Colonies to Commonwealth: Familial Ideology and the Beginnings of the American Republic*. Baltimore: Johns Hopkins University Press, 1985.

Young, Elizabeth. *Disarming the Nation: Women's Writing and the American Civil War*. Chicago: University of Chicago Press, 1999.

THESES AND DISSERTATIONS

Adams, Carrol Franklin. "A New England Teacher in Southside Virginia: A Study of Emily Howe, 1812–1883." M.A. thesis, University of Virginia, 1954.

Alexander, Ronald Ray. "Central Kentucky during the Civil War." Ph.D. diss., University of Kentucky, 1976.

Bell, Christine Anne. "A Family Conflict: Visual Imagery of the 'Homefront' and the War between the States, 1860–1866." Ph.D. diss., Northwestern University, 1996.

Carmichael, Peter S. "The Last Generation: Sons of Virginia Slaveholders and the Creation of Southern Identity." Ph.D. diss., Pennsylvania State University, 1996.

Dicker, Rory. "Home Repair: Reconfigurations of Domesticity in American Fiction of the 1860s." Ph.D. diss., Vanderbilt University, 1998.

Fife, Iline. "The Theater in the Confederacy." Ph.D. diss., Louisiana State University, 1949.

Prichard, James M. "Champion of the Union: George D. Prentice and the Civil War in Kentucky." M.A. thesis, Wright State University, 1988.

Roth, Sarah Nelson. "Rebels and Martyrs: The Debate over Slavery in American Popular Culture, 1822–1865." Ph.D. diss., University of Virginia, 2002.

Rubin, Anne Sarah. "Redefining the South: Confederates, Southerners, and Americans, 1863–1868." Ph.D. diss., University of Virginia, 1999.

Shuster, Richard. "American Civil War Novels to 1880." Ph.D. diss., Columbia University, 1961.

Smith, Rebecca Washington. "The Civil War and Its Aftermath in American Fiction, 1861–1899." Ph.D. diss., University of Chicago, 1932.

Index